CONSTANT VIGILANCE

CONSTANT VIGILANCE

The RAF Regiment
in the
Burma Campaign

NIGEL W. M. WARWICK

Pen & Sword
AVIATION

First published in 2007
and reprinted in paperback format in 2014 by
PEN & SWORD AVIATION
An imprint of
Pen & Sword Books Ltd
47 Church Street
Barnsley, South Yorkshire
S70 2AS

ISBN 978 1 47382 284 9

A CIP catalogue record for this book is
available from the British Library

Typeset in Sabon by Phoenix Typesetting, Auldgirth, Dumfriesshir

Printed and bound in India by Replika Press Pvt Ltd.

Pen & Sword Books Ltd incorporates the Imprints of Aviation, Atlas,
Family History, Fiction, Maritime, Military, Discovery, Politics, History,
Archaeology, Select, Wharncliffe Local History, Wharncliffe True Crime,
Military Classics, Wharncliffe Transport, Leo Cooper, The Praetorian Press,
Remember When, Seaforth Publishing and Frontline Publishing

For a complete list of Pen & Sword titles please contact
PEN & SWORD BOOKS LIMITED
47 Church Street, Barnsley, South Yorkshire, S70 2AS, England
E-mail: enquiries@pen-and-sword.co.uk
Website: www.pen-and-sword.co.uk

Contents

Maps

See colour section

The South-East Asia Command Theatre 1943–6

The Arakan Line of Communication

The Imphal Battlefield

The Kabaw Valley

South Arakan

Mandalay – Meiktila

Southern Burma

© Crown copyright material is reproduced with the permission of the Controller of HMSO and Queen's Printer for Scotland

Sketch Maps

'. . . and with the dangers of infiltration ever present, the need is for constant vigilance.'

Operations Record Book, 1307 Wing HQ, RAF Regiment, October 1945

Dedication

'WHEN YOU GO HOME, TELL THEM OF US AND SAY,
FOR YOUR TOMORROW, WE GAVE OUR TODAY.'

The Kohima Epitaph

Foreword

'The Forgotten Army', the famous and poignant soubriquet of the Fourteenth Army in Burma in the Second World War, applied just as much to the Air Forces that supported it within South-East Asia Command (SEAC); arguably even more so. SEAC was 'forgotten' because of the homeland's focus upon its own immediate survival against Germany. Yet this great Command, the poor relation of the Allies' share in the titanic global struggle, utterly destroyed the land and air forces of the Japanese Empire in South-East Asia, in the process pioneering the most effective air/land cooperation ever seen in conflict, under a British Supreme Allied Commander (Lord Mountbatten) and arguably the finest fighting general of the twentieth century (Lord Slim), together with another great but unsung commander, Air Marshal Sir John Baldwin, commanding SEAC's 3rd Tactical Air Force.

Never before had a major land force ever depended completely throughout a strategic theatre upon air power, not only for close air support, but for all its logistics, reinforcements and aero-medical evacuation, as well as its fighter cover, interdiction of enemy logistics and theatre-wide strategic bombardment. Lord Slim himself said that without the Air Force, the Army could never have won. However, as is very apparent from the various RAF tributes quoted by the author, the RAF Commanders considered that air power might not have remained viable without its own force-protection, provided mainly by the infant Royal Air Force Regiment.

SEAC, centred upon Burma as the keystone and comprising British, Indian, Gurkha and African troops, together with its Air Command, South-East Asia (which was made up of men from throughout the British Empire and also had elements of the United States Army Air Force in support), saved India from savage conquest and inflicted the largest land defeat of the war on the Japanese. This was no 'diversionary colonial sideshow' as held by some revisionist historians today. It was a terrible but glorious episode in Allied history, an episode in which the RAF Regiment should take great pride for its own part.

This book therefore is a salutary reminder of the crucial part played in the efficacy of the RAF in SEAC by its youngest fighting arm. The RAF Regiment was created in 1942 and sent men out in their thousands; they were untried and untested, in some instances not even properly trained, formed, acclimatised or properly equipped to fight, to face a hitherto invincible enemy in one of the worst combat environments imaginable. Participating in some of the most bitter fighting of the war, including the most important battle the RAF Regiment has ever fought to this day as the 'lead' arm, in defence of the airfield at Meiktila, the new Corps truly earned acclaim in the 'forgotten' theatre. But 'forgotten' elsewhere it remained and the RAF Regiment's place in it unknown, until a group of old comrades formed the RAF Regiment SEAC Association forty years after the war.

It is fitting therefore that this book, stemming primarily from the collaboration of Mr Henry Kirk MBE, a SEAC veteran and Founding President of the Association, with Dr Nigel Warwick, a military historian in Australia, and strongly supported by Air

Commodore P.J. Drissell, Commandant General, RAF Regiment, should be published during the lifetimes of those remaining few to whom we owe so much. It thus becomes a historic source of impeccable first-hand provenance for future historians, capturing something of the atmosphere and attitudes of the men who were in the line in those days. Concentrating as it does upon the personal accounts of today's few surviving veterans, albeit always set in the context of the wider war and of RAF and SEAC policy, its focus is not on Grand Strategy nor High Command. Rather it focuses upon the man with the rifle and the fascinating, amusing, heroic and sometimes tragic stories and opinions of individuals at the 'slit trench' and gun-pit levels.

Air Commodore Marcus Witherow RAF (Ret'd)
Director RAF Regiment 1987–1990
Patron RAF Regiment SEAC Association 1986–2005

Appreciation

On behalf of all ranks of the Royal Air Force Regiment who served in India, Burma and the Far East in the Second World War, I wish to thank the author, Dr Nigel Warwick, who for the past ten years has done deep research culminating in this excellent book. It is a fitting tribute to men who had to operate in severe tropical conditions and at the same time fight a vicious enemy.

Out of this close comradeship a unique veteran's Association was formed, Air Commodore M.S. Witherow being our Patron. His leadership and guidance over the years was very much appreciated.

Finally our thanks must go to the Commandant General, RAF Regiment, Air Commodore P.J. Drissell for his interest and valued help in bringing this book to fruition.

Mr Henry Kirk MBE
President RAF Regiment SEAC Association

Preface and Acknowledgements

The story of the Royal Air Force Regiment and its achievements deserves to be more widely known. While reading extensively on the Burma campaign, I was struck by the paucity of published information on the Regiment. There were fleeting mentions in some recent histories, while most of the RAF Squadron histories, fairly enough, concentrate on the flying operations. Ground defence is rarely mentioned. The British Official Histories of the War against Japan mention the Regiment on one or two occasions per volume. They do not, however, make any reference to the Regiment's involvement in the action at Meiktila, one of its greatest battle honours. In pursuit of more information, I wrote to the RAF Regiment SEAC Association where I made contact with its President, Henry Kirk. The correspondence arising from this contact made it clear that they had a great story to tell.

This book draws on the personal reminiscences and diaries of those airmen of the Regiment who served in Burma. To provide a framework to these accounts I have used the Operations Records Books (ORBs) and official reports of the RAF Regiment units. Fortunately the RAF Regiment SEAC Association has been active in gathering information on their deeds in Burma. In this context they contributed a great deal to the preparation of Michael Turner's painting depicting the siege of Meiktila, which was commissioned as part of the RAF Regiment's Fiftieth Anniversary in 1992.

The Fourteenth Army was always short of men and equipment and the RAF Regiment was no different in this regard. Many of those who reached Rangoon in 1945 had been in India and Burma since 1942, and some earlier. Most had received no leave for three years and had suffered from one and, more commonly, two or three tropical diseases. In reading the personal diaries and the ORBs it must always be remembered that they were being kept under the most hideous conditions; at best in a bamboo basha, possibly under canvas, or often in a slit trench, all in conditions of extreme heat, high humidity, mud and incessant rain and in a struggle against a ruthless foe. Above all, however, one is struck by the rapid development of a strong *esprit de corps*, comradeship and professionalism in the newly formed RAF Regiment.

One of the great difficulties of writing and reading history is that one is in a privileged and comfortable position of knowing the outcome of the events at hand. The reader should bear in mind that the participants were not as assured of the eventual outcome. Based on the earlier year's experiences in the Arakan, the airmen of the Regiment could have been forgiven for expecting further disaster. They did have two factors that gave them optimism for the future. Firstly, they had two exceptional senior commanders, Lord Louis Mountbatten and General William 'Bill' Slim. The RAF was well served with leaders of similar calibre. The Command Defence Officer Group Captain (later Air Vice-Marshal) Harris deserves special mention for his crucial role in the development and success of the Regiment in SEAC. Secondly, new tactics had been developed whereby the Army would be supported by air supply, thus nullifying the Japanese Army's most effective ploy, the ability to surround and cut off an Army tied to road-bound supply lines. Air supply and air superiority and, consequently, the ground defence of airfields and radar stations in forward areas would, therefore, be a crucial element in the eventual victory.

There are many people who have made a contribution to this book and without which it would be much the lesser. Most importantly, I thank Henry Kirk, ably supported by his wife Margaret, for providing many vivid accounts and recollections from his time in SEAC and for his constant inspiration, enthusiasm and friendship during the writing of *Constant Vigilance*. It has been a great privilege to have been invited to tell the story of the RAF Regiment airmen who served in SEAC. I also wish to thank the following men, some now sadly deceased, and who, directly or indirectly, provided commentaries, reminiscences, diaries and photographs: Hartley Blairs, George Briggs, John Buckman, Tom Collier, Ted Daines, Norman Gerrish, Stan Hutchinson, Les Jewitt, Charles Killeen, Colin Kirby, Alan Knight, Alexander Miller, Randle Manwaring, Cyril Paskin, Bill Raymond, Jim Robinson, Ian Welch and Sid Wood.

The ORBs and reports held by The National Archives of the United Kingdom were an excellent resource and I thank them for permission to quote from this material. I am grateful to the Director of the Australian War Memorial, the Trustees of the Imperial War Museum and the National Archives of Australia for permission to reproduce photographs from their collections. I also thank The Controller of Her Majesty's Stationery Office for permission to reproduce the maps from the Official Histories of the War against Japan. I especially wish to thank Sebastian Cox and Mary Hudson of the Air Historical Branch in the Ministry of Defence for their great efforts in selecting photographs relevant to the RAF Regiment from the AHB collection. Thank you also to Wilf Goold DFC ex-607 (Spitfire) Squadron for permission to use a photograph from his personal collection and Chris Johnson for his assistance with details of the defensive 'boxes' at Imphal.

I wish to thank Squadron Leader Paul Bruning and the late Owen Thompson and his wife Betty, who showed such kind hospitality when I visited the RAF Regiment Museum at Honington in 1997. I am also appreciative of the assistance of Wing Commander Martin Hooker, Director of the RAF Regiment Museum during the final stages of preparation. My sincere thanks go to Air Commodore Mickey Witherow for his astute reading of the final manuscript and writing the Foreword, and to Group Captain Kingsley Oliver, who provided invaluable comments and great assistance in obtaining photographs from his two excellent histories of the RAF Regiment *Through Adversity* and *The RAF Regiment at War 1942–1946*. I extend particular thanks to Air Commodore Peter J. Drissell, Commandant General RAF Regiment, who provided unfailing support and assistance in bringing this project to a successful conclusion.

I also wish to thank my Uncle and Aunt, Roy and Barbara Morris, for their hospitality during my visit to the United Kingdom while doing research on the book. I particularly thank Roy (ex-28th LAA Regiment, Royal Artillery) for inspiring my interest in the Burma campaign. Particular thanks go to my mother Betty Warwick and late father Sydney Warwick (ex-5th Battalion, Grenadier Guards) who encouraged my enthusiasm for military history from a very young age.

Finally, I would like to express my deepest gratitude to my wife, Caroline, who has been a constant source of encouragement, advice and provision of practical help with proof reading, document and image preparation, and to my daughters, Elinor and Clare, for their patience and tolerance (to a degree well beyond their years) of the time that I had to dedicate to research and writing.

Dr Nigel W.M. Warwick
Armidale, New South Wales, Australia

Glossary

ACSEA	Air Command, South-East Asia
AFV	Armoured Fighting Vehicle
AHQ India	Air Headquarters India
ALFSEA	Allied Land Forces, South-East Asia. Formed following dissolution of the 11th Army Group
AMES	Air Ministry Experiment Stations, a pseudonym for all types of RAF ground radar stations throughout the Second World War. As 'radar' was top secret the word could not be used in unit nomenclature
AOC	Air Officer Commanding
AOC-in-C	Air Officer Commanding-in-Chief
AFV	Armoured Fighting Vehicle
basha	thatched building with a bamboo frame
BORs	British Other Ranks, generic term for all British service personnel who were NCOs and private soldiers
Bren	standard British 0.303-inch light machine-gun
CDO	Command Defence Officer
charpoy	a simple bed often made of rope mesh
chaung	a dry or wet water course
chota monsoon	a heavy downpour prior to the start of the monsoon proper
COL	Chain Overseas Low radar
CRA	Commander, Royal Artillery, the senior artillery officer in a division
D Day	the day of an amphibious landing is called D Day, hence D+5 the fifth day after the landings
dacoit	robber or bandit
DTI	Defence Training Instructor
DUKW	an American 6x6 amphibious truck. They were used extensively by the Fourteenth Army on the Chindwin and Irrawaddy, but there were only limited numbers available
FAMO	Forward Airfield Maintenance Organisation established the airhead which included all installations, depots and dumps following the establishment or capture of an airfield
GCI	Ground Control Interception radar
GDO	Group Defence Officer

gharri-wallah	driver of a gharry
gharry	Hindi word for any wheeled cart or carriage but in RAF parlance a lorry
GHQ India	General Headquarters India, located in New Delhi
ground gunners	so-called to distinguish them from aircrew who manned machine-guns and hence were called air gunners
HAA	heavy anti-aircraft
HMG	heavy machine-gun
i/c	in charge
IFF	Identification, Friend or Foe. A transponder installed in an aircraft to send out a pulse when triggered by a radar station
INA	Indian National Army
IWT	Inland Water Transport
jawan	an Indian soldier
Jifs	Japanese Indian Forces
KAR	King's African Rifles
khisti	an Arakanese dugout boat
KOYLI	King's Own Yorkshire Light Infantry
kutcha	roughly or badly formed
LAA	light anti-aircraft
LCA	Landing Craft, Assault
LCI	Landing Craft, Infantry
LCM	Landing Craft, Mechanised
LCT	Landing Craft, Tank
LMG	light machine-gun
LSI	Landing Ship, Infantry
MC	Military Cross
MFCU	Mobile Fighter Control Unit
MM	Military Medal
MMG	Medium Machine Gun
MT	motor transport
NAAFI	Navy, Army and Air Force Institute
Naik	the Indian Army rank of Naik is equivalent to a Corporal in the British Army
NCO	Non-commissioned officer. The ranks of Corporal, Sergeant, Flight Sergeant, Warrant Officer
nullah	dried up watercourse
OC	Officer Commanding
OCTU	Officer Cadet Training Unit

ORB	Operations Record Book
ORs	Other ranks
pani	water
PIAT	Projector, Infantry Anti-Tank was the standard issue British hand-held anti-tank weapon
pukka gen	proper or reliable information
R&R Party	refuelling and rearming party
R&SU	Repair and Salvage Unit. Responsible for salvaging and repairing crashed aircraft
R/T	radio telephony
RAAF	Royal Australian Air Force
RAPWI	recovery of Allied prisoners-of-war and internees
RSM	Regimental Sergeant-Major
SEAC	South-East Asia Command. Established in November 1943 with Vice-Admiral, Lord Louis Mountbatten as Supreme Commander
stand-to	the period an hour or so before dawn and in the evening when an enemy attack is considered most likely. All personnel would stand ready with their weapons at their posts until ordered to stand down
Sten	British sub machine-gun developed during the war of simple design and cheap to produce. It suffered from several faults, including accidental discharge if dropped and a weak magazine spring that led to jamming
tonga	two-wheeled carriage hauled by a pony
USAAF	United States Army Air Force
VCP	Visual Control Post. Consisted of an RAF officer with flying experience and two signallers with either a jeep or light pack set. Developed during the advance to Rangoon to coordinate close air support
W/T	wireless telegraphy
WVS	Women's Voluntary Service
Z Force	This organisation dealt with internal security in India and the collection of information by patrols in enemy territory up to a distance of some 60 miles ahead of the fighting formations

Operations in which the RAF Regiment was involved in SEAC

Capital	The land offensive for the recapture of north and central Burma in early 1945
Cloak	The deception operation to cover the Irrawaddy crossing of February 1945
Dracula	The combined sea and air assault on Rangoon, May 1945
Extended Capital	The adjustment of *Capital* to include the capture of Meiktila
Ha-Go	The Japanese offensive in the Arakan, February 1944
Mastiff	The delivery of supplies and support to the prisoner-of-war camps in the SEAC area of responsibility during August and September 1945
Matador	The amphibious landing on Ramree Island, January 1945
Romulus	The offensive in the north Arakan in late 1944 and early 1945
Talon	The amphibious landing on Akyab Island, January 1945
Tiderace	The emergency operation for the quick occupation of Singapore in September 1945
U-Go	The Japanese offensive against Imphal and Kohima, March 1944
Zipper	The invasion of Malaya, September 1945

RAF Ranks

Airmen

AC2   Aircraftman 2nd Class. Entry level rank for airmen
AC1   Aircraftman 1st Class
LAC   Leading Aircraftman
Corporal
Sergeant
Flight Sergeant
Warrant Officer

Officers

Pilot Officer   The lowest commissioned rank and equivalent to Second Lieutenant
                 in the Army
Flying Officer
Flight Lieutenant
Squadron Leader
Wing Commander
Group Captain
Air Commodore
Air Vice-Marshal
Air Marshal
Air Chief Marshal
Marshal of the Royal Air Force

CHAPTER ONE

Ground Defence and the Formation of the RAF Regiment

'All over the camp there were well-educated chaps and skilled tradesmen walking around with puzzled expressions: "What is this Ground Defence?"'
LAC Colin Kirby, Ground Defence Branch, RAF

As the first glimmer of dawn touched the distant hills, thirty or so men with rifles and Brens at the ready, climbed out of slit trenches and made their way through a barbed-wire apron before cautiously heading off across the baked red soil to a dusty airstrip. There was no cover on the airstrip and only a few patches of short dry scrub around the edges and in a belt between the two parallel runways. The only significant building was a small shell-damaged pagoda, the bells of which still rang softly in the light breeze. An abandoned steamroller lay on its side some distance away and a Dakota lay broken and smouldering in the near distance. The men spread out and began a sweep of the airstrip and its perimeter. Every ditch, slit trench and patch of scrub had to be examined. They were searching for Japanese soldiers who had infiltrated the airstrip and its surrounds during the night. In the darkness they had heard the Japanese moving around their positions, digging themselves into new strongpoints or crawling in close and trying to draw fire from the British, Indian and Gurkha defenders. The patrol would take just over two hours to complete the task but this was the only method to ensure it was safe for aircraft to land.

It was March 1945 and the airstrip was located east of a town called Meiktila on the central plain of Burma. These men were playing a vital part in what is considered the masterstroke of the Burma campaign, the thrust for, and capture of, Meiktila. The town was a major supply and administrative centre and if captured and held, would break the back of the Japanese Army in Burma.

An armoured and infantry column of the 17th Indian Division had moved secretly down the Myittha Valley, crossed the Irrawaddy River and then sped some 85 miles through enemy territory to take Meiktila. Initially taken by surprise, the enemy soon reacted with characteristic determination and now sought to recapture the town and strip. The men of the Fourteenth Army and RAF, who had captured and secured Meiktila town and the airfield, were now solely dependent on supply by air. The transport aircraft were most vulnerable to ground fire on take-off and landing, and the capacity of the airstrip to take aircraft would be strangled if the flight paths were not cleared of hostile forces. Petrol, oil and spare parts for the tanks and other vehicles, along with food, medical supplies and ammunition, were needed for the 255th Indian Tank Brigade and 17th Indian Division to sustain their defence and strike capacity.

The men moving across the airstrip, however, were not soldiers of the British-Indian Army; they were airmen of the Royal Air Force Regiment, a Corps that had only been in existence for just over three years. The RAF Regiment was formed in the exigencies of the early years of the Second World War, and their achievements meant that, in common with The Royal Marines Commandos, The Parachute Regiment and The Special Air Service, they would be retained in the Order of Battle of Britain's post-war armed forces.

'The Royal Air Force Regiment', which came into existence in the United Kingdom on 1 February 1942 following the signing of the Royal Warrant by King George VI, was the title conferred upon the newest Corps of the RAF. Its personnel were drawn from the old 'Ground Defence Branch' of the RAF and the intent, expressed in the Air Ministry memorandum of 5 February 1942, was to be more than just a formation of aerodrome guards:

> While the strategic function of the Corps is inherently defensive, it is essential that it should be trained to act tactically on the offensive, and that its title should be one which will foster a fighting spirit and high morale and not lay emphasis on the defensive role.[1]

Prior to the Second World War the Army held responsibility for airfield defence. Once the war began, however, few Army commanders had the manpower to spare for this task as troops were desperately needed according to Army priorities and not those of the RAF. For the first three years of the war, close defence of airstrips was the responsibility of station and squadron defence flights of about thirty-six airmen of the Ground Defence Branch. The airmen were referred to as Ground Gunners and wore a badge on the lower sleeve with the letters 'GG'. As had been demonstrated clearly in France in 1940 and again in Greece and Crete in 1941, control of the air had become a vital factor in the domination of the battlefield; hence airfields had become important targets for enemy air forces and parachute troops. All too frequently RAF aircraft were being destroyed on the ground by enemy fighter sweeps, and with the successful invasion of Crete by German parachute troops, it was finally determined that there was a need for a specialist and dedicated RAF Corps trained to provide close defence of RAF assets against air and ground attack.[2] In particular, the RAF needed a force that would not be siphoned off for Army tasks at times of crisis and thus the RAF Regiment came into being.

The Japanese invaded Hong Kong and Malaya in December 1941 and by February 1942 had invaded the Netherlands East Indies[3] and had passed through Indo-China and Siam to threaten Burma. Burma was unprepared for war and with the British only possessing two divisions of poorly equipped and largely raw troops, the end result was inevitable. By May 1942, the British Army had endured the longest retreat in its history, and all of Burma was in Japanese hands (Map 1).

The RAF had played a part in the early stages of the retreat but had only a few squadrons, though ably assisted by the American Volunteer Group. While scoring some notable successes, the eventual outcome of the air war was also in no doubt. The parlous state of ground defence of airfields in Burma in 1942 is best described by two instances.

The first relates to the anti-aircraft defence, which was extremely limited with only two HAA and LAA batteries to defend the entire Army and Air Force and limited AA defence was scratched together from whatever could be found. So inadequate were the armaments available that an infantry battalion of the KOYLI had their Vickers medium machine-guns taken from them and given to a Burmese unit for AA defence of an airfield, and it was believed that they were never fired in anger.[4] Following the loss of Rangoon the RAF had withdrawn to an ex-civilian airfield located up the Irrawaddy valley at Magwe. Having completed a successful raid on the now Japanese-held airfield at Mingaladon, near Rangoon, the enemy retaliated the following day and Magwe was attacked several times over the next forty-eight hours by groups of up to twenty-seven bombers and fifty fighters. As the early warning system was extremely primitive and unreliable the raid caught most of the aircraft on the ground. No satisfactory AA barrage could be put up in response and a large part of the fighter and bomber force in Burma was destroyed and as a result the RAF soon after withdrew to Akyab.

The second was the situation that greeted the newly appointed commander of Burcorps, General Slim, who flew into Magwe airfield a few days after the raid. Arriving around sunset, Slim's Lysander circled the airfield waiting for a signal to land. None was received so his Sikh pilot landed the plane and taxied up the runway. He found Magwe deserted and was able to stroll freely amongst the only remaining RAF fighter aircraft in Burma. Finally a Burma Rifles truck happened to pass on a nearby road and Slim hitched a lift into Magwe town to the RAF Wing HQ. There, he found 'everyone in good heart and cheer'. Slim suggested that 'it was bit rash to leave so many aeroplanes on a deserted airfield in the midst of a not too reliable population'. He was told that safety of the aircraft was the 'Army's business'.[5]

The monsoon of 1942, the severest since 1897, had finally halted the Japanese on the India-Burma border. The enemy were held in three areas: south of Chittagong, at Tiddim-Imphal-Tamu in Manipur and north of Mogaung-Myitkyina. By April 1942, Ceylon (now Sri Lanka) and the eastern coast of India were being threatened by a Japanese naval group, which carried out bombing raids and sunk naval and merchant shipping. From late 1942 barely three raw Indian infantry divisions faced the Japanese Army. The Allies were still locked in the decisive struggles against the German-Italian Army in North Africa, the Battle of the Atlantic and the build-up of a large force for the invasion of German-occupied Europe. Britain and the United States of America had decided on a policy of beating Germany first and as a result, the Army and Air Forces in India were at the bottom of the list in priority for manpower and for modern arms and equipment. In the first eight months after the withdrawal to India in 1942, it was only possible to hold the positions along the India-Burma border while the Army and Air Force were built up. Offensive action by the Allies was planned for late 1942 but the resources available fluctuated depending on the situation in other theatres.

The story of the RAF Regiment in India and the Burma campaign begins in May 1942 when AHQ India informed the Air Ministry in London that additional defence flights would be needed by early 1943, and moreover, that there were a limited number of AA machine-guns available for airfield defence. The RAF Director of Ground Defence from the Air Ministry in the London arrived in India in June 1942 to assess the situation almost five months after the Corps had come into existence in the United Kingdom. He reported the following:

Little had been done by AHQ India in ground defence matters in response to signals from the Air Ministry in London concerning the formation of RAF Regiment AA flights,

1. Indian Army garrison companies had not been allocated for defence of airfields and formation of mobile relief columns of first-line troops had not been considered,

2. Aerodromes and airfields had not been classified as to their defence priority,
3. Ground Defence staff had not been organised and Ground Defence officers and men were being misemployed and,
4. Estimates of the number of Ground Defence personnel required far exceeded those available.[6]

Rather than being attached to particular Air Stations, as in the United Kingdom, the majority of RAF ground defence personnel in India were in squadron defence flights that were permanently attached to, and travelled with, a particular flying squadron. As with many aspects of the war in South-East Asia, equipment, and even manpower allocations, were much reduced when compared with European scales. For example, a squadron defence flight in the United Kingdom consisted of two officers, eleven NCOs and forty-five airmen, compared with those in India, of one officer, four NCOs and thirty-two ground gunners – a deficit of twenty personnel for India flights. Smaller defence flights were also attached to Wing HQs consisting of one Sergeant and eighteen ground gunners. A Wing Defence Officer was responsible for training and supervision of flights under his command along with 'backers-up'. The 'backers-up' were ground crew who, if able, assisted in ground defence or manned AA machine-guns should the airfield come under attack. They received additional pay for taking on the extra tasks.

Prior to the visit of the Director of Ground Defence in June 1942, the training of station and squadron defence personnel in India was virtually non-existent, and discipline in some cases was not what it should have been. Ground defence was not considered a glamorous role for many of the men who joined the RAF, particularly those who had dreamt of becoming pilots or aircrew. A few happily went into ground defence; while many, after initial scepticism, took great pride in the achievements of the RAF Regiment.

George Briggs volunteered at 18 years old, but after reporting to the new recruits Depot was sent home on deferred service and was recalled in June 1941. After six weeks training at Filey on the East Coast he was posted to an airfield at Stanton Harcourt to guard against air raids and saboteurs. The equipment was outdated twin Lewis and Vickers machine-guns. After a few months at RAF Stanton Harcourt, George Briggs answered a call for volunteers to serve overseas. He recalls:

> . . . myself and another couple of guys put our names forward and we were duly despatched to RAF Abingdon and after a few days we were sent by train to Blackpool where we were given our tropical kit and inoculations. Our number had swelled by now with some of the Abingdon guys having joined us. We sailed from Liverpool in March 1942 landing eventually at Karachi in the Scinde. There we were allocated to units and our party travelled across India by train to Calcutta. Myself and a few more bods were attached to No 75 Air Stores Park, and our duties were to guard a large warehouse containing spare parts and equipment.

Ian Welch was only 17 years and 4 months but was keen to join the RAF, so he put his age up to 18 years old, was accepted and sent to ground defence. Randle Manwaring, who was later to command an RAF Regiment Wing HQ during the advance through Burma in 1945, had enlisted in the Royal Air Force Volunteer Reserve in 1939, and though he had volunteered to be a wireless operator, was asked to go into ground

Henry Kirk while on a gunnery course on the Isle of Man, aged 18 years, July 1940. (Henry Kirk)

defence. He started as an AC2 and was then promoted from AC1 to LAC and finally Corporal before being commissioned in 1941. Henry Kirk had similarly joined the Royal Air Force Volunteer Reserve and was called to service in July 1940. He volunteered to be an air gunner/wireless operator but was considered too tall to fit in an aircraft turret (6ft 1in). He was sent to RAF Benson as a Ground Gunner and was then posted to 99 Squadron Defence Flight in March 1942.

Ted Daines had joined ground defence on enlistment and was posted abroad in the defence flight of 160 Squadron RAF, first to the Middle East and then by early 1942 to India. By mid-1942, 160 Squadron was stationed at Salbani on the Bay of Bengal. In early 1943 his defence flight was posted away in its entirety from 160 Squadron to 180 Wing at Kumbhirgram in Assam in north-east India.

Les Jewitt entered ground defence early in the war and had arrived in India during 1942. He remembers that there was a common feeling that the rankers had been sent to ground defence against their better judgment, most having been duped into defence flights after completing basic training. However, he felt that most had put this resentment behind them and training was entered into with a high degree of goodwill, but with no extra pay!

Some of the first ground gunners had arrived in India from the United Kingdom on 21 September 1941, a few months before the Japanese launched their infamous attacks on Pearl Harbor and Malaya without first declaring war. Alan Knight had volunteered for overseas service in June 1941 and along with sixteen others was sent out to India:

> We sailed in the *Windsor Castle*, leaving Glasgow 29 July 1941; and as the ships 'ack ack' gunners we had to pick cabins close to the main staircase for quick access to gun-posts, above the 'bridge'. The 'ack ack' guns were old French Hotchkiss machine-guns and we had duty hours of four on four off. On 16 August in mid-Atlantic in dense fog we were ordered to disperse convoy; but at 2100 hours another convoy ship rammed into our starboard side, penetrating about 5 feet at our cabin level. The prow missed me by about 6 feet and I was thrown from my bunk onto the deck. We listed heavily and off we went to lifeboat stations. There were no lifeboats for us as they had been carried away in the collision. Fortunately, the ship didn't sink.

Next day, our ship was alone, however, the Walrus amphibian from the escort cruiser found the *Windsor Castle*. At 12.30 pm my mate spotted a U-boat periscope. After seeing it pop-up twice he climbed down to the bridge and approached the Officer on the Watch and said, 'Excuse me Sir, there's a U-boat to starboard, I think you ought to know'. After the panic the Walrus took care of it with depth charges but we were unaware of any results.

We arrived in Bombay on 24 September 1941 and sixteen of us were posted to Kohat on the Northwest Frontier. The RAF Squadron had Westland Wapitis and the Indian Air Force Westland Lysanders. The Japanese had invaded Burma so we were posted to Dum Dum near Calcutta, then a few days later to Dinjan in Upper Assam. The airfield was just an open space surrounded by jungle. We had Christmas there in 1941, and lived in bashas.

He was soon in the thick of the action as Burma fell to the Japanese:

In 1942 with the retreat in Burma in full swing we only had four Hawker Audax biplanes to defend us. One flew with a wing low in an attempt to increase armament by strapping a 0.303 machine-gun under that wing. During the early period the airfield personnel were suddenly evacuated and the sixteen of us ground gunners were ordered to fight to the last man if the Japanese overran us. Unfortunately the sandbags of the gun posts had rotted away and were only two bags high at the most and the twin 'Lewis' could not be trained along the ground as they were mounted against air attack. We were thankful when the ground personnel returned next day, and we were informed it was just a 'flap'.

Many things happened after that. The air evacuation from Burma was taking place, using Dakotas being flown in the main by American pilots. They asked for volunteers to help drop supplies to the Army retreating from Burma, so I went on two trips. The last trip over the Chindwin area we were followed by a Japanese 'Betty' bomber trying to find our operating base. I took two photos of the Chindwin, but I couldn't photograph the bomber as he kept high and behind us. I also tried to get a shot in with my Thompson sub machine-gun but to no avail.

During the Burma retreat the air evacuation took place from the airfield at Myitkyina in Northern Burma. Many terrible scenes came out of the Dakotas and I once counted nearly sixty people come out of one plane, including a terribly burnt soldier.

In the final stages of the withdrawal the RAF Regiment personnel were paraded and volunteers called for to accompany a four-man demolition team that was to fly in to Myitkyina, blow up installations and walk back about 180 miles though jungle hills. Fortunately a Blenheim bomber did a recce over the airfield and found the Japanese had taken over and we weren't required. We were very lucky. My family twice had telegrams to say I had been killed. Very discouraging, it could put people off war!

Cyril Paskin volunteered for the RAF and wanted to be an air gunner, but was not accepted and was sent into ground defence:

My first posting was in Penross in Wales where we were sent to defend against a possible invasion. We had no ammunition but we looked the part!

Along with a number of ground gunners he was despatched to Singapore in late 1941 as the situation in the Far East worsened. He continues:

We were almost at Singapore when we were diverted to Bombay Docks where they didn't know what to do with us so we were hanging around there for a long time before being sent to the Northwest Frontier.

Had his ship reached Singapore before it fell in February 1942, he would have inevitably become a prisoner of war of the Japanese and would have had only a slim chance of surviving the war given the harsh treatment and conditions.

With the Japanese advancing rapidly, more reinforcements were sent from the United Kingdom to bolster a rapidly deteriorating situation. LAC Henry Kirk of 99 (Madras Presidency) Squadron Defence Flight sailed with the squadron ground crew from the United Kingdom in March 1942 and reached Bombay on 20 May 1942. There followed many futile train journeys across India and much confusion as to where 99 Squadron was to be located and accommodated. It was mid-October before they finally settled at Digri to the west of Calcutta. The Bengal cyclone of 1942 hit the airstrip just prior to the squadron's arrival, causing considerable damage to domestic accommodation and the living conditions were not healthy. Most of the Ganges Delta was underwater. Henry Kirk continues:

. . . the runway was on a ridge and the only place not waist deep in water. An Armoury Sergeant asked if I was okay and I said 'No', and collapsed and fell into unconsciousness. I was flown immediately to Calcutta in a Wellington piloted by the South African CO, Squadron Leader Rose. I was diagnosed with pneumonia and pleurisy and my parents received a telegram saying that my condition was critical. I took three months to get back on my feet. Others were not as lucky. I lost two close friends out there to disease. One, who was married only a week before leaving the UK for India, died of cerebral malaria and the other succumbed to typhoid.

The photograph taken by Henry Kirk using a 'Box Brownie' camera of the tiger that surprised the homing-beacon party at Jessore airfield in 1943. (Henry Kirk)

In June 1943 the squadron moved east to the better-equipped airfield at Jessore. As was often the case in India and Burma, the dangers were as much from the terrain, vegetation or wildlife as the enemy. The defence flight and signals personnel would go out each evening to set up the homing beacon on the high banks of the nearby river to guide in the returning bombers. They had been warned on arrival at Jessore to be careful when out on the strip and to keep a constant watch. 'Keep your eyes open, this is tiger country!' they were told by Station Officers. With the Japanese many hundreds of miles away, LAC Henry Kirk thought they were trying to keep them on edge and that those giving the warning were exaggerating the dangers. He continues:

> As dawn broke, we scanned the sky for the last Wellington. All of a sudden there was a scuffle and I found myself alone on the river bank. Looking around I noticed that everyone else had piled into the back of the Bedford lorry parked nearby. Unbeknownst to me a tiger had padded stealthily out of the jungle nearby and had moved towards the party. [Fortunately it wasn't hungry or it didn't have a taste for airmen and it kept its distance.] I had a Box Brownie camera with me and I was able to snap a quick photograph of the beast, from the back of the Bedford, as it moved down the riverbank and swam across the river.

Although kept busy with many tasks within 99 Squadron, the defence flight operated very much independently of other flying squadron defence flights. They did patrols around the squadron aircraft but there was little tactical coordination with other flights or station personnel at the same airfields.

Colin Kirby gives a vivid account of the state of the defence flights prior to the formation of the Regiment, and how an *esprit de corps* gradually evolved in the newly formed Corps. Colin had joined the RAF in July 1941 and reported to an air station in the south of England. He had no qualifications or trade, as his father had stopped him sitting for a scholarship for a high school place. Colin recalls:

> I thought I would make a pretty good air gunner. The officer at the intake base laughed in my face and said he would put me down for Ground Defence. All over the camp there were well-educated chaps and skilled tradesmen walking around with puzzled expressions 'What is this Ground Defence?' After five weeks square bashing and arms drill at Skegness and four weeks field training and unarmed combat at Whitley Bay, I was posted to an aerodrome on the banks of the Mersey near Birkenhead. With only a few twin Browning machine-guns for AA defence, and an Army Sergeant determined they should learn everything possible about the Vickers water-cooled medium machine-gun, I found many of my colleagues applying to get out of Ground Defence. The Army had told the Air Force they would have to take care of airfield defence and in one great swoop men with all kinds of education, trades and experience had been drafted in as Ground Gunners.
>
> With the drudgery and lack of activity I leapt at the chance to volunteer for overseas service. It was January 1942, and the first steps were being taken to form the RAF Regiment, however, rather than being put in the first squadron to be formed in the UK, I was instead attached to 413 Squadron Royal Canadian Air Force equipped with Catalina flying boats. After a horrendous trip on a troopship I arrived at Lake Koggala on the southern tip of Ceylon. About three-dozen of us were attached to the Canadians and a similar number

'. . . first class; in fact, an outstanding officer . . .' Squadron Leader George Arnold RAAF of RAF Station Koggala, Assault Wing RAF Regiment Depot Secunderabad and 2944 Field Squadron. (National Archives of Australia A9300)

to 205 Squadron RAF and an HQ Flight. Everybody had arrived in Ground Defence against their will, and just about everybody had applications going through the Adjutant's office for re-mustering in some RAF trade or as aircrew. Morale was pretty low and we mooched around doing guard duty, sat in gun pits waiting for Jap Zeros that never appeared, practised Morse code; as fluency in the same was reckoned to be a help if the call ever came to appear before a Trade board.

Having been placed in this somewhat dismal situation, matters were not much better than they had been in the United Kingdom. Soon, however, there were significant changes for the better for the airmen at Koggala. Colin continues:

Enter Flight Lieutenant George D. Arnold. An Australian . . . It was announced that henceforth he would be in charge of all defence and security matters at RAF Station Koggala, and so it came to pass. Arnold was about six foot three inches tall, built like a heavyweight wrestler, grey hair, bushy grey brows, florid complexion and a morose temperament.[7] Gradually he began to pull things around. Parties of men were up at dawn, rations drawn, and off along jungle tracks through the heat of the day, arriving back about sundown, hardly able to stand, with this elderly man jauntily in front with the ghost of a smile on his face. He had us crawling through thick jungle in the interior, wading through paddy fields in the heat of the day and then taking cover. This meant lying in ooze and smelly slime. The man was relentless. When you were thinking, surely he'll give us a ten-minute break, he'd send you off across country to rendezvous with somebody he'd left observing a Buddhist temple. Weapons training, aircraft recognition, unarmed combat, he pushed everybody to the full. Some of us started getting keen on super-fitness. We rigged up a gym with rings, parallel bars etc. We dropped sandbags on our guts to strengthen the stomach muscles and ran miles on the sand.

The RAF and RCAF air and ground crews laughed at us as we had returned exhausted each evening from exercises and route marches. We soon had revenge, as it was announced that all station and squadron personnel had to spend time on route marches. The Ground Defence personnel took these in their stride but the others found them to be purgatory. As far as Southern

9

Ceylon in 1942 was concerned, the man solely responsible was Flight Lieutenant Arnold . . . Australia could be proud of him. Without actually having affection for the man, everybody had enormous respect.

Following the critical report of the Director of Ground Defence, AHQ India took decisive action to improve the training, morale and effectiveness of the RAF Regiment. Wing Commander J.H. Harris from the Directorate of Ground Defence in the United Kingdom was appointed Command Defence Officer (CDO) and arrived in Delhi to take up his appointment at AHQ India on 20 December 1942.[8] Harris's appointment was a sound decision; he was a former pilot and infantry officer and had a particular aptitude for staff work. A Group Defence Officer (GDO) was appointed to each of the seven RAF groups (Nos 221–7).

After a tour of inspection, Wing Commander Harris reported that most defence flights were badly equipped and in most places the men were being used as general 'dogs-bodies' and were 'eating their heads off' in misemployment.[9] Plans were afoot to convert many of the ground defence men into technicians for employment as ground crew. Even by July 1943, eight months after the first serious steps had been taken to improve ground defence, the exact strength of RAF Regiment personnel in India was not known. The CDO then had the difficult task of creating sufficient RAF Regiment AA flights to cover future operations, from those of the required medical standard amongst the estimated 3,750 ground gunners in the command.

During November 1942 the Air Ministry allocated the numbers for the RAF Regiment AA flights to be formed in India. By December 1942 AHQ India had started to draw together the 4,500 RAF ground defence personnel scattered in disparate groups across the sub-continent. They were sent to a central Training School that was being established to ensure consistent and higher standards of training for anti-aircraft and ground defence of airfields. No 1 RAF Regiment Training School opened at 'Wellesley Lines' Begampet near Secunderabad on 2 October 1942. The first Commanding Officer was Squadron Leader C.G.E. Kennedy, with Chief Instructor Flight Lieutenant W.A.P. Gardner, five other officers and forty-six airmen for administrative duties.

Secunderabad was a garrison town and a pleasant, clean place with a decent climate, plenty of restaurants, two cinemas, sports facilities and a large hospital. The area surrounding Secunderabad was ideal for training and, as it turned out, was very similar to central Burma (Map 1).

A three-week course was designed for

Air Vice-Marshal Jack Harris CB CBE played a major part in the establishment and ultimate success of the RAF Regiment in SEAC. He later became the first RAF Regiment officer appointed as Commandant General of the RAF Regiment from 1959 to 1961. (RAF Regiment Museum) blocks of ninety airmen with a capacity for three concurrent courses or 280 airmen. The course provided instruction in the organisation, tactics and skills required for ground defence. In keeping with any new venture of this kind, none of the necessary forms, manuals, weapons, transport or furniture was available. No time was allowed for settling in, as the first airmen arrived almost immediately. Depot transport was borrowed from the Nizam of Hyderabad's State Railway,[10] and within five days, six Lewis machine-guns for AA training had arrived, although they lacked spare parts. Few of the airmen arriving had boots or anklets and some did not even have topees. The welfare of many of the airmen had not been looked after and morale was not good. Some were not even aware of why they had been sent to Secunderabad or of the formation of the RAF Regiment of which they were now part.

The Training School at Begampet was in permanent buildings, which were part of the Nizam of Hyderabad's aerodrome and an Elementary Flying Training School. Les Jewitt was one of the first airmen to be sent to the Training School and came to realise that things were looking up for those in the RAF Regiment in India:

> The accommodation was immaculate throughout . . . greatly superior to anything I had so far found anywhere in India, and this seemed to presage well for the future of a newly-formed Corps which had aspirations of becoming an elite unit . . . and the all-important 'maidan' or parade ground was surfaced with tarmac which provided the necessary snap for drill movements. The overall message that seemed to come through to all there for training was, raise your performance NOW and raise it to undreamt of heights!

To the credit of those involved in setting up the No 1 RAF Regiment Training School, the first training course of ninety airmen started ten days from its establishment and a new course was started every seven days after that. The course was made up of sessions of weapons training, field craft and field works instruction and anti-gas and artillery classes. Night operations were carried out three times a week. By November 1942 it had been decided that the month-long course was inadequate and the first six-week course was started. The RAF Regiment airmen had to learn all the skills in defence and attack of airfields, radar and radio installations. By early 1943, additional exercises were being carried out in field signals, use of cover, machine-gun tactics, the individual and section stalk, sentry duty and fighting patrols. A daily routine was soon in place as Les Jewitt recalls:

> Saturday mornings were reserved for CO's parade, when trainees along with instructors paraded for inspection by the CO, Squadron Leader Kennedy, and later a foot inspection was held by our Flight Lieutenant instructor; whether this was peculiar to our flight I do not recall, but emphasis was placed on the great importance of keeping our feet and footwear in tip-top condition at all times. Each morning at 0305 hrs the duty cooks would place a one-gallon billy can of piping hot 'Sergeant-Major's tea' on a small stone cairn outside the cookhouse, freely available for anyone wishing to partake of the brew at this unearthly hour; anyone having tasted this nectar had no qualms about rising early in order to get another helping. However, the billy can was removed from the cairn promptly at 0400 hrs! Nobody seemed to know just how this beverage was made, but it was hot, strong and sweet and, if not mistaken, there was a flavour of Darjeeling in it. This daily ritual ceased when we left Begampet for the new camp and was never reinstated.

11

Initially the men had been required to wear the near useless solar topee, but the more practical bush hat eventually replaced this. Les Jewitt continues:

> Dress at the Depot normally consisted of denim boiler suits over cotton underwear with sleeves folded back in daylight. Sleeves were buttoned at the wrist for protection against mosquitoes during hours of darkness. Boots were regulation 'ammunition' type topped with webbing gaiters or short khaki puttees. Headgear for normal use was the Australian bush hat with puggaree, on the left side of which was attached the RAF Regiment flash, which effectively prevented the wearer from wearing the hat with the left side-brim in the raised position. The issue of this headgear caused us to be known as 'Kennedy's Cowboys' . . . a reference to the Depot Commanding Officer, Squadron Leader Kennedy.

A high priority was put on endurance during training. Les Jewitt recalls being sent out on route marches and exercises in the surrounding rough, dry, scrub-covered country surrounding the Depot:

> On one occasion, led by our instructor, Flight Lieutenant Gilchrist, we set off on a cross-country march bearing a Lewis gun, but after a short while we noticed the Flight Lieutenant was getting further and further ahead of us, despite our high level of fitness. After a while he turned and walked back to us and gave a rollicking for lagging behind, then set off again. Once more he gained ground on us and there was not a thing we could do to catch up. He came back a second time and tore into us. The bloke who had been toting the Lewis gun exclaimed 'It's alright for you Sir . . . you aren't carrying a ruddy Lewis gun!' The response was for the Flight Lieutenant to pick up the gun and set off at a cracking pace once again . . . and again we simply could not keep up . . . Conclusion . . . we were not fit enough . . . extra PT was ordered!

John Buckman had trained as an RAF Regiment officer in the United Kingdom. He remembers the training and route marches at Secunderabad and the high standards now expected of the airmen:

> We were put through rigorous training, including assault courses and up to 20 miles of rough rock walking in climates of 100 degrees Fahrenheit plus. After these gruelling marches, there were understandably a number who did not finish the course. In all, I consider that the training was more rigorous than OCTU [Officer Cadet Training Unit] training with the Brigade of Guards.

> Colin Kirby, with 413 Squadron Defence Flight at Koggala, recalls men being selected for posting to the RAF Regiment Depot and other airmen arriving from there to replace them. It now appeared that ground defence was getting on to a much sounder footing:

> News filtered through that the RAF Regiment was in being, with a Depot at Secunderabad. Men in groups of four or five began to be posted there. Then an RAF Regiment AA Flight [4413] arrived during July 1943. We admired their bush hats and puttees and they took over some of the area defence. I received the call to go to the Depot with five others. By this time everybody

had forgotten about wanting to be anything but part of RAF Ground Defence. Calling us a Regiment would be fine.

Soon after reaching the Depot they were experiencing the tough new training regime. Fortunately, their previous experience at Koggala held them in good stead. Colin recalls:

> We went on long route marches, manoeuvres, rock climbing and swinging about and down the escarpments on ropes with kit and weapons. The country around the Depot was rough, undulating plain with high, rocky outcrops.
>
> I remember one day particularly well. We were out at first light and on the go all day marching, counter-marching, ambushing imaginary enemies, being ambushed in turn, all with full packs and minimum rations in torrid heat, climbing, firing weapons, until we set off back to the Depot. By this time we could hardly put one foot before the other, eyes glazed, faces caked with sweat. We looked like a scene from a melodramatic French Foreign Legion film, and as someone had the strength to mutter, he wished he had joined the Legion. Back to our bashas at last, collapse onto bunk . . . unable to move for a few hours. The next day back on parade, back on exercises etc. Relentless. Some men by this time were falling out and were posted away, others suffered with horrendous skin complaints. Those of us who had been through Arnold's regime in Ceylon seemed to cope.
>
> Some days we had to run miles with full packs and finish firing ten rounds rapid at a distant target with our Lee-Enfield rifle. Hands shaking, sweat stinging and filling our eyes. Sarcastic comments about accuracy.

After three weeks of training the airmen would be posted to field squadrons or AA flights, and would spend the remaining time at the Depot as an identifiable unit (Appendix 1). After the trials of weapons training, route marches and assault courses, leave could be taken in Secunderabad and nearby Hyderabad. Les Jewitt recalls that simply getting to and from the Depot, however, was a process fraught with difficulties:

> On arrival at the Depot one of the first things pointed out to us was the neces-sity of paying gharri-wallahs the officially agreed rate of transportation to and from Secunderabad, and the inference we gathered from this was that anyone contravening this instruction would find himself in trouble with the hierarchy. Our first trip to town, however, was in a local eighteen-seater bus powered by a charcoal-burning device and everything went according to the book. Later journeys by tonga were eventful as all manner of pressures were exerted on us to pay at least double the official rate and it soon came to be demanded of us that we pay the official rate before the journey commenced. Smelling a rat, but being determined to stick to the official rate, we paid up, but then had the mortification of having the gharri-wallah stop the tonga when only half way to town and order us to either pay again or get out of his tonga! Our motto for this favour was to 'fight fire with fire'. So we then began a process of 'out-conning' the con man by first arguing with him (no chance of success) then telling him 'OK chum . . . can you change a twenty-rupee note?' Which of course he could not, so then we went into the next phase of our operation, which consisted of telling him what a 'damn good gharri-wallah' he was, and that we wanted him to transport us round town, so if he would take us to the

WVS canteen on the racecourse, we would go in there for a cuppa and get change; so if he would wait for us outside we could then either take out the money to him or he could transport us round town and we would pay him whenever . . . ! The drill was then to have a meal at the WVS canteen and afterwards saunter across the racecourse to one of the cinemas, leaving the would-be con artist high and dry.

Gradually, as the position regarding transportation worsened, we found it best to walk into town and back, a journey of several miles each way. While it remains a well-established fact that our fellow countrymen and women resident in India at the time displayed nothing but disdain and contempt for 'rankers' such as we, there was a particular group of ladies who formed themselves into a charitable concern, which was known as 'The Hyderabad Women's War Work Committee', and they organised social evenings, garden parties, etc. and their kindness to RAF Regiment Depot staff was legendary.

Despite the improvements brought about by the establishment of the Training School, in January 1943 the Army still held prime responsibility for airfield defence in India. The RAF could only assume the AA defence of its airfields with light machine-guns against low-flying aircraft. Many of the Army troops allocated for airfield defence were not of the highest calibre and no provision had been made for airfield defence specialists trained to oppose an attack on the ground by high-grade enemy troops. Furthermore, as in other theatres, the Army troops were liable to be called away in times of crisis. The gap between the number of airmen required and the number available was large. In the United Kingdom, requests were already being made of the Air Ministry to cut numbers in the RAF Regiment in all theatres of operations.[11]

Estimates made at the time indicated that the RAF Regiment would require fifteen field squadrons and ninety AA flights for the task.[12] With restrictions placed on expansion of the RAF Regiment by the Air Ministry, and after the medically unfit had been eliminated, the existing strength would mean only fifteen squadrons and thirty-one AA flights could be formed. An option for recruitment of some of the 12,000 Indian Army personnel already being used on airfield defence was considered but eventually rejected by the Army. Thus, AHQ India was faced with the prospect of making do with the pool of airmen it already had in ground defence. After extensive discussions and negotiation between AHQ India and the Air Ministry in London, permission was obtained during May 1943 to implement what became known as the 'First Reorganisation'. Permission was finally given to form six field squadrons and seventy AA flights, appoint thirty Staff officers and train eleven officers and 300 NCOs as instructors. With a wastage pool of fifteen officers and 372 ORs, this gave a total pool of 162 officers and 4,092 NCOs and ORs in the RAF Regiment in India.

The proposal that the RAF Regiment could provide local airfield defence using additional Indian troops augmented by RAF Station personnel was not achievable and, therefore, the Army would still be required to provide general and local defence assisted by the RAF. RAF Regiment units were, however, to be allocated to those airfields accessible to Japanese ground forces and then, based on importance and location. The RAF Stations most vulnerable to enemy air attack were those in Assam, Bengal, Ceylon and on the east coast of India.[13] RAF Station personnel were to provide the bulk of resistance, with the RAF Regiment where provided, forming the hard-core of defence. They were to have particular roles in provision of LAA cover, dealing with pockets of the enemy and leading counter-attack.

To implement the change to properly trained and equipped RAF Regiment units, the Training School was renamed the 'RAF Regiment Depot' on 1 March 1943, and the number of staff increased. Under the new arrangements, the role of the RAF Regiment Depot would be training, equipping and forming field squadrons and AA flights; rather than training airmen in ground defence and returning them to their station or squadron defence flights. The Depot expansion meant that it now consisted of a CO, a Chief Instructor, a Medical Officer, an Adjutant, three formation wings, three squadron wings and three AA wings. The primary role of the field squadrons was ground defence of airfields, Air Ministry Experiment Stations (AMES) and wireless facilities, whereas the AA flights were to provide local AA defence of airfields with nine twin-Browning LMGs.

With the increase in size and responsibilities, it became necessary to move the Depot to a new site. From 1 to 12 March a move was made to Usofgooda, a mile or so to the west of Begampet, and, with the usual urgency, the Depot received the first airmen four days later at the new location (Sketch Map 1). The first task facing the Depot staff was to select those airmen who were medically fit and physically capable of carrying out the tasks now required of the RAF Regiment. The first draft was to make up the first field squadron to be formed and trained at the Depot and in India (Appendix 2). During the first weeks of the course No 1 Squadron, as it was popularly known, was to change its name and number on a regular basis; the first change was to 'Special AA Squadron', then 2901 Field Squadron, and finally to 2941 Field Squadron. Training commenced on 16 March for the field squadron, and four AA flights. No 2941 Field Squadron completed training on 9 April 1943 and departed by 17 April for Agartala in Bengal. On 14 April, 4401 to 4404 AA Flights[14] completed training and they were followed by 2942 Field Squadron in late May. Within two weeks another

Airmen of the newly formed squadron and AA flights crawl under barbed-wire while attempting the assault course at the RAF Regiment Depot Secunderabad, July 1943. (Air Historical Branch RAF Crown Copyright)

Airmen of the RAF Regiment swim with full kit across a tank forming part of the Battle Inoculation Course at the RAF Regiment Depot Secunderabad, July 1943. (Air Historical Branch RAF Crown Copyright)

squadron and four flights had been formed and were training at the Depot. This six-week cycle of formation and training of urgently required squadrons and AA flights for despatch to airfields in Bengal, Assam and Manipur was to continue unabated for the next eight months.

The officers and airmen of the RAF Regiment were proud of the toughness of the Assault Course at Secunderabad. Under various incarnations it assumed some notoriety and was reputed to be the most exacting in India; a fact proudly trumpeted by senior RAF officers at the time. To demonstrate the toughness of the new RAF Regiment, airmen would be sent through the course under the observation of senior Army and RAF officers. The Army officers who came to watch considered it tougher than anything the Army had and, moreover, unfair to ask men to attempt it. A certain percentage always came to grief and ended up in the local military hospital. The airmen would begin by crawling under a net 18 inches off the ground, then vault a 3 foot high wall, move up to a 7 foot 6 inch high ramp, jump off with a front roll, climb over a further 4 foot high wall, wade through a water tank and climb another wall, this time over ten foot high, jump off with another front roll, double 50 yards, crawl under a car ramp, double another 70 yards and vault over barbed wire entanglements to five square holes, varying in depth and spaced at 1.5-yard intervals. At each hole the men made a point with the bayonet at a dummy then dived under another net, ran through a long and winding trench filled with dannert wire and smoke, crossed a 15 foot plank and grabbed on to a rope from which they swung over wire to a distance of 10 feet to represent swinging over a chasm. They then went on to a steel rope along which they moved hand over hand, on to another rope, also hand-over-hand, doubled 200 yards and then completed six bayonet thrusts at dummies.[15] This rather clinical description from an Operations Record Book (ORB) is given a more human perspective when described by one of the airmen who helped to design, build and demonstrate the assault course. Les Jewitt remembers the preparation required before it could be attempted:

> The Begampet Assault Course was a killer; savage and severe, and before it could be tackled our physical fitness had to be built up to what was considered an adequate level. This brought us into contact with the Depot PT Instructor, Sergeant 'Nick' Carter, who also taught us martial arts and 'the silent kill'. Nick was a legend in his own lifetime, dreaded by most, feared and hated by so many, yet deeply respected by quite a lot of us. In my opinion he did more to instil toughness and fighting qualities in us than any other individual or collection of individuals. He taught us a form of what he always referred to as 'Karoti' and one day some of the 'bods' came across a magazine article which identified the subject as 'Karate'; [they] had the temerity to reproach 'Nick' for his mispronunciation of the word, which brought forth his response, 'If I say it's f . . . ing Karoti, it's f . . . ing Karoti! OK?'
>
> The build up to the assault course consisted of a row of bricks, one course high, set in the ground; a few yards further on another row of bricks two courses high; then three courses, etc. etc. and each of these mini-obstacles had to be overcome under the eagle eye of 'Nick' . . . which we thought was ridiculous in the extreme, until he sent one bloke back to negotiate the two-course high row of bricks, having noticed the chap dodge around the end of the obstacle. In the event it transpired that the bloke did not have the nerve to go over the obstacle, so he was given a form of counselling in a kind, fatherly manner to try to help him overcome his phobia but without success. The airman departed the Depot soon after.
>
> The two outstanding features of the assault course, so far as I was concerned, were, (a) the smoke-filled trench, several feet deep, filled to waist height with muddy water and barbed wire entanglements both above and below water level (it would have been easy to get trapped below water in one of the deep holes criss-crossed at angles with trip wires), and, (b) the wall . . . eight feet or perhaps ten . . . It was a nightmare to scale after having traversed the other obstacles, but one received encouragement to climb it by 'Nick' Carter who suddenly appeared alongside the wall and, in very rude military language informed us that if we didn't get up that 'f . . . ing wall' he would 'Tear it down and shove it up your a . . . brick by brick!' To give emphasis to his words Bakelite grenades would begin to explode around one's feet. Somehow or other we all managed, with varying degrees of extreme difficulty, to master the obstacles.

A Battle Inoculation or 'Blitz' Course with live firing was set up later. It was approximately 2,000 yards in length and the airmen were expected to move at the double all the time. The course culminated in a swim in full equipment through an 80-yard long tank. Bakelite grenades were tossed about and machine-guns fired live rounds on fixed lines at selected locations on the course.

With the move to the new RAF Regiment Depot, the Assault and Battle Inoculation Courses had to be created anew. Ted Daines, who had come to the Depot from 160 Squadron Defence Flight at Kumbhirgram in Assam, had a hand in setting up the new Battle Inoculation Course (Sketch Map 2):

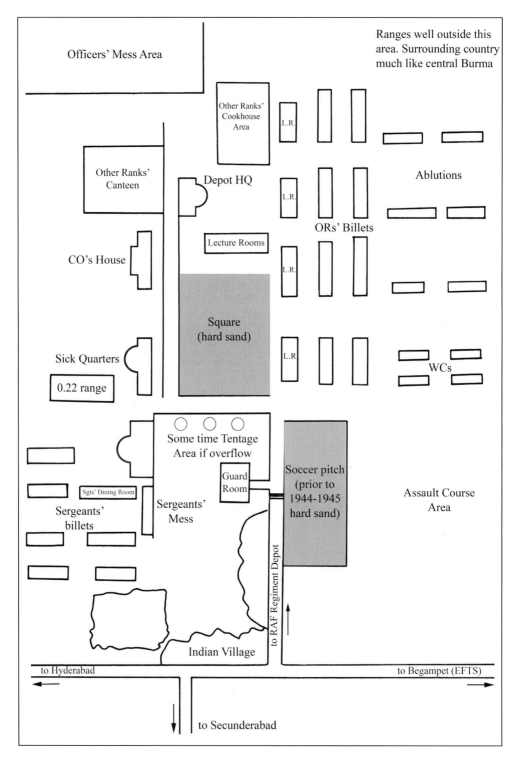

Ranges well outside this area. Surrounding country much like central Burma

Officers' Mess Area

Other Ranks' Cookhouse Area

L.R.

Ablutions

Other Ranks' Canteen

Depot HQ

L.R.

ORs' Billets

Lecture Rooms

CO's House

L.R.

Square (hard sand)

Sick Quarters

L.R.

WCs

0.22 range

Some time Tentage Area if overflow

Guard Room

Soccer pitch (prior to 1944-1945 hard sand)

Assault Course Area

Sgts' Dining Room

Sergeants' Mess

Sergeants' billets

to RAF Regiment Depot

Indian Village

to Hyderabad

to Begampet (EFTS)

to Secunderabad

1 *The RAF Regiment Depot, Secunderabad circa 1944–5. (From a map drawn by Ted Daines.)*

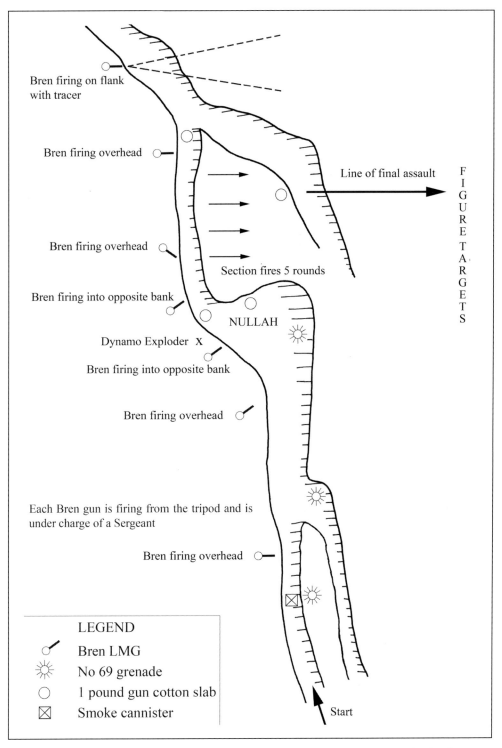

Bren firing on flank
with tracer

Bren firing overhead

Line of final assault

FIGURE TARGETS

Bren firing overhead

Section fires 5 rounds

Bren firing into opposite bank

NULLAH

Dynamo Exploder X

Bren firing into opposite bank

Bren firing overhead

Each Bren gun is firing from the tripod and is
under charge of a Sergeant

Bren firing overhead

LEGEND

Bren LMG
No 69 grenade
1 pound gun cotton slab
Smoke cannister

Start

2 *The Battle Inoculation Course at the RAF Regiment Depot Secunderabad February
1944*

A member of staff at the time was Squadron Leader Gilchrist, a short, very dour Scot. We were aiming a Bren for firing on fixed lines. Gilchrist was armed with a short cleft stick, which had a white disc jammed into the cleft. Gilchrist said 'I am going out about two hundred yards; I will climb onto a boulder, when I raise the disc, aim and lock the aim on. When all is ready I shall shout "fire!" [and] one round will be fired.' We were ready, and he shouted 'Fire!' One round was fired; he promptly went over backwards and disappeared from view. We all thought we had shot him. The relief was great when two or three minutes later he appeared limping and very dusty. At the exact time the trigger was pressed, he had slipped and gone over the back of the rock. Apart from a few scratches he was fortunately OK.

Following the construction of the Battle Inoculation Course a Squad was formed, which would be based at the Depot and would be involved in training new personnel 'by example' or 'demonstration'. Those selected were immediately formed into a separate unit. Les Jewitt recounts the early development of the 'Demo Squad':

At the conclusion of our course we would in the normal course of events have been posted, either back to our own units or elsewhere. Now the CO announced that he would be selecting personnel from our ranks to form a demonstration flight or 'demo squad'. The flight would be instrumental in assisting the training of future units.

Around this time it was announced that the Depot was being moved to a new site, a few miles away, where contractors were constructing billets. Sergeant 'Nick' Carter was detailed to take half a dozen men of 'Demo Squad' and proceed to the new campsite to assist in the development. Being one of the half-dozen, I looked forward to moving to the new site. On arriving there, however, I began to entertain grave doubts about the suitability of the site as there was no tarmac anywhere; only bare earth for a parade ground, bashas under construction for us to live in and a cross-country trek of some two miles to the nearest metalled road, then several more miles to Secunderabad. The reason for Sergeant Carter's working party soon resolved itself into being a task force charged with the construction of a new assault course! Great stuff this, it would give us the opportunity of showing folks what an assault course ought to be like, and we gave pretty free rein to our imagination in this respect, finally coming up with a course from which a number of obstacles were deleted before anyone even had the chance to try them! That still left one awesome course, though, knowing full well that we would not be required to ever negotiate it, we felt rather smug about it.

Eventually, the day came when trainees were being introduced to the assault course and the CO in addressing the assembled [airmen] stated something to the effect that 'This assault course has been described as very tough, but this is nowhere near as tough as people make out and to prove this Sergeant Carter and his merry men will go round the course now by way of demonstration.' Talk about being nonplussed and crestfallen. This was terrible! It rested with 'Nick' to get us off the hook and he did this most diplomatically by suggesting that we go round it obstacle by obstacle, pausing at each to describe it in detail, so that everybody would be *au fait* with it all and not be overawed by it.

The dubious privilege of being the first unit in training to try the new Battle Inoculation Course fell to 2942 Field Squadron. The course simulated the complete field squadron in attack and was designed to expose the airmen to the firing of live rounds over their heads and close proximity to explosions. It used Bren LMGs firing on fixed lines and gun cotton explosive set at intervals along the route. The course was by no means safe and casualties often occurred. Even the instructors were exposed to danger, as Ted Daines recall:

> Sergeant Davies was part of the live ammunition demonstration and got a bullet through his shoulder. Sergeant Cole, his partner in the demo, got a broken arm. Being an instructor at the Depot was not the safest occupation. It was not long before I received a fragment in the arm.

Les Jewitt remembers some of the tensions that developed with a situation fraught with danger:

> Not long after the new course was opened Johnny 'Muscles' Bearpark of the 'Demo Squad' was wounded in the left shoulder by the lead ball from a grenade which exploded alongside him as he dropped off the wall. A particular Corporal in the 'Demo Squad', who liked to be noticed, had left his position during a 'fire and movement exercise' with live ammo, to run across in front of his section as it began to lay down fire on its target area. In the billet that night this caused a rumpus with the [man] who had almost shot him accidentally. The row ended with the Corporal pulling rank while the 'bod' warned against any recurrence of the incident. Next day saw a repetition of this exercise and, unfortunately, a repetition of the Corporal's misbehaviour. Suddenly, amidst a volley of shots, there was a scream as the Corporal moved across in front of his section; his steel helmet flew up in the air and he dropped like a log. A .303 bullet had struck his left arm and had been deflected upwards by the bone, emerging through his shoulder and knocking off his tin hat. A training accident . . . ?

With such a tough regime and the harsh climate, there were always men going sick or injured. Colin Kirby recalls the 'medical parades' and the unsympathetic hearing given by the then Depot Medical Officer:

> The MO at the time was a 'nutcase' who took medical parades where he walked down the lines of men, each having to display their identity discs worn around the neck. This was followed by a lecture on the necessity of wearing these, followed by strong hints that the medical room would not welcome men reporting sick. Anyone suffering with the 'runs', nausea or general fatigue brought about by the regime was given short shrift. 'Medicine and duty' was usually the verdict. The unfortunates crept back to their training sections and the sergeant in charge would decide how much 'duty' and how much 'medicine' (maybe half a day's rest).

The airmen proceeding on exercises in the red-soiled, dusty, dry and scrub-covered country surrounding the Depot needed to keep in mind the presence of the large numbers of venomous snakes. Ted Daines recalls:

Snakes were common in the area. Out on the Assault Course one day, Sergeant Cole was firing one of the Bren guns. He decided to have a brew up and with plenty of wood lying about it was only a matter of a few minutes before a fire was blazing. To keep the fire going the Sergeant collected some more wood, including a nice little log, throwing this on the fire, and being rotten it burst open, and out slithered a Krait, a most deadly snake indeed. A week or two later he was writing a letter in his hut under the light of an oil lamp when another Krait fell from the roof of the basha. It landed on the table and slithered away.

The presence of snakes, however, was not necessarily completely bad . . . at the Depot, Frank Lowers, with the nickname 'Snakey', had the rather unusual task of capturing venomous snakes which were then kept in special containers. Frank would then 'milk' the creatures and the venom procured was used for the preparation of suitable antidotes.

An armourer was required for each of the RAF Regiment units and, therefore, as each squadron and AA flight was formed, one or two airmen were selected and despatched to No 1 School of Technical Training at Ambala in the Punjab. Arriving at Secunderabad in late 1943, LAC Henry Kirk of 99 Squadron Defence Flight was selected to be an Armourer along with twenty-four other airmen. At the time the RAF Regiment was coming under increasing pressure to cut its numbers and despatch suitably qualified tradesmen to technical positions in the flying squadrons and Henry's attendance and success at the Armourer's Course nearly ended his association with the RAF Regiment:

What I didn't know at the time was that the RAF in India had orders to run down the RAF Regiment and remuster them because they were short of men on RAF squadrons. They were short of all sorts of trades. They said, 'We'll pinch them out of the RAF Regiment.' What they didn't know was we didn't even have enough RAF Regiment men to do what they had to do, because the Army wasn't defending airfields, as they didn't have the men. That was before Imphal. So off I went on this course to Ambala in the Punjab. There were twenty-five on that course and I came top.

A Squadron Leader Nightingale sent for me, and he said, 'You've done well on this course. I want to remuster you'. There was no promotion for an armourer in an RAF Regiment Field Squadron. The posting was for an LAC from November 1940 until I came out in 1946. No promotion possible. That was it. Now I didn't know anything about this until after the war. I remember thinking how can he transfer me out of the RAF Regiment, I've got to go back to Secunderabad? The lads I'd been with in 99 Squadron, thirty or forty of them, were now all in 2944 Field Squadron. I was with them in England, and at Digri and Jessore, and I wanted to stay with them out here. He said 'I want to remuster you; you can stop here another month or so for another course that's going to start and I promise you that you'll go out of here as a Corporal and be sent to a fighter squadron.' I ummed and aahed and said, 'I'll think it over. I'll let you know by tomorrow.' I remember at the time thinking, 'How can he do that?' Obviously he could.

I turned the offer down and when I got back to Secunderabad they went and put me in another Field Squadron! I went to the Adjutant and said, 'I needn't have come back here.' He looked at my record and said, 'I see you did well on that course.' I told him what they wanted to do with me and he said, 'Oh did he!' I said, 'I wanted to be with the lads, but they've already got an armourer.' He said, 'Well I'll take it up.' And that was how I got back with the lads in 2944 and spent the next 15 months sleeping on Mother Earth.

In June 1943 the Depot acquired a further role when it was ordered to train a few hundred RAF Regiment personnel, with the rank of Sergeant or Corporal, as Defence Training Instructors (DTIs). These NCOs were to go out to airfields and other RAF facilities and transfer their knowledge on airfield defence and survival techniques to RAF aircrew and station personnel. Jim Robinson recalls the DTI Training Course and his new responsibilities:

I passed out on that course as a Sergeant Instructor [DTI], and with four corporals was posted firstly to RAF Station Agartala and subsequently to RAF Stations Chittagong and Comilla. Due to the apparent lack of individual defence training . . . Lord Louis Mountbatten had decided that all personnel should attend a cadre course [known as a 'backers-up' course]. No one excluded! Officers, aircrew, ground staff and Army personnel that were attached to the [air] station such as Heavy AA and Signals . . . it appeared that tradesmen such as cooks, signals and admin were not trained to defend themselves . . . everyone had to become reasonably self-sufficient.

The course would include field craft, unarmed combat, the use of rifle, pistol, a little aircraft recognition, firing on the range, priming and throwing grenades and jungle training. To get through the number of personnel, the course was limited to just one week. I would take classes of officers, senior NCOs and aircrew and my Corporals would take the ORs.

I might add that it was not a popular course and it was especially resented by some officers and aircrew, but at the end a great percentage had enjoyed it. It was a diversion from normal duties . . . they learned something new, and appreciated the need for such a course, and now felt they were able to contribute to their own well-being and to that of others. This, of course, was going on at other RAF Stations with other groups of instructors, of whom all had come out of the Depot. I was also responsible for a monthly report and update of all arms and equipment held by Air Force and Army units on the station to GHQ Delhi.

I think it was fair to say that most had received more training and knowledge in that one week than possibly in all their previous military service. Although a short course, it was very comprehensive. We felt quite proud that it fell to the RAF Regiment to train so many to help them save their own skins . . . I felt it was well worthwhile and a great achievement.

A necessity for the RAF Regiment Depot and the new Corps was to have a band. The Nizam of Hyderabad kindly donated the instruments and the magnificent leopard skins were given by the daughter of his Senior Physician.[16] Les Jewitt was the first Drum Major of the RAF Regiment Depot Band and describes the events leading to its formation:

A rumour believed to have emanated from the Orderly Room, made the rounds of the new camp, to the effect that personnel from the 'Demo Squad' would be undergoing training as musicians, drummers etc. and would then form a marching band. In due course we of the 'Demo Squad' were told that some of us would be going to the Gordon Highlanders for tuition on bagpipes. On the appointed day it was announced that there had been a change of plan. Along with a number of others, I found myself at a mechanised cavalry regiment being instructed on the merits, and otherwise, of the General Grant tank, after which we all piled inside and went for a spin around the tank-testing ground under the auspices of an Hussar sergeant.

The piping lessons never did materialise, but one day the CO picked out the nucleus of what he then announced would be the band. Some individuals had limited amounts of drumming ability and some had an aptitude for the trumpet, but there was no musical library with the various instruments and it was pretty rough going at first, however, things improved as we went along. The CO informed me that he had been a Drum Major with the Band of the Manchester Regiment for a number of years, and he proceeded to give me all the instruction for the efficient discharge of the duties of Drum Major; right there on the flat roof of his detached house. Long before we felt ready to cope with any public performance; we were told that we would 'play out' units leaving Secunderabad for active service and our first such parade was carefully planned. It had to be; we only knew two trumpet marches, and these had to be spread out to cover a march of almost half a mile. So, on the Saturday evening prior to the march, the CO, the Adjutant and I 'walked the course' and laid our plans. Thus it was on the following Monday evening when the march began, it did so with the rather unusual formula of two seven-pace drum rolls, followed by a fanfare of trumpets (four paces), another seven-pace drum roll

Two drummers from the RAF Regiment Band at Rangoon in June 1945. The band instruments were paid for by the Nizam of Hyderabad and the leopard skins given by the daughter of his Senior Physician (RAF Regiment SEAC Association)

The RAF Regiment Depot Band and the 'Demo' Flight at Mountbatten's SEAC HQ at Kandy Ceylon in 1944. The Drum Major was Sergeant Geoffrey Eggleton. (RAF Regiment SEAC Association)

and four paces of the fanfare of trumpets, then into the trumpet march from 'Semper Fidelis' and, hey presto, we were almost halfway to the railway station.

An RAF Dance Band was also formed from a few of the jazz enthusiasts at the Depot and was a resounding success from the word 'go'. They kept abreast of the latest hits of popular music and all were very good musicians. Ironically, none played in the Depot Band.

Every day a duty trumpeter played all the calls through 'Reveille' to 'Lights Out'. On one particular occasion, trumpeter 'Ginger' Riseley was playing 'Last Post' from atop a mound. He was rather near to the billets of trainees who had had an extremely trying day and were not in the best of tempers. Part way through the trumpet call a vast chorus of voices erupted in fury and demanded 'Shut up you noisy Bastard!' and a few other choice comments; as the trumpeter in question had not had a good day himself, he broke off the call around the halfway stage and yelled back at his tormentors 'Bollocks!' and then calmly resumed his call.

From imperfect beginnings the Depot Band grew. It gained a section of pipers, and was eventually in great demand for ceremonial occasions. A commemoration of the third anniversary of the Battle of Britain was held in September 1943 at a drumhead service at Secunderabad and the RAF Regiment Band played a significant part. All twelve of the AA flights then in training were also present with the British Resident, The Honourable Sir Arthur Lothian, taking the salute at the 'March Past'. In January 1944 Flight Lieutenant Gosnell and Flying Officer Payne, along with the demonstration flight of thirty-two men and four trumpeters, left for Bhopal to act as guard of honour on the occasion of the presentation of Honorary Rank of Air Commodore to His Excellency The Nawab of Bhopal. On 17 September 1944 the Band was in attendance at the nearby Secunderabad No 1 Elementary Flying Training School for a 'Battle of Britain'

Parade. All units of RAF Station Secunderabad were represented, with the RAF Regiment having 300 men on parade.

During November 1943 Wing Commander Kennedy was repatriated to the United Kingdom due to illness. As a result Squadron Leader McKirdy became Chief Instructor while Squadron Leader W.A.P. Gardner assumed command of the Depot until the arrival in March 1944 of Wing Commander J.L. Fowke, previously Ground Defence Officer for the 3rd Tactical Air Force. In September 1944 Fowke departed on temporary attachment to ACSEA and McKirdy became CO of the Depot in his absence.

By January 1944 all the authorised squadrons and AA Flights had been trained, however, there still remained a pool of surplus personnel resulting from the disband-ment of the station and squadron defence flights. The Air Ministry in London, which was now taking renewed steps to minimise the number of personnel in the RAF Regiment, was unlikely to authorise the formation of additional flights. AHQ India, therefore, authorised the formation of a further twelve AA flights on a lower manpower 'Indian' establishment; many with a Flight Sergeant in command and a few less airmen than the AA flights. The India AA flights, as they were known, were numbered from 1 to 12 until the Air Ministry could allocate the appropriate four-digit number beginning with 4. These numbers were never allocated and they remained as Nos 1–12 (India) AA Flights for the six to eight months they were in existence.

Large numbers of airmen had now passed through the RAF Regiment Depot, having been trained to a previously unimagined level for their specialist role in ground defence. In just over ten months the RAF Regiment in India was transformed from a group of disparate flights of varying quality, experience and capability into a uniform and highly trained specialist Corps. Six Field Squadrons and sixty-two AA Flights had been formed and trained at the RAF Regiment Depot (Appendix 2). Moving off to battle stations, they were to play an important role in the coming crucial battles for the defence of India in the Arakan and at Imphal. The Depot would maintain a steady flow of reinforcements for the units in forward areas until decisions at higher levels would lead to the requirement for reorganisation and training of new RAF Regiment units.

Notes

1   Air Ministry Memorandum quoted in M.S. Witherow, 'Flying Soldiers in Blue Khaki, The Royal Air Force Regiment Part 1' *Army Quarterly & Defence Journal.* 118, 1988, pp. 187–8.

2   RAF assets included not only airfields and aircraft but radar and wireless installations, Group, Wing and Squadron HQs, Air Stores Parks, Repair & Salvage Units and Supply and Transport columns.

3   If the Allies needed any further affirmation that a dedicated airfield defence force was required, it was given when the Japanese attacked Palembang airfield on the island of Sumatra on 14 February 1942. While 258 (Hurricane) Squadron was airborne the airfield was overrun by parachute troops. Flying Officer Matthys Tauté of the RAF Regiment (the Regiment had only been in existence for 14 days) led counterattacks with a Squadron Defence Flight of only 20 airmen in an attempt to drive back the Japanese as they attempted to take control of the airstrip. This was the only force available to defend the strip other than a few Army AA gunners. He was subsequently taken prisoner but survived the war and in March 1946 was awarded the Military Cross for his actions at Palembang. As such, his recommendation for the MC was the last to be gazetted for service during the Second World War due to his long imprisonment with the Japanese. Moreover, he was the first RAF Regiment officer to perform an act leading to the award of the MC. A detailed account of

this action is provided in *In Adversity*, N.G. Tucker, Oldham, Lancashire, Jade Publishing 1997, pp. 101–103.

4   This was the 2nd King's Own Yorkshire Light Infantry. Hingston, W. *Never Give Up. History of the King's Own Yorkshire Light Infantry 1919–1942*. Vol. V. York: Published by the Regiment, 1950, p. 145.

5   Slim, W. *Defeat into Victory*. 2nd ed. London: Cassell, 1956, pp. 21–2.

6   *Ground Defence and the RAF Regiment in India and South-East Asia 1942–1945*, RAF Regiment Museum, Honington, Suffolk, p. 6.

7   George Doughty Arnold had served for nearly three years during the First World War in the artillery of the 1st Australian Imperial Force, including a period on the Western Front. He had joined the RAF Volunteer Reserve in May 1941 in Australia and arrived in Ceylon on 28 February 1942. He was posted immediately to RAF Station Koggala. He was born on 15 May 1896 and thus he was 45 years old when he began his period of active service with the RAF Regiment.

8   Later Air Vice-Marshal Jack Harris CB CBE (1903–1963).

9   *Ground Defence and the RAF Regiment*, op. cit., p. 8.

10 At the time the Nizam of Hyderabad was reputedly the richest man in the world.

11 A reduction of 35% in the global ceiling of the RAF Regiment had been ordered in December 1942 and the original saving of 10,000 was later increased to a total of 30,000.

12 This was based on a minimum of one field squadron and three AA flights to each wing in forward areas.

13 These areas were the responsibility of 221, 222, 224 and 225 Groups.

14 Originally numbered 4351 to 4354.

15 AIR 29/716, *No 1 RAF Regiment Training School, later RAF Regiment (ACSEA) Secunderabad (with Appendices)*.

16 The leopard skins are now held at the RAF Regiment Museum at RAF Honington, Suffolk.

CHAPTER TWO

First and Second Arakan – The RAF Regiment Deploys

'Units of the RAF Regiment have proved themselves of the greatest value in this campaign, of which the insecurity of airfields and warning establishments in forward areas has been a feature . . .'

Air Marshal Sir John Baldwin KBE CB DSO,
Air Commander, 3rd Tactical Air Force

The war in North Africa, the Battle of the Atlantic and the defence of the United Kingdom were of greater priority to the Allies in 1942 than the war in the Far East. The few RAF units that could be spared were despatched to Malaya, Singapore and Burma. With inadequate and outdated air and naval forces and an Army that had yet to learn how to fight an efficient, well trained and ruthless foe, these countries were quickly overrun in a few months by the seemingly unstoppable Japanese Imperial Army. The monsoon of May 1942 had fortunately caused the Japanese to halt on the eastern borders of India. Only a small British-Indian force could be put in place to oppose them. There were two main fronts; that of IV Corps at Imphal with 23rd Indian Division and the remnants of the Army that had withdrawn from Burma being the main component, and to the south-west, 14th Indian Division, which held a defensive line around Chittagong. Apart from small patrol actions, the monsoon prevented any large-scale military operations until October 1942.

Despite limited resources, political pressures required that an offensive be launched against the Japanese as early as possible after the end of the monsoon. The British-Indian troops in the east of India were placed under the command of the Eastern Army, which was charged with launching the offensive. The Eastern Army lacked adequately trained troops and landing craft for an amphibious landing on the Arakan coast and, therefore, a limited land advance was all that was possible. Other theatres had higher priority for landing craft necessary for amphibious landings and this was to plague the Allied military planners in South-East Asia for the remainder of the war. The First Arakan offensive lasted from September 1942 to March 1943, with the limited objective being to reoccupy north Arakan and capture Akyab Island with its harbour and airfield. It should be recalled that at this time the Eighth Army was fighting to prevent the fall of Egypt and the British position in the Middle East to the German-Italian Army.

The offensive went well at first and the 14th Indian Division met limited opposition, with the advance progressing at a reasonable pace until February 1943. Poor lines of communication and inadequate coastal shipping limited the pace of the land advance. With intensifying Japanese resistance and supply difficulties, the advance bogged down south of the line from Maungdaw to Buthidaung. The reprieve gave the Japanese time to dig-in and in doing so they constructed a series of virtually impregnable defensive positions. British and Indian battalions spent themselves in repeated and ultimately futile attacks to take these positions by frontal assault. Unfortunately, due to intense political pressure for success, attacks were persisted with when it should have been apparent that further action was wasting lives with little chance of success. Matters then deteriorated rapidly. In early February the Japanese launched a counter-offensive and applied their usual encircling tactics; Japanese columns moved up through the Kaladan Valley and launched themselves on the Eastern Army's tenuous supply lines (Map 2).

With the crisis deepening, XV Indian Corps HQ under the command of Lieutenant-General W.J. 'Bill' Slim was brought forward during April to take over the unwieldy and poorly organised command structure. Slim persisted with the offensive for two more months but the impending monsoon, exhaustion and the further threats by the Japanese to the left flank forced a withdrawal in early May to the start line from which the Eastern Army had departed so hopefully in the previous year. The monsoon line was established by the end of May in the Cox's Bazaar-Ramu-Ukhia area. The Japanese could not bypass this position and it at least allowed for the retention of the forward airfields at Chittagong, Cox's Bazaar and Ramu. Slim was able to extract the bulk of the demoralised force, and, importantly, he gained further worthwhile experience in fighting the Japanese. His only option had been to withdraw and take stock of the failings of the campaign. New tactics and attitudes to fighting in the jungle against the Japanese had to be developed.

A highlight of the otherwise disappointing First Arakan campaign was the performance of the RAF, which with limited resources had staunchly supported the Eastern Army. Military operations in India had always had their main focus on the Northwest Frontier and, as a result, India was not well prepared for either land or air action against an aggressor coming from the east. The RAF had few all-weather airfields from which it could support offensive operations. Forward landing grounds had been desperately needed for the RAF to launch sweeps over Burma and to support the land offensive. An active programme of airstrip construction meant that by 1943 numerous forward airstrips, albeit mostly fair-weather, were operational. Having steadily built up its resources since mid-1942, the RAF had operated in the First Arakan campaign at maximum effort. No. 221 Group at Calcutta, with responsibility for bomber, coastal and fighter squadrons, defended the city, while 224 Group at Chittagong controlled the fighter and light bomber squadrons operating over the entire Burma front from Assam to the Bay of Bengal. Equipped predominantly with the Hurricane fighter, which was considered inferior to the Japanese 'Zero,' and the Blenheim light bomber, the two Groups had at least prevented large scale raids on towns and airfields of south-east Bengal. They had also provided more effective air to ground support than the Japanese Air Force had to their own troops. The RAF had achieved temporary local air superiority over the Arakan. This had allowed the Eastern Army to operate without constantly glancing skyward for enemy aircraft as had been the case for British and Empire troops in France, Greece and Crete during the early years of the war and in Malaya and Burma in 1942.

By November 1942 approximately thirty ground defence flights were distributed across the flying squadrons or were attached to Station and Group HQs, while other detachments were with Radar, Wireless, Recovery & Salvage and Air Stores Parks units (Appendix 3). It will be recalled that at this time ground defence was in a parlous state with regard to equipment and personnel. This is exemplified by the experience of the 'Tezpur' and 'Bombay' Defence Flights. The 'Tezpur' Flight had arrived at Chittagong from its previous station in the Upper Brahmaputra Valley on 27 December 1942. 'Bombay' Flight had arrived in Chittagong from Bombay (made up of personnel recently arrived from the UK) on 1 January without automatic weapons and, in *lieu* of any others, was armed with Bren LMGs of which at that time they had little knowledge. One section of the 'Tezpur' Flight was, therefore, posted to 'Bombay' Flight in exchange for one section of that unit. Within a fortnight the airmen of the latter flight were on air and ground defence duties at the forward airstrip at 'Hay' near Ramu.

With the apparent early success of the First Arakan offensive by the Eastern Army, some squadron defence flights had moved forward in early December independently of their flying squadrons. During January 1943, 79, 135, 136 and 607 Squadrons' flights were moved to 'Hay' and Nidania and the forward airstrips at Maungdaw North and Maungdaw South, respectively. Most of these strips were primitive in their construction. 'Reindeer I' at Ramu had been scraped out of a large expanse of paddy field. Nidania (code-named 'George') was 14 miles further to the south and adjacent to the beach on the Teknaf Peninsula and described as 1,000 yards by 70 yards of grass and powdery sand laid with steel mesh. The airstrip code-named 'Hove' (also known as Beach Strip), located south of Nidania, was merely a sea beach useable at all times except high tide.[1] The two Maungdaw strips were vital for the RAF and Eastern Army at this time, with 28 Squadron flying tactical reconnaissance sorties and detachments of 79 and 615 Squadrons on fighter operations. Some of the defence flights moved closely behind the advancing troops to provide protection for the mobile short-range radar units (AMES). Just as importantly, therefore, Maungdaw was the location of a forward AMES providing early warning for incoming air raids and allowing accurate and rapid interception. The 'Tezpur' Flight commanded by Flying Officer G.T. Bell had an important and special role given to it when it was ordered forward on 7 January to Maungdaw North. It was to protect the GCI radar and transmitting station, which was to be established 35 miles further south at Foul Point following its occupation by the 14th Indian Division. The planned move proved optimistic, as the advance stalled and Foul Point at the tip of the Mayu Peninsula and the jumping off point for the move on Akyab Island was not reached. However, the flight did move as far south as Indin before being withdrawn. Early air interception was essential to protect the forward airfields and to divert attacks on the major cities and towns to the north, so the AMES and their defence flights were not moved back until the last possible moment. No 4401 AA Flight was sent as far south as Teknaf on 3 May, where it remained until three days

Nidania airstrip on the south Bengal coast. Although this photo was taken in March 1945, it shows the rudimentary nature of the airstrips and the close country surrounding them. (Australian War Memorial SEA 0202)

LAC Challmer and LAC Padgin of gun post 'Robinson Crusoe' at 'Hove' airstrip. The Browning LMGs were the heaviest weapons the Regiment possessed until the arrival of large numbers of Hispano 20-mm cannon in mid-1944. (Air Historical Branch RAF Crown Copyright)

before the Army withdrawal from Maungdaw to Cox's Bazaar began on 11 May.

By April 1943 nine defence Flights were operating around Ramu, with two Flights at Maungdaw and an R&SU Flight[2] at Teknaf on the Naf Peninsula (Appendix 4). During the First Arakan offensive the Japanese Air Force flew 1,159 sorties with airfields being the primary targets. The 224 Group airstrips were attacked repeatedly during March, April and May 1943 and Ground Defence personnel were frequently and directly involved. However, their capacity for an effective response was limited by the range and power of their AA machine-guns.

On Sunday 27 March 1943 the 'Bombay' and 165 Wing HQ flights engaged a Japanese 'Sonia' light bomber flying over 'Lyons' and 'Reindeer' but no hits were observed. On 5 May, only three days after arriving from the RAF Regiment Depot, 4402 AA Flight at Dohazari strip suffered its first casualties. An attack by Japanese aircraft destroyed two Blenheims on the ground, wounding LACs J. Eland and Naveen, while Corporal G.E.V. Garratt was killed immediately and LAC N.D. Harrison died of wounds the following day. On 21 May at 0900 hours 136 Squadron Defence Flight saw fifteen enemy aircraft approaching the 'Lyons' strip from the west. Four twin-Browning machine-guns opened fire at about 500 feet and hits were observed. A few minutes later 79 Squadron Defence Flight at nearby 'Hay' strip saw the same enemy aircraft at 1,000 feet and hits were also claimed by three of the gun posts. Unfortunately faulty ammunition and jamming weapons prevented some of the Browning LMGs from firing.

The raid of early May was to have great significance for the air war over Burma. Observing events was Wing Commander Paul Richey DFC & bar, an experienced fighter pilot who had fought in the Battle of Britain and over occupied Europe. He had been sent to the Far East to report on fighter control and tactics. His report criti-cised the way that enemy attacks were tracked and intercepted. Moreover, he emphasised that the RAF could only achieve air superiority over the Japanese Air Force if equipped with Spitfires rather than the trusty but slower and less agile Hurricanes.[3] The latter recommendation was eventually implemented in late 1943.

As soon as the monsoon started most air operations ceased and aircraft were with-drawn to the all-weather airfields. Prior to the monsoon of 1943 twenty-five airstrips were available, but by the time it was in full spate, only eight were serviceable. As the weather worsened during May the forward squadrons of 165 Wing and the defence flights were moved back to the few all-weather airstrips at Chittagong and Dohazari to see out the monsoon. Fortunately the Japanese Air Force was reluctant to fly in the monsoon so enemy air activity correspondingly declined and by June 1943 the RAF was in complete control of the skies over the Arakan. For the RAF, valuable lessons had been learned, however, the First Arakan campaign was best described as a draw rather than a victory.

As a result of the 'First Reorganisation' of the RAF Regiment in India, completely formed and autonomous units had begun arriving from the RAF Regiment Depot at Secunderabad. From April 1943 Field Squadrons and AA Flights were deployed in defence of airstrips of 221, 224 and 231 Groups. By June 1943 and the end of the First Arakan offensive, these totalled four squadrons and twelve flights: two squadrons and nine flights in 224 Group, one flight in 221 Group and two squadrons and two flights in 231 (Appendix 5). By the end of the year the RAF Regiment had deployed five squadrons and twenty-six flights in 224 Group (Appendix 6), one squadron and ten flights in 221 Group (Appendix 7), eight flights in 231 Group and four flights in 222 Group (Appendix 8). This gave a total of six field squadrons and fifty AA flights. The field squadrons and AA flights had immediately relieved some of the squadron and station defence flights that had been engaged in the First Arakan offensive for more than six months. Those units were withdrawn and sent to Secunderabad for a course of instruction and reorganisation to provide personnel for the formation of more field squadrons and AA flights.

The tradesmen and enrolled followers at Singarbil had been mounting guard duties as they were uncertain as to the friendliness of the local population. They were much relieved when 4426 AA Flight, under the command of Flight Lieutenant Dutton, arrived to take on this onerous task.

Airmen of an AA flight at 'bayonet practice' at an airstrip on the Bengal coast, January 1944. (Air Historical Branch RAF Crown Copyright)

Slim and XV Corps, and AHQ India, now set about correcting the failings of the previous campaigning season. The infantry was trained to treat the jungle as a friend and to meet the Japanese on equal terms. All administrative, clerical and service corps personnel were given realistic infantry training under active service conditions. Medical problems arising from jungle warfare, in particular tropical diseases, received attention and improved malarial precautions were developed. Meanwhile the command structure for the theatre was completely reorganised so that operations would no longer be the direct responsibility of GHQ India in New Delhi. South-East Asia Command (SEAC) came into being on 15/16 November 1943 and was charged with the direction of operations based in India and Ceylon against Japan. Admiral Lord Louis Mountbatten was appointed Supreme Allied Commander and Lieutenant-General Slim promoted to command the Eastern Army, which was renamed the Fourteenth Army. The Fourteenth Army would be responsible for offensive action from Assam and Bengal.

All the Allied air forces were passed to the new Air Command, South-East Asia (ACSEA) under Air Chief Marshal Sir Richard Peirse.[5] Of direct importance for the campaign to retake Burma was Eastern Air Command, which was established in Calcutta. It was to have three major components: 3rd Tactical Air Force, a Strategic Air Force; Troop Carrier Command; and a Photographic Reconnaissance Force. The 3rd Tactical Air Force, under the highly capable Air Marshal Sir John Baldwin,[6] was to consist of 224 Group RAF in support of XV Corps in the Arakan, 221 Group RAF in support of IV Corps at Imphal, and the Northern Air Sector Force USAAF in support of the Northern front. We will be concerned with the actions of 221 and 224 Groups RAF and the RAF Regiment units associated with their activities. After consultations between HQ SEAC and GHQ India, it was agreed that west of 90 degrees (East) longitude no static ground defence garrisons were needed, while to the east the Army would provide garrisons for RAF Stations, according to resources and merit. Army units would be allocated where superior Japanese forces threatened RAF stations, however, any allocation of Regiment field squadrons by SEAC would correspondingly decrease the Army garrison.

The First Arakan campaign had shown that an offensive based around vulnerable supply lines would not succeed against the Japanese. A new method for supporting and supplying troops well forward in the jungle was required. The Japanese response when attacked was to move quickly around the flanks of the attacking force and to come out of the jungle in the rear. They would cut the road-bound supply lines and attack the vulnerable administrative units. They would then roll up the surrounded and weakened formations and use the captured supplies to support their advance. Supply by air had been used in only limited instances by this stage of the war. Dropping supplies by parachute had been refined for jungle operations to the greatest degree in early 1943 during Wingate's first Chindit operation. Following the First Arakan offensive air dropping would thus become a vital component of the Fourteenth Army's success against the Japanese encircling tactics. When the lines of communication were attacked the troops of the Fourteenth Army were ordered not to retreat, as they had done previously, but to form defensive 'boxes'. Supplies would be dropped by parachute from the invaluable C46 Commando and C47 Dakota transport aircraft. If unable to break into the defensive 'boxes', the Japanese attacking force would run short of their own supplies and become weakened and those encircled in the 'box' could then go over to the offensive.

Airfields were now being constructed much closer to the front line – a front line, however, that stretched over more than 800 miles. In March 1942, there were only sixteen airfields with all-weather runways in all of India. By November 1943, after mobilising the large manpower resources of India, there were 140 airfields with double all-weather strips completed and a further 135 with single all-weather and fair-weather strips. The massive increase in aircraft, personnel, radar units and airfields in preparation for the new offensive significantly increased the number of defensive tasks requiring RAF Regiment units. Squadron Leader H.J. Forbes, commanding 2941 Field Squadron, had reached Agartala on 18 April 1943. Agartala was a very different place to Secunderabad. Located east of Calcutta in eastern Bengal (now Bangladesh), the land is very flat and fertile and comprises mainly rice paddy fields, scattered through heavily timbered and thick jungle areas. The area was susceptible to flooding during the monsoon and mosquitoes bred in profusion. The Bengal climate was particularly unpleasant, with heat and high humidity.

The squadron camp, located near a kutcha airstrip at Agartala, was not suitable for permanent occupation and thus the squadron set to clearing jungle around the buildings, as the area was overgrown. Cooks were called for as only one was listed in the field squadron establishment of six officers and 150 ORs, and volunteers initiated into the mysteries of cooking. Other volunteers became masons and constructed field kitchens, ablution blocks and wells. Huts were usually timber-framed with hard-packed mud or brick floor and reed or brush walls and thatched roofs. After a week conditions were much improved for the visit of the Group Defence Officer. Training then commenced on jungle warfare, field engineering and range firing.

With the monsoon easing, the Japanese Air Force returned and made its presence felt over the 224 Group airfields. During November 1943 the Japanese launched a series of offensive sweeps over the airfields in southern Bengal, Calcutta was bombed and in December attacks began on the Chittagong airfields. Neither side could claim complete air superiority, although the Allied air forces outnumbered the Japanese. The

A twin Browning LMG crew of the RAF Regiment at 'Hove' airstrip on the coast of Bengal, India, watch a 20 Squadron RAF Hurricane return from a sortie over the Arakan, January 1944. (Air Historical Branch RAF Crown Copyright)

Japanese Air Force had been depleted due to demands in other theatres, while the RAF had received more modern fighter aircraft, particularly the Spitfire. In the next few months 224 Group RAF was to fight for, and secure, mastery of the air over the Arakan. By January 1944 the fair-weather strips had reopened at Cox's Bazaar and Ramu and 20 and 258 Squadron had moved to the forward airstrips of Nidania and Hove, respectively. Nine squadrons were soon deployed in support of 5th and 7th Indian Divisions as they moved south to regain the territory given up the previous May with Maungdaw being recaptured on 6 January.

The ORB of 2942 Field Squadron, the second field squadron to deploy, describes the typical activities at this time:

> After a period of training at Comilla in late 1943 during which airfield patrols were maintained the move to 'Hay' in the Ramu area brought us to the most forward landing strips. Here we had to build our own roads and bridges, lived under canvas, and carried out refuelling of aircraft for both RAF and USAAF for five months, more airfield patrols, guards on crashed aircraft and other useful assignments.[4]

George Briggs had spent a few weeks guarding the 75 Air Stores Park before moving to the RAF Regiment Depot, where he was posted to 2942 Field Squadron:

> Our Squadron moved up to Ramu where Hurricanes were operating, harassing the Japs and trying to make their airstrips unserviceable. At this time our Squadron were deployed in gun pits for defence of our airstrip. Some days some of us would help with refuelling of the aircraft, other times we went on training exercises or for some practice on the firing range. This involved finding a gully in a safe area and firing a few rounds from a Bren gun. Very rarely a 'Zero' would chase a Hurricane home, which had used up all his ammunition, and then we were able to have a go at him with our Brens.

With the Japanese targeting the forward airstrips, strafing and bombing attacks were a common and ever-present threat. Despite the new aircraft and tactics, the fighter screen could still be by-passed or taken by surprise. Once through, the Japanese fighters and light bombers were faced with the limited AA defence around the airfields. Standing orders given to RAF Regiment AA flight commanders on their primary and secondary roles and responsibilities in airfield defence in forward areas were as follows:

> [The] Primary role is defence against low flying aircraft. [The] Secondary role is to provide a hard core of defence of an airfield or vital position against enemy ground forces.[7]

Airfield defence by the AA flight was to be organised as follows (Sketch Map 3):

> Maintain nine light machine-gun posts[8] in groups of three, post to have good field of fire, both for ground to air and ground to ground.
>
> (a)   Man post fully on stand-to at dusk and dawn and during six nights either side of full moon and during night flying. Man post fully when air raid is on and air sentry during daylight hours.

(b)   Patrol locality of each post from dusk to dawn, when guns not manned at night.

(c)   Perform allotted role in ground defence.[9]

In the first week of February the Japanese, not unexpectedly, launched their counter-offensive Operation *Ha-Go* in the Arakan against XV Indian Corps. The 7th Indian Division, on the eastern side of the Mayu Range, was encircled and immediately formed into defensive 'boxes'. The most famous being the 'Admin Box', which was composed initially of predominantly administrative, supply and medical personnel. To the west of the range enemy columns reached Taung Bazaar and a detachment of the Japanese *Sakurai Column* was ordered to cut the Maungdaw-Bawli Bazaar road on the coastal plain. In response to this XV Indian Corps launched 26th Indian Division from the north to deal with the offensive, while the 5th and 7th Indian Division 'boxes' held on and were supplied by air.

After completing training at Secunderabad, 4443 AA Flight had arrived at Comilla during September 1943. After a few months the flight moved forward to 'Reindeer II' on the Cox's Bazaar-Ramu road, where it established an AA defensive layout based on its nine Browning machine-guns to cover the strip. On 9 February 1944 the airstrips in the Ramu area, including that defended by 4443 AA Flight, came under enemy air attack:

At 1050 hours on this morning, five Oscars penetrated the air defences by approaching from the south-east, two flying at a height of 200 feet and three at 600 feet. Nos 1, 2 and 3 Sections situated on 'Reindeer II' opened fire but

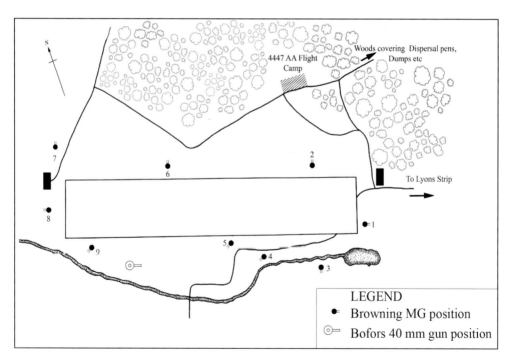

3 The AA defensive layout for Hay airstrip near Ramu, February 1944. (The Browning gun posts were manned by 4447 AA Flight. Based on a sketch drawn at the time by Flying Officer P.H. Brice, OC 4447 AA Flight.)

due to the speed of the aircraft, hits could not be observed. One Spitfire aircraft led an Army 01 [Oscar] over the ground AA defences at approximately 50 feet on which No 1 Section gun posts directed their fire until it passed out of range, when another Spitfire approaching from the south-west engaged it and shot it down about a mile away. The pilot of the Spitfire which decoyed the enemy aircraft over the AA defences visited the CO and congratulated No 1 Section on the effectiveness of their fire.[10]

A fortnight later 4443 AA Flight was moved south to Bawli Bazaar to protect 224 Group HQ and the nearby strip. It was to hold itself in readiness to give cover for any forward strip cleared of the enemy and required for RAF use. On 22 February a senior RAF officer in the vicinity requested No 2 Section move 15 miles further south to Chota Maunghnama to protect an R&R Party. A pair of AA machine-guns was manned for defence of the strip. The ORB continues:

> At 2230 hours a Japanese patrol made a local attack in the vicinity, which was repulsed by a contingent of the 2nd East Lancashire Regiment. During this time No 2 Section took up defensive positions in rifle pits, which were situated in 'box' fashion to defend the R&R Party. Although fire appeared to be directed on their positions no direct encounter with the enemy was achieved . . . the NCO in charge of No 2 Section [Corporal Lumsden, reported that] the men under his charge displayed admirable coolness and self possession and a strong desire to come to grips with the enemy. The defensive positions were fully manned until first light of the following day when normal duties were continued. Meanwhile No 1 and 3 Sections were carrying out routine patrols at Bawli Bazaar in the vicinity of the domestic site and the strip, two twin AA LMGs being manned on the latter.
>
> [Three days later No 2 Section] were informed that they were to move back to Bawli South landing strip, as their presence at Chota Maunghnama was considered unnecessary . . . On their arrival, a domestic site was chosen and two twin Brownings were mounted in disused Bofors sites for the defence of the strip, also a patrol consisting one NCO and ten men was maintained between the hours of first and last light to ensure security of the airfield from attack.[11]

2944 Field Squadron had departed the RAF Regiment Depot on 21 June 1943. It moved to Barkakana near Ranchi in Bengal, where it underwent further intensive training and five months later travelled by train to Chittagong airfield (Appendix 9). As Squadron Armourer, LAC Henry Kirk had been sent back to Secunderabad to collect the squadron's allocation of Bren guns. After collecting them he then boarded a train where he was locked in a second class compartment with his charges. This was a safety measure as there had been reports of civil disturbances and rioting on the line and this would provide some protection should the train be attacked *en route*. At one halt in the journey a carriage with a Vickers machine-gun detachment was shunted on to the front of the train as trouble was expected. Henry recalls:

> Fortunately the journey was uneventful and I arrived at Howrah station at Calcutta in the afternoon. As all the trains to Chittagong were full I was told that I wouldn't be leaving for another day. I signed over the Bren guns to the MPs and was sent to a transit camp. There I met a Corporal of the 2nd King's

Own Scottish Borderers who was also trying to get back to his battalion. The next day we decided to go off to the Metro Cinema to pass the time till our train departed. Coming out of the cinema in the late afternoon we stood for a minute on the relatively wide pavement adjusting to the light. The next thing I woke up and I was lying in a bed in the 47th British General Hospital, next to me was the Corporal with one leg, broken in two places, held in the air. A jeep loaded with drunken American servicemen, and being driven recklessly, had mounted the pavement and ploughed into myself and the KOSB Corporal. Despite being knocked unconscious I had no broken bones. I was able to complete my journey to Chittagong a few days later.

By this time nearly half the squadron were suffering from malaria and were confined to quarters, as the hospital was full to overflowing, and the healthy personnel were spread thinly across the various tasks. Henry Kirk was on aircraft refuelling duties on Christmas Day 1943 when the Japanese raided Chittagong. He continues:

Looking upwards we could see a group of twelve or so 'Sally' bombers at about 10,000 feet. We heard the distinctive double burst of machine-gun fire from the lead bomber, which contained the bomb aimer, to indicate that all planes should drop their loads. Most fell at the far end of the runway, but a Japanese 'Zero' fighter then came in and strafed the strip. We dived under the vehicle nearest to us and watched as the sparks flew off the runway as the bullets hit. After the 'all clear' we crawled out only to realise we had been sheltering under the petrol bowser. Not a safe place should a bullet have hit, but at the time we had simply went instinctively under the nearest cover.

Despite the high sickness rate of the squadron, and with the success of XV Corps dry season offensive, the men were soon despatched to Maungdaw on AMES protection duties. Early warning of the approach of enemy air aircraft was essential as it gave intercepting aircraft time to scramble, climb and choose their moment of attack. Thus it was essential to establish the AMES as far forward as possible. The AMES that 2944 Field Squadron was looking after was located between the forward infantry positions and the artillery. Henry Kirk remembers the stay at Maungdaw:

. . . when the guns fired the dug outs shook and stones flew about. I slept under an Army lorry with orders to destroy the AMES if the Japanese broke through, with a bag of gun cotton explosive. The area was desolate, with charred trees and a terrible stench, two graves of our soldiers were on the road edge marked with sticks and their dog tags and here we saw the first sights of the horrors of war.

The advance of the *Sakurai Column* as part of Operation *Ha-Go* meant that the AMES at Maungdaw was soon in a precarious position. Orders were received to withdraw immediately back to Dohazari airfield, south of Chittagong. Leaving at first light the vehicles of the squadron and the AMES moved north from Maungdaw. Henry Kirk remembers the trip back to Dohazari:

Suddenly one morning we were ordered out by the Army in a hurry and were not told what was happening. The Squadron left quickly in the 3-ton Bedford lorries with canvas tops bound northwards for the airfield at Dohazari. It was a very hot and sunny morning as we travelled back up this rough coastal road paved with bricks and rubble. Along with LAC 'Taffy' Griffiths we sat with our backs to the cab on cases of 303 ammo and grenades which were right up to the top of the sideboards. Looking out of the back and to the right there were two or three rice fields then palm trees and a beach. Out on the left were the same rice fields and thick jungle leading up to the Mayu Range. We had been going for some time and were nearing a small village when we heard what sounded like fireworks going off: a typical start to an Indian Festival Day. I looked out of the back of the vehicle and saw a number of figures dressed in khaki near the jungle edge, which I thought odd because our forces were dressed in jungle green.

Shortly after this we were stopped at a road block manned by the York and Lancaster Regiment. A Sergeant looked into the back of our lorry and said 'Where have you come from?' and we replied, 'Maungdaw'. He replied 'You can't have, because the Japs have broken through and cut the road.' He then told us to get out and pointed to the lorry's sideboard where there were several fresh chips of wood gouged out by bullets, and at the same time said 'You two bods have been very lucky!'

Henry Kirk and 'Taffy' Griffiths were indeed lucky as no bullets had gone higher than the wooden sides of the 3-tonner and this had saved their lives. Henry then realised that the 'firecrackers' he had heard were in fact the sounds of rifle fire coming from the khaki-clad figures that the convoy had passed. Those figures most likely belonged to the *Sakurai Column* moving down from the Mayu Range to cut the road.

2944 Field Squadron arrived at Dohazari airfield to find everybody on 'high alert'. As the Squadron Armourer, Henry Kirk was responsible for checking, cleaning and replacing the empty ammunition drums on a number of machine-gun posts placed around the airstrip for AA defence. While carry out the task one morning he faced yet another life-threatening situation. He continues:

At the southern end between two strips of trees was a battery of 3.7 inch anti-aircraft guns with their long barrels pointing and manned by well trained Sikh gunners. Round the airfield were red earth gun pits about 4 feet deep and a row of sand bags around the top. Mounted on tripods were Vickers 0.303 pan-fed air-cooled machine-guns with covers on. In a raid anyone could use these to fire on the enemy.

One morning I arrived at one near a dispersal where two fitters were working on the engine of a Hurricane. They put a hand up to me and I acknowledged them. I put my cleaning gear down on a sand bag and jumped into the pit. On lifting up the canvas cover I realised something had dropped down and saw it was cobra! Before I could get out of the pit it struck out and I felt a sting in the calf muscle of my left leg. I shouted out to the two fitters who rushed over. Using my 'four by two' cleaning strips they put a tourniquet tightly above my knee and rushed me in their vehicle to sick quarters. The MO said 'You're lucky the venom is on your trousers. Keep still while I cut the cloth off.' He then injected me and treated two fang wounds. The scars are still there today. The snake was killed and brought back to the MO for identification. I was in dock under observation for two days and then it was back to work again. After that I lifted the covers off with a length of bamboo.

Around the time that 2944 Field Squadron had been ordered to Maungdaw, 2945 Field Squadron was sent on a defence task with a more nautical flavour. It was decided to set up an AMES at St Martin's Island, located 10 miles off the Mayu Peninsula and 14 miles south-west of Maungdaw. In preparation for the move the Group Defence Officer, the OC 2945 Field Squadron, a Medical Officer and two Technical Officers embarked at Chittagong to undertake a reconnaissance. St Martin's Island is nowadays marketed as a tropical paradise with white sandy beaches and swaying palms; in 1944, located well forward of the Allied positions on the mainland, it was not viewed with the same relish. It was found to be unoccupied by the Japanese and the villagers were quite friendly. A suitable landing place was located and the ground would provide a suitable defence area for the COL barge, which was to be moored 200 yards offshore from this point. On 31 January 1944, 2945 Field Squadron embarked at Chittagong to establish and protect the AMES on St Martin's Island and completed the 130-mile journey on 2 February. The squadron's arrival coincided with the launch of Operation *Ha-Go*. Fortunately the enemy did not take any action against 2945 Field Squadron and the COL barge and they were not required to withdraw. They could, however, see the fighting occurring on the mainland. In late February, Nos 5 Army Commando and 44 Royal Marine Commando disembarked on the Island and then departed on 10 March to attack Alethangyaw on the mainland to the north-east.

After a month and a half on St Martin's Island the AMES received the order to withdraw and on 18 March the COL barge departed. No orders, however, were communicated to 2945 Field Squadron as to its future movements. The squadron did not have any W/T equipment of its own so it was unable to communicate with the mainland. Now began a period of difficulty that would have fatal consequences for one member of the squadron. For the next few days the squadron personnel watched to the north-east in the hope that a ship would be sent to pick them up. On 20 March an LCM went past the mouth of the Naf River but it did not move towards St Martin's Island. Furthermore, signals were fired off to a steamer seen off the north-west part of the island, but it failed to answer them and moved off the following day towards the Naf River mouth. The following day three motor launches came in and the Captain of one promised to report their predicament when he returned to the mainland. On the 25 March, with still no sign of assistance, a khisti with Corporal Lawes and LAC Boland was despatched to Teknaf to try and make contact with a Senior Naval Officer.

The ration situation had now become serious, and probably as a direct result of this, on 25 March Flight Sergeant W.J. Morrice was taken ill with a high temperature, sickness and vomiting. Sergeant Hetherington and two nursing orderlies stayed with him during the night. It was not possible to move him by khisti to the mainland as the tide was too low and it was hoped that Corporal Lawes' mission would bear fruit. T-strips were placed outside indicating an ambulance was required and an airman stood by to signal passing aircraft or shipping. At 1800 hours another boat passed the island but failed to notice any signals. At 1730 hours Flight Sergeant Morrice collapsed and he died 45 minutes later. Artificial respiration was continued for another one and half hours, but to no avail. The cause of death was thought to be due to a combination of spinal malaria and food poisoning caused by eating bully beef from a tin that had been open for two days.

Anxious though they were to get Morrice's body to Teknaf for a proper determination of the cause of death, the suggestion was sensibly overruled by Squadron Leader T.R. Garnett. The squadron was now down to only ninety-four men and seven of them could not be spared for the trip to Teknaf by khisti. At 0600 hours on 27 March a Section of No 3 Flight prepared a grave for Flight Sergeant Morrice on the north-west corner of the island on a slight rise. His body was sewn into a blanket and tent flooring and at 1015 hours he was buried in the prepared grave. Garnett read the service and a firing party of fourteen men fired three volleys in salute. A bamboo cross and an inscription in concrete were prepared and the grave was fenced and paved with coral from the nearby beach.[12]

They were now down to the last sack of sugar and other rations would last less than a week. It was decided that the evacuation of the island by khisti would start on 29 March if no help arrived, with fours days required to complete the exercise. The following day, two khistis returned from Teknaf and reported that Corporal Lawes would return with a steamer in two days. Finally, on 28 March an RAF Tiger Moth landed and later the officer in command of Inland Water Transport arrived to explain their enforced stay on the Island. The ship that had been seen on 20 and 21 March had been the SS *Dhamra*, which had been detailed to collect the squadron. It had ignored the signals sent from the island as it had no signaller on board and it had then laid up in the Naf River for some days with boiler trouble. The following day an LCM arrived and transferred the squadron to the SS *Dhamra* now lying offshore. By 1 April 2945 Field Squadron was back at Feni airfield in Bengal. In response to enquiries by Squadron Leader Garnett about his problems in communicating with the mainland, he was simply told that a W/T station should also have been set up on the island along with the COL.

Despite the difficulties experienced by 2945 Squadron in the latter part of the operation, the AMES at St Martin's Island, located well forward of the front line, and that protected by 2944 Field Squadron at Maungdaw, provided useful cover and had assisted with successful interceptions of intruders off the Arakan coast during a decisive period in the campaign in Burma.[13]

Although initially surprised by the Japanese counter-offensive, Slim quickly regained the initiative. The XV Indian Corps objective was now to push the Japanese back to allow the establishment of monsoon positions around Maungdaw. To the east, the Japanese had still to be driven out of positions on the Mayu Range, but the 'boxes' had held out, supplied by air, while surrounded by the Japanese columns. After a few weeks of bitter fighting, Operation *Ha-Go* was called off and the 5th and 7th Indian Divisions linked up with the 25th Indian Division moving from the north. By early April the 25th and 26th Indian Divisions had taken over from the 5th and 7th Indian Divisions after they were ordered to Imphal and Kohima to deal with a new and more threatening Japanese offensive.

Back at Dohazari 2944 Field Squadron continued its patrol work and manned the outer defences of the very busy airfield. In March the squadron moved back to Maungdaw with the AMES, however, within a matter of days the men were ordered to return to Dohazari as the squadron was urgently required at Imphal. On 19 March 2942 Field Squadron, under the command of Squadron Leader E.M. John, had crossed into Burma for the first time and moved to Maungdaw to relieve 2944 Field Squadron of its AMES protection duties. Around this time they received a visit from Admiral Lord Louis Mountbatten and, following his visit, the order was given to 'splice the main brace' and an extra rum ration was issued. The plan was for 2942 Field Squadron to remain at Maungdaw for the duration of the coming monsoon. On 13 April two flights were moved to North Island Maungdaw to protect a second AMES and they immediately set about constructing bashas and bunds for monsoon accommodation. After discussions with senior officers from the 25th Indian Division, the remainder of the squadron, located further south, was informed that it was actually outside the Army's monsoon defensive line. Sensibly, it was decided to consolidate the two AMES and the squadron in North Island Maungdaw and this move was completed by 3 May. A few weeks later the monsoon broke and the road south of Bawli Bazaar became unreliable, meaning that supplies would often have to come by steamer into the port of Maungdaw. 2942 Field Squadron was arguably the most forward RAF unit in South-East Asia, located in sight and sound of the enemy forward positions and subject to the attention of Japanese patrols.

The original objective for the Second Arakan offensive had been the recapture of Akyab Island before the 1944 monsoon. However, the Japanese counter-offensive did not leave enough time to achieve this and the offensive was called off. The Japanese forces in the Arakan were now only a limited threat and the Allied air and land forces could be used more profitably on the Central Front around Imphal where the crucial battle for India was to be fought. Despite the small numbers of soldiers and airmen involved, the important feature of the Second Arakan campaign was that the enemy's offensive had been defeated and turned back, thus destroying the myth of Japanese invincibility.

The Air Commander, 3rd Tactical Air Force, Air Marshal Sir John Baldwin made the following comments regarding the conduct of the RAF Regiment during the Second Arakan Campaign:

> Units of the RAF Regiment have proved themselves of the greatest value in this campaign, of which the insecurity of airfields and warning establishments in forward areas has been a feature. When Radar Stations were established at St Martin's Island and later in the Maungdaw area, the unusual situation existed of Radar Stations being actually well in advance of the front line and within range of the enemy's guns and night patrols. It says much for the RAF Regiment personnel that the Radar crews enjoyed undisturbed conditions in which to carry on their work under such trying conditions. It has proved to be quite unsound to rely on the Army maintaining troops for local defence in times of crisis when the land situation deteriorates. This is the time when they are really needed by us, but this is the time when they are invariably withdrawn to take part in the land battle.[14]

Notes

1 Roberson, N.J. *The History of No. 20 Squadron Royal Flying Corps Royal Air Force.* Weeze: Privately Published [Printed by Palka-Verlag], 1987, p. 47.
2 This mobile Repair & Salvage Unit (Forward Areas) had been specifically formed to deal with recovery, salvage and repair of crashed aircraft south of Chittagong and into the Arakan. It was a form of 'Flying Squad' made up of the appropriate tradesmen. The unit was defended by a flight of thirty-six RAF Regiment gunners under Flying Officer Garnett. Sansome, R.S. *The Bamboo Workshop: The History of the RAF Repair & Salvage Units India/Burma 1941–1946.* Braunton, Devon: Merlin Books, 1995, p. 40–41.
3 Richey, P. and N. Franks. *Fighter Pilot's Summer.* London: Grub Street, 1999 (1993), pp. 194–7.
4 AIR 29/134, *Operations Record Books RAF Regiment Squadrons 2934, 2935, 2941–2943.*
5 Air Chief Marshal Sir Richard Peirse KCB DSO AFC (1892–1970).
6 Air Marshal Sir John Baldwin KBE CB DSO (1892–1975).
7 AIR 23/2050, *1942–44 Aerodrome Defence: RAF Regiment Instructions.* HQ 224 Group to OC AA Flights, Operational Standing Orders 21 December 1943.
8 Each post had two 0.303-inch Mk II Browning LMGs on a Motley Stalk mounting.

9   op. cit. AIR 23/2050.
10 AIR 29/886, *Operations Record Books and Appendices RAF Regiment 4436–4450, 5756, 6201, 6203, 6204, 6206 AA Flights.*
11 ibid.
12 Flight Sergeant Morrice was 27 years old and came from Aberdeenshire. His body was later re-interred in the Taukkyan War Cemetery near Rangoon.
13 Air Marshal Sir R.E.C. Peirse KCB DSO AFC, *Third Supplement to the London Gazette,* Tuesday 13 March 1951, Air Operations in South-East Asia 16 November 1943 to 31 May 1944, p. 1,401.
14 Air Marshal Sir John Baldwin KBE CB DSO, quoted in ibid., p. 1,404.

CHAPTER THREE

The Siege of Imphal

'. . . nothing very heroic, just a hard slog. We had done our job and everything that had been asked of us.'

Corporal Colin Kirby, 4440 AA Flight

Fortunately for the Allies, the Japanese had not launched an offensive against Imphal in 1942 when it was most vulnerable. Slightly more than one infantry division had stood between the Japanese and the plains and rivers of Eastern India. The area lacked decent roads and had no railways, and while the mountainous and jungle-clad terrain made it difficult for the British to build up supplies and reinforcements for their defensive positions, it also made it difficult for the Japanese to launch a fresh offensive. The Japanese High Command had decided in 1942 that the country west of the River Chindwin was impassable to the forces required to launch an effective attack on the British-Indian positions at Imphal. Both armies had contented themselves with small fighting patrols and limited actions to improve their defensive positions and lines of communication. Wingate's first Chindit expedition of 1943 demonstrated, however, that infantry columns large enough for offensive action could still cross this country hitherto thought impassable. By mid-1943 the Japanese were aware that the British were building up men and materials on the Central Front for an offensive from Imphal, as it was considered the best jumping-off place for the reconquest of northern and central Burma. To forestall this the Japanese were to launch a major offensive called Operation *U-Go* against Imphal and Kohima in early 1944, subsequent to the moves in the Arakan. The green hills of Manipur would see some of the heaviest hand-to-hand fighting of the Second World War, with no quarter given, and the Battles of Kohima and Imphal would rank alongside Stalingrad and Alamein in their significance for the defeat of the Axis. The RAF Regiment would be well represented and would play an important role in the great battle and siege of Imphal (Map 3).

The town of Imphal is set in a green valley about 20 miles wide and 35 miles in length in the Indian state of Manipur. It is surrounded by high mountains around 5,000 feet high and mostly covered in thick jungle. Although it lies some 3,000 feet above sea level, it is a large valley of mostly flat land, dense with paddy fields. At the southern end is Logtak Lake, the largest expanse of fresh water in north-east India and home to large populations of water birds. The darker side to the area, however, is the presence of many tropical diseases, such as spinal and cerebral malaria, typhoid, black water fever and scrub typhus, along with blood-sucking leeches and swarms of mosquitoes. Furthermore, there are various other bites, sores, prickly heat and rashes that add to the misery.

Access to the Imphal Valley in 1944 was limited and this made for long and difficult supply lines from India. It was most easily reached on the narrow road from the railhead at Dimapur in Assam to the north-west. Some 47 miles from Dimapur in the Naga Hills was the small town of Kohima, which had a military hospital and reinforcements and supply depots. Imphal was just over 60 miles further south on a narrow tortuous road. A rough, undulating track unsuitable for motor vehicles led from Bishenpur, to the south of Imphal Town, to Silchar in the Surma Valley. There were two roads leading to the India-Burma border. A primitive road went directly south from Imphal for 110 miles to Tiddim in the Chin Hills. At the south-east end of the valley was a road from Palel through the Shenam Pass to Tamu on the India-Burma border, which lay at the head of the Kabaw Valley.

Operation *U-Go* was launched in three prongs by the Japanese *15th Army* during the first week of March 1944, and with the troops confident of the quick capture of enemy stores they carried only twenty days' supplies. The first and most northerly prong consisted of the *31st Division* of 15,000 men, which crossed the River Chindwin in three columns between Homalin and Tamanthi and headed north over 160 miles to cut the Dimapur-Imphal Road around Kohima. It converged on and lay siege to the Kohima garrison of only 3,500 men, and threatened the much more important railhead and stores depot further west at Dimapur. Further south, the middle prong was made up of five columns of the *15th Division* and *Yamamoto Force*. The northernmost of the five columns bypassed Ukhrul and moved on to attack Imphal from the north and to cut the Imphal-Kohima road. To the north-east, the 23rd Indian Division, which had been at Imphal since 1942, along with the recently arrived 50th Indian Parachute Brigade, was covering any movement via the tracks from Ukhrul and they were soon to clash with these columns. Meanwhile, the main southerly columns fell on the 20th Indian Division and its forward positions, which extended to the banks of the River Chindwin. The Division withdrew steadily up the Kabaw Valley through Tamu and moved back to positions on the western side of the Shenam Pass. Moving with the enemy columns were elements of the *1st Indian National Army Division*. The third prong was the *33rd Division*, which moved off from Kalemyo in three columns and attacked the 17th Indian Light Division, which was operating on extended lines of communication around Tiddim. The 17th Indian Light Division had been gradually pushing the road to Tiddim southward from the Imphal Valley from late 1943. The 17th Indian Light Division delayed its withdrawal to Imphal until Japanese intentions were clear and, therefore, it had a difficult time fighting its way back through the road-blocks established by the columns of the *33rd Division*.

The British, Indian and Gurkha troops in the Imphal area were in IV Corps under the command of Lieutenant-General Geoffry Scoones. On 5 December 1943, Air Commodore Rowley with 221 Group RAF HQ had moved from Calcutta to Imphal to work in close cooperation with IV Corps. On 16 February 1944 Air Commodore S.F. Vincent[1] took command of 221 Group. Vincent was a determined but likeable and generous character. He had been a fighter pilot during the First World War and had also fought in the Battle of Britain. He saw the importance of a strong working relationship with the ground forces commander and was to develop this, almost to perfection, with Slim and the Fourteenth Army during the advance into Burma in 1945. At a planning conference at IV Corps HQ shortly after taking command, he indicated his determination to keep 221 Group HQ and as many RAF units as possible in the Imphal Valley during the siege, rather than operate from airfields over the mountains to the west. Vincent had been in Singapore, Sumatra and Java in 1942 and said he had done enough retreating from the Japanese in the past and didn't intend to do so any more and wanted to stay put. He was confident they could beat the Japanese thoroughly. Thus, the RAF was to stay in the valley and preparations were made for the coming struggle.

As in the Arakan, the Japanese tactics for the attack on Imphal were founded on the encirclement of the enemy, the blocking of road-bound supply lines, and the use of the captured supplies to support a further advance. On the Imphal Plain there were large depots, dumps, administrative elements, hospitals and labour camps. It was, therefore, an invaluable base for the Allies, but also a coveted prize for the Japanese. Most importantly, there were two all-weather airfields, Imphal Main in the north and Palel in the south, and four fair-weather airfields at Kangla, Tulihal, Wangjing and Sapam. These airfields would provide the means by which the Imphal garrison would halt, defeat and pursue the Japanese divisions. At Imphal there would be no distinct front line, rather defended areas with large gaps between, and the Japanese would be easily able to infiltrate onto the plain. No position would be safe from enemy attack and everyone was a combatant. Defences were organised around 221 Group HQ, and the airfields, flying squadron dispersals, AMES and signals facility. Bunkers and slit trenches were dug and small arms, ammunition and rations were allotted.

The role of the RAF Regiment was essential if the RAF was to 'stick it out' in the valley. The Defence Training Instructors (DTIs) enlarged and intensified their training courses in ground defence, of which all at Imphal had to become proficient. From February 1944 onwards, RAF Regiment personnel oversaw intensive training of pilots, ground crew and station defence personnel in the use of rifles, Sten and Thompson SMGs and hand grenades. Flight Sergeant Alan Knight, who we last heard of at Dinjan in the Assam Valley in 1942, had completed training as a DTI and was then retained as a Regimental Instructor at the Secunderabad Depot. In September 1943 he was posted to 221 Group Calcutta.

> My job was to train RAF personnel in Airfield Defence before they moved to forward areas. The Group then moved to Imphal, where, in early 44 the Japanese attacked and surrounded Imphal. Our 221 Group was formed into a defence 'box' in a side valley. I was given responsibility for siting and getting the defence positions dug; which included toiling each day up to a ridge about 4,000 feet high.
>
> Digging in one day on the ridge, one of the men pointed to three aircraft flying towards us, and asked me to identify them. I said, 'It's okay they're Mohawks [which looked very much like the Japanese "Zero"].' As they passed level and quite close we saw in fact they were 'Zeros'. The lead pilot half-raised a hand. I didn't live it down for some time.
>
> On 12 March 1944 I was wounded, with bullets through both knees. I was lucky as I only had about ¼ second to make my mind up, so I jumped and as I reached the top so the bullets hit. If I had dropped I wouldn't have been writing this. I was operated on in a grass hut on a trestle table. A few days later I was flown to Comilla, then by train to Chittagong, where on board a hospital ship the docks were machine-gunned by 'Zeros'. To add to this discomfort I then found I had an insect crawling inside one of my leg plasters. A sister promptly found a 'Flit' Gun and poked the nozzle down the plaster and squirted.

The Japanese thrusts through the Arakan and in Manipur were fortunately staggered, and this enabled Lieutenant-General Slim to parry the attack in the Arakan and then deal in strength with the later and larger attack on Imphal. Slim withdrew arguably his two best divisions, the 5th and 7th Indian Divisions, from the Arakan, and moved them by air to Imphal and Dimapur from mid-March to early May. The large-scale movement of troops by air served to emphasise the importance that air transport had assumed. It gave great flexibility to field commanders. However, the RAF had to have air superiority to permit the safe movement of large bodies of troops over long distances. Although supplies were dropped by parachute in many circumstances in the Burma campaign, the most efficient means of delivering large numbers of troops, heavy tonnages and sophisticated or heavy equipment required airfields on which transport aircraft could land safely. There would be periods of crisis during the siege when ration allocations would need to be halved. However, from 29 March when the Japanese cut the Dimapur-Imphal Road until the reopening on 22 June 1944, transport aircraft of Troop Carrier Command would fly in all of the rations, supplies, armaments, ammunition and reinforcements required by the Imphal garrison.

By March 1944 221 Group RAF had fourteen squadrons, nine of which were located in the Imphal Valley under the control of 170 Wing. Two squadrons equipped with Spitfire Mark Vs and later Mark VIIIs were given the task of air defence to protect the air supply operation. Nine Hurricane squadrons, four equipped as fighter-bombers, and three Vengeance dive-bomber squadrons based both in and out of the Valley, were used in ground strafing and close support of Army formations. A detachment of Beaufighter night fighters of 176 Squadron was permanently located at Kangla throughout the siege. Secure and well-defended airfields were essential for these squadrons to operate effectively. The landing strips had to be in close proximity to forward areas and have the capability for refuelling and rearming aircraft to maintain the high state of readiness.

The RAF Regiment had been gathering at Imphal and in the Surma Valley well before the Japanese offensive began. The first Depot-trained unit to arrive at Imphal was 4408 AA Flight under the command of Flight Lieutenant G. J. Grierson. Formed on 9 May 1943, the unit moved from Secunderabad via Calcutta, Silchar and the Manipur Road and arrived at Imphal Main airstrip on 1 June 1943. The flight would stay in the valley for fifteen months without relief (Appendix 8).

Just over a year after arriving in India, LAC Cyril Paskin had been sent to the Depot in August 1943. After a period of training he was posted to the newly formed 4417 AA Flight. From Secunderabad the flight was sent directly to the Silchar Valley, 70 miles to the west of Imphal, and to the airfield at Kumbhirgram. The flight's role, along with that of 4416 AA Flight, was to protect the Vultee Vengeance dive-bomber squadrons of 168 Wing. These squadrons would play an important role in attacking lines of communications targets and supporting the ground troops during the siege of Imphal.

By December 1943 2943 Field Squadron and ten AA flights were located in all parts of the Imphal Plain and the Surma Valley in air and ground defence of airfields, and close-protection of wireless stations and AMES units. The RAF Regiment commitment would increase by another one and half flights in early 1944, with each airstrip eventually having two to five rifle or AA flights at the height of the siege.

Colin Kirby[2] had successfully completed his training at Secunderabad and arrived with 4440 AA Flight at Imphal during November 1943. He recounts the move:

We left the Secunderabad Depot on 27 October. The Flight had eight Browning machine-guns in four pairs mounted and calibrated for AA purposes against low-flying aircraft, much 0.303 ammunition for same and Bren guns and our Lee-Enfield rifles. We procured sacks of tea, sugar, tins of condensed milk and bully beef, hard tack and ginger marmalade to sustain us on our journey to Manipur. 'Where's Manipur?' asked Flight Sergeant Rawlings.

'Somewhere on the border with Burma, I think.' Anyway, first major stop Calcutta, 0945 hours and we are on our way. Two days later we arrive in Calcutta at Howrah station, having journeyed in open-sided carriages. Guards at night because if the train stopped local natives appeared out of the darkness and tried to reach in to grab what they could.

Whenever we stopped during the day somebody climbed down with an old petrol can we had, ran to the loco and placed it under a convenient pipe. The driver pulled the appropriate lever and filled the can with hot water. Brought back to the carriage, a few handfuls of tea into it, stirred vigorously with a bayonet. A can of condensed milk was pierced with bayonet and poured into the brew. A few fistfuls of sugar, more stirring and it was ready to drink. Sweaty bodies were refreshed with hot tea.

We spent two days in a transit camp; one of my section did guard duty at Howrah station. It must be remembered that there was much internal strife in India, with various factions calling for home rule, activity encouraged by Japanese sympathisers. After that we moved across the great Hooghly River Bridge to Sealdah station, from which the railway led to the north and east. After spending the night of 1 November in a siding at Sealdah station the flight pulled out the next day. The guns and ammunition and other stores were in a freight wagon and I was installed in it with two of the lads. We opened the side door and perched on ammo boxes watching Bengal and then Assam roll by. The train moved at no great speed on the single track. Every few hours there was a loop to enable trains going in the opposite direction to pass. Sometimes we pulled in to one of these and were stationary for a few hours. On the evening of the 3 November we stopped at Dhubri and spent the night in a transit camp before boarding a river steamer next day for a journey of about a day down the Brahmaputra River to Pandu. Another transit camp, the next day another train, then about a further 24 hours to reach the railhead at Dimapur.

Early next morning we boarded trucks with all our supplies to take us to up the Manipur road to the Imphal Plain. It took all day, climbing on a road that was one hairpin after another, usually with sheer drops down the mountainside. The drivers were Indian troops who had only recently learned to drive, and consequently we saw many crashed vehicles. Pretty nerve-wracking, but we arrived in one piece at a site near Imphal town, which was really only a village increased by the military buildings erected around it. We pitched our tents and experienced our first Jap air raid. With the tortuous supply line from Bengal making logistics difficult, it seemed that airstrips would be vital if planes could get through the very hazardous flying conditions and past Jap fighters.

Up to this time Flight Sergeant Rawlings had commanded the flight. On 20 November, however, Flight Lieutenant Wilmot arrived to take command of 4440 AA Flight. On 5 December we were transported south to Sapam, the satellite strip of Palel, almost to the point where the plain ended and the mountainous jungle began. There was a dirt airstrip made from a flattened paddy field at the foot of the hills and a native village a mile or two away. We set about making a camp, camouflaging, digging latrines etc. We dug four gun pits near the airstrip, some distance from camp. We had been equipped with a pick-up truck, and I was sent to Imphal to collect timber suitable for making a base for each of the gun mountings. This was not easy but I managed to load the truck and scrounge a saw. Sergeant Rawlings demonstrated his joinery skills in making a good job of the cross pieces which formed a base for the gun mountings. By the end of the day we were ready for action.

To gain hands-on experience in patrol work in forward areas, RAF Regiment detachments were sent out with infantry units of IV Corps. The first group was from 2941 Field Squadron, which from September 1943 was attached by flights to 3/10th Gurkha Rifles at Shenam for training in jungle warfare. The Group Defence Officer visited the flight of 2943 Field Squadron, protecting the AMES at Tamu during January 1944, and reported that the officers and men were anxious to stay forward. They had been out on patrols with 2nd Border Regiment through arrangements made with 100th Indian Brigade of 20th Indian Division. The arrangement was for all NCOs to take part and when all Sections had participated, the entire flight would form a patrol and then take over a sector from 20th Indian Division. Operation *U-Go* put a halt to these plans. Tamu came under pressure from the enemy and the AMES early warning set was destroyed by shelling.[3] The detachment from 2943 Field Squadron and 4423 AA Flight, which had arrived on 5 February, was withdrawn from Tamu on 18 March, only a few days before the rearguard of 20th Indian Division.

Slim had prepared a carefully planned withdrawal of the Fourteenth Army to the Imphal Plain if the Japanese launched an offensive. IV Corps could then fight the Japanese on ground of its own choosing. The withdrawal during March from the forward outposts, however, did have a serious effect on the capacity of 221 Group RAF to defend the Imphal airstrips. Prior to the Japanese attack there were three AMES located well forward at Tamu to the south-east, Tiddim far to the south and at Wabagai, providing general cover of the area. In addition, there were radar sets at Moirang 28 miles to the south of Imphal town, Kangla to the north-east and another, out of the valley, north of Dimapur.[4] Tamu also had a useful forward and emergency landing strip, but more importantly it was the only site where radar could locate Japanese aircraft movements to the east of the high mountain range that separated the Imphal Plain from the Kabaw Valley.[5] A landline then stretched back from Tamu to 221 Group HQ at Imphal, which gave an immediate warning of some 100 miles. Unfortunately the planned withdrawal meant that forward radar units and their RAF Regiment detachments had to move from carefully chosen positions, going in some cases to unprepared and operationally inferior sites. At Moirang a mobile GCI station, No 857 AMES, had been providing early warnings of Japanese air attacks since late January. The pressure of the enemy advance from the south meant that the Army could no longer prevent Japanese patrols from breaking through and could not guarantee the position would not be outflanked.[6] With only a small number of RAF Regiment and radar personnel to defend the site, the AMES was rapidly withdrawn to Burri Bazaar, much closer to Imphal town. The AMES at Tiddim and Kangla were also withdrawn at the same time. This loss of radar coverage was overcome later, to a limited extent, by placing Air Liaison Officers with R/T sets on the surrounding hills to give early warnings and to direct close-support aircraft. The hills were often held or patrolled by the enemy and in many instances an RAF Regiment gunner accompanied these officers as a personal bodyguard.

The main defended locality at Imphal, known as the 'Keep', was located 2 miles to the north-west of Imphal town astride the Imphal-Kohima road. The 'Keep' included large stocks of ammunition and food, and along with Palel had the only two all-weather airfields in the valley. Along with the bulk of the hospitals, workshops and ordnance depots, there was also the IV Corps and 221 Group HQs and a vital wireless station for communication out of the valley.[7] It was composed of a series of defended localities called 'boxes', which were set out along the hills to the north-east and south-west of the Imphal Main airfield (Sketch Map 4).[8] The 'boxes' were self-contained in terms of supplies and ammunition. They were mutually supporting and if

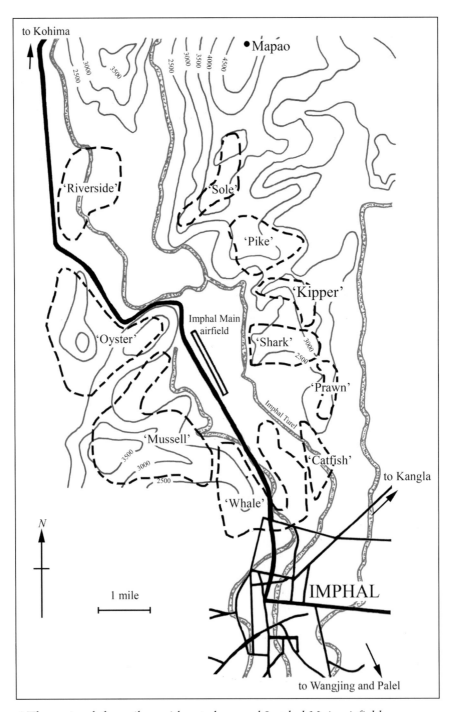

4 The major defence 'boxes' located around Imphal Main airfield.

necessary could hold out for two weeks. They were garrisoned by detachments from Corps artillery, engineers, admin units and any infantry that could be spared.[9] At the beginning of the siege there were many 'boxes' around the valley and they were dispersed as a precaution against air attack. This was believed to be the greatest threat at that time, however, later in the siege when it became apparent that infantry, not air, attack was more likely, the 'boxes' were amalgamated and concentrated around the main airfields.

The RAF Regiment would be heavily involved in the protection of the two vital areas in the Imphal Plain, these being the Imphal Main airfields. Located some 25 miles apart, if they were not held securely the operations to repel the Japanese surrounding the plain would fail. Air Commodore Vincent described the situation as IV Corps readied itself for the Japanese columns and his efforts to inspire the airmen of 221 Group:

> I wrote out an 'Order of the Day' as follows: If a 'box' is attacked it must, I repeat *must*, hold out, reporting the attack to Group or Corps, who will send tanks which can mop up the enemy. We must keep our landing strips safe to use and our aircraft to fly. We can beat the enemy for certain. Air Force humour will beat the Jap, who has none. Good Luck! Good Shooting![10]

At Sapam strip, just north of Palel, 4440 AA Flight had quickly settled into a routine of manning the AA Brownings and sending out night patrols. The men were soon made aware that trouble was expected and that they should be prepared. Colin Kirby continues:

> Every fourth night as Orderly Corporal I had to visit each gun post, armed with a Sten gun, usually very dark and very spooky. Flight Lieutenant Wilmot was driving us in building slit trenches and little manoeuvres for expected situations. The days were burning hot and the nights freezing cold. Water was frozen solid by morning and had to be thawed to make tea. Just before Christmas an RAF padre gave us a visit; until then we thought our existence had been forgotten about. On Christmas Day 1943 we went in small parties down to Imphal to have a Yuletide dinner with 5 Squadron who were flying Hurricanes. On Boxing Day Corporal Gates and some of the men went into Imphal and collected a motorbike and 1,000 sandbags. The bike was American 750 cc. It was probably of great use in Europe and anywhere else on decent roads. Here there was only one forty-mile stretch of road where it could be handily used.
>
> More backbreaking work was carried out filling the sandbags with dirt. They were placed around the rim of the gun pits to make a protective parapet and also around the slit trenches. On 9 February I was in one of the gun pits, ostensibly checking that the lads had cleaned the guns but actually to have a chat and keep out of Flight Lieutenant Wilmot's way for an hour. In the distance I noticed a group approaching out of the heat haze. As they came closer I could see red tabs on uniforms. Top Brass! We extinguished cigarettes and I jumped out of the pit. Then I thought perhaps I should have stayed inside, but then it was too late. The normal sweating increased. Admiral Lord Louis Mountbatten, 'Supremo' of SEAC, approached. I called the lads in the pit to attention and gave a trembling salute. The big chief hardly noticed me. He conferred with his staff officers; pointing to the jungle behind us and

sweeping an arm toward the airstrip, before wandering away back to our camp. When they were out of sight we relit our cigarettes and mopped our brows.

Flying from the airstrips in the Imphal Valley, the fighter squadrons could provide immediate close-support to the troops in the surrounding hills. In some instances the enemy positions were so close that the Hurricanes could, in effect, do an airfield circuit to complete their support mission. In the space of a few minutes they would take off, head towards the area targeted by forward troops, strafe or bomb the target, turn and land on the strip and then prepare for the next sortie. Some dived in very close to their targets and would return with parts of tree branches sticking out in the air intakes and wings. No 4440 AA Flight took on the job of rearming and refuelling the Hurricanes of 5 Squadron RAF. Colin Kirby recalls the arrival of the Hurricanes:

Two weeks later the Japanese launched an attack on Imphal [against] our sector. Every day three or four Hurricanes hopped up from Imphal at first light. They sat on our strip with radios tuned. From time to time they would take off and then dip over the jungle behind us. We could hear the bombs explode on the occasions they dropped them, and the sound of gunfire. A couple of RAF armourers would also travel from Imphal in a light plane to service the guns. After a time they stopped and our lads serviced the guns. We were also able to ply the pilots with tea as they sat and waited in their

Lord Louis Mountbatten, early in the siege, addresses the ground and aircrew of 607 (County of Durham) Squadron RAF who flew Spitfires in defence of Imphal. Many of these men were flown out soon after to save on food and to keep the aircraft safe at night. Air Commodore S.F. Vincent, AOC 221 Group, stands at the rear of the jeep. (RAF Regiment SEAC Association)

Hurricanes on the strip. Now the pressure was on we had little sleep, the noise of Jap mortars 'crumping' in the jungle on and off all day. Patrolling around the camp with a dawn stand-to. Rations were reduced. Hurricanes in and out, Jap planes overhead. Strangely they left us alone and concentrated on Imphal and other points.

The Japanese columns moved ever closer to the defensive 'boxes' and airstrips and occupied strong positions in the surrounding hills. They were now only a few miles from some of the RAF Regiment field squadrons and AA flights. At Sapam airstrip, 4440 AA Flight felt very exposed. Colin Kirby describes the serious situation that developed as 20th Indian Division came back across the Shenam Pass:

On the evening of 21 March a Brigadier arrived from Imphal and mustered as many of us as possible in the mess basha. He gave us a talk on the seriousness of the situation, and on this gloomy note departed. Later that night Flight Lieutenant Wilmot went off on the motorcycle to Imphal. When he returned he gathered those available into the basha. He told us that he had been to a briefing. The Japs were expected at any moment to break into the plain at about Sapam. We had to stand fast. 'Probably we will not see the dawn,' he said quietly. We looked at each other in the light of the solitary oil lamp.

We filed out into the night and went to spread the word to the others. We manned the gun posts and trenches; it was a very dark night and cold as usual. Peering through the blackness, nerves twanging, our ears tuned to every imagined sound, fingers on triggers. Hoarse whispers, 'Did you hear that?' 'Over to the right!' and so on. The night moved slowly on. Eventually daylight and the sun came over the mountain tops. No enemy assailed us. We stood-to all day, hungry, bleary-eyed and now boiling in the heat. What were we defending except ourselves? The RAF had ceased using the strip and there was no contact with anyone. Gunfire and mortars could be heard, seeming quite close. In the jungle in front of us units were in contact with the Japs. At least we were having it easier than they were. 'Skip' Rawlings came round and after a few words of encouragement moved on to another.

Toward evening some were stood down to hurry back to camp for food and drink. Eventually I went back to find 'Fatty' Darby brewing tea and dishing out hard tack and jam. It went on like this for a day or two. In spite of everything I should emphasise that morale was high. Without any 'gung-ho' attitude we thought we were a pretty good unit. Even so we realised we could not hold back hordes of Japanese had they come at us out of the jungle at Sapam. Also at the back of one's mind was the knowledge that the enemy rarely took prisoners, and those would ultimately receive a horrible death.

With some relief, given the apparent futility of their situation, 4440 AA Flight was moved to the northern end of the Imphal Valley. Colin Kirby continues:

Sapam airstrip was unused and it came as no surprise that a day or two later a senior officer came out from Group HQ in Imphal with orders to move to another location. We moved to a spot nearer Imphal, an almost pastoral area with a small river and a few shady trees overlooking a grassy surface. We dug more trenches, holes in the ground, camouflaged them, guarded the area at night and looked earnestly for some Jap planes to shoot at during the day.

After much work, in a few days new orders came to move again on 26 March. We moved to another dirt strip near Imphal called Wangjing. The Japs had broken through between Kohima and Imphal and now controlled the road. Wangjing was south-east of Imphal Main airfield. The Imphal airfield was the end of the lifeline from Bengal; transport planes landing and taking off continually from dawn to dusk bringing in vital supplies. On arrival we set about digging in. The Hurricanes of 5 Squadron were now flying from Wangjing; defending Imphal and the transport planes from Japanese aircraft, carrying out strafing runs over Japanese airfields and escorting Vengeance dive-bombers on ground support missions. 4440 AA Flight had to defend their strip. An important assignment again left to a small unit of the RAF Regiment.

It was back-breaking work. We dug down several feet in squares about the size of a small room, linking them together with the usual trenches. When completed we covered them with tents laid flat and camouflaged. It rather reminded me of pictures of dugouts and trenches in World War I on the Western Front. Also, of course, the gun pits with our Brownings were set up to keep low-flying attacks at bay; we hoped. Heavily laden planes circled waiting their turn to land. From time to time Japanese fighters roaring in to get to them, Hurricanes buzzing about to get them in turn, mortars crumping in the jungle and occasionally exploding planes crashing. We were so near the airstrip that when the Hurricanes took off they kicked up a dust storm so that we were caked in it as it adhered to our sweating bodies.

'When completed we covered them with tents laid flat and camouflaged . . . it rather reminded me of pictures of dugouts and trenches in World War 1 on the Western Front.' A 'domestic area' for pilots and ground crew in the 'box' at Wangjing. (W.A. Goold DFC)

As the sun set the heat abated, but the activity did not. Routine night or 'prowler' patrols were sent out to prevent the Japanese approaching the strips undetected. It should be remembered that these patrols were carried out without fail by all detachments of the RAF Regiment for the thirteen weeks of the siege. Colin Kirby vividly describes a routine night patrol:

> With the dark hours there was a stillness contrasting with the heat and noise of the day. We had to stand-to facing the hills from where the Japs may appear as the light faded quickly, Brownings lowered and turned in the same direction. Later some men were stood down to get some sleep, some still on guards, others on patrol. The Corporals had to lead a patrol of six men toward the hills for two hours, so we never had much sleep. The belief was that the Japs would send out small suicide parties to raid the strip and do any other damage they could. As they were fanatical and did not seem to mind dying for their Emperor, it was a daunting prospect making contact with them. We would walk quietly for a mile or so, and then start to crawl over the rough ground. We halted from time to time for a breather, listening for any suspicious sounds. Muttered conversation, then I would spread them out in a diagonal line maybe 20 yards apart, with myself in 'point' position. Then every man was alone with his thoughts but I hoped still alert. From time to time I would move back and pass among them. 'How long have we been out Corp?' 'I don't know, I can't see my bloody watch, but there's a long time to go.' 'It's f . . . . . . cold!' 'I could sink a pint right now.' 'Well you won't for a long time, if ever.' Thus the conversation. I would decide if it was time to move back to camp. We approached cautiously until near enough to make contact with the relief patrol. The men would dive for their sleeping space and I would report to the Flight Commander who had his own tent.

As he entered the tent to report, his Flight Commander had the disturbing habit of reaching for his torch with one hand and at the same time picking up his service revolver in the other. He would then switch on the torch and shine it into Corporal Kirby's face. Colin Kirby was understandably concerned that one night the Flight Lieutenant would forget which hand held the revolver and pull the trigger of his revolver rather than switch his torch on!

Most of the patrols neither saw nor heard any enemy infiltration parties, while others were nerve-wracking. Colin Kirby continues:

> By late April the number of men out on patrols had been reduced to allow for a little more sleep. . . . No respite for the Corporals though. That night I took out four men on patrol. It was the middle of the night. We had heard of the daring Jap raiding parties who ventured on to the Plain to inflict what damage they could. . . . I led them out some way; before us open ground. It was very dark. By now we were finding moving over the ground more difficult; 100 yards began to seem like a mile. I dropped two after we had gone some distance, and then after a little more distance covered, the other two. I pressed on alone for a little longer, keeping what I hoped was straight line. I stopped with my back resting against a small tree, Sten gun on lap. The only sound was an occasional hyena with its mournful cry. I felt very much alone. I heard a noise to my front and moved into a crouch position and cocked the Sten. I told

myself it was my imagination or perhaps a hyena or wild dog? It was there again! I gulped and pointed the gun ahead and let off a few rounds, turned and hurried back. I bumped into one of the others, his mate had already moved back to the first two. I collected them and we approached the camp cautiously. 'Corporal Kirby's patrol returning!' I shouted. Everybody was already on stand-to peering anxiously into the night.

By 4 April the three infantry divisions of IV Corps had withdrawn successfully and were concentrated in and around the Imphal Plain, albeit with differing degrees of difficulty. On 6 April 4408 AA Flight located at Imphal Main airstrip saw enemy ground forces moving near the strip and dispersal areas and the unit stood-to, but was not attacked. Many times during the month, small arms fire could be heard as Army patrols encountered Japanese infiltration parties. Three enemy shells fell in close proximity to the Imphal strip on 19 April at 1530 hours. Although no damage was caused, this was the first of many shellings that Imphal and Palel airfields were to receive over the next three months as the Japanese moved in and captured hill features close to the two airfields.

The defensive 'box' at Palel would be a major objective for the enemy. Wired defensive positions were arranged around a large pimple located at the eastern end of the strip. Radiating from the base of the pimple, on which was located an Army Bofors gun, were the dispersal bays for the Hurricanes. Unfortunately, the preparation of the defensive 'box' had been relatively hasty and no communications trenches were dug. As a result, after dark it became very difficult, if not fatal, for the defenders to move easily from one position to another. The airmen could soon hear the sounds of heavy fighting in the hills around the airfield and thought of what that might mean for those waiting in the slit trenches should the Japanese break through. Most of the actions by the enemy occurred during the night hours and this was when the 'box' defences and RAF Regiment patrols had to be on full alert. By night, Japanese 'jitter' parties would move around the perimeter of the 'boxes' attempting to draw fire to give away positions. 'Jifs' would crawl up to tempt Indian and Gurkha troops to come over to their side; in this endeavour they were never successful.

By early April it was apparent that the personnel of the RAF flying squadrons in the 'boxes' were exhausted, owing to ground defence commitments. Absolute silence and the strictest blackout were kept from dusk to dawn; 25 per cent of air and ground crew were on guard duty at night during quiet periods, rising to 100 per cent as the enemy closed in. Flying and servicing of aircraft had to continue during the day; therefore, it was not long before personnel of 221 Group were showing signs of exhaustion, particularly on those airfields only a few miles from the enemy such as Palel. Sentry duties and night patrols that were considered in the first weeks as a 'bit-of-a-hoot' by some pilots, now made heavy demands and the numerous night alarms added further to the strain. Aircraft serviceability and operational efficiency would seriously decline if RAF personnel continued with their dual responsibilities. The Army was fully committed to repelling the offensive and no troops could be spared for airfield defence. This was contrary to an agreement reached in November 1943, that the Army would withdraw garrisons from airfields remote from enemy action and provide them where attack was possible. As a result, during May, six of the flying squadrons were withdrawn from the plain to airfields in the Surma and Assam Valley, with the last fighter-bomber squadron withdrawn during June. The RAF would still closely support IV Corps, but the fighters and fighter-bombers would fly into the plain early each morning to airstrips made safe by the RAF Regiment. The transfer of the flying

The personnel of an RAF fighter squadron at Palel stand-to while the Squadron Dance Band entertains them. Responsibility for ground defence, along with flying and maintenance duties, was soon found to be unsustainable for the air and ground crews. (Australian War Memorial P02491.356)

squadrons did have one benefit, as it reduced the tonnage of rations required to be flown in for the garrison.

The limit of the Japanese advance was reached on 21 April but the struggle would continue for the next three months. *Yamamoto Force* fought to break through the positions held by the 20th Indian Division on the Shenam Pass, with the aim of capturing Palel airstrip, on which much of the air supply of the garrison depended. The AFV Flight of 2943 Field Squadron was lent to the 20th Indian Division and attached to the 100th Indian Infantry Brigade to carry out armoured patrols to help with keeping the road open to these forward positions. The British, Indian and Gurkha troops on the Shenam Pass were in close contact with the Japanese and both sides lived in conditions similar to those of the Somme in the First World War. Positions were lost, retaken and lost again, while each side fought for control of the Pass.

Enemy air activity increased during April, with attacks being made on ground targets in the Imphal area. Formations of up to thirty fighters, sometimes accompanied by medium bombers, would attack in the early morning. Many were intercepted by the Spitfires, which caused such heavy losses that the Japanese returned to night attacks. During the third week of April the Japanese attempted to put the airfields at Imphal, Palel and Tulihal out of action, but little damage was done and runways were closed for only a few hours after each raid. Those Japanese raiders that got through the fighter screen to attack the airfields would encounter a limited barrage from the small number of Army AA guns. The AA defence at Imphal was still primarily the responsibility of IV Corps and consisted of the Corps Artillery: the 67th Heavy AA Regiment with 3.7-in HAA guns, the 28th and 78th LAA Regiments with Bofors 40-mm LAA guns,

An RAF Regiment Armoured Carrier (Indian-Pattern) belonging to an AFV Flight. 2943 Field Squadron put these to good use patrolling the Shenam Pass during the siege of Imphal. (Air Historical Branch RAF Crown Copyright)

and the 2nd Indian, 55th and 82nd LAA/Anti-Tank Regiments, also equipped with Bofors with the infantry divisions. Not as well endowed with AA ordnance as their RAF Regiment brothers in the European and Mediterranean theatres of war, at Imphal they could only provide close air defence to airfields. The twin Browning AA guns had a limited range and hitting power and their primary effect was to divert Japanese fighter aircraft from strafing attacks. They could, however, also be used if necessary for ground defence against Japanese infantry attacks against the airfields.

The RAF Regiment gunners had to be continually on the alert for Japanese fighters swooping in on strafing runs, medium to high altitude bombing attacks and rumoured infantry attacks. For those manning the Brownings, there would only be a short warning period before enemy fighters streaked across the strip. The strafing attacks lasted only a few seconds and were often preceded by days or weeks where no enemy aircraft had put in an appearance. Gun positions were manned during daylight hours, at night during moonlight periods, plus six days either side. The ORBs of the AA flights at Imphal from March until July are replete with the statement 'Gun posts and Guards' day after day (Appendix 11). There were periods of intense activity with warnings of air attack, signalled by three shots fired from an Army Bofors gun located on the strip. The warnings 'red', 'yellow' or 'white'[11] occurred two to three times a day when the Japanese Air Force was active. These were, however, often false alarms as the raiders veered off to attack another target. Fifteen air raids warnings were given at Imphal Main during April, on occasions twice a day. On 15 April nine Japanese 'Sally' bombers and ten 'Oscars' approached the camp site of 4408 AA Flight from the south-west at low level. The aircraft strafed the dispersal bay nearby and an anti-personnel bomb fell between two foxholes occupied by airmen. Though not killed by the explosion, they suffered serious shock and were sent away for treatment. Small arms fire and shrapnel pierced the tents and orderly room. The flight's 15-cwt truck caught fire after being hit by cannon shells and incendiary bullets and considerable damage was caused to the airmen's kit. The flight was fortunate as eight Indian Pioneers nearby were killed and nine severely injured. The Browning AA guns had some success when they engaged the aircraft and hits were registered on two aircraft, but they did not crash immediately.

Both 4430 and 4444 AA Flights had arrived at Palel during the latter months of 1943 and had remained there since. There were sixteen air raid warnings during May, of which four resulted in direct attacks by enemy aircraft on or near the strip. On the ground the Japanese were moving ever closer to Palel. On 1 May at 2430 hours small arms fire was heard on the hills east of the airfield and by 0200 hours a strong battle could be heard raging, which lasted until daylight. The 5.5-in guns and 25-pounder batteries located nearby opened up and continued firing for long periods to break up the Japanese attack. 4444 AA Flight moved into 42 (Hurricane) Squadron's defence area during daylight, manning rifle pits and twin Brownings while others stood-to in bunkers. No direct attack was made on the 'box', although heavy fighting was going on all around and streams of tracer bullets were constantly passing overhead. At dawn Japanese stragglers were observed being chased by Bren carriers in the foothills and bashas were set on fire to chase them out. On 3 May the enemy pressure on the strip forced 42 Squadron to move out. Three days later the airmen watched as twenty-four Vultee Vengeance and twelve Hurricanes dive-bombed and strafed the enemy positions east of the strip. The Japanese artillery was now in range of the airstrip and on 9 May eight shells landed harmlessly on the south end of the strip; however, at 0815 hours the following day enemy shells landed on the dispersal occupied by 4430 AA Flight at the northern end. Corporal Harold Barlow was killed immediately. LAC Thomas Harris died of wounds later that day, while LAC Coleman was wounded but survived. Thus the flight had the first RAF Regiment airmen to be killed in action during the siege.

RAF Regiment reinforcements were urgently despatched to the valley, though the Regiment would always be thin on the ground for the tasks required. In late March and early April 2944 Field Squadron and two flights of 2941 Field Squadron were flown in from Dohazari and Agartala, respectively (Appendix 10). It will be recalled that 2944 Field Squadron had been deployed to Maungdaw in the Arakan on AMES protection but had been recalled without delay to Dohazari. Henry Kirk remembers the move:

In the first few days of April we heard that Imphal was besieged and we received orders to prepare to move there after stand-to the next morning. Each man was restricted to 20 lb in weight of personal kit. At 0430 hours we were relieved by another Regiment squadron and taken by road to Dohazari. There we were packed into six Dakotas of the USAAF, which had been diverted from the Calcutta-China hump run. After a flight of some 1½ hours, the last part over jungle-clad hills held by the Japanese, we landed at Kangla. As we alighted from the aircraft non-combatants took our place. It was a case of; if you cannot fire a weapon, get out, as others needed the available food. We were given a small box of American K rations about the size of a present day carton of 200 cigarettes. This was classed as an emergency meal for one man; we were told not to eat it all at once, as they did not know where the next meal was coming from. In fact that's all we did receive for over 24 hours. An Army officer directed us to some small hills about 1,200 feet above sea level, these being the foothills of a much higher range. After being given a password, we were told to dig in and get below ground, no easy task in this rock and shale.

On the heights above were strung out units of the 20th Indian Division; during the night our medium artillery kept dropping shells in the saddles between the peaks to stop the Japanese breaking through . . . Quite an experience when

A flying controller at Imphal Main airfield signals from his two-storey, log and corrugated iron control tower. The hills in the background are typical of the locations of the defensive 'boxes'. (Air Historical Branch RAF Crown Copyright)

the order is 'Shoot to kill anything that moves'. Later in the siege this was changed to hand grenades only, due to the flash of weapons giving the defence positions away. This was our first night in the siege of Imphal; we had very little time for sleep in between our stag [guard] duties and even less for breakfast as we nibbled at the remains of our K rations.

After all the hard work spent in preparing dugouts, we were moved the next morning to the all-weather airfield Imphal Main. This had two parallel runways, the shorter one for use by fighter aircraft. The fighters flew out each night for safety from ground attack, leaving the ground crews in a 'box'.

On 30 March and 1 April two flights of 2941 Field Squadron were landed at Imphal and Sapam. They immediately moved by road to a high hill overlooking 221 Group HQ north of the Imphal Main airstrip and began preparing defensive positions. Kanglatongbi, a few miles to the north-west of Imphal, fell to the Japanese on 8 April and the two flights went on 100 per cent stand-to. On 10 April at 1000 hours six enemy aircraft dived on Imphal Main strip. A terrific barrage met them as they dived in, and the Brens of No 1 Flight of 2941 Field Squadron, firing from their hill positions above the strip, claimed a hit on one of the aircraft.

The stay was relatively short as on 24 April both flights moved east to Kangla, where they joined 4418 and 9 (India) AA Flights. Kangla had a dirt strip with a few bashas and was completely surrounded by hills. Night flying was in operation and No 1 Flight took up defensive positions at the north end of strip to defend against any incursions from the north-east and to watch over the unloading of aircraft. After discussions with the officer-in-charge of the Bofors detachment at Kangla,[12] the 'Kite Box' was formed under the command of the 2941 Field Squadron CO, Squadron Leader R.A. Plank. It was to be completely administered by RAF Regiment staff. 4423 and 4434 AA Flights moved in over the next few days with the latter Flight to take on a protective role for an AMES being re-established near the strip.

The squadron patrolled extensively for more than a month through the hills over-looking the strip to the north, east and south-east. Any attempt by the Japanese to occupy these hills would curtail flying at Kangla. Although there were never clashes with the enemy, there were indications of their presence. Flight Lieutenant Stewart led an eight-hour patrol west of Kamhongphul, on 2 May, which climbed a spur to 4,500 feet where the men found prepared, but fortunately unoccupied, Japanese bunker posi-tions. Just before dawn on 11 May the occupants of 'Kite Box' received an air raid warning. However, rather than being bombed the airmen were showered with leaflets, which after translation by the Manipur Police were found to be an appeal for recruits to the Indian National Army, complete with instructions on how to join.

The day that 2941 Field Squadron departed for Kangla, it was replaced by 2944 Field Squadron, which moved in to take over the hill feature, known as 'C' for Charlie. The defensive position, of which it was part, overlooked Imphal Main airfield.'[13] Indian Line of Communication Troops had previously been in occupation on parts of the feature and had dug only shallow weapon pits. The squadron set to, and a lot of work was put in to toughen up the defensive positions; bunkers were camouflaged, slit trenches and Bren posts re-sited and the hillside cleared to improve fields of fire. Nos 2 and 4 Flights of 2944 Field Squadron with Flying Officer Gordon took over positions on 'C' for Charlie, which overlooked 221 Group HQ, while No 1 Flight established itself with 355 Wireless Unit near Group HQ. The protection of this radio post was vital as it provided the main link with the world outside the Valley. Flying Officer Evington with No 3 Flight was established in the Saddle, located between the two hills, while Field Squadron HQ and the Orderly Room were set up below it. The squadron would remain here until mid-August. Henry Kirk continues:

> I was the Squadron Armourer and HQ was a basha built into a hillside, next door was the Chindit's HQ. Every part of the valley was split up into inde-pendent 'box' defences. The outer defences of our box were a range of high hills with the radio post 'D' for Donald. This afterwards got the nickname 'Nightmare Peak', from the valley floor it was like looking at a wall, you had to put your head right back to see the tops and on these heights our Field Squadron had to dig in and fortify the area and we muleteers had to supply all their needs.
>
> The Japanese or 'Jifs' regularly moved between the posts at night as the limited manpower of the Squadrons and Flights could not cover all the paths across the hills. Such infiltrations were relatively common, although many were of only nuisance value. When moving along the jungle tracks around the 'box' during daylight it was not unusual to come across freshly broken twigs and branches, disturbed soil and rubbed bark where climbing ropes had been tied by enemy parties moving about the previous night. 'D' for Donald was the peak with the main radio transmitter for Imphal. There were two landlines that followed the tracks up 'D' for Donald; one went to 221 Group HQ and the other to IV Corps HQ. Any loss of either of them could have had serious consequences for the defenders of Imphal.

At times during the siege the rate of delivery of supplies by air could not match demand and as a result, on a number of occasions cuts were made to rations for the garrison. Henry Kirk describes the typical fare consumed during the siege and the means by which 'supplementary' rations could be obtained for the squadron:

LAC A. Nickson and LAC Frank Yewbrey of 2944 Field Squadron discuss the siting of a Bren gun with the 221 Group Defence Officer, Squadron Leader T.F. Ryalls, and Flying Officer J.D. Crowhill. (Air Historical Branch RAF Crown Copyright)

Food in the first part of the siege was so called half rations i.e. hard biscuits and jam for breakfast and tea, dinner was again biscuits and a small tin of bully beef between four men, this was poured out never cut, a dixie of tea at each meal always without sugar and sometimes milk, the ration of cigarettes was fifty 'V's a week; made in India and often mouldy. Before stand-to at night a tot of rum was issued to all ranks. So it was a big improvement when along came Australian dehydrated potatoes and mutton. The Cook's special for this was his stew and [I] must say that not very appetising after seeing the perspiration dripping off his face into it. In addition to the swarms of flies having a meal off us they were also attracted to the stew and if we complained about these insects being in it all we got was 'What are you complaining about, you're getting extra meat!' One thing for sure you ate it as there was nothing else. The biscuits we were issued with were hard and made to last and it was amusing to watch a mule deal with one, pointing its nose to the heavens as it turned one round and round in its mouth, you can only guess it was deciding what on earth it had got hold of. Our first allocation of bread was twenty loaves and our Commanding Officer remarked to us that these are not on our ration scale and am sure he thought we had stolen them. He was partly right although he never knew it. As it happened I went to school with the officer who was issuing them. I well remember him lifting up a tarpaulin sheet and seeing these lovely loaves underneath, he told us to quickly fill two empty sugar bags and keep quiet. So you can imagine we did not need twice telling.

Every morning during the siege we collected drinking water from a treatment plant on the Imphal Turel [River], this was carried in two-gallon petrol tins with ten such tins carried on each mule. One morning we were held back under the cover of some trees waiting to go forward, normally it was straight in and out. This morning when we eventually got our load we were stopped by an Army NCO who remarked 'Don't tell your people we have been fishing Jap bodies out of here this morning' – we were both parched dry and dare not touch it. When we arrived back at base HQs before going to the heights we found the cook had used the water he had in stock salted for the daily dose of one pint per man and it was this we drank, regarding the rest the CO gave the order to boil the lot and keep the smoke signals down, some job that with damp wood. The total number of round trips we made with the mules was 187, each one a marathon in its own right, and looking at photographs now we look more like greyhounds, but must say the fittest I ever was in the four years spent in the Far East.

The war in Burma could not have been won without extensive use of the mule. Much-maligned beasts, they were an efficient means of transporting armaments and equipment through all kinds of rough terrain and particularly the jungle-clad hills. Many of those who served in Burma and worked with the animals have fond memories of these tenacious, intelligent, strong and sometimes obstinate animals. Henry Kirk continues:

I never did get to know how I got the job but was put in charge of supplies. It might have been the fact that I was brought up with horses and my mate to be, Bert Robson, who hailed from Carlisle, was a slaughterman in civilian life. What was to follow was a hair-raising experience and we became quite likely the only muleteers to serve in the RAF Regiment.

. . . We collected them after stand-to and breakfast each morning from the Indian Army mule lines. There seemed to be hundreds of them and we had to be in early to get the same ones, always two, sometimes four and then with an Indian Army muleteer. The mules were all ready to take away, completely harnessed and each having a feedbag. These Army mules were well cared for and continually checked by Army Veterinary Officers and at the end of each day we had to report if we noticed anything amiss with them. We were told the mules had been shipped from the Argentine but I always doubted this as they responded well to directions in Urdu. The mule is a much-maligned animal but we found them more intelligent than given credit for and sure footed traversing difficult parts of our route to the heights. They liked a free head and did not object to us hanging on to their tails. If you overloaded or put an uneven load on them they stood rock solid with their ears up like goal posts. The sound of the heavy gunfire or from the fighting nearby which rolled around the hills, also the low flying aircraft, never seemed to bother them.

We did have one very frightening experience with them; this was on Tuesday 6 June 1944, the day we heard of the Second Front in Europe, very low clouds covered the valley floor and it was terribly hot and humid. We had set off with four mules with water and dry rations and we made our way upwards through the cloud and came out into the clear blue sky and sunshine with the peaks some 7,000 feet high sticking up through black menacing clouds, transport aircraft were going round in the circuit dropping their supplies by parachute through the cloud to the valley floor, high above our Spitfires could be seen patrolling and protecting the air corridor back into Assam.[14] I have never forgotten the scene that I suppose was a photographer's dream.

We got rid of our loads and began our return loaded with empty water tins when we were surrounded in thick cloud, sheet lightning and thunder, you could feel the electricity in the air and the heavens opened with torrential rain. Due to this we had decided to lead the mules down when they suddenly stopped going round a ledge, it was just a rock path with a sheer wall on one side and a drop on the other of hundreds of feet looking down into the treetops. I was in the lead and my mule brayed and raised its front feet in the air. I managed to pull its head down and it put its nose under my arm, I spoke to it and stroked it and managed to quieten it down then led them forward off this dangerous ledge and under some trees where we stayed until the storm passed.

We arrived back at HQ soaked to the skin and covered in mud and together with the mules must have looked a very sorry sight. Our CO Squadron Leader Arnold[15], a big powerfully built Australian, told us to get rid of the mules and stay in the HQ basha for the night, this was something because everybody at night at this time went into dug-outs and took turns at manning the airfield inner defences. Something we also learned about the mules is that while a horse will drink any water, it has to be good for a mule and the Indian muleteers used to tell us that if a mule drinks the water then you can.

Nearly every morning when collecting the mules we could see the Major come towards us and we would look at each other and say wait for it. He would call out to us 'Bring them back to us – I can replace you but not them.' I have often wondered if he had got the message that my mate Bert Robson was a slaughterman in civilian life and thought he was going to lose one so we could have fresh meat.

The defenders of 'Nightmare Peak', Imphal, 2944 Field Squadron. The thick-set man on the left is the cook, Corporal Harper. Note the khaki shirts and shorts, before the issue of jungle green, indicating the early days of the siege. Taking a photo on this track would not be possible within a few weeks as grouping would draw sniper fire. (RAF Regiment SEAC Association)

To the north-east of the 'boxes' the columns of the *15th Japanese Division* were making a major effort to break into the Imphal Valley. Some 6 miles to the north-east was Nunshigum Hill, the occupier of which could look down directly on Imphal town and airfield. Nunshigum had seen heavy fighting during April as the 5th Indian Division fought to drive the Japanese from their vantage point. After changing hands several times it was finally retaken with heavy casualties on 13 April. This was the nearest that any Japanese force larger than a patrol ever got to Imphal. Two Japanese battalions later occupied a village and hill feature called Mapao, located only a few thousand yards to the north. From 'Nightmare Peak' the airmen of 2944 Field Squadron could almost see the progress of the siege unfolding before their eyes. Henry Kirk recalls:

> From the hills you had a panoramic view of the heights surrounding Imphal and aircraft movements on the main airfield looked like toys. One got a grand-stand view of the warfare going on around you, we did not know at the time but the Japs had got on to the heights across the valley from us and they were in positions overlooking the airfield and the IV Corps HQ. Going up with the mules we stopped and watched Vultee Vengeance dive-bombers and Hurricane fighter-bombers circling round and diving on to this ridge and all 'hell' seemed to break loose when batteries of heavy guns started to shell the Japanese posi-tions. We learnt later they had been driven off.
>   Another morning, 9 May, Wellington bombers went over escorted by the ever present Spitfires and Hurricanes and we watched them run in and drop their bombs in the Bishenpur area. Other Wellington aircraft from my old Squadron,[16] I know were ferrying in 250 lb bombs, which Hurricane IICs carried, one under each wing, to attack the Japanese positions. American B-25 Mitchells were being used to bring in urgent medical supplies carried in canis-ters in the bomb bays.

Living in the Valley was not only a struggle against the Japanese but also against the weather, the jungle and its nastier inhabitants. Henry Kirk continues:

> In spite of the terrible conditions we operated under morale remained high. The climate was hot and humid in the period approaching the monsoon. Just to stand was like having a shower with the perspiration rolling off. Imphal was in an area with one of the highest rainfall levels in the world and when the monsoon did come it was the heaviest for years with over 400 inches of rain. In the sunny periods between the storms one was in a steam bath, everything you had went green and clothing rotted, if left for just a few days there would only be bones left on a body.
>   Imphal at first sight looked a beautiful place with its greenery and flowers but there it ended, the hills or should we say mountains, jungle covered, carried every tropical disease and some scrub typhus. Everybody dreaded this and many died, and along with sores, bites and rashes added to your misery. Mosquitoes, which we called 'Mark Vs', came out at dusk so thick you might have cut the air in blocks. We had long forgotten what it was like to sleep in a charpoy, it was the ever-ready ground sheet and Mother Earth. All this and besieged by an enemy so ferocious that some of the acts they committed were beyond belief. We were told by an Intelligence Officer 'If the Japanese break in here remember you have nowhere to go, drop a hand grenade and take them with you', 'Do not get taken prisoner, we know they will use you for bayonet

practice'. The siege brought young men together sharing everything they received even down to a cigarette being cut in half. By the end of the siege of 80 days the so called half rations we knew were in danger of being cut further despite the air transport working flat out to bring in supplies. It was said that shells and ammunition had priority over everything else.

Reading this you will have picked up in this desperate situation all ranks closed and each helped one another, mere lads became men overnight. This was no place for a 'loner' and nothing stood in the way of propping one another up. This was typical throughout the besieged forces whatever the branch of service they belonged.

Malaria and typhus were a constant and common threat and in the first years of the Burma campaign there were about a hundred sick due to disease to every man wounded in action. Anti-malarial precautions were introduced and the taking of suppressive drugs such as mepacrine, the covering of exposed skin at night and use of repellent were enforced. Special units were formed and trained to carry out anti-malarial procedures, such as spraying in areas where the disease was endemic. By 1944 these efforts had been rewarded with a substantial reduction in the incidence of the disease. Despite this many men still came down with the disease or suffered recurrences of fever from malaria contracted earlier. In these situations the sufferer had to be taken as soon as possible for treatment. Henry Kirk was involved in the evacuation of one such individual:

On Monday 15 May 1944, a night operation which even today gives one shivers at the very thought of it. This was at the height of the siege and the Japanese had closed up to most of the defences and [were] making fanatical attempts to break through into the valley before the monsoon broke. In our sector they were getting through a saddle between the peaks near 'D' for Donald Radio Post. They were more of a nuisance than anything else with their nightly cutting of the telephone lines and cries in the night of 'Come on Johnny' keeping men on these forward posts alert and depriving those who should be resting of their sleep.

At 2000 hours we had just stood down when the CO sent for me, he said, 'The land line is still open and we have received an urgent message from Flying Officer Evington that he has a man unconscious with suspected spinal or cerebral malaria on one of his posts. Nobody knows the track like you, will you volunteer to be the guide and escort the medical orderly to go up there and see what you can do – we could lose him if left. This is not an order!' Together with Corporal Hindmarsh of Leeds we set off with a stretcher. I had four hand grenades; two hung each side of my belt. The password was 'Orange' that night. We left a Bren gun post and picked up the telephone lines and went up the first steep rock gully. Due to the low drifting clouds it was a dark night broken by the flashes from our heavy guns pounding Japanese positions and drifting Very lights. The whole route was covered with small trees, bamboo and much undergrowth, it was a case of no talking, checking and careful movements. Not easy when disturbed monkeys were screeching and moving about. We were met below the saddle as pre-arranged, challenged by the patrol and exchanged passwords. We were soon to discover our patient was one of the unit's heavy gang, LAC Vic Busby, a Londoner, a good job we were going down with him and not up.

LAC Henry Kirk of 2944 Field Squadron adjusts a load in his new job as a muleteer, 'Nightmare Peak', Imphal, 1944. (Photograph courtesy of the Imperial War Museum, London IWM CI 684)

After a short rest and some cold tea we set off with the heavily laden stretcher. The same patrol went ahead and left us at the saddle. We had just gone round the rock wall when the cries of 'Come on Johnny!' echoed around the hillside from down below us. A Japanese 'jitter' party must have got through the saddle while we were at the top post. We moved off the track and took cover behind bamboo; it seemed like an eternity but in fact it was only minutes before they came climbing up the track led by an officer or Warrant Officer with a sword, followed by four men dwarfed by their long rifles with bayonets fixed. They passed the other side of us, only six to eight feet away. We heard them go away towards the rock wall and we moved out and the rest of the climb down was uneventful.

On reaching the forward Bren gun post the patient was taken from us and removed to a field hospital. He recovered and later rejoined the Squadron. This successful operation took nearly four and a half hours. On Tuesday 16 May we were both informed that we had been recommended for the award 'mentioned in despatches'. Corporal Hindmarsh received the award.

Prior to the siege, Imphal had been a garrison town with the usual camp followers, labourers and other non-combatants. As many as possible were flown out during the siege to reduce the ration strength, however, there were still individuals or groups that had become confused by the fighting, had fled their posts and were wandering the valley. It was common to have intrusions of many kinds into the defensive 'boxes', particularly at night. Anyone moving outside the perimeter at night was treated as hostile and likely to receive a grenade tossed from a slit trench. Parties of 'Jifs' of the Indian National Army moving about during the night often dressed similarly to the Indian troops of IV Corps, which made identification of friend or foe difficult. Some disturbances were easily explained as Japanese 'jitter' parties while others were more mysterious and explanations were never found. One such incident, typical of many, occurred on the night of the 24/25 May 1944 when Flying Officer Evington of No 3 Flight, 2944 Field Squadron, heard footsteps leading to the wire surrounding the positions on the top of 'D' for Donald. He reported the incident as follows:

At approximately 2300 hours my southernmost bunker position advised me that they had heard definite footsteps leading to the defence wire which surrounds their bunker positions, at the same time they heard the tin cans rattle on the wire after being touched. I advised them by field telephone to halt and enquire the password from whoever may be there; it was too dark to see 20–30 feet away. They did so but received no reply, a scuffle was heard and loose stones were heard falling down the hillside at the Imphal (south-west) side. I advised them to listen carefully for any further movements, my orders generally being that fire is to be held until the object is well sighted and at close range.

Having recently had the patrol which covers these hills near to my position, I decided to contact 221 Group HQ and ascertain if they were out at that hour, and if they had altered or were likely to make a wrong detour. In the meantime I ordered a full stand-to and I learned from the Group Defence Officer that the patrol was expected back any moment. I phoned 'C' for Charlie and advised them that we were not very happy about the position and to remain on the 'Alert'.

At approximately 0030 hours I learned from the GDO that the patrol previously mentioned, had returned to its base, and had not been near to our positions. At the same time my southernmost and south-east positions advised me that they heard definite noises in the 'dip' between 'C' for Charlie and 'D' for Donald.

I phoned 'C' for Charlie and Group, the former being told that they were not to fire in my direction until I had satisfied myself as to the noises heard. I sent a patrol of three men to the extremity of my defences, where they concealed themselves, and half an hour later heard five rifle shots. I again advised the GDO and 'C' for Charlie that my men were dealing with the matter, and once again the latter to refrain from firing (long range) until the patrol made its report. I was on the telephone with Group when my patrol returned. This is significant, because a few seconds later the line was dead: on interrogation they said they lay concealed for 'some time' and saw some black objects moving in the dip whereupon they opened fire . . .

At this time I attempted to phone 'C' for Charlie to tell them we were now in our own positions, but found the line 'dead'. I, therefore, decided to send out a patrol again with a linesman to repair the line, if possible. At the same time we 'listened in' with our own transmitter and were able to contact Group who in turn contacted 'C' for Charlie and HQ 2944 Field Squadron. A shot was fired from Group direction as the patrol left the position. My patrol and linesman returned with 30 feet of cable, one end of which was definitely cut straight in two, the other end was an old joined end; the significant thing was that the cut end was tied and knotted around a tree.

We maintained ¼ hourly communications with the GDO until 'first light' when the patrol went out again to mend the breakage. I may add that I was of the opinion that some Japs or 'Jifs' may have left the area south-west of our positions, where continual fighting seems to have been in progress for some days. Some evenings ago, I reported a 'figure' wandering forlornly at the Imphal side of our hill, who looked as though he may be battled 'dazed'.[17]

Further reinforcements, in the form of 4407, 4424 and 4433 AA Flights, were flown to Kangla from Feni in the second week of May. These units were unable to bring any transport vehicles but were still required to take all armaments, stores and provisions as shown by the items flown in with 4407 AA Flight:

Eighteen Browning [light] machine guns and their nine Motley Stalk mountings, five Bren guns, ammunition, thirty-eight No 36 grenades, four pickaxes, four shovels, a stretcher, four No 108 radio sets, an armoury tool kit, a first aid kit, all their cooking utensils and all orderly room papers . . . Each man was to carry two days reserve rations, which consisted of two tins of bully beef and six packets of biscuits.[18]

All three flights were placed under the control of 181 Signals Wing[19] with 4407 AA Flight being sent to Burri Bazaar to protect an AMES in the 'Starling Box' while 4424 and 4433 AA Flights went to protect the AMES at Sawambung near Kangla and Yairipok, respectively. These stations were crucial to the air defence of the Valley.

By June the lot of the defenders at Imphal had improved, while for the Japanese it was now apparent that the offensive had faltered. Three field squadrons and seventeen AA flights were now stationed on the Imphal Plain (Appendix 8). For 2943 Field Squadron and 4430 and 4444 AA Flights at Palel airstrip, June had passed in a similar manner to the previous two months of the siege, with constant manning of AA positions interspersed with periods of enemy ground activity around the airstrip and surrounding hills. In late June, however, the Japanese made their last effort to break through and capture Palel. 4418 and 4423 AA Flights were sent as reinforcements from Kangla. The 23rd Indian Division, which had taken over from the 20th Indian Division, was fighting a renewed and partially successful attempt by the *Yamamoto Force* to capture important features on the Shenam Pass Road. The Division had been ordered to hold its positions at all costs. A major reason was to ensure that no Japanese guns could be put where they could bombard the Palel airstrip. Some did get close but they were firing at maximum range, and the aircraft continued to take off and land. During July the local Japanese commander, Nukui, decided that small but determined parties of saboteurs would have a greater chance of reaching the Palel main base and airfield. 4444 AA Flight was ordered to abandon its AA role and concentrate on the protection of aircraft in the dispersal bays. The wire was strengthened and listening posts were established. Guard duties and patrols were aimed primarily at protecting aircraft and airfields from parties with the intent to damage or destroy aircraft on the ground.

A party of Japanese made a fanatical attack on 29/30 June on the Palel Bridge but was beaten back. On the afternoon of 1 July, shells began bursting near the Palel airstrip and continued for two hours. As the shells were falling rather haphazardly it was deemed sensible by the airmen to take cover once the bark of the enemy guns could be heard. On 5 July a party of one officer and thirteen men raided the Palel airstrip. They were from the *Nukui Column*, which had been involved in fighting around Tegnoupal on the Shenam Pass in late June as part of *Yamamoto Force*. The strip was no longer used by the air transports because, as a result of the continuous use during the siege, it had suffered severe surface cracking. Hurricane fighter-bombers, however, were still using it to attack Japanese positions beyond the hills above the airfield. The ORB of 4444 AA Flight describes the raid from their positions:

Around 0100 hours . . . 4444 AA Flight personnel heard a burst of rifle fire coming from the main aircraft dispersal at the south-east end of the strip and the Camp patrol reported immediately afterwards that an aircraft parked there was on fire. A 100% stand-to was at once ordered and contact made with the Heavy AA who, however, had no information. The intensity of the fire increased and there were several loud explosions from bursting ammunition. The Flight Commander was about to proceed to investigate when a 'phone message' was received from 2943 Squadron that a party of saboteurs had penetrated the wire and damaged aircraft. All round defensive positions were taken up but no enemy were observed.[20]

At Palel there was an Army Bofors gun position located on a small rock pimple, into which had been cut the dispersal bays for the fighter aircraft. Unbeknown to the Bofors gunners the party had crept in, blown a hole in the wire and placed timing devices on the aircraft air intakes directly below their position. A two-man patrol of 2943 Field Squadron challenged the raiding party as they were leaving and then opened fire. About this time a party of 'Jifs' ran into a position held by Indian troops; after being greeted they thought that our Indian troops would change sides and join them, however, they were turned upon and all were killed.

A report submitted by 221 Group HQ to the 3rd Tactical Air Force describes the sequence of events on the night of 4 July:

> . . . the RAF Regiment patrol had heard sounds in the neighbourhood of two Harvards, one belonging to 113 Squadron and the other to 152 Squadron. On their approach there were explosions in the two Harvards and in two Hurricanes on the opposite side of the taxiing track. They saw some men run away into the darkness and fired on them and followed. In the meantime, more members of the enemy patrol took advantage of the disturbance and came in behind the patrol, and placed their bombs in the three Spitfires, making off immediately into the darkness to the south.
>
> These were also fired at by the Bofors gun crew located on the top of the pimple, but without success. This Bofors gun crew failed to see or hear anyone approach, but this was no doubt due to the fact that our own 5.5-inch and 25-pounder guns were firing at the time, less than half a mile away to the south. The raiding party had taken full advantage of this gunfire to cover their movements, and were familiar with the position of the aircraft, and also with the general layout of the aircraft themselves. Bombs were placed in air intakes, front of radiators and in the back locker of one Harvard, and had apparently only a short delay action. A bomb was also thrown into a workshop basha, but without doing any harm. This was probably thrown thinking that airmen might be sleeping therein.
>
> A Bangalore torpedo was found near one of the Spitfires and was doubtless brought to blow a hole in the barbed wire. This proved unnecessary as the barbed wire was only thin, and had been cut under cover of the noise of gunfire. The party of about 10–20 men strong, then ran away into the darkness to the south, turning east to a re-entry in the hills, and climbed up the hillside into the trees. This area was combed out by Indian troops and the RAF Regiment so far with no success other than signs that the enemy had gone that way. There were no personnel casualties.[21]

The raiding party was led by Captain Inoue Sukezo and he eluded capture; however, this was not to be his last encounter with the RAF Regiment. We will read of him again in a later chapter. The raid cost the RAF seven aircraft but fortunately no casualties. While the raiding party had successfully achieved its aim, this episode serves to emphasise the real and serious threat faced in protecting the aircraft on the ground and the essential nature of the task being carried out by the RAF Regiment in close defence of the airstrips. The RAF Regiment units had spent the entire siege on alert and this was the only successful sabotage attempt on RAF aircraft on the Imphal airfields.

LAC Henry Kirk (left) and LAC Bert Robson (right) of 2944 Field Squadron mule supply team on 'Nightmare Peak'. In the background can be seen the aerial for 'D' for Donald Radio Post, the Imphal garrison's radio link with the outside world. (RAF Regiment SEAC Association)

In response to the threat posed by the close proximity of the Japanese to Palel, 2944 Field Squadron and two AA Flights were soon moved south to the airstrip.[22] The actions of *Nukui Column* were the last gasp, however, and soon the *15th Army* was ordered to withdraw to the Kabaw Valley. The siege was in the final stages and on 11 July 1944 units of the 5th Indian Division, fighting their way north up the Imphal-Kohima Road, met units of 2nd British Division coming south from Kohima. The 2nd British and 7th Indian Divisions had endured much bloody fighting clearing out the enemy and opening the road from the north. The siege was raised and the road was open. Despite this, it would be a few more weeks before the Japanese could be driven from the hills overlooking the valley. There was still much heavy and bitter fighting to drive the Japanese back to the River Chindwin.

Once the monsoon broke the Japanese knew that the *U-Go* offensive had failed. Although they still held positions around the Plain, the ammunition, food and supplies were held by IV Corps. The Kohima-Imphal Road was open and lorry-loads of supplies were now reaching the garrison. The Japanese had gambled on capturing the stores depots at Imphal, Kohima and Dimapur; they had failed at the very gates. The Japanese could see everything they needed to carry them through to India from where they sat. The combined efforts of the Fourteenth Army and not least the airmen of 221 Group and Troop Carrier Command, had thwarted them in that aim. At the time the Dimapur-Imphal road was cut there were 155,000 men, including 6,000 RAF personnel, and 11,000 animals besieged in the Imphal Valley. They had been completely dependent on stocks already at Imphal and then on supplies that could be delivered by air. By mid-April reserves at Imphal had reached a low level and the RAF initiated Operation *Stamina* with the aim of delivering 245 tons per day by air to build up reserves on the Plain. By May the garrison had been reduced to 118,000 men and only 1,000 animals, as large numbers of non-combatants had been either flown out or walked out along the Silchar track. Despite some setbacks with aircraft numbers, weather and problems with runway failure, by 1 June IV Corps had received on average 373 tons per day and 60 tons for the RAF.[23]

The Commander-in-Chief of the 11th Army Group, General Giffard, wrote to General Slim on 28 July, congratulating him and the Fourteenth Army on their victory. In reference to the airmen of Eastern Air Command he wrote:

. . . I have not forgotten the immense debt which the Army owes to Air. It is no exaggeration to say that without the really magnificent assistance given by the Eastern Air Command, the Army would never have won its victories.

I am sure no one who watched them is likely to forget the courage, determination and skill of the aircraft pilots and crews who have flown through some of the worst weather in the world over appalling country either to attack the enemy in front of the Army . . . or to deliver reinforcements, supplies, ammunition, etc., to the troops isolated in the Arakan, Imphal and Central Burma.[24]

The airmen of the RAF Regiment are owed a share of that debt. The RAF Regiment had made a significant contribution to the defence at Imphal. In IV Corps area no airfields were defended directly by the Army. Surely, this was strong supporting evidence of the need for the RAF Regiment to maintain its numbers and continue its vital role. The alternative at Imphal would have been complete withdrawal of local air support.

For the RAF Regiment at Imphal the Japanese threat had lessened but the men could not relax their vigilance and, therefore, patrolling and manning of AA guns continued. One benefit of the arrival of the monsoon was, however, that enemy air activity eased. 4430 AA Flight reported only three air raid warnings for the entire month of June. The monsoon did not favour one side over the other and the Imphal garrison suffered under heavy and continuous rain. 4440 AA Flight was now located on the hills to the north of the 'Keep' protecting the wireless station. The living conditions as the monsoon rain sheeted down were very unpleasant. Colin Kirby continues:

It's difficult to describe the monsoon rain day after day. It had to be experienced. Suffice to say that we spent a lot of 'free' time digging trenches to try and run water away from our tents and to keep some clothing dry. Everything was wet. Some men would sleep in the canteen tent on the rough furniture we had, others in a sitting position propped against a tent pole with feet and behind in water. There would be occasional hours and day when the rain stopped, the sun came out with its usual intensity and everything steamed. It was like being in a Turkish bath as we slithered around in the mud. Meanwhile, we carried on with our patrols. On 6 June somebody strolled over from the wireless unit, 'Heard the news?' 'The Second Front's started.' 'Oh is that all.' Thus the lukewarm enthusiasm with which we greeted this momentous fact. Frankly, we could not have cared less. Nobody mentioned it again, and we continued doing what we were doing.

We still carried out our guard duties on the wireless post, but now the tension was evaporating some of the men became ill. Nothing very specific. Morale was high, but physically they seemed spent. One day a group of them reported sick to Rawlings and he ordered them into Imphal to see the MO . . . The men were dosed with some potion to revive their flagging bodies a little. In due course, but some time later, some who served on the Flight did return to India for non-combatant duties, and . . . one or two were sent back to the UK.

Once the monsoon had broken, jungle paths and roads became quagmires and normally placid jungle streams became raging torrents. It was now virtually impossible for the Japanese to get supplies forward and RAF fighters attacked anything that moved on the roads and tracks leading north and west across the River Chindwin. The shattered remnants of the three Japanese divisions that had confidently crossed the India-Burma border in what some called 'The March on Delhi', were now fleeing back into Burma or lay dying from starvation, disease and inadequate medical treatment. The Japanese plans had assumed the quick and easy capture of large quantities of the ammunition and supplies. Deprived of these by the staunch defence of the Kohima and Imphal garrisons, the Japanese suffered their greatest land defeat of the Second World War. The British and Commonwealth casualties had been 4,064 and 12,603 at Kohima and Imphal, respectively. Of the 84,280 Japanese soldiers who marched into Manipur in early 1944, 53,505 were killed in action, missing or had died of disease or malnutrition. The remaining 30,775 were suffering from light wounds or malnutrition or both. Many of them were to die on the retreat back across the River Chindwin. The Fourteenth Army had inflicted a crushing and decisive defeat on the Japanese *15th Army*.

Colin Kirby and 4440 AA Flight were ordered to return to India, where they would be absorbed into a new field squadron. With the battle over, he summed up the feeling after the siege and relief of Imphal:

> On the 12th August we filled in all the trenches and on the 14th August dismounted the Brownings. On the 16th we left the Imphal Plain. What the hell were we going to do at Comilla? For myself I suspected the days of 4440 Flight were numbered. In any case, the saga of the Flight and the siege of Imphal had drawn to a close. A small unit had flowered and was soon to disappear, leaving not a ripple in military history; nothing very heroic, just a hard slog. We had done our job and everything that had been asked of us.

Notes

1   Later Air Vice-Marshal S.F. Vincent CB DFC AFC DL (1898–1976).
2   Corporal Colin Kirby, 4440 AA Flight, RAF Regiment, Imphal Valley, November 1943–August 1944.
3   Hamilton, A. *Canadians on Radar in South-East Asia 1941–1945*. Fredericton, N.B. [Canada]: ACH Publishing, 1998, p. 82.
4   2943 Field Squadron detachment and 4423 AA Flight, 4418 and 2 (India) Flights, respectively.
5   It was estimated that there was a loss of nine minutes in warning of approaching aircraft.
6   op. cit., Hamilton, A., pp. 50–54.
7   Prasad, S. N., K.D. Bhargava, and P.N. Khera, eds. *Reconquest of Burma 1942–45: June 1942–June 1944*. Vol. I, *Official History of the Indian Armed Forces in the Second World War, 1939–45*. New Delhi: Combined Inter-Services Historical Section, India & Pakistan. Orient: Longmans, 1958, pp. 418–5.
8   The 'boxes' around the Imphal 'Keep' were named after animals, birds, fish or other forms of marine life e.g. 'Salmon', 'Perch', 'Pike', 'Mussel' and 'Sardine'. The famous 17th Indian 'Black Cat' Division was given the appropriately named 'Catfish Box'.
9   For an excellent account of the struggles of 'Lion Box' at Kanglatongbe a few miles to the north see C.D. Johnson, *The Forgotten Army's Box of Lions*, privately published by the author, 2001.
10 Vincent, S. F. *Flying Fever*. London: Jarrolds, 1972, p. 157.
11 Increasing from 'white', 'yellow' to 'red', the colour indicated the proximity of the raiders and their likelihood of attacking the strip.
12 A detachment of 112 Battery, 28th Light AA Regiment, Royal Artillery.
13 The RAF Regiment units at Imphal Main were responsible for Group HQ, a Wing HQ, a Fighter Operations Unit and RAF Signals.

14 At times when the airstrip at Imphal was closed due to shelling or other enemy activity, the supplies had to be dropped by parachute as the delivery of rations etc. could not cease for any length of time.

15 Squadron Leader George D. Arnold had became OC 2944 Field Squadron at Secunderabad on its formation during June 1943, after fourteen months at RAF Station Koggala. He was transferred to the Depot Assault Wing for a few months before returning to 2944 Field Squadron. Henry Kirk was in the HQ Section of 2944 Field Squadron and so knew him first hand: 'He was a first class, in fact, an outstanding officer. He never asked anybody to do anything he would not do himself. He always asked for volunteers. He used to say that one volunteer was better than three pressed men. The siege of Imphal was a ready-made situation for a leader of his quality.' Arnold departed in late July 1944 while the squadron was at Palel having completed a three-year (for married men) tour of duty in the tropics and returned to Australia.

16 The 99 (Madras Presidency) Squadron.

17 AIR 25/915, *Operations Record Book and Appendices, 221 Group, May 1944*. Report on activities on 'D' for Donald hill – The night of 24/25 May 1944.

18 AIR 29/884, *Operations Record Books, 4401–4408 AA Flights*.

19 No 181 Signals Wing RAF was responsible for control of all radar units in the Imphal area.

20 AIR 29/886, *Operations Record Books and Appendices, 4436–4450, 5756, 6201, 6203, 6204, 6206 AA Flights*.

21 AIR 25/917, *221 Group, Appendices Only, July 1944*. 4 July 44, Report on ground attack on aircraft at Palel.

22 There was a story current at the time 2944 Field Squadron arrived at Palel that the airmen who had been on a two-man patrol in front of the airstrip at the time of the raid, and who had failed to detect the presence of the saboteurs, had been put on a charge for neglect of duty. At the time of the raid the artillery had been firing a heavy barrage, the noise of which made detection of any activity difficult. In addition, no other personnel on the airfield perimeter saw the attackers. Shortly after the incident the Orderly Room of the RAF Regiment unit received a visit from Major-General Douglas Gracey, the highly-respected GOC of 20th Indian Division. He demanded to speak to the unit CO. Being absent, he asked to see the charge sheet. He read it and then said 'My men have been fighting for thirteen weeks up on the Shenam Pass. Many are falling asleep at their posts through sheer exhaustion.' He continued 'If I was to charge every one of my men who had been in a similar position to these airmen, half of my division would be on a charge. We've all been hard at it and are all worn out, we can't ask anymore than the men have been giving.' With that he tore the charge sheet up and put it in the nearest rubbish bin, and as he left said 'and tell your CO that I've been here'.

23 Kirby, S.W. et al. *The War against Japan. The Decisive Battles*. Vol. III. London: HMSO, 1961, pp. 311–312.

24 ibid., pp. 373–4.

CHAPTER 4

Reorganisation, Re-equipment and Reinforcement

'The reactions of the Air Commander were natural . . . His chief point was that the Air Ministry cannot be expected to appreciate the difficulty in this theatre, of putting adequate Army troops on the ground defence of airfields.'

Wing Commander J.L. Fowke, Ground Defence Officer, HQ 3rd Tactical Air Force

The Air Forces in India had been gradually built-up from early 1943 and this gained greater impetus with the creation of South-East Asia Command. More squadrons and better aircraft were arriving, although many were obsolete or outdated in other theatres. The RAF Regiment had been placed on a sounder footing by the end of 1943 as a result of the 'first reorganisation' and the squadrons and AA flights were now located where RAF airfields, radar stations and other installations were most threatened by enemy action. It must, therefore, have caused considerable consternation and frustration for the ground defence staff at HQ ACSEA and 3rd Tactical Air Force, when the decision was made by the Air Ministry in London in early 1943, that a large reduction was required in the size of the RAF Regiment in the India-Burma theatre. The RAF Regiment reached its maximum global size of around 50,000 officers and men in July 1943. After four years of war, however, the Army was short of manpower. Pressure was being applied to the Air Ministry, including that from the Prime Minister Winston Churchill, to decrease the size of the RAF Regiment in what he later referred to scathingly as the Royal Air Force's 'Private Army'.[1]

The Air Ministry in London ordered AHQ India to make severe cuts, firstly, to obtain airmen who could be transferred to trades positions in flying squadrons[2] and secondly, to put the RAF Regiment in India on a similar organisational basis to that in the United Kingdom. The requirement was to cut the number of personnel from more than 4,000 to 2,000 and replace ground defence forces required in excess of this number by recruitment of Indian personnel. High-level approaches by AHQ India to the Army to provide Indian garrison troops proved fruitless and this was ruled out as source of manpower for airfield defence. A see-saw battle of letter and counter-letter commenced. It would take nearly a year to resolve, and the final result would significantly alter the structure and composition of the RAF Regiment in SEAC.

This process was implemented at the very time that the Fourteenth Army and the RAF were fighting the early stages of the great battles in the Arakan and Imphal. The directions for the 'second reorganisation' were finally released on 28 February 1944. ACSEA indicated that although it could achieve the reduction target, it would take many months to implement. The Air Ministry responded by insisting it be achieved by

March 1944; ACSEA countered that with current operations it could only be done by June 1944. The reorganisation involved the elimination of the six field squadrons and disbandment of all sixty-two AA flights. In their place the RAF in India would be allowed only twelve Mobile Light AA Squadrons, each with twenty-four 20-mm Hispano cannon. The LAA squadrons would only be available for deployment to 221 and 224 Groups of the 3rd Tactical Air Force. Including Command, Group, RAF Regiment Depot and Defence Training staffs, this plan gave a target of 2,510 officers and airmen.[3]

The Command Defence Officer at ACSEA, Group Captain J.H. Harris, outlined the steps that would have to be taken to make the required reductions but at the same time maintain ground and AA defence of forward airstrips:

> The Regiment survivors will all be converted to 20-mm work, and the station personnel will have to man any .303 guns. That is one reason why we have been pressing to increase 'backers up" training. Guns will be handed over by the Regiment in so far as the Station personnel can man them. That .303 guns may, in most cases, have to be near places of work at the expense of the normal fire plan will have to be accepted. We must try to have at least eight Browning posts at each airfield. This would not be so bad if we had enough 20-mm Squadrons (in addition) for all airfields. But we haven't.[4]

As was typical for the India-Burma theatre, what was planned and what was achievable with the resources provided were two very different matters. By March 1944 there were still only forty-eight Hispano cannon in the country, enough to equip only two LAA squadrons. The remaining squadrons would have to be equipped temporarily with Browning AA machine-guns until more arrived.[5]

While the Fourteenth Army had spent the monsoon building and preparing for the coming struggles, the RAF Regiment was being ordered to undo the hard work of the last year at the time of greatest need. It was obvious to those in ACSEA that the RAF Regiment was the only Corps able to carry out the specialised airfield and other defence tasks. The six field squadrons would be required to withdraw from their current deployments at Imphal and the Arakan to reorganise as six LAA squadrons. For the airmen of the RAF Regiment at Imphal and in the Arakan, all this administrative activity was of little consequence as they concerned themselves with living and surviving under the difficult conditions and repelling the Japanese onslaught.

The frustration of those in senior RAF Regiment appointments, who were now dealing with the Japanese offensives in the Arakan and Imphal, was most apparent in the correspondence between the Command Defence Officer, Group Captain J. H. Harris, at ACSEA in New Delhi, and Wing Commander J.L. Fowke at the 3rd Tactical Air Force and the Group Defence Officers with 221 and 224 Groups. Fowke wrote to Harris in early February 1944, pointing out two of the problems with the 'second reorganisation':

> Reduction in number means reduction in protection and from here we can suggest how this may be done without the possibility of disastrous results. I feel we cannot risk the Regiment letting down the rest of the RAF through no fault of its own.
>
> I note with some apprehension a reference in a letter . . . to all units returning to the Depot. The movement of these bodies [the field squadrons] will be a formidable task . . . if done it must be . . . [6]

Group Captain Harris made it quite clear to Wing Commander Fowke that ACSEA realised the difficulties and that the Air Ministry had been made aware of them repeatedly over the last six months, but further argument would be futile:

> . . . and you may be assured that everything will be done to soften the blow from the 'forward area' viewpoint . . . .
>
> I must tell you categorically that these major items of policy are unalterable, that we know that from the ACSEA aspect they are very serious and most distressing, and that we have fought tooth and nail during the last twelve months to stave them off. However, we have definite instructions from the highest source, and if you do submit your views that they are undesirable – we shall tell you that we agree with you – but direct you to get on with it nevertheless. That is just to save you wasting your time!!
>
> . . . You will see that we are being reduced below bedrock, and that the reduction must first fall upon the commitment for which we are not legitimately responsible.[7]

In his reply Fowke reiterated that the reduction would have serious consequences for the coming Japanese offensive, as he wrote in the following paragraph taken from a letter of 29 February 1944:

> I have received your . . . letter of February 22nd 1944 and passed it forthwith to the Air Commander [of the 3rd Tactical Air Force] . . . The reactions of the Air Commander were natural and you may hear of them following his visit to Delhi now. His chief point was that the Air Ministry cannot be expected to appreciate the difficulty in this theatre, of putting adequate Army troops on the ground defence of airfields.[8]

With no possibility of a change of plan, the first steps were reluctantly taken in the 'second reorganisation'. The original instructions were for units in the north-eastern sector of India, directly under command of the 3rd Tactical Air Force and 231 Group, to be dealt with first, followed by the southern sector, containing 222 and 225 Groups and the RAF Regiment Depot. However, this order was sensibly reversed, as outlined in a letter of 14 March. Fowke informed 221 and 224 Group GDOs, Flying Officer Hunter-Arundel and Squadron Leader G.D. Andrews, of the plan, which would minimise disruption to the squadrons and AA flights in the forward areas:

> First all flights from South India and Ceylon will be reorganised to form the first LAA Squadron . . . Then one (or two) field squadrons will be converted at the Depot. At present there are only enough guns in the country to equip two Squadrons so the conversion will be dependent on the rate of supply of guns.
>
> . . . DTIs on a scale of one Sergeant and one Corporal per airfield will be employed where required to be responsible for all weapons (particularly 12 Brownings per airfield) used by Defence AA and Rifle Flights.[9]

On 30 March 1944 a letter from HQ ACSEA gave details of the 'G' (going) and 'S' (staying) Flights and nominal rolls of airmen to be retained or remustered. While the LAA squadrons would be formed from this pool, any excess airmen would be remustered to RAF trades. By 2 April, while the struggle at Imphal intensified, the GDO

at the 3rd Tactical Air Force was stressing to ACSEA the practical difficulties of initi-
ating the reorganisation:

> It is understood that it was intended to commence the reorganisation of the
> RAF Regiment by converting Field Squadrons, starting probably with 2941
> Squadron. Your attention is drawn to the fact that four Field Squadrons are
> now heavily committed in operations, leaving only 2945 Squadron in a static
> defence role:
>
> | | |
> |---|---|
> | 2941 Squadron (3 flights) | Imphal |
> | 2942 Squadron | Maungdaw |
> | 2943 Squadron | Palel |
> | 2944 Squadron (3 flights) | Maungdaw |
>
> . . . the other four squadrons cannot be released from their operational role
> without exposing at once vital and vulnerable installations.[10]

Some sense finally prevailed as the crisis at Imphal reached its peak and there was no
possibility that the units in the north-east could be withdrawn. The Allied Air
Commander-in-Chief ACSEA urgently signalled the 3rd Tactical Air Force and 231
Group to defer action to reduce the RAF Regiment in their areas until further notice.
The field squadrons were to be maintained at their original number. On 14 April the
following instructions were issued to the GDOs of 221 and 224 Groups RAF:

> In particular reference to . . . ACSEA letter . . . of March 30th, 1944, the Air
> Commander, Third Tactical Air Force has directed that no moves of RAF
> Regiment personnel in or out of the Imphal Valley are to be carried out until
> the situation clears up sufficiently to allow reinforcing flights to reach the
> Valley before 'going' flights are withdrawn . . . Transfer of personnel in or out
> of the Valley is impracticable and such postings are to be effected on paper but
> the personnel are to remain attached to their parent unit.[11]

Despite this temporary reprieve for the field squadrons and AA flights of 221 and 224
Groups, the 'second reorganisation' remained a firm policy to be implemented when
enemy offensive action had eased. The return to the Depot and disbandment of AA
flights stationed with 222 and 225 Groups was to be continued.

The RAF Regiment's responsibilities had always been predicated on the capacity
of the Army to provide part of the garrisons for airfield defence. The agreement was
that an RAF Regiment unit sent to a forward area would be provided in diminution
of the Army contribution, and this would hold until the end of the campaign.[12] In
late March 1944 ACSEA received a document from the 3rd Tactical Air Force that
set out starkly the inadequate contribution that the Army was currently making to
airfield defence. Of the fifty-three static RAF airfields and establishments in eastern
India, only eleven had Army or RAF Regiment units on ground defence and of these,
seven were defended by RAF Regiment field squadrons. Furthermore, in the IV Corps
area there were no Army garrisons at RAF Stations. Consequently, on 10 April the
Allied Air Commander-in-Chief ACSEA, Air Marshal Sir Richard Peirse, informed
the 11th Army Group of this deficiency and requested Army support as had been
agreed in November 1943. The alternative was withdrawal of flying squadrons and

consequent reduction in air support. The Air Commander-in-Chief described the agreement as follows:

> The strength of the RAF Regiment throughout has been insufficient to justify the acceptance of full responsibility for the local defence of Royal Air Force Stations and to meet the threat of infiltration by enemy ground raiding parties to airfields and radar stations. A remedy was sought in November, 1943, whereby the Army agreed to withdraw all static garrisons from RAF Stations in areas remote from enemy action, and to provide them at stations where attack was possible. The RAF was to have made a contribution to the defence of its stations within the limit of available resources.[13]

On 5 May 1944 the Allied Air Commander-in-Chief ACSEA had signalled the Air Ministry to indicate that seven of the eight flying squadrons were being withdrawn from the Imphal Valley as the Army was incapable of meeting its commitments for defence of the forward airfields. Station and maintenance personnel had been employed in a part-time defensive role. With many pilots and servicing personnel facing severe fatigue, the general standard of flying and aircraft maintenance was endangered. Any further reduction of the RAF Regiment through the 'second reorganisation' would be detrimental to ground defence at this moment of greatest need. He later wrote:

> I had no alternative but to direct that further reduction of the Regiment, already down to 3,434 all ranks, should be suspended.[14]

To explain the difficulties created by the changes and to present the arguments for a reprieve face-to-face, the ACSEA Command Defence Officer, Group Captain J.H. Harris, was despatched to London during May 1944. His two-fold mission was described as follows:

> . . . to explain the circumstances and to request, not only that suspension of the Regiment reduction should be confirmed, but that a force adequate for the task of defending airfields and ancillary stations in the battle area be provided.[15]

Harris did an excellent job and the Air Ministry accepted the gravity of the situation at Imphal and in the Arakan. Steps were finally taken to make a serious assessment of the existing situation for the RAF Regiment in ACSEA and to determine future operational requirements. Ground defence policy was, as a consequence, altered significantly from that pending for the last year. The RAF Regiment strength was confirmed at 3,300 officers and men, 800 more than previously permitted. Other trades in the Command, however, had to be kept at 800 fewer.

The requirements for future operations were now set at twelve field squadrons and eighteen LAA squadrons; an increase of thirteen squadrons over the seventeen that could be formed from the existing strength in India. During May 1944 consideration was given as to where the extra seventeen squadrons were going to be found. Initially it was thought five surplus LAA squadrons in the Central Mediterranean could be acquired, but the problem would be to find the remaining eight. This plan was rejected and it was decided in June that thirteen squadrons would be sent directly from the United Kingdom.

On 4 August 1944 a directive was issued that finally clarified the situation with regard to the RAF Regiment in SEAC. It stated that:

The future Ground Defence and RAF Regiment organisation in ACSEA will be as follows:

(i) Ground Defence staff officers at formations (having RAF Ground Defence responsibilities) down to Groups;
(ii) RAF Regiment Wing HQs;
(iii) Field Squadrons, RAF Regiment;
(iv) Light AA Squadrons, RAF Regiment;
(v) The RAF Regiment Depot:-
    (a) Secunderabad;
    (b) Forward Echelon;
(vi) Station Personnel Instructors (officers and NCOs of the RAF Regiment).[16]

The Regiment would emerge from this 'third reorganisation' on a sounder, albeit limited, footing, both from an organisational and a tactical viewpoint. Despite this it would always be thin on the ground in Burma and there were never enough squadrons for the tasks in hand.

A Ground Defence Adviser was appointed at HQ Eastern Air Command[17] and other senior staff appointments upgraded in rank. The Wing Headquarters were formed for the control of two or more squadrons in the field and consisted of a Wing Commander assisted by a Flying Officer and a small staff of two Corporals and three airmen (Appendix 1).

RAF Regiment personnel pass across an obstacle as part of the 'jungle warfare' course. (Australian War Memorial SUK 13500)

RAF Regiment personnel climb a wall as part of the 'jungle warfare' course. (Australian War Memorial SUK 13502)

Field squadrons were reorganised to become fully mobile and were to consist of an HQ section, three rifle flights and an armoured fighting vehicle flight (AFV flight). They would be further modified the following year as experience and a shortage of airmen forced alterations. The LAA squadrons would be composed of an HQ section and three flights manning twenty-four 20-mm Hispano cannon (Appendix 2). By mid 1944 the RAF had achieved a large measure of air superiority and there was a decreased need for AA defence. The requirement, therefore, was changed, with the new plan being to form eighteen field and twelve LAA squadrons (instead of the original plan for twelve field and eighteen LAA squadrons).

The RAF Regiment Depot at Secunderabad had received limited quantities of 20-mm Hispanos by May 1944 and training courses could, therefore, commenced for the new LAA squadrons (Appendix 2). The Hispanos did not have the range and power of the 40-mm Bofors light AA guns, which were standard issue to the Regiment in the Mediterranean and North-West Europe theatres. Unfortunately the ammunition was not self-destroying so the field of fire and the likely trajectory of any barrage had to be carefully considered to avoid causing damage to equipment, injury or loss of life to RAF or Army personnel in the vicinity. The Hispanos were, however, an improvement on the 0.303-in Browning LMGs. The RAF Regiment in SEAC would still, therefore, have to rely on the Army for heavy and light AA defence of the airstrips.

A training and refitting facility known as 'Forward Echelon' was established under the 3rd Tactical Air Force in the steamy atmosphere of Agartala in Bengal, to provide advanced training and acclimatisation for the field squadrons arriving from the United Kingdom. After this task had been completed, the Forward Echelon and its 'Battle School' would provide modern advanced training for field squadrons that had been formed in SEAC and a reinforcement and wastage replacement depot closer to the RAF Regiment units advancing into Burma. It must be remembered that the distance between Secunderabad and the River Chindwin is about the same as the distance from London to Warsaw (Map 1).

The first five United Kingdom squadrons were despatched in a convoy arriving in October, with a further eight planned to arrive in January 1945. By end of the campaign thirteen squadrons from the United Kingdom would be operating in SEAC, in addition to the seventeen SEAC-formed units (Appendix 2). Thus the desired strength of thirty squadrons would be attained. Some initial problems were encountered when it was found that there were restrictions on the eligibility of some personnel from the United Kingdom to serve in SEAC. This resulted in the loss of a number of squadron specialists prior to departure. Consequently, men untrained for specialist duties had to be selected and trained *en route*, to be ready on arrival in India.

Thus, it was only two months following the departure of the last AA flights from the RAF Regiment Depot that four flights from 222, 225 and 231 Groups returned for disbandment and creation of the first 'Mobile LAA Squadron'. Ted Daines, an instructor at the Depot, describes the new role:

> Each course we took lasted about two to three weeks' duration, sometimes longer. As the units came in to refit and re-kit for the conquest of Burma, additional things were added to the courses. They had to supply people to drive, every Squadron had to become self-contained and I believe the only non–Regiment person carried was an MT fitter. We had our own cooks and also a medical orderly.

The first LAA squadron course began on 11 April 1944 with organisation of the new squadron, followed by training for motor-transport drivers and despatch riders and the formation of a 'Demo Flight' for Hispano 20-mm training. On 1 May the first Hispano AA gun training began and consisted, in the first week, of classes on parts, mechanisms and stoppages. The second week covered gun drill, mounting and dismounting from vehicles and the last week, range training. The squadron received instruction on advancing into and occupying airfields to give AA protection, the siting of Hispanos to cover the strip and withdrawing the guns and moving off. On 28 May under the command of Squadron Leader G.K. Dean, the AA 'Training' Squadron was renumbered as 2958 LAA Squadron and it departed for Bengal and the airfield at Chittagong two days later (Map 2).

Seven days later 2959 LAA Squadron began training and it departed on 1 July for the forward airstrip at Cox's Bazaar. On 5 July 1944 ten more AA flights arrived from Chittagong for conversion to two LAA squadrons, 2960 and 2961.[18] The course for each LAA squadron concluded with a twenty-four-hour convoy exercise, one of which was recounted in the ORB of 2960 LAA Squadron:

> They departed the Depot in glorious weather and proceeded to a previously selected spot where guns and trucks were dispersed for the night. The weather deteriorated in the evening and despite the heaviest rainfall of the season, patrols guarded the area all night. In the early hours, the convoy re-formed and proceeded to a nearby airfield, where guns were dispersed for protection of the strip. During the course of the morning 'enemy' patrols were sighted near the area occupied by 'A' Flight. The 'enemy' was engaged and several prisoners taken. 'A' Flight lost two guns during the course of the day. The exercise finished successfully with extermination of the 'enemy' invaders.[19]

On 17 August these two squadrons were inspected at a parade by Air Marshal A. Lees GB CBE DSO DFC, the officer-in-charge of ACSEA Administrative HQ. 2961 LAA Squadron personnel marched past, while 2960 LAA Squadron drove past in full transport on thirteen 3-tonners and four jeeps. Gun drill was demonstrated by two detachments of a Corporal and three airmen of the 'Demo Flight', with two Hispanos going 'into' and 'out of' action. 2960 LAA Squadron had its first significant victory on 21 August when it defeated 2961 LAA Squadron in a football match 5 goals to 1. The ORB of 2960 LAA Squadron describes the last days at the Depot and the eagerness of the airmen to perfect their new role:

To wind-up the training programme a gun drill competition, in which 24 teams took part. All personnel entered into the competition enthusiastically in a spirit of friendly rivalry, and some very commendable displays were witnessed. First and second places were won by teams from 'A' and 'B' Flights. [20]

In a report written by the CO of 2960 LAA Squadron in May 1946, it seems that events during the final days at Secunderabad had obviously entered squadron folklore:

> . . . the Squadron was considered operationally sound by the Commandant of the Depot [Wing Commander Fowke] after a passing out parade. It might be added that a 'passing out' dinner of some magnitude was held in the officers' mess the self same night. [21]

A new field squadron, 2968, was formed on 28 August and moved off three weeks later for Dimapur, followed a month later by 2963 LAA Squadron, which moved to Imphal. The RAF Regiment Depot received a visit from Lord Louis Mountbatten on 7 October 1944. He lunched with officers of the permanent staff, officers under training and some of the large number of officers who had recently arrived from the United Kingdom. He then proceeded to the Depot HQ where a cross-section of NCOs and airmen from the permanent staff and personnel under training was presented to him. Following this he addressed the entire strength of officers and men on the parade ground. This certainly gave a boost to the Regiment and provided an affirmation of the importance of their role in the reconquest of Burma.

By the end of October three new field squadrons and five new LAA squadrons had

Lord Louis Mountbatten addresses the airmen of the newly formed 2963 LAA Squadron during his visit to Secunderabad, October 1944. The Depot CO, Wing Commander Tom McKirdy, stands at the rear of the jeep. (RAF Regiment SEAC Association)

Lord Louis Mountbatten meets a group of RAF Regiment officers who had recently arrived at Secunderabad from the United Kingdom, during his visit, October 1944. On the right introducing them is Squadron Leader (later Wing Commander) C.M. Lander. He was to play a crucial role in the action at Meiktila the following March. (RAF Regiment Museum)

been created and were located in, or were *en route*, to the forward areas of 221 and 224 Groups. To speed up the formation of units by avoiding the long journey back to Secunderabad, two field squadrons, 2966 and 2967, had been formed at Comilla and Agartala, respectively.

One of the flights chosen to form 2966 Field Squadron was 4440 AA Flight, which, with Colin Kirby, we had left at Imphal seeing out the monsoon. The flight finally departed the Imphal Valley on 16 August and was ordered to move to Comilla for reorganisation and amalgamation with other 'staying' flights to form the new field squadron. Colin Kirby describes the move:

At 7.20 am we were on our way, crowded into four 3-ton trucks with all our kit, guns, tents etc. The lads were sprawled all over the place; it must have been an uncomfortable ride for them as our little convoy wound its way down on the rough mountain road to Bengal. For myself I had more physical comfort as Flying Officer Wilmot decided he would bring up the rear, and chose me as his travelling companion. I would have preferred to be amongst the others and more mentally relaxed . . . He had a pack of cigs on the dash-board, and from time to time I had to light one for him. At that time I didn't smoke. The road with its steep gradients and one hairpin bend after another with a precipitous drop over the edge did not need the distraction of lighting a cig, so I was happy to oblige. Gradually he softened and began to talk about rugby and his memories of watching internationals at Twickenham. I told him about professional Rugby League in the north of England and watching games at Headingley.

After a few hours our truck broke down, and much tinkering with the engine had no result. Fortunately we had a tow rope, and we had to be towed by one of the others . . . We reached a transit camp at 8 pm. We were on our way again at eight the next morning, still being towed. Our progress was necessarily not very fast. We reached the railhead at Dimapur by four in the afternoon. Much had happened since we passed through here about nine months earlier. We spent two days here in the transit camp and the local transport unit fixed the truck. We took the opportunity to give all our clothing a good wash. On 20 August we were on the road again and making faster progress. We drove all day until arriving at another transit camp at 9 pm. We made a later start the following day, and had only an hour's run to Gauhati which had a superior transit camp. Also, a group of American missionaries had a canteen there which was quite pleasant. We remained there on 22 August and left the following day at 7 am . . . and reached Shillong after three hours.

Shillong was a hill station where the Europeans sent their families in pre-war days to escape the worst of the heat in Delhi, etc. Certainly with its gardens, lake, greenery, clean streets and substantial but not intrusive buildings it was a very pleasant place. The camp we stayed at was outside town and we left at 10 am the next day to arrive at Sylhet by 11 pm . . . We stayed a day at Sylhet and said goodbye to the trucks. We had to unload all the gear and reload it on to a train for the next stage of the journey was by rail. We boarded at 5 am, but the train did not leave until 8 am. We arrived at our final destination, Comilla, at 10 am on the 27 August and went into camp. It had been a long, tiring journey.

2966 Field Squadron was constituted at Comilla on 31 July and, along with 4440 AA Flight, was to be formed of airmen from 4412, 4416, 4434 and 6 (India) AA Flights. Over the next month the squadron experienced some growing pains. The most apparent difficulties were in maintaining the training schedule, with personnel on numerous escort duties and others undergoing 'blanket' treatment following anti-malarial suppressive treatment. Some airmen were sent on leave to hill stations, in most cases the first for eighteen months to two years! The lack of leave was a recurring problem mentioned in many of the SEAC RAF Regiment ORBs. There did not seem to be a well-planned and organised leave system for the Regiment personnel. Notwithstanding these problems, and the difficulties of life in the monsoon, more than half the personnel had by the end of the month received a fortnight's individual train-ing and fired all unit weapons. Taking five independent units with different experiences and degrees of *esprit de corps* and forging those into one unit also gave rise to teething problems. Colin Kirby describes the effects of the amalgamation on personnel and the dynamics arising from the creation of the new unit:

At some point we had ceased to be 4440 AA Flight and became part of 2966 Field Squadron under the command of Squadron Leader [sic] Furneaux. The next day we were on parade at first light, and spent the rest of the day cleaning our weapons . . . on 3 September we moved to another camp outside town. This was fairly extensive, hutted accommodation laid out in military fashion with parade ground, etc. Comilla was a garrison town, and Slim had his HQ there before moving on to Imphal about the time we had left. There was now a time of coming and going among personnel. The other Flight from Imphal, 4434, suffered likewise. Imphal had taken its toll. The remnants of the two Flights formed the nucleus of the new Squadron. At the beginning there was mutual dislike and a childish 'ya-boo!' attitude between the two factions and each party kept to themselves as much as possible. Then reinforcements began to arrive, mainly chaps new to the Orient. Instantly there was rapport between the two bands of 'old-stagers' from Imphal. We, yellowish-brown with leathery skins and a fund of stories from the siege, these fellows were fresh-faced and light skinned, babes not versed in the mystic ways of the tropics. We were the graduate who 'knew what it was all about' and our disdain showed. Most of us picked up a smattering of Hindi and Urdu, enough to hold brief conversation with each other when the new men were in ear shot, pushing our 'superiority' down their throats . . .

'A', 'B', 'C' and 'D' Flights were formed, and I was in the latter, along with Henry Livesly, one of the four Corporals from the old 4440 . . . 'Skip' Rawlings had gone and also Wilmot . . . The Squadron was run on a day to day basis by two Warrant Officers . . . the Corporals were sent off with the men to give lectures. Over the following two weeks I gave instruction on the Sten gun, Bren gun, grenade, map reading, use of cover, etc. It was useful in finding out how good the new men were. One day we went firing on the range. Then with great enthusiasm the two Warrant Officers arranged a football match between Flights 'A' & 'B' and 'C' & 'D'. They captained the sides. It was a victory to the former by 7 goals to 5.

One wheeze they thought of was to pile everybody into trucks with the canopies tied down so nobody could see out. They drove around circuitously for about half an hour before releasing us. Each Corporal had to lead his Section back to camp – first back would receive a new pair of socks for each man. Where they got them from I couldn't guess! The Sections stood on the road watching the departing trucks and wondering in which direction to strike out. 'Do you mind getting your feet wet?' I asked my lot. 'No' they replied. 'Then follow me and don't complain if the going gets a bit sticky.' I branched off the road and headed through the trees. I led them over muddy ground and through paddy fields, and we were first back. One of my wartime triumphs. Anyway, we had time to shower and clean our boots before the next section arrived.

New Squadrons were being formed with AA guns . . . Some Corporals new to us were off again with instant promotion, but I remained. I had conflicting feelings about this . . . Staying with 2966 seemed to offer more exciting possibilities . . . Perhaps my youthfulness was against me, or maybe I was more suited to a Field Squadron.

AFV flights had been integral to the units of the RAF Regiment in North-west Europe and the Mediterranean since early 1942. In India, however, they were not included in the first field squadron establishments. It was not until December 1943 that authorisation was given for the allocation of AFVs to the field squadrons. A number of AFVs were tested to determine their suitability. The armoured vehicles chosen were known as Armoured Carriers (Indian-Pattern) or AOVs (Armoured Observation Vehicles). Assembled in Indian workshops using imported Canadian Ford Quad 4x4 chassis, these four-wheel drive vehicles had a maximum armour thickness of just over half an inch, mounted one or two Bren guns, were fitted with a wireless set and had a crew of four. The AOVs were used widely in the British and Indian Army in North Africa, Italy and Burma.

The first five of the six field squadrons formed in 1943 at Secunderabad had converted a rifle flight to an AFV flight by February 1944. When it appeared the Regiment was going to face a severe reduction in the number of AA flights, it was decided that a troop of three AFVs would be allocated to certain airfields within the operational areas of the eight RAF Groups under the control of ACSEA. A Regiment NCO would be troop commander as well as instructor for the station personnel who would crew them. This ambitious plan was, however, discontinued when it was decided to form an AFV flight within each of the SEAC-formed field squadrons created from the merging of the AA flights. One such unit was Colin Kirby's squadron, and he was soon sent on a course to train for this new role:

On 17 September there was a call for volunteers to go on an armoured car course. The Squadron had to be equipped with some of these. Ever eager to try something new I put my name down. Henry Lively agreed to come along and did the same, and on 19 September a group of us left for Agartala some miles away.[22] The course was under the command of Flight Lieutenant Steele, a charismatic character whose style of leadership suited me. The next day I was sitting in the driver's seat of a 7-ton armoured fighting vehicle . . . and told to drive. My only previous experience of engine-propelled vehicles had been the motorbike of unhappy memory at Imphal. For a start, this monster had two sets of gears, with levers to match. I looked at the Corporal Instructor. 'Er, how do I start the thing?' He gave me a pitying look and sighed, but after a few false starts following his 'push this, pull that' the wheels began to roll. The following day I was driving solo. We had a crew of four. One man was in the turret with a Bren gun which he could swivel round. His legs dangled each side of the driver's head. In the back was the wireless operator. Next to the driver the fourth man had a forward-firing machine-gun. The next three weeks were enjoyable. We drove around the countryside on manoeuvres, practised all kind of drills travelling across rough terrain, and learned how to operate the radio with AFVs calling each other names until the Sergeant would break in to stop it. We had exercises with explosives going off under the wheels and on the side, and with the visor down so that the driver was looking through a slit. Everybody had to become proficient in all four posts. Often we would cross deep rivers with a long drop and only a wooden bridge to support us, swaying under our weight and barely wide enough to give us a passage. A lot of the district was the estate of some Rajah, who complained about damage to his land and trees. Sometimes a fussily important Indian would pop out of the undergrowth with pad and pen and make a show of recording all the 'damage' we were causing to his Excellency's estate.

On another occasion Henry was driving, and four of us were hanging on the outside. We were travelling over a narrow strip of land across the paddy fields and a bullock-cart was coming toward us. There seemed hardly room for one to pass the other. Always the gentleman, Henry moved over a little to accommodate the cart, and we toppled over into the paddy. I was on the inside of the fall and jumped clear. The other man on my side was thrown and landed in the paddy with arms and legs outstretched. When he stood clear, covered with mud, he had left an indentation in it which looked like those drawings of a cartoon character blasted through the wall. The two on the other side were able to jump down and we pulled Henry out, who suffered only a few bruises. We were all muddy. The bullock-cart and its driver trundled on, unconcerned at our antics. We looked at each other and at the AFV settled on its side in the ooze. What to do? Another AFV turned up a few minutes later and they reported to HQ on their radio.

Steele arrived shortly after in his jeep. Jumping out, he gazed reflectively at the scene for a few moments. He then asked who had been driving and how it had happened. Henry explained that he had moved over slightly to allow a bullock-cart to get past. 'You have an armoured car weighing over 7 tons and you gave way to a bullock-cart?' he exploded in disbelief. 'If the cart had gone into the bloody paddy the bloody bullock would have pulled it out! How the bloody hell are we going to pull this out?' He waved an arm at the recumbent vehicle. He summoned more AFVs and towing chains, and there followed a magnificent act of recovery which took several hours. The problem was that first the vehicle had to be pulled upright. Using the chains and the other AFVs, inching a few inches in one direction, stop, another AFV inching then the other way, stop, start, on a narrow strip of ground, the AFV gurgled its way upright. It was an extraordinary display of skill by Steele. But the problem was only half solved. It had to be returned to the 'road', and all the manoeuvring recommenced. The roaring engines and thickening fumes in the air brought an audience of the local populace who looked on in wonderment at the silly games of the British. What had seemed an impossible task some hours earlier was eventually accomplished, and the muddied vehicle was towed back. Henry vowed that the next time he was driving and saw a bullock-cart coming toward him he would drive right over it. On the 10th October the course finished and we returned to Comilla with our AFVs. I was the proud holder of a service driving licence.

On the 5 November the Squadron left Comilla for Dohazari, back under canvas. Our two amiable WOs departed for pastures new and there was still movement in the Squadron of personnel with some posted away and others arriving. Gradually things pulled together. We now had a mortar section under Sgt Brown, separate from the Flights. My 'D' Flight was a pretty mixed affair – part AFV and part Rifle. Sgt Mann was in charge. Part of the time I was carrying out duties of a normal Flight, other times those of us AFV-trained (as was Mann) went out in our cars, or more probably washed and generally cleaned them for Mann's inspection. He was a keen type but generally easy to get along with.

Another matter of interest which affected everybody was a change in our pay. I don't know the structure of today's RAF, but at that time there were five different pay rates according to trade: aero engine mechanic, airframe fitter, armourer, transport and so on. The Regiment was in Group 5, the lowest. We had all thought for a long time that this was unfair, and eventually somebody at the Air Ministry must have agreed because the Regiment became Group 2. This bumped up our pay considerably.

As the end of 1944 approached, the squadron knew it was to be deployed for the re-conquest of Burma but as yet its task had not been made clear. The new squadron gradually honed its skills and the airmen settled into their new role and responsibilities. Life continued steadily for Colin Kirby. There was driving practice, engine maintenance, wireless maintenance, parades, and being Orderly Corporal, giving lectures, drilling, field training and so on. A lot was expected of a junior NCO in the Regiment. After the rigours of the siege of Imphal, however, there also was enough time for other activities of a less physical nature, which helped rebuild the mind and morale:

One of the Corporals in 'D' Flight was Clem Hales, whose home was in Kettering. Tall, large, athletic build, he was very light on his feet, explained in fact that in civilian life he had been a professional ballroom dancer, teaching and giving exhibitions across the country. He was very fit and tough under an easy-going exterior. He had with him a copy of *Palgrave's Golden Treasury* of poems, and as we shared a tent we spent much time reading these to each other and generally discussing them.

Clem was a keen bridge player, and set about teaching me, Henry and Corporal Jack 'Ginger' Adams at least the rudiments in our spare time.

Sometime later he also started dancing classes. It was quite a sight to see some of the lads waltzing, doing fox-trots, etc. with serious concentration. It was taken very seriously, and Clem drew charts of where the feet should be placed, and so on. They wanted to improve their social skills, and really they were receiving expert tuition for free what would have been expensive in 'civvy street.'

I can't recall where it came from, but we had an old gramophone and one record. Both sides were the violinist Fritz Kreisler playing solo. One side was 'Caprice Viennois' . . . We had a ritual every night when we turned in on our charpoys. Clem had the gramophone next to him and he would dim the oil lamp and put on the record. He played each side twice. It was very soothing. Down the years, whenever I have heard that tune or indeed the playing of Fritz Kreisler, my mind goes back to that tent in Bengal.

In early 1945, after more than a year of use, it was concluded that the AFVs would seldom be able to operate effectively over the rough terrain encountered during the advance from Imphal to the Irrawaddy. ACSEA sent the following instruction to RAF Bengal-Burma detailing the future of the AFV flights:

> The inclusion of armoured flights as an integral part of RAF Regiment Field Squadrons (although tactically desirable) has proved uneconomical at the present phase of the war in this theatre. Owing to the terrain in the zone of immediate operations, it has not been possible for armoured flights to accompany field squadrons in their forward movement, and the cumulative neutralisation of manpower, fire potential and material has been considerable. Furthermore, squadrons to be transported by air, or engaged in certain types of amphibious operations would not be accompanied by armoured flights.[23]

In January 1945 the decision was taken to place all the AFVs from the field squadrons in three armoured squadrons (Appendix 1). These would be holding units from which armoured flights could be detached where required and practicable. The AFVs were unused for the remainder of the campaign and only one armoured squadron, 2970, was eventually deployed. Lack of shipping space precluded the use of the armoured squadron for the advance into Burma and it finally deployed by sea to Rangoon in October 1945. Each of the AFVs was equipped with one or two Bren LMGs. To compensate in some measure for the loss of firepower occasioned by the withdrawal of armoured flights, a small LMG group (equipped with four Bren LMGs) was added to the headquarters of each field squadron. Further changes were made to the field squadrons formed from July 1944 with the Squadron HQ to include a 3-inch mortar section. The mortar section was a useful, if belated, innovation, and would have a profound effect on the firepower of the field squadrons that possessed one.[24] The LMG group, along with the mortar section, would provide a further useful support element under the direct control of the Squadron Commander.

Despite the arrival of reinforcements from the United Kingdom and the 'third re-organisation', many of the RAF Regiment units were still heavily depleted through illness and exhaustion. Furthermore, many experienced airmen were now returning to the United Kingdom having completed their overseas tour; three years for married men and four years for single men. There was a desperate need for reinforcements and the training role of the Depot was tailing off. Consequently, many of those at the Depot were sent forward to join the field and LAA squadrons for the final drive into Burma.

Ted Daines had been a member of the 'Demo Squad' and an instructor at Secunderabad from the early days, but in late 1944 he was sent off to Delhi to attend a mortar course. He continues:

> When training was nearing completion a new specialist weapon was going to be introduced to the field squadrons. I was ordered to attend a course to learn all about the 2-inch and 3-inch mortars. This was held by 2nd KOYLI at New Delhi and would last five weeks.[25]
>
> . . . When the course reached a certain stage we went to the mortar firing range, by which, in my opinion, rank bad planning had placed near one of the major airports. A man had to be placed in such a position as to be able to watch out for aircraft taking off. If he could see one moving for taking off, he would raise a red flag. So it was with great dismay we saw a Dakota airborne several hundred feet as our mortar bomb left the barrel. I can see it now, the bomb sailed away in an arc over the port wing of the aircraft. A sigh of relief, tempered with red flares flying all over the place. I imagine there were very harsh words sent back to the control tower.
>
> When the course was over we were to go to Forward Echelon at Agartala, where we would be running a short mortar course for the designated Field Squadrons. When it was over I was to report to 2943 Field Squadron, located on the Imphal Plain at Palel. I eventually reached them at Wangjing.

The first United Kingdom squadrons, 2706, 2837 and 2854 LAA Squadrons, reached the Depot at Secunderabad on 29 October. So great was the need, they were destined for immediate action. They were kitted out to 'East of Brahmaputra' scale and moved off for operational duties with 224 Group in just fourteen days. The ORB for the Depot records their short stay thus:

> During their stay they had little training apart from PT. The majority of time being taken in kitting up . . . re-forming to Indian establishment and general acclimatisation including sport and swimming.[26]

2739 and 2759 Field Squadrons arrived at Secunderabad as the first three United Kingdom LAA squadrons departed, but after the same short stay they also headed for the Arakan to join 224 Group.

The final eight field squadrons arrived from the United Kingdom in early January and were reorganised into the new Indian establishments. Six were to remain as field squadrons (2708, 2743, 2748, 2802, 2810 and 2896) while two were converted to LAA squadrons (2846, 2852). In contrast with the October arrivals these squadrons would undergo preliminary training for a number of weeks at Secunderabad. The first two squadrons would receive their 'advanced battle' and 'jungle' training at Forward Echelon Agartala, while the third was sent to Comilla. 2708 and 2743 Squadrons were to be ready for deployment by the beginning of March 1945.

A further amended establishment for field squadrons would be introduced in February 1945 with an HQ of fifty-eight airmen including Bren and mortar sections, but only three rather than four rifle flights of thirty-six officers and airmen (Appendix 1). The firepower of the field squadron and its offensive and defensive capacity had improved significantly since 1943, however, the standard of arming for the RAF Regiment in SEAC, particularly for AA defence, was always some three to four years behind that of other theatres. Furthermore, many squadrons would not attain even this establishment until the campaign had ended. However, despite these limitations, the 'third reorganisation' meant that the Regiment now had a structure and order of battle that would allow it to fulfil its specialised and crucial role in the reconquest of Burma.

Notes

1   M.S. Witherow, 'Flying Soldiers in Blue Khaki' – The Royal Air Force Regiment Part 1,' *Army Quarterly & Defence Journal*, Vol. 118, 1988, p. 190.

2   It will be recalled that LAC Henry Kirk of 2944 Field Squadron was nearly transferred as an Armourer to a flying squadron as part of this programme.

3   This was not the only time that the RAF in India had had a vehement disagreement with policy generated at the Air Ministry in London. In August the previous year the AOC-in-C Air HQ India, Air Vice-Marshal Sir Richard Peirse, had written: 'Since, however, it seems clear that Air Ministry is in a better position to judge the defence needs of India than I am, it is plain that the alternatives are either to withdraw me and conduct matters from Whitehall or to relieve me by someone possessing a modicum of operational ability,' quoted in Probert, H. *The Forgotten Air Force: A History of the Royal Air Force in the War Against Japan.* London: Brassey's, 1995, pp. 122–3.

4   AIR 23/2051, *Policy concerning the reduction and reorganisation of the RAF Regiment,* correspondence, Group Captain J.H. Harris HQ ACSEA to Wing Commander J.L. Fowke HQ 3rd Tactical Air Force, 22 February 1944.

5   ibid., correspondence, Wing Commander J.L. Fowke HQ 3rd Tactical Air Force to 221 and 224 Group Defence Officers, 'Reduction and Reorganisation – RAF Regiment' 14 March 1944. Two hundred and eighty-eight Hispano 20-mm guns were required to form the twelve squadrons.

6   ibid., correspondence, Wing Commander J.L. Fowke, HQ 3rd Tactical Air Force to Group Captain J.H. Harris, HQ ACSEA, undated, ca, 20 Feb.

7   ibid., correspondence, Group Captain J.H. Harris, HQ ACSEA to Wing Commander J.L. Fowke, HQ 3rd Tactical Air Force, 22 February 1944.

8   ibid., correspondence, Wing Commander J.L. Fowke HQ 3rd Tactical Air Force to Group Captain J.H. Harris HQ ACSEA, 29 February 1944.

9   ibid., correspondence, 14 March 1944, Wing Commander J.L. Fowke HQ 3rd Tactical Air Force to 221 and 224 Group Defence Officers.

10   ibid., correspondence, 2 April 1944, Wing Commander J.L. Fowke HQ 3rd Tactical Air Force to Group Captain J.H. Harris HQ ACSEA, 'Policy for reorganisation of field squadrons into AA squadrons'. A matter of interest is that this letter makes no mention of 2946 Field Squadron, which had been at stationed at RAF Chittagong with 224 Group HQ since arriving from the Depot in November 1943. It had, however, been classified as a 'going' unit and was thus headed for disbandment.

11   ibid., correspondence, Wing Commander J.L. Fowke HQ 3rd Tactical Air Force to 221, 224 and 231 Group Defence Officers, 'Reduction of RAF Regiment – Posting Instructions', 14 April 1944.

12   AIR 24/1375, *Operational Record Books Appendices, SEAC, Indian Observer Corps, Ground Defence, January–August 1945,* Appendix GD/A/4/45. The Army had agreed in late 1943 that it provide airfield infantry garrisons. However, it was only in January 1945 that instructions to provide these were issued to local commanders.

13   *Third Supplement to the London Gazette,* Tuesday 13 March 1951. p. 1403–4.

14   ibid.

15   ibid.

16   AIR 24/1374, *Operations Record Books Appendices, SEAC, Indian Observer Corps, Gas Defence, Ground Defence, Engineer 1943–1944.* RAF Regiment, Third Organisation.

17   In December 1944 the 3rd Tactical Air Force was disbanded and the command of 221 and 224 Groups placed directly under Eastern Air Command.

18   Consisting of 4402, 4406, 4414, 4432, 4443, 4438, 3 (India), 5 (India), 7 (India) AA Flights and one flight from 2946 Field Squadron.

19 AIR 29/137, *Operations Record Books RAF Regiment Squadrons 2960–2970.*

20 ibid.

21 ibid., *Résumé of operations undertaken by No 2960 LAA Squadron, RAF Regiment.*

22 Two Sergeants, four Corporals and twenty-six ACs formed 'D' (Armoured) Flight and were detached to the RAF Regiment Domestic AFV School at Agartala for the Armoured Flight Course.

23 op. cit., AIR 24/1375 14 January 1945. Letter from HQ ACSEA to HQ RAF Bengal-Burma and OC RAF Regiment Depot.

24 AIR 29/134, *Operations Record Book, RAF Regiment Squadrons 2934, 2935, 2941–2943.*

25 The 2nd Battalion of the King's Own Yorkshire Light Infantry had been one of the regular Army battalions that had participated in the retreat from Burma in 1942 and performed admirably despite the trying conditions. The men had suffered severe casualties and spent the remainder of the war on internal security and training duties. Equipment supplies were so dire that they had spent the entire retreat without an issue of tin helmets. Ted Daines recalls talking to the RSM of the 2nd KOYLI and he expressed concern that the battalion was to return to the UK. Ted thought he would be happy. As a regular soldier, however, he had been moving around the globe for some twenty-six years and had not returned to the UK during that time. The First World War hadn't even ended when he began his overseas tour!

26 AIR 29/716 *No 1 RAF Regiment Training School later RAF Regiment (ACSEA) Secunderabad (with Appendices).*

CHAPTER FIVE

The Kabaw Valley

'We thought what we had seen before and been through was the worst, but nothing prepared us for what was to come in the seven weeks we spent going down this jungle valley.'

LAC Henry Kirk, Armourer, 2944 Field Squadron

For the first two years of the Burma campaign it had been usual once the monsoon had broken for both sides to 'draw stumps' and retreat to prepared positions. From there, they would carry out limited patrol activity but no large-scale offensive action. This time, however, Lord Louis Mountbatten, 'Supremo' of SEAC, did not plan to leave the Japanese to withdraw unimpeded and allow them to rebuild their strength. He directed XXXIII Indian Corps and 221 Group RAF to 'fight-on and fly-on through the monsoon'. Those Army troops not involved in the pursuit were withdrawn to India or remained in the valley where the monsoon period would be used to rebuild, reinforce and train for the coming dry season campaign.

By the end of July the hills around the Imphal Plain had been cleared of the enemy and the Fourteenth Army was preparing to drive the enemy back to the India-Burma border. Infantry columns fanned out from Imphal to pursue and harry the defeated remnants of the Japanese *15th Army*. One of these columns comprised a company from the 14/13th Frontier Force Rifles of the 20th Indian Division and they were despatched on a thirty-day patrol during mid-August. Accompanying them was No 1 Flight of 2943 Field Squadron under Flying Officer W.M. Graham. The flight was on attachment to give training in active patrolling and to accustom the unit to jungle conditions to the east of Imphal. The column was to assist with mopping-up operations for Japanese stragglers remaining west of the River Chindwin (Map 3). The airmen marched some 200 miles carrying every item of kit on their backs along tracks winding up mountains up to 7,000 feet. Supply by air had been precarious owing to bad weather and rations were frequently in short supply. Incessant rain poured in torrents and frequent river crossings meant little opportunity to dry clothing, while the attention of mosquitoes and other insects made sleep difficult. At least 2,000 Japanese dead were counted *en route*, along with numerous caches of discarded Japanese lorries, and items of equipment including rifles, bayonets, maps and even some excellent soap! The column never caught up with the retreating Japanese but did gain valuable experience in patrol work and jungle-craft. The men eventually reached a point 4½ miles east of the River Chindwin. By the end of the month the airmen were just as at home in the jungle as the seasoned jawans of the 13th Frontier Force Rifles. The Command Defence Officer, Group Captain J.H. Harris, inspected No 1 Flight at Palel on their return and congratulated the men on their performance. A newspaper article written at the time applauded the joint exploits of the Indian troops and RAF Regiment:

For the Indian troops the RAF Regiment have nothing but praise, and admiration and friendship sprang from their month-long campaign together. 'Those Indian troops are marvellous soldiers; they were always on the go' . . . Describing the kindness and patience of the Indians, another LAC said 'They gave us everything from food to rifle oil, taught us how to build bamboo bashas, and showed us how to make chapattis, which we found very good.'[1]

While most of the AA flights had departed from Imphal for disbandment, the field squadrons of the RAF Regiment that had been present throughout the siege had remained, continuing with air and ground defence of airstrips, AMES, wireless units and protection of RAF convoys. Reinforcements arrived from the Depot and one or two complete AA flights were absorbed into the three field squadrons. They were now seriously depleted by the rigours of the previous months. An RAF Regiment Defence Training Centre was established at Wangjing. It was necessary to restart training for the squadrons, to bring the reinforcements and those from the AA flights up to speed on the operation of a field squadron. It was also necessary to restore to fitness or replace those airmen who had been at Imphal through the siege and had suffered physical debilitation by months spent in static positions and in the awful monsoon conditions. Despite the best intentions, only 114 airmen completed the course at Wangjing in September due to as many men as possible being sent on leave and the high sickness rate in many units. From early November twelve RAF Regiment personnel per squadron and 10 per cent of all RAF personnel liable to operate against the enemy were to receive training in the detection and neutralisation of mines and booby traps. This was an unpleasant danger the airmen would increasingly face during the forthcoming advance.[2]

2941 Squadron had sent three flights into Imphal during the siege but Squadron HQ had remained outside the Valley. With the end of the siege, however, 2941 Squadron consolidated at Tulihal on 8 July. The ORB of 2941 Field Squadron describes the morale and attitude of the airmen at this time:

> The month [August 1944] started with an atmosphere which was a mixture of relief and apathy. Relief that things in the Valley had turned out better than anyone had a right to expect, and apathy which is the inevitable aftermath of a state of suppressed excitement. Certain guards are being maintained, but now they have become largely anti-saboteur in character, there is not the same enthusiasm which has been so marked a feature of activities of the past few weeks . . . Food has improved beyond one's wildest hopes. The cooks galvanised into a state of great activity, evoked largely by the sight of so much food, have excelled themselves . . . The third reorganisation is well underway and the eagerly awaited details are to hand. The general impression is that the Field Squadron is a very fine fighting force.[3]

Since June the 23rd Indian Division had been involved in a bitter struggle with *Yamamoto Force* on the Shenam Pass as it attempted to reopen the Palel-Tamu Road. In mid-July a successful offensive drove the enemy from their hill positions and on 4 August the town of Tamu with its valuable airstrip was recaptured. The Group Defence Officer, accompanied by Flight Lieutenant Gosnell of 2958 LAA Squadron and Flight Lieutenant Edwards of 2943 Field Squadron, reconnoitred the airstrip on 21 August and made arrangements for the re-establishment of an AMES. Ten days later a flight of 2943 Field Squadron and No 569 AMES arrived in Tamu. It was just over five months since the RAF Regiment had withdrawn from the devastated town. The men immediately set about preparing defences and were ordered to locate, capture or destroy any Japanese stragglers found in and around the airstrip. On 31 August the remainder of 2943 Field Squadron were relieved of their tasks at Palel. The squadron had been there since December the previous year and had been on constant alert since the first Japanese incursions across the Shenam Pass in April. Squadron HQ and two flights were moved to Wangjing, however, the AFV flight still continued on special duties with the Army, while the remaining rifle flight was occupied at Tamu airstrip.

From August 1944 the LAA and field squadrons formed from the 'third reorganisation' began arriving at Imphal. The first was 2958 LAA Squadron, which made an epic three-week 800-mile approach march over the hills from Chittagong. In spite of many difficulties encountered through shocking weather and road conditions, the squadron arrived intact and immediately took over the AA defence of Palel with 'A' and 'B' Flights and Imphal with 'C' Flight. During September they were joined in the Valley by 2960 and 2961 LAA Squadrons. The former squadron was deployed on the Imphal Main airfield where the flights and sub sections coordinated the placement of its Hispanos with the Army's 267 LAA and 189 HAA Batteries. The latter was split between Tulihal and Kangla. Three more squadrons, 2963 AA and 2946 and 2968 Field Squadrons, arrived in November. The RAF Regiment was now in place for the first steps back into Burma (Appendix 12).

As a further consequence of the 'third reorganisation' two Wing HQs were established in preparation for the impending advance. On 7 September 1324 Wing came into being at Imphal with personnel seconded from 2941 Field Squadron and by early October it was under the command of Wing Commander N.G. Whitfield. 1324 Wing had responsibility for AA and ground defence at Tulihal, Imphal and Kangla. In early October 1323 Wing was formed at Palel, commanded by Wing Commander R. Gladding, and assumed control of the squadrons at Palel and Wangjing. Over the next few weeks as preparations for the advance into Burma were intensified, there were regular alterations made to the squadrons under the control of each of the two Wing HQs. The first major move forward came on 22 October when 2941 Field Squadron, on completion of a special training programme, set off from Tulihal for the six-hour journey to Tamu. All the 15-cwts belonging to the squadron had been exchanged for four-wheel drive 3-tonners, as these were the only vehicles permitted on the Imphal-Tamu road. On arrival, they dug-in and cleared vegetation and were soon providing two aircraft guards and one refuelling team to 243 Wing. They were joined by 2958 LAA Squadron, which was charged with AA defence of the strip.

On 5 November 1944 the Japanese Air Force returned to Manipur and 2958 and 2960 LAA Squadrons took part in the first AA actions of the campaign using the 20-mm Hispano AA cannon (Appendix 11). Intelligence reports of the previous evening had indicated a probable air raid against Tamu airstrip. A despatch rider had to warn all the Flight Commanders of 2958 LAA Squadron as no telephones or wire had yet been received. At 0530 hours the next day an air raid warning was given and all the guns were fully manned. Fifteen minutes later enemy aircraft were heard at high altitude while Spitfires were seen patrolling the area. Twelve 'Oscars' were observed heading west to Palel, where at 0615 hours 2960 LAA Squadron opened fire, but the aircraft did not come within range. Anti-personnel bombs were dropped harmlessly in bare paddy fields near the north end of the strip, and each aircraft in turn then carried out a strafing run. One of these was directly over the 34 Squadron dispersal area, where, fortunately, an oil drum was the only casualty. Three-quarters of an hour later at Tamu two 'Oscars' swept in on a low-level attack and were immediately engaged by

95

the Hispanos of 2958 LAA Squadron and the Bofors of the 44th LAA Regiment RA. A disused Mitchell bomber was shot up and dogfights continued above the strip until 0650 hours when the all clear was sounded. The airmen of 2958 LAA Squadron were elated as this was their first action and morale was boosted, particularly as hits on three aircraft were claimed by three of the guns that went into action.

With the weather clearing and the advance pending, the RAF Regiment was required to provide a guard of honour for visiting dignitaries on a number of occasions. 2968 and 2944 Field Squadrons were present for the farewell visit of the AOC-in-C of ACSEA, Air Chief Marshal Sir Richard Peirse during November to Imphal and Palel, respectively. The official press release described his visit as follows:

> The Air Chief Marshal inspected on the airstrip a guard of honour provided by the men of the RAF Regiment field squadron. Many of these men had been in action against the enemy in the Palel area defending airfields. Today they formed a picturesque sight as they presented arms, wearing battle green [sic] and blue berets.[4]

Meanwhile, 2946 Field Squadron had the honour to be present at Imphal on 14 December when Lieutenant-General Slim and his three Corps Commanders, Lieutenant-Generals Christison, Scoones and Stopford, were knighted by the Viceroy, Field Marshal Wavell, for the successes of the Arakan and Imphal-Kohima campaigns. The RAF Regiment Guard was the subject of a complimentary letter to Air Vice-Marshal Vincent AOC 221 Group from the Fourteenth Army commander.

While the experienced 5th Indian Division pursued the retreating Japanese down the Tiddim Road, the newly arrived 11th East African Division had passed through Tamu on 12 August and set off down the Kabaw Valley (Map 4). Until the monsoon, abated the roads could not be kept in a reliable state and both divisions would be heavily dependent on air supply. However, this would also be severely limited by the monsoon weather. The Kabaw Valley had a deserved reputation as one of the most disease-ridden places in the world. It was a windless depression of thick teak forest and clinging mud. The vegetation was continuously drenched during the monsoon and visibility was limited to at most 100 yards. It was commonly known as the 'Valley of Death' as malaria and scrub typhus were rampant and easily contracted, and this was exacerbated by the monsoon conditions. Some 10 to 20 miles wide, the Valley was hemmed in on each side by high ranges. Beyond the eastern range was the River Chindwin, which marked the last barrier before the Fourteenth Army could move onto the central plain of Burma.

Impossible weather had slowed the advance of the 11th East African Division in early September. Conditions improved, however, in late October as the monsoon eased and the advance down the Kabaw Valley from Yazagyo was resumed on 1 November. This was somewhat of a false start as the 21st East African Brigade was held up at Mawlaik and the 26th East African Brigade north of Indainggyi. To maintain momentum, Major-General C. C. Fowkes, the Divisional Commander, ordered his reserve, the 25th East African Brigade, to by-pass Indainggyi on the west and to move direct to Kalemyo and make contact with the 5th Indian Division coming from Tiddim.

To gain more experience in patrolling for the RAF Regiment field squadrons, it was arranged that individual flights should be attached to the East Africans. From 8 to 24 November thirty airmen of No 2 Flight of 2941 Field Squadron, under command of Flying Officer R.H. Barnes,[5] were sent to work with an infantry battalion of the 25th East African Brigade (Sketch Map 5). During this time they were to participate alongside the East Africans in actions that would finally drive the enemy back across the River Chindwin. On 8 November No 2 Flight reported to the 25th East African Brigade HQ, just north of Honnaing. The brigade had just moved from reserve and was implementing Fowkes' new orders. Small parties of Japanese were moving around the area east of Fort White and the Tiddim Road and were attempting to reach Kalemyo and Kalewa as they were pursued by the 5th Indian and 11th East African Divisions. As a result the brigade was now dealing with pockets of Japanese resistance north of the Kalemyo-Kalewa road. The flight was welcomed on arrival by an air raid. Six 'Tojo' fighters appeared and quite unmolested proceeded to shoot down five of the Dakotas dropping supplies. Anti-personnel bombs were then dropped near the flight, causing a number of casualties among the Regiment gunners, fortunately none of them fatal.

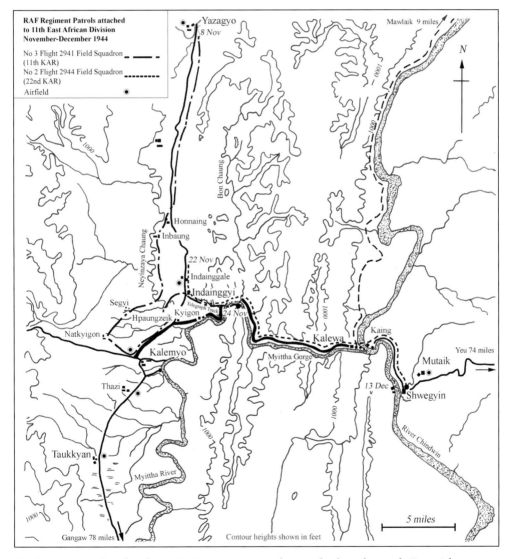

5 *The routes taken by the RAF Regiment patrols attached to the 11th East African Division during the advance from Yazagyo to Shwegyin, November to December 1944*

Leaving Brigade HQ, No 2 Flight moved south to join the 11th (Kenya) Battalion, The King's African Rifles (KAR). This time they were welcomed by an unpleasant half an hour of heavy shelling from a Japanese 75-mm gun with one shell pitching only 30 yards away, killing two KAR officers. The first night, as with most, was spent in silence and on full alert with orders to use only the bayonet or grenade should they come under fire. The shelling continued the following morning for a short time before the battalion moved south. Local patrols had reported Japanese in twos and threes moving through the area and obviously seeking a means of escape.

On 10 November the battalion moved across the Neyinzaya Chaung. The march was hard work due to the heavy brushwood and thick elephant grass. Two companies were detailed to attack and capture Segyi and No 2 Flight provided the escort to the mule train with essential supplies for the consolidating companies. While moving up, a shot was fired at the column from a nearby village and the RAF Regiment deployed to attack but found no sign of the enemy. On 12 November heavy fighting broke out around the Battalion HQ, of which the RAF Regiment was now in a protective role, and much firing could be heard. These incursions threatened the battalion supply lines and rations had become dangerously low for the scattered companies. No 1 Section under Flying Officer Barnes was, therefore, ordered to return to the Neyinzaya Chaung crossing with a mule train and bring back food supplies. Just as No 1 Section arrived at the river the mist lifted and the Japanese shelled the crossing. All hell was let loose, mules scampered around and the Askaris and Indian muleteers dived into slit trenches. Quickly summing up their predicament, the airmen decided the best action was not to sit out the shelling but to load up and get out of it. Between shell bursts the mules were caught and loaded, fortunately, without mishap.[6] When told of their exploits, the Battalion CO, Lieutenant-Colonel Birkbeck, congratulated the RAF Regiment on their return for the good work they were doing.[7] The actions of No 1 Section were a fine example of courage, devotion to duty and team work.

The battle now intensified as the 5th Indian Division drove the enemy eastwards towards the East Africans and on 13 November 11th KAR linked up with a patrol of the 4/7th Rajput Regiment to the west of Kalemyo. The objective of the two-prong monsoon advance had been achieved. The 25th East African Brigade was now ordered to advance eastwards towards Kalewa at the eastern end of the Myittha Gorge. Having been attached to Battalion HQ up to this point, the Flight Commander requested that No 2 Flight be given an opportunity to carry out patrol work. Birkbeck indicated he had been grateful for their presence at Battalion HQ and that the flight had performed magnificent work. Kalemyo had fallen and they would be attached to 'B' Company to get their patrol experience.

With the 5th Indian Division mopping up the Kalemyo area, the East Africans were now free to concentrate their strength for the capture of Kalewa and the establishment of a bridgehead over the Chindwin. No 2 Flight moved off with the Company. Their objective was Hpaungzeik, where the Japanese had constructed a floating bridge as a major escape route for those fleeing from Tiddim. A strong enemy position was located before Hpaungzeik and a platoon of 'B' Company patrolling along the road was ambushed. The remainder of 'B' Company deployed to attack the position to help the stricken platoon, while No 2 Flight formed a roadblock and casualty-clearing station. There was much firing and No 2 Flight was able to bring out one wounded and one dead African. The RAF Regiment Nursing Orderly acted with great coolness and efficiently bandaged the wounded man and sent him back to base. Though not taking the position, the platoon was successfully extracted and 'B' Company withdrew without further loss.

Askaris of the 11th East African Division on the road to Kalewa, December 1944. (Photograph courtesy of the Imperial War Museum, London, SE 1884)

Fowkes now ordered the 25th Brigade north to help the 26th East African Brigade, still held up in front of Indainggyi. The next day the 11th KAR were moved to a position south of Indainggyi. From here the men could cut the road to Kalewa from the north at Kyigon. To do so they had to take and hold Kyigon Peak. On 18 November the battalion moved up with No 2 Flight escorting HQ Company and sent out patrols around the planned route. After a 4-mile march taking seven hours over heavy country, the battalion successfully reached its objective. The 26th East African Brigade had been attempting to take Indainggyi from the north and the sudden appearance of the 25th Brigade to the south of the town took the enemy by surprise. Despite heavy air support, attempts to take Indainggyi had been frustrated. However, the appearance of the column, including the 11th KAR and its attached flight to the south of the town, had convinced the Japanese to withdraw. From its new positions the flight was able to watch Japanese lorries escaping down the road. A party of Japanese was caught by surprise by the East Africans while bathing and was wiped out.

A strong bunker position was then located further up the road and the battalion ordered to take it. Prior to the attack No 2 Flight saw the 'pleasant sight' of an air strike by twenty-four Hurricanes on the bunker position. On 21 November the 11th KAR, supported by a troop of tanks of the 7th Light Cavalry, secured Kyigon. Casualties amongst the East Africans were high particularly due to the accurate shelling by the enemy, but the flight emerged unscathed. While escorting both the CO to inspect company positions and also a line-laying party, the section was heavily shelled and an airman hit by shrapnel, again fortunately causing no injury. No 2 Flight seemed to live a charmed life. The enemy was not easily dissuaded and after the 11th KAR and No 2

Flight had dug-in, there was much activity from Japanese 'jitter' parties. It was a very unpleasant night when a grenade thrown by a nervous Askari killed two Africans, and a British officer sleeping in a trench was blown up by his own grenade. No 2 Flight greeted the arrival of dawn with great relief, as there had been more danger from East African bullets than from the Japanese.

On 22 November No 2 Flight was despatched across the Myittha River with orders to patrol inland then work back to the south bank of the river. The men found un-occupied bunker positions and saw a single Japanese soldier watching them from a distance. However, he eluded capture. Keeping pace with the battalion as it moved along the north bank of the river, the flight reported Japanese 'sampans' moving on the river and found many useful papers. This, however, was to be the flight's last day of work with the battalion and on 25 November the men departed by lorry for Tamu, arriving on 26 November.[8] The CO of the 11th KAR in his farewell message thanked all concerned for the excellent way in which they had carried out their various assign-ments and finally added, 'I am proud of you and will miss you all. Good Luck'.

While No 2 Flight was making its way back from the attachment with the East Africans, at Tamu the AFV flight of 2941 Field Squadron was continuing with patrol duties at the north end of the airstrip. On 26 November No 1 Flight of 2941 Field Squadron, under the command of Flying Officer S.W. Cook, had been ordered to proceed to Mawlaik on the west bank of the River Chindwin for AMES protection duties. This town had fallen to the 21st East African Brigade on 10 November. After travelling for four hours by lorry to Teinkaya where they spent the night, the men then moved on foot for the next 3½ days along a bad track. Ankle deep in mud, in rocky and steep conditions, they trekked over the hills that defined the eastern side of the Kabaw Valley. To save their jungle rations they lived off food found in an old camp. They moved on to Yezon and again found unused rations but the river had nearly dried up and thus they were short of water. Moving on the next morning, the track improved but there was little shade for the next 8 miles. At Sadwin No 1 Flight met a mule team from the Assam Regiment. They were the first people they had seen for three days. The villagers brought them cooked rice and fruit and they spent the night in an old elephant shed. After a six-hour march the next day they reached Mawlaik and made contact with the Supply Officer on the airstrip. He expressed amazement that they had done the 25-mile trip over such difficult country on their own and without mules.

Meanwhile, the longest of the RAF Regiment's attachments with the East Africans began when thirty men of No 3 Flight of 2944 Field Squadron, under the command of Pilot Officer A.W. Newton,[9] departed from Palel on 20 November (Sketch Map 5). They travelled by road through to Tamu airstrip, spent the night under the hospitality of 2941 Field Squadron, and then moved south to Yazagyo. Two days later they reported to the 11th East African Divisional HQ south of Yazagyo and were sent to work with the 22nd (Nyasaland) Battalion, The King's African Rifles of the 26th East African Brigade. The attachment was originally planned as two weeks 'training' on patrol work and jungle craft. However, unforeseen circumstances led to the 22nd KAR being urgently committed to an operational role, and with them went No 3 Flight.

No 3 Flight was sent to the 'C' Company position and was allocated the southern perimeter only 200 yards from the enemy. That night the men observed the usual rules of defence: no firing, only bayonets or grenades, with Bren guns covering likely lines of approach. On 23 November the company moved off along the road to Indainggyi with No 13 Platoon in the lead, with 15 and 14 Platoons followed by No 3 Flight. They passed through Indainggyi and then moved along the 'Telegraph Track'. This track went east until it met the north bank of Myittha River gorge and was being used by the retreating enemy. In some places on the track the elephant grass bordered the road on both sides and visibility was limited. At the river they linked up with the 25th East African Brigade coming from the west and were informed that No 2 Flight, 2941 Field Squadron, was covering the Kalemyo to Kalewa road directly opposite them from the south side of the river.

There followed a further night with 'jitter' parties disturbing the peace. The following morning firing was heard and Japanese runners were observed making for the 'Telegraph Track'. The 'C' Company Quartermaster Sergeant and LAC Vic Busby gave chase and shot a runner.[10] Papers were found on the body and handed over to the Battalion Intelligence Officer. For the next three days 'C' Company and No 3 Flight waited while other units of the division moved east along the Myittha River. Early morning and evening clearing patrols consisting of either a Section from the flight or a mixed group of Askaris and airmen went out to mop up enemy stragglers and provide intelligence on possible Japanese positions and campsites. On 1 December a move was made a few miles to the east and No 3 Flight set up a self-contained defensive position. The battalion waited a further two days while the division prepared to cross the River Chindwin and establish a bridgehead.

The crossing on 3 December by the 26th East African Brigade marked the return of the Fourteenth Army to Burma proper. No 3 Flight moved up to Kalewa with the battalion and crossed on timber rafts on 5 December, thus becoming the first RAF Regiment unit to cross the Chindwin. No 3 Flight disembarked first and formed the

A view of the 1,100-ft Bailey bridge across the Chindwin River as it nears completion, less than twelve hours after the Fourteenth Army captured Kalewa, 2 December 1944. (Photograph courtesy of the Imperial War Museum, London, SE 835)

covering party for the battalion landing. The men then moved on to Kaing and after the 34th KAR had taken a strong bunker on a nearby ridge, No 3 Flight took up position on the western perimeter with two companies of the 22nd KAR. On 6 December the airmen apprehended ten Burmese and took them for interrogation to Battalion HQ. Fire came in from nearby Japanese positions during the following night. The battalion moved and took over positions from the 34th KAR, which overlooked the river, and 'C' Company and No 3 Flight were ordered to fire on any boats moving along the river. A patrol consisting of Captain Mossley (KAR) and two Askari, along with LAC W.J. Whibley, who had volunteered to accompany them, set out to make contact with the 21st East African Brigade moving in from the north along the east bank of the River Chindwin. The link up allowed the Paung Chaung to be opened for mule pack trains and evacuation of the wounded from the 25th East African Brigade.

The movement east continued and on 9 December the position received a visit from none other than Lieutenant-General Sir William Slim, the Fourteenth Army commander, and Lieutenant-General Sir Montague Stopford, XXXIII Corps commander. The reason for the visit soon became apparent when on 10 December 'C' Company moved forward and took the lead for the advance to Shwegyin, the next objective of the 11th East African Division. Shwegyin had been the location of the last major battle before Burcorps retreated from Imphal in 1942 and there was strong Japanese opposition to the advance.

The situation in the positions occupied by the 22nd KAR and No 3 Flight that evening was chaotic; telephone lines were cut and a forward platoon was accidentally shelled by its own artillery. The airmen frequently came under fire from 'jitter' parties and machine-guns sweeping the defensive perimeter, and a shower of grenades was thrown into the company positions. Early that evening Pilot Officer Newton identified enemy movement on a feature to the east of No 3 Flight's positions and requested supporting mortar fire. The East African mortars opened up and further enemy responses ceased. At stand-to the next day, No 3 Flight fully expected an attack but fortunately none came. During the night two of the Askaris had taken fright and deserted, and a Burmese interrogator had run away and falsely reported to Battalion HQ that the company had been overrun. Fortunately, once the telephone line to the company was repaired it was discovered that this was not the case.

No 3 Flight moved forward that morning to clear the area to the left of the Shwegyin road, while a KAR platoon cleared the right. Sergeant Garner and No 1 Section patrolled up to the twin hills from which the enemy fire had come the previous night. They found the enemy positions and a large amount of spent ammunition. The enemy had departed and the position was held by No 1 Section until relieved by 'D' Company. The remaining section under Pilot Officer Newton cleared the area below the hills. The 13th KAR now took the lead and moved on to take Shwegyin. On 13 December the attachment came to an end and No 3 Flight moved back across the Chindwin and travelled in 2nd British Division vehicles to rejoin 2944 Field Squadron, now located at Yazagyo. The attachment of No 3 Flight from 2944 Field Squadron had been a resounding success and the Flight Commander, Pilot Officer Newton, reported as follows:

The Flight mainly comprised men who had done an average of three years' service in this theatre of war . . . the attachment for training became an attachment for operational duties due to the fact that 11th Division were near the end of their operational commitments and as such were badly in need of replacements for casualties incurred during the previous months . . .

The Flight was committed to an operational role as soon as they arrived at 'C' Company and the first few days' climb and march were such to test even the most seasoned of troops . . . the RAF Regiment men responded very well and learning all the while they soon became efficient and held their own in the repeated marching, digging-in, and patrolling, comparing favourably with the Company to which they were attached.

The CO of the Company himself on a number of occasions expressed his satisfaction at the demeanour and keenness of the men and was particularly impressed by the men's soldierly behaviour under heavy enemy fire at night . . . The CO of the Battalion . . . expressed the wish that the RAF Regiment Flight remain with him until 11th Division were withdrawn from the front, for their well earned rest.[11]

With the tasks of the 11th East African and 5th Indian Divisions now successfully completed, the Fourteenth Army could now concentrate on the banks of the Chindwin ready for the move forward. This was not easy as the track down the Kabaw Valley had disintegrated during the monsoon and forward airfields were scarce. The engineers were given road repair and airfield construction tasks as top priorities and of getting the material to Kalewa to bridge the Chindwin. Taukkyan airstrip was captured intact by the 5th Indian Division on 13 November, while the Yazagyo airstrip was opened on 16 November. Despite this, the East Africans were still largely dependent on supply drops. The two way fair-weather road reached Indainggyi on 28 November. As the Army moved forward, captured airfields were improved and enlarged, while new airfields were constructed. Yazagyo and Taukkyan were extended 2,000 yards to take fighters and larger-capacity Commando C46 aircraft and new fighter strips were built at Thazi and Kalemyo, a pair of runways at Indainggale (1 mile north of Indainggyi) suitable for transport aircraft and an airstrip for light aircraft at Inbaung (5 miles north of Indainggyi).[12]

November had been set as the month for the reopening of the Allied campaign and 1 November was, therefore, set as the target date for all RAF Regiment squadrons to be fully trained and ready for action. The RAF Regiment moved *en masse* during the last week of November and the first weeks of December with the object being to get as many squadrons as possible forward to Yazagyo for deployment on recaptured airstrips. After the trials and vicissitudes of the last two years and the dour struggle during the siege of Imphal, everyone was grateful to be finally moving forward. Within a few days the following moves took place: 2968 Field Squadron and two flights of 2958 LAA Squadron and 2941[13] and 2944 Field Squadrons moved from Tamu; 2943 Field Squadron moved from Palel; 2960 LAA Squadron from Kangla; and Wangjing and 2961 LAA Squadron from Sapam and Wangjing.

The stay at Yazagyo by the two flights of 2958 LAA Squadron and 2968 Field Squadron[14] lasted only a few days before they moved on to Kalemyo. All seven squadrons were to come under the control of 1324 Wing, which had been located at Yazagyo since 23 November. 1323 Wing remained at Tulihal to organise and prepare the newly arrived 2946 Field Squadron and 2963 LAA Squadron for movement forward by the end of December.

LAC Henry Kirk had kept a diary during the siege, but eventually had to stop writing after the move to Palel due to the horrendous monsoon conditions. Over 400 inches of rain fell in a seven-week period with an average of ten inches in one day. It had been planned that 2944 Field Squadron would be given leave one flight at a time. The first flight was duly flown out to Calcutta and was billeted on the transit camp at the main race course. The other flights never had the opportunity for leave as the squadron was soon put on full readiness, was issued with wet weather gear, and ordered to proceed to the Kabaw Valley. Leaving Palel on 26 November, the first stop for 2944 Field Squadron was Tamu. There was still evidence of heavy fighting and loss of life on the Shenam Pass and although it had been three months since the capture of the town, the death and destruction almost defied the imagination. Henry Kirk continues:

> After Imphal we expected to have some rest and recuperation; everybody was jaundice yellow from mepacrine, the anti-malarial drug, and underweight from months on half-rations with no fresh meat or vegetables. Instead of going back we were issued with monsoon gear in November and moved in an RAF convoy over the Shenam Pass to Tamu. We left Palel airfield with two loads of armoury equipment on the road to Tamu, just 28 miles over the hills and at the head of the Kabaw Valley. A deadly winding road climbing up and around the mountain tops, a clear hot day and lovely view over jungle covered mountains and valleys. Once the area was reached where 20th and 23rd Indian Divisions had fought to keep the Japanese from Palel, there was a stark contrast and we found a scene of desolation and scarred hillsides. Japanese bunkers and trenches were everywhere, and bomb craters nearly joined one another where our aircraft had repeatedly blasted the gateway to the Imphal Valley.
> The Japanese had been cleared from Tamu but their dead lay everywhere. The stench was inescapable. There was a Field Hospital with a wrecked Jap ambulance outside. The Japanese, still in their beds, had all been shot, we were told, by their own troops because they had no means of transport for them.[15] At Tamu we had a job in finding where we had to go but an MP directed us to the edge of a small airstrip. He said 'You're going with the 11th East Africans down the Kabaw Valley.' Our job was to protect an AMES unit.

On 1 December 2944 Field Squadron was ordered forward from Tamu. The AMES was still highly secret and it was vital that it did not fall into enemy hands. Henry Kirk was issued with a haversack containing wet and dry gun cotton and lengths of line, and was instructed to blow up the AMES if it was likely that it was to be captured. The ORB describes some of the difficulties and frustrations encountered in 2944 Field Squadron's first major move:

> The rapid advance of the Army and the resultant occupation of forward airstrips has made the unit prepare for greater mobility and a state of preparedness to move. After having been at Tamu for only six days, there was little surprise when HQ 221 Group ordered the unit to move to Yazagyo . . . a distance of some 61 miles. Motor transport was inadequate and some difficulty was experienced in obtaining additional transport. This was eventually lent by 2941 Squadron. Seven Armoured Fighting Vehicles which would have been of assistance in a move were ordered to be left . . . pending a decision as to the ultimate use of these vehicles within the Squadron. The AFV Flight commander Flying Officer P.H. Brice, after having completed a specialised course at [Agartala], Bengal, was disappointed too at the possible disbandment of the Flight as an armoured unit.[16]

With the Army moving forward, the radar stations were moved closely behind with their RAF Regiment guardians to give the maximum warning of incoming Japanese aircraft intent on disrupting air supply operations or attacking airstrips. Despite the poor road surface the bulk of 2944 Field Squadron had taken only a day to reach Yazagyo, where the men took over the site previously occupied by 2968 Field Squadron. The squadron set about preparing defensive positions and then the following day the Flight Commanders commenced training, stressing the methods of jungle attack, active patrols and tactical exercises. Basic features of training were carried out, including weapons training, physical training, map reading, aircraft recognition and R/T intercommunication. Henry Kirk recalls the difficult conditions encountered as 2944 Field Squadron moved further down the Kabaw Valley and two incidents which occurred on the journey:

The distance from Tamu to Kalewa on the River Chindwin was about 112 miles. We thought what we had seen before and been through was the worst, but nothing prepared us for what was to come in the seven weeks we spent going down this jungle valley. It was a hell hole, dense jungle with a top cover of massive teak trees and bamboo. The unmade road was knee deep in mud slurry and littered with the wreckage of rusting vehicles abandoned on the retreat from Burma in 1942. Japanese bodies were being piled up and destroyed with flame guns to prevent disease. We were sprayed at intervals by an aircraft with DDT to deal with the mosquitoes.

Trees were sawn down and elephants moved them onto the bad parts making a log road. It was a battle alone to keep vehicles moving. Sometimes when stuck a long cable was attached and they were winched out by a Bren gun carrier. The engineers eventually laid a sort of road surface using hessian soaked in tar and called bithess. The wooden bridges had been blown-up by the retreating Japanese. It must have been one of the most pestilential places on earth with every known fever and tropical disease. Death and destruction was everywhere. When the sun shone the trees and undergrowth were so thick we only saw beams of light. One was never dry, soaked by the heavy rain and in the breaks in the monsoon by perspiration due to the heat and high humidity.

Above all you made sure you never got in front of the East Africans. The Valley was ambush country and the Askari officers were constantly concerned about this. Often they put a man forward to draw enemy fire and then observed the direction from which it came.

The AMES radar had at that time a short range of 30–50 miles depending on how it was sited. We moved off down the Kabaw Valley tailing the advance of 11th East African Division and shortly before dark each night we moved up to them and formed a box defence. The AMES was towed with a tracked Bren gun carrier through the sea of mud and water.

The Kabaw Valley left its mark on the memories of those who went forward through it in that monsoon of 1944. Two incidents come to mind. Just before Myittha Gorge we formed a 'box' defence near a large flooded chaung. The road here went over a rough timber bridge, to the left of which was long sloping bank covered in small trees and much bamboo, beyond was the flooded chaung. Just as dawn broke we all stood-to. Some of us were behind the chaung bank and an RSM of the East African's crept up to me and said 'They tell me you're a hot shot. Take your bush hat off and come with me and keep down'. It was not very far and he said, 'Peep over the top, there is some-body in front of us beyond the bamboo, this side of the chaung.' I spotted a khaki-clad figure with a soft hat and the RSM said 'It's not one of your lads is it?' I said 'No, they're all like me in jungle green, it's a Jap.' A voice, I learnt later was that of an Askari officer, said 'Take him out with a single shot, a second one will give our position away.' There was only a small window between the clumps of bamboo and he seemed to keep bending down. I carried a US M1 carbine which fired single or auto shots which I had acquired at Imphal. I fired one shot at him and he went down. A short time afterwards a patrol of East Africans went out and reported back that it was a Jap sergeant. They took possession of some maps and papers brought back a haversack and asked if I wanted anything out of it. We were at the time under orders not to be caught by the Japanese with as much as one of their pay books on your person. I spotted an oblong leather case, it was a Kodak 127 folding camera wrapped in a silk handkerchief.[17]

The other incident was with the same RSM. There was what looked like a Burmese with a large straw brimmed hat ploughing with a bullock in a flooded paddy field. The RSM said to LAC Frank Greenwood, 'Bring that man in and watch him he's a Jap.' Something was said about the depth of the water and Frank was told to do the same as him and take his boots off and roll up his trousers. He brought the man in and he was Japanese. It appeared he had got on with a local woman and had stayed put when the others retreated. We never got to know how the RSM knew he was a Jap.

Prior to moving from Palel on 3/4 December, 2943 Field Squadron suffered a severe blow to the strength of the unit when forty airmen were posted to Forward Echelon at Agartala on medical grounds. They had still not been replaced by the end of the month. After a stay at Forward Echelon Agartala as a mortar instructor, Ted Daines was ordered to Imphal to join 2943 Field Squadron. Two days after he arrived they were on the move:

I was lucky to get a lift on a supply truck and make it to Imphal. I was able to trace my unit after a few days . . . they were in fact at Wangjing. The following day my trip down Burma really started. We moved up to Palel . . . on a small hill at the south end of the airfield.[18] Looking up the road one could see the gap in the hills where the Japs had dragged a 105 mm gun to fire at us over open sites. We were, however, not here long. HQ and 'A' Flight were ordered forward to Yazagyo in Burma.

The engineers had slowly been re-forming the Kabaw Valley road. The road would be feet deep in mud but days later it would dry to a fine red powdery dust. Ted Daines of 2943 Field Squadron recalls the move:

The occupants of our convoy sitting on the backs of the open lorries were covered from head to foot in this red dust. Stopping the convoy on the way the Flight Lieutenant decided to hold an inspection for non-shavers and to check for clean gear in general. Can you imagine a mile or so of airmen and lorries just sitting there, no sentries or AA guns manned, the Flight Lieutenant up the line looking at dust-covered men. Then suddenly it broke up, the Squadron CO drove up and told us to get moving.

Arriving at Yazagyo the Flight Lieutenant called up all the senior NCOs and started to rip into us, saying we were a disgrace. The Squadron CO came up, listened for a few seconds, dismissed us, and led the officer away. I would have liked to hear what was said. He should have returned him to the Army from where he had come. Can you imagine it? Already reduced to a pint of water a day, saving some for a shave was the last thing we thought of, especially as we knew what sort of road we were going to drive along. Then what about the 'sitting ducks' just lined up and waiting for the Japanese 'Zeros'. I can fully understand why the Army had allowed him to transfer to us.

Yazagyo was the first stop for 2943 Field Squadron after crossing the India-Burma border and, along with 2941 and 2944 Field Squadrons, provided guards for No 569 AMES. 2943 Field Squadron encamped just off the southern end of the rough small airstrip suited only to L5 Sentinels and other light ambulance aircraft but with Spitfires operating from it. A patch of scrub and then a wood with a crashed Commando C46 separated the squadron from the airstrip. A crash guard was provided for three nights on the strip for the damaged Commando. Ted Daines continues:

> Nearby was a river, we could at least have a good wash, during a patrol we came across a Japanese patrol that had been caught by a fighter in the open, six or eight bodies and not one under six feet two, so much for the myth that all Japanese are small . . . on the airfield, if you could call it that, was a paddy field with the bunds cut off where you would think landing a Spitfire was a hazard in itself.

On 17 December 1944 at about 1630 hours a Mosquito aircraft was heard approaching Yazagyo airstrip.[19] The aircraft crashed at the south end of the strip, about 500 yards from the end and 400 yards from 'B' Flight HQ of 2960 LAA Squadron. Pilot Officer J. Firth of this flight and a number of RAF Regiment personnel from various squadrons ran to give assistance. Ted Daines continues:

> At Yazagyo was a tragedy that should never have happened. A Mosquito clearly in distress crash-landed at the top of the strip. The first we heard was a rough sounding engine, then the noise into a rumble, cum scraping sound of an aircraft on its belly. When we arrived the stricken aircraft was approachable although smoking.

The plane had a broken back and the plane had twisted so the main plane and cockpit were upside down and the tail upright. The pilot's head and arm were protruding from under the trailing edge behind the port engine. The observer's body was trapped but his legs protruded from the fuselage. Struggling to release the crew proved futile as they were well entangled. Stripped to the waist, the airmen tried to pull the tail section with the observer clear but to no avail. Ted Daines continues:

> One of our officers spoke to the pilot who was just about conscious and said his feet were trapped in the rudder bar, no way could we do anything, but as the plane began to show signs of bursting into flames the fire wagon rolled up. The tragedy then unfolded, the foam tank was empty, ammo now began to explode, we were forced back and had to watch the incineration of two Australian aircrew. We arrived back at camp sickened by what we had just

witnessed. Somebody said to me you're bleeding like a stuck pig; sure enough blood was dripping off my fingertips. I had indeed suffered a deep cut to my right elbow. I must admit I have no knowledge of being hit, although there was plenty of stuff flying about. We did hear later that [the] Corporal in charge of the fire wagon had only just relieved the previous crew and so was unaware that the tank was empty. Even today I think what a tragedy.

On 14 December Squadron Leader E.S. Gosnell, the 2944 Field Squadron HQ and two rifle flights were ordered to move to the recently captured and undamaged airstrip at Taukkyan (Appendix 13). This was to be the most forward airstrip operating at the time. Orders were received at 0410 hours and the two rifle flights moved at 0630 hours, followed by Squadron HQ with thirty-six airmen at 1030 hours. Flying Officer Brice and Pilot Officer Newton with seventy-two airmen remained at Yazagyo for patrolling duties until they were relieved by a follow-up squadron. AA protection was realised with the appearance at the same time of two flights of 2958 LAA Squadron. Henry Kirk recalls that 2944 Field Squadron HQ arrived to find the strip in illustrious hands:

> The 3/1st Gurkha Rifles had moved further south and captured the airstrip at Taukkyan, which the Japanese had carved out of the jungle. I suppose a lovely setting in the hills with a plain to the south. Then 17 Squadron flew in on the same day with their Spitfires along with their CO, Squadron Leader 'Ginger' Lacey of Battle of Britain fame. Their job was to protect the Bailey bridge over the River Chindwin. The longest Bailey bridge built during World War 2.

The 3/1st Gurkha Rifles developed a great friendship with the fighter pilots and refused to hand over the airstrip as they saw themselves honour-bound to defend the newly arrived 17 Squadron. Their request to their CO was that they had defended the airstrip without aircraft and would continue to do so with aircraft. An interesting demarcation dispute developed when the Gurkhas were:

> . . . Told politely that the RAF Regiment had come for that purpose, the little men drew up their own guard roster and continued with their duties as though the latter were not there.[20]

Only training and local camp patrols were, therefore, carried out by 2944 Field Squadron until 29 December when the Gurkhas departed. Taukkyan had been

Men from a section of 2944 Field Squadron at Taukkyan proudly display a Japanese battle flag captured during their journey down the Kabaw Valley, December 1944. (RAF Regiment SEAC Association)

constructed by the Japanese and was closed in on three sides by hills with a wide plain to the south. Thick jungle could have hidden an army in the surrounding hills and six to eight feet high elephant grass grew up to the edge of the strip. This was so thick that it was almost impenetrable. Henry Kirk recalls the problems this caused:

> Our Squadron sent out patrols on a compass bearing to search out any pockets of Japanese. Christmas Day was spent in searching for LAC Brisco and another airman who [had] gone out two days earlier to buy chickens from a nearby village and had not returned. It was like looking for a needle in a hay stack. They arrived back under their own steam. We all had the usual bully beef for Christmas Dinner.

For the airmen of 2943 Field Squadron at Yazagyo, who were also on relatively short rations and dependent on air supply, Christmas Day was much more satisfying. About mid-morning, thoughts had turned to whether they would have any special fare appropriate to the festive season. All of a sudden the airdrop arrived with Christmas lunch delivered as part of it. Ted Daines continues:

> We could serve the men in time-honoured fashion; we got the lot, tinned turkey, and chicken, even Christmas 'pud'. Beer and spirits, the only lot we ever had during the campaign; we often used to wonder who had snaffled the rest. The only drawback was the fact we had to move up at 0300 hours the next day, Boxing Day.

A Concert Party called the 'Forty-Three Road Show' was organised by the 2i/c and the Welfare Officer. This was performed on Christmas Eve and Christmas Day, and again on 30 December for 2958 LAA Squadron. A surprising amount of talent was discovered in 2943 Field Squadron and the concerts were a great success. Soon after, 2943 Field Squadron took over the defence of the AMES at Kalemyo from 2968 Field Squadron, which was to move forward across the River Chindwin. Meanwhile, 2961 LAA Squadron had been in action on 23 December with its Hispanos used against enemy aircraft, which attacked Kalewa in an unsuccessful attempt to destroy the newly constructed pontoon bridge over the Chindwin.

For 2968 Field Squadron, one of the lead squadrons, Christmas in the Kabaw Valley had not been as pleasant. Cyril Paskin had joined this squadron when his AA flight had been absorbed into it at the Depot three months earlier.[21] He continues:

> We were sent to an airstrip . . . [and] arrived on Christmas Eve. The Japanese had all gone although there were lots of dead Japs together with Geisha girls all with their heads cut off. The East Africans had got there before us and done the job on our behalf! We spent the night there but there was no action.

Ted Daines' story regarding the overzealous ex-Army Flight Lieutenant had an amusing and revealing sequel a few weeks later. He continues:

> . . . Kalemyo became very quiet and our next move was across the pontoon bridge over the Chindwin on [passing through] to Kalewa. One night [31 December] we had orders to stand-to [along with 2960 and 2961 LAA Squadrons] as the Japs were expected to make a paratroop drop on us to re-capture the airfield. Happy we were when rather than attacking they withdrew.

The only thing I remember about this airfield was its very hard ground. I think it took me three hours to dig down two feet. Don't forget, no food until the slit trench had been dug.

When moving a few weeks later to a small light plane airstrip called Mutaik, we heard that the steep-sided road had collapsed. We would have to be prepared to march about twenty miles, of the 'up hills and down dales' variety, full packs would be carried by all regardless of rank. A list was read out to all indicating what was to be taken and that there would be an inspection before we were taken to the start of the march by road. The Squadron assembled, the CO walked round the men, lifting a pack here and there. Then when he went around the officers, coming to the ex-Army type, he lifted his pack. He then whispered in his ear. He marched off and returned after about ten minutes. He had tried the old Army trick of putting an empty cardboard box in his pack.

The last weeks of 1944 were filled with preparations for the move onto the central plain of Burma. The East Africans and the 5th Indian Division were soon to be relieved by the 2nd British Division, which had moved to Yazagyo, while the brigades of the 20th Indian Division were now located at Kalemyo and Khampat near Htinzin. XXXIII Corps HQ was now in place south of Yazagyo. The relentless pursuit of the Japanese *15th Army* through the monsoon had succeeded, but at the cost of some 50,000 casualties or about 55 per cent of the strength of XXXIII Corps. Of these casualties, 90 per cent were due to sickness.[22] The results were, however, considered worthwhile as the Fourteenth Army was poised, ready to move at the earliest opportunity and with the larger part of the dry season still available for campaigning.

1323 Wing HQ now moved forward from Imphal with its two squadrons and by 29 December it was located at Indainggyi airstrip, 3 miles north of Kalemyo. 1324 Wing HQ moved south from Yazagyo on 31 December and joined them. The final arrival of the year was that of 1307 Wing HQ. This wing had originally served in France after D Day. It had been disbanded in September 1944 and was re-formed at Bombay on 4 December 1944 on arrival of personnel from the United Kingdom. It moved to Secunderabad, where it spent only eleven days before moving via Calcutta, Agartala, Comilla and Imphal. On 21 December Wing Commander C.M. 'Bill' Lander, previously CO of 2968 Field Squadron, assumed command.

Seven squadrons were now deployed across the airstrips and AMES that would be used to support the advance into Burma. They were responsible for: ground and AA defence at Yazagyo, Kalemyo and Taukkyan airstrips; AA defence at Kalewa and Indainggale airstrips; and protection of AMES at Mawlaik, Mutaik, Sittaung and Kalemyo. By 1 January 1945, 1307, 1323 and 1324 Wing HQs were in position at Indainggyi alongside the 221 Group RAF Forward HQ. The divisions of the Fourteenth Army had begun moving forward in the last week of December. The stage was set for the reconquest of Burma.

Notes
1   *The Statesman*, Delhi, 19 September 1944.
2   AIR 29/134, *Operations Record Books RAF Regiment Squadrons 2934, 2935, 2941–2943*. The ORB of 2941 Field Squadron gives an idea of the number of men that could be away on training courses at any one time. During October 1944 there were three NCOs on a Warrant Officers' course at the RAF Regiment Depot; three junior NCOs and one LAC on a mortar course at Forward Echelon Agartala; two LACs on a signallers' course at RAF

Station Tulihal; one LAC on an administration course and a complete flight at the AFV Domestic School at Agartala.

3   ibid.

4   AWM 173 4/13 Official Press Note Com/236, 5 November 1944.

5   ibid., Flying Officer Barnes was not only to gain mention in his role as a patrol leader. The chronicler of the unit ORB noted that he had also produced a unit concert called 'Pukka Gen' in his role as Entertainments Officer prior to leaving Tulihal. This had been presented more than five times that month, not only to his own squadron, but to a number of other flying, maintenance, admin and Regiment units. The production was 'eminently successful and all performers are to be congratulated on producing what has been described as one of the best shows east of the Brahmaputra'.

6   AIR 29/138, *Operations Record Books RAF Regiment Squadrons 2941–2950, 2953–2955, 2957–2962, 2964, 2966–2970, Appendices Only.* The Operational Report on the attachment of the flight states: 'I cannot understand how we came out of that shelling without casualties.'

7   Anon. *The Eleventh (Kenya) Battalion King's African Rifles 1941 to 1945.* Ranchi, Bihar: Privately published, 1946, pp. 16, 21. The attachment of No 2 Flight of 2941 Field Squadron to the 11th KAR made an impression as it received a significant mention in the Battalion History as follows: 'The battalion now had under command a Flight of RAF Regiment, who had been sent down to get active experience; they got on well with the askari and were a very useful extra platoon. They assisted now in protecting the mules, a number of which had been allotted to the Battalion. When the mist had lifted, shelling began and they had a difficult time with the animals.' And later 'For the next two days the advance continued along the road without incident save the killing of a few Jap stragglers. The road lay along the north bank of the Myittha River, with high ground on the left which had to be cleared, while the Flight of the RAF Regiment moved along the south bank parallel with the battalion's advance.'

8   loc. cit., AIR 29/138. The flight was congratulated for its fine work and for the valuable information gained during the last two days. There were no casualties other than six malaria cases and one man 'ruptured'.

9   Pilot Officer Newton had arrived from the United Kingdom only a few months earlier in a large draft of officers and had joined 2944 Field Squadron during October. LAC Henry Kirk recalls meeting Newton. As Squadron Armourer he was supposed to issue Newton with a Sten gun but instead gave him a Thompson sub machine-gun. During the siege 2944 Field Squadron had acquired a number of these as they were considered to be a more reliable weapon. Henry had obtained them via an old school chum, Lieutenant Brian Beal RASC. Beal was in charge of supply dump at Imphal and had told him the orders were that any weapons he had were to go out immediately to the troops defending the Valley. No signatures were required. Henry sought permission from his squadron CO, George Arnold, and hence the squadron was well endowed with a very efficient jungle weapon. Henry also told Newton it was best he removed his rank slides as the enemy would easily identify him as an officer and pick him off. Everyone in his flight would recognise him so he didn't need to wear rank insignia.

10 LAC Busby was the airman that LAC Henry Kirk and Corporal Hindmarsh had carried down from Nightmare Peak with suspected spinal or cerebral malaria the previous May at Imphal.

11 loc. cit., AIR 29/138.

12 Kirby, S.W. et al. *The War against Japan. The Reconquest of Burma.* Vol. IV. London: HMSO, 1965, p. 156.

13 Less AFV flight at Tamu and No 1 and 2 Flights at Mawlaik and Sittaung on AMES protection, respectively.

14 Under command of Squadron Leaders G.K. Dean and C.M. Lander, respectively.

15 Khera, P. N. and S. N. Prasad, eds. *Reconquest of Burma 1942–45: June 1944–August 1945.* Vol. II, *Official History of the Indian Armed Forces in the Second World War,*

1939–45. New Delhi: Combined Inter-Services Historical Section, India & Pakistan. Orient: Longmans, 1959, pp. 60. 'Tamu bore closer resemblance to hell than to any place on this green earth. When next day the Allied troops set fire to every building that had a corpse in it as the quickest method of cleaning up and disinfecting the town, the picture of Dante's "Inferno" was complete.'

16 AIR 29/136, *Operations Record Books RAF Regiment Squadrons 2944–2959*.

17 This camera is now at the RAF Regiment Museum at RAF Honington, Bury St Edmunds. When Henry came home from the Far East he took the film to be developed at a local chemist. When he went to collect the photographs the proprietor asked how he had come by the film. He told the story of how he had acquired the camera. He was then informed that the film included photographs of Japanese comfort girls, taken by the previous owner. As a consequence the film could not be returned to him and had to be destroyed.

18 This was the pimple that had been the site of Captain Inoue Sukezo's sabotage attempts in July.

19 Jefford, C.G. *The Flying Camels. The History of No. 45 Squadron RAF.* High Wycombe, Bucks: CG Jefford, 1995, pp 283, 506. The Mosquito belonged to 45 Squadron RAF and had just carried out a raid on a military camp at Yeu and suffered an engine failure. The pilot had been able to nurse the aircraft back as far as Yazagyo where the fatal crash occurred.

20 Bickers, R.T. *Ginger Lacey, Fighter Pilot.* London: Pan, 1969 (1962), p. 153.

21 On 18 August 1944 Cyril Paskin and 4417 AA Flight had departed Kumbhirgram for Secunderabad, having been stationed there for nearly a year. The flight now only consisted of one NCO and nineteen airmen out of an establishment of thirty-six.

22 Kirby, S.W., et al., op. cit., p. 160.

CHAPTER SIX

The Arakan Monsoon and After

'Flying Officer Mitchell displayed great courage in accomplishing an extremely difficult and hazardous task. His conduct definitely influenced the situation . . . .'
Company Commander, 6th Ox and Bucks Light Infantry

The monsoon had broken on 15 June 1944, a few weeks later than expected, however, it did so with extreme ferocity. There had been 50 inches of rain in July and over six inches fell in a single day on a number of occasions. In the Arakan, activity of a military nature other than patrolling slowed as men struggled to simply cope with living under the incessant rain, the humidity and the mud, not to mention the insects and leeches and the increased incidence of life-threatening tropical diseases such as malaria and dengue fever. In addition, the enemy was still close by, albeit reduced to a bare minimum of troops in forward positions. Regular patrolling was necessary to ensure the men had not occupied any tactical feature that would make the 25th Indian Division's own positions unsound or to check whether there were any signs of a new enemy offensive.

With the monsoon halting most air activity, the AA flights had withdrawn to the all-weather strips in the north Arakan and south Bengal (Map 2). At the end of April there had been two field squadrons and thirty-three AA flights with 224 Group. However, with the implementation of the 'second reorganisation' by September 1944 only two field squadrons, 2942 at Maungdaw and 2946 at Chittagong, remained.

Those AA flights that had not returned to Secunderabad had been ordered to merge with the SEAC squadrons deployed with 224 Group. Their place in the order of battle was gradually taken in the second half of the year by the newly formed 2966 and 2967 Field, and 2958[1] and 2959 LAA Squadrons. 2959 LAA Squadron assumed part of the AA defence of the airfield at Cox's Bazaar, where 224 Group had its Advanced HQ.

The most forward representatives of the RAF Regiment in Arakan until November were the airmen of 2942 Field Squadron. They had remained at Maungdaw since April, a town situated behind the mud and mangroves along the Naf River, in bamboo bashas and in prepared positions. As well as their AMES protection duties, the airmen were also involved in routine patrolling and air-sea rescue work as the following report describes:

10 September. A Spitfire reported crashed on St Martin's Island south of Teknaf. Squadron CO Squadron Leader E.M. John, Squadron Leader Hay, Flying Officer A.I. Mitchell and three armed guards from the unit leave by IWT launch as search party. The first map reference given proves wrong, but another Spitfire circling over St Martin's Island well to the south leads the

party to that location where they encounter a Royal Indian Navy patrol boat. The naval launch puts off a dinghy, but the current and the rocks delay the landing so Squadron Leader Hay swims ashore 600 yards. The pilot, Flying Officer Piper of 273 Squadron, is brought off unharmed and the aircraft IFF equipment destroyed. Flying Officer Mitchell and the three guards [Corporal Johnston, LAC Andrews and Birchall] are then landed with 48 hours rations and left as guard party, while the remainder embark on the launch, which owing to the darkness cannot move and so the party returns to Maungdaw at 0800 hours on 11 September. The aircraft is salvageable and orders are awaited regarding arrival of the Recovery & Salvage Unit crew.

12 September. Flying Officer Dankwerts takes relief guard to the island by launch. Guard consists of Sergeant Neave and twelve men with tentage, arms and rations for seven days. Sun and windburn are the main ailment of Flying Officer Mitchell and three guards on return.

13 September. 131 R&SU arrive for salvage job. Arrangements are made for an LCT but delayed due to engine problems.

17 September. Flying Officer Dankwerts, Medical Officer, Warrant Officer Sims, salvage crew, driver and 3-tonner from this unit leave on LCT for Island. Air cover provided by two Spitfires at 0600 hours and 1730 hours over the mouth of the Naf River owing to the military situation near Bolsterhead Beach. Truck landed successfully in running sea and driven to crash site.

21 September. Flying Officer Dankwerts proceeds to St Martin's Island with Lieutenant Moran of IWT on a tug and an LCT. The entire party complete with 3-tonner and salvaged aircraft is embarked successfully at 1100 hours, brought back to Maungdaw at 1330 hours. The salvage crew, 3-tonner and aircraft leave on 22 September en route for 131 R&SU.[2]

The severe monsoon conditions had taken a toll on the health of the troops who were required to endure it and, as a result, many of the Army units were well below strength. The 25th Indian Division was stationed around Maungdaw and 2942 Field Squadron was asked to contribute to infantry patrols to gain experience but also to make up for the Army shortages in personnel. The main activities of the enemy during the monsoon had consisted of raids in the coastal plain south of Maungdaw to seize food and supplies and to forcibly recruit local native labour. During July the airmen had accompanied a patrol of the 16/10th Baluch Regiment but, apart from the severe climatic conditions, they had little to report on their return.

As the weather improved the forward troops of XV Corps and the Japanese *Sakurai Detachment* reoccupied points of tactical importance and patrol activity intensified in readiness for the resumption of the campaign in the dry season. Two sections of 2942 Field Squadron had proceeded on a week's attachment to the 25th Indian Division for battalion duties and patrols, while the crashed aircraft was being dealt with by the detachment on St Martin's Island. A section consisting of Sergeant Clark, two Corporals and ten men went out with the 9th York and Lancaster Regiment to the infamous Tunnels area[3] while the other section, consisting of Sergeant Williams, two Corporals and ten men, went with the 8th York and Lancaster Regiment to the Ngakyedauk area. This section was then relieved by another on 25 September.

On 30 September the latter detachment returned to Maungdaw, where it had carried out numerous patrols. Although the men made no contact with the enemy, from a small hill at the end of the pass they had been able to look across a small valley to where the Japanese were camped. The airmen attached to the 9th York and Lancaster Regiment, however, had a more arduous time. They were out on fighting patrols for most of the time, and in one case for six days, as part of the 25th Indian Division's Operation *Spread*. This operation had been organised to provide estimates of the Japanese strength in the area. The airmen saw the enemy on a number of occasions but had not been able to engage them. The battalion and the airmen had, however, during its patrolling, been able to locate four 75-mm guns, which had subjected them to some shelling. This section stood up so well to the rigours during their time with the York and Lancasters that they happily remained with them for a further week.

On 23 September another section of 2942 Field Squadron was sent out on a week-long attachment to the 6th Oxfordshire and Buckinghamshire Light Infantry (Ox and Bucks), now located in the Chiradan-Godusara area, about 10 miles south-east of Maungdaw. The officer commanding the RAF Regiment detachment this time was one Flying Officer Ian Mitchell, whom we had seen busy a fortnight earlier on the successful search and rescue operation to St Martin's Island. Immediately on their arrival, Mitchell's section was given responsibility for the defence of the Air Dropping Station of the 25th Indian Division. This was where messages and photographs delivered by tactical reconnaissance Hurricanes were collected for immediate despatch to Divisional HQ. In early September the Ox and Bucks had begun a month of inten-sive patrolling. The highest point of Mayu Range, Point 1433, had recently been captured and the new operations aimed to exploit this success with a plan to dominate the coastal plain to the south of this feature. The first operation was planned for 29 September with an attack by 'B' Company on a feature 8 miles south-east of Maungdaw, forming part of the Suniamapara Pimples. The feature was inelegantly known to the attackers as 'South Tit'. The RAF Medical Officer in-charge at Maungdaw, Flight Lieutenant J. B. Fawcitt, was able to provide a report on the events of that day:

On the morning of 29 September 1944, I was present at Battalion HQ of the 6th Oxfordshire and Buckinghamshire Light Infantry and was able to obtain a minute-to-minute appreciation of the action in which Flying Officer Mitchell was involved.

It had been decided to capture a small feature known in the area of the 'South Tit' with a force of rather more than a company, and with artillery, mortar and MMG cover. This was the sole remaining feature occupied by the enemy in that small massif, and it was not anticipated that there would be much opposition. The feature was covered with dense scrub jungle, and was of a precipitous nature.

Flying Officer Mitchell and an orderly were the sole RAF Regiment repre-sentative of the force, and Flying Officer Mitchell transmitted information direct to the battalion command post by a telephone line that was laid as the party climbed the feature. By this means it was possible to obtain a very accu-rate idea of what occurred.

The artillery and mortar barrage commenced at approximately 0930 hours and continued till rather after 1100 hours by which time the assaulting force had reached within a reasonable distance of the summit. It lifted, and the

MMGs on Point 109 put a barrage, first on the top, and then over it. During this time, Flying Officer Mitchell had been giving a résumé over the telephone line of what occurred.

The Company Commander and a Corporal reached the summit and disappeared over the top; there was the sound of grenades bursting and LMG fire, and the Company Commander and the NCO did not return. The Company retired to re-form about 80 yards below the summit and Flying Officer Mitchell asked the Colonel Commanding the Battalion who was in the Command Post, if he should take over the command of the Company and continue the assault. The Colonel agreed to this, and Flying Officer Mitchell took over at approximately 1200 hours.

When the Company had re-formed he sent out two recce parties, one to each flank of the feature, and awaited their reports. He also arranged for the final advance to be covered by MMG fire from Point 109. The recce parties returned, and the final advance to the top took place at approximately 1230 hours. There was no enemy opposition, but a bunker was found about 12 feet below the summit on the reverse slope. Flying Officer Mitchell then consolidated the position, and remained there until the platoon that was to occupy the feature arrived. The body of the company commander was found just over the summit.[4]

The Colonel expressed considerable satisfaction in the manner in which Flying Officer Mitchell had handled a situation of which he had no previous experience, and which was far from simple.

On 2 October Flying Officer Mitchell was again in the thick of the action. The platoon patrol of about eighteen men, including a mortar section, was sent out at about 0200 hours under command of Lieutenant A.E.B. Pope. At 0600 hours the patrol reached a feature overlooking the Ton Chaung to observe the enemy lines of communication. The country surrounding the hill features was very thick scrub jungle with visibility of about 40 yards, not paddy as the map had led them to believe. Splitting into two groups, one was to cover the position on the hill and it was this group that had the platoon commander and Flying Officer Mitchell and LAC Tom Collier. The patrol was unaware at this stage how many of the enemy were on the feature, however, over the next few hours they observed many Japanese and 'Jifs'.

Two 'Jifs' were seen by the patrol and in attempting to capture them one was killed and the other wounded by a grenade thrown by Flying Officer Mitchell. The enemy were alerted to their presence and they were subjected to intense bombardment by mortars and MMG fire. The enemy also put in several attacks, some getting within four yards of the patrol positions. More Japanese appeared from the east and north-east and a fire-fight ensued until 1300 hours, causing two casualties to the patrol. Over the next two hours four attacks of about thirty Japanese and 'Jifs' were repelled with LMG fire and grenades. The last attack was accompanied by shouts calling on the patrol to surrender. The situation became serious, as reinforcements were not forthcoming. The Company Commander continues the description of the ensuing action:

On 2 October, Flying Officer Mitchell took part in the Battle of the Pimple. At about 1300 hours when the situation was extremely serious, Lieutenant A. E. B. Pope ordered Corporal Maidment to reconnoitre a route for one man to get back to base with information. Corporal Maidment reported that he could find no escape route as the position appeared to be completely surrounded by enemy.

Flying Officer Mitchell at once volunteered to go off alone. [He removed all his equipment and started crawling down the slope; when he saw two Japanese crawling towards him. He turned back to warn his party.] He then crossed an open piece of ground and was fired on but reached a small chaung safely [where he lay with his camouflage veil over him]. The enemy spotted him, fired and missed, and came after him. Flying Officer Mitchell again dashed for further cover, while under fire. He contacted 'V' Force who guided him to Thayegonbaung where I met him myself as I'd had information from villagers that he was on his way back. This information enabled me to arrange artillery support and bring down the reinforcement platoon, which helped to withdraw the covering section.

Flying Officer Mitchell displayed great courage in accomplishing an extremely difficult and hazardous task. His conduct definitely influenced the situation and if the patrol had not been able to withdraw after his departure it would have made an enormous difference, as no information had been received from the patrol all day.

LAC Tom Collier, who had accompanying Flying Officer Mitchell on the ill-fated patrol, was last seen crawling off into the bush with wounds to his legs. He continues:

We had been under fire for some considerable time . . . I was lying next to the Ox and Bucks officer. After 'Mitch' left one of the lads got badly wounded in the chest and we had some minor casualties. It was when they got near enough to throw grenades, one of which effectively cancelled out my walking and shattered the officer's heel that the cry came, 'Every man for himself!' There was a dash and hope for safety, but unfortunately I couldn't follow them, nor could the lad who was wounded in the chest. Thinking back now it seems quite strange, but I actually sat down, took my field dressing out and tried to look after my wounds. They were unfortunately too extensive, and I suddenly realised that apart from the two of us we were on our own. Any minute the Japs would be here, so I crawled into what I thought was enough cover to hide me. I had only just got out of sight when the Japs arrived and saw the other lad who was wounded. They finished him off and then proceeded to jump on him. They stopped within five yards of me and discovered my discarded field dressing, nattered away for several minutes, then left in chase of the others. I heard sporadic gunfire for the next ten minutes and then silence for about a half hour. I reckoned 'Mad Mitch' must have got back to Battalion HQ because the hill became subject to gunfire for about ten minutes. I thought, 'What a way to go,' but luckily it was all around me and not near enough to harm me.

I lay where I was till dark and then crawled up to the summit of the hill, down the other side and finished up in a chaung. That night it rained heavily and I never felt so miserable. By dawn the following morning the realisation that I was exposed made me crawl along the chaung into a paddy field with about six inches of water in the bottom, and eighteen-inch stalks above which provided shelter. Occasionally I would pop my head up to get my bearings and found that there was a village called Suniamapara about a quarter of a mile away. I managed to crawl my way there by dusk and had to get across a nine-inch plank, which spanned the chaung. I then hid under the bushes until I realised I had to have a drink, so I crawled out again and found some water lodged between the stones, then had a 'pani' booze up.

It must have been 2100 hours or thereabouts, when I thought I was done for, when two natives came to me and motioned to be silent. They said they would come back later. This they did, and they took me and positioned me in what can only be termed an outside plot. Contrary to what may have been said I was never hidden in a hut. It would have been too dangerous as their village was constantly patrolled. I lay there for over twenty-four hours and during this period the flies had got to wounds that were crawling with maggots. Some time later I was told that this probably saved my leg from gangrene. The following night they decided to move me, and I was carried some three or four miles to the river, put in a boat and covered with leaves. We paddled for God knows how far and then we ran into 'V' Force who advised where to go for help. We eventually arrived on some mud banks at about 0500 hours, shouted our lungs out, and I some time later arrived at the Casualty Clearing Station. By this time I was pretty far gone, but I will always remember an officer coming along who played hell with his staff because they had left me on a stretcher spreading maggots on his nice clean floor.

Two medical officers, one RAF and one Army, disagreed on what should be done with my leg. The RAF officer wanted to amputate, the Army one didn't. Thank God the latter was the senior officer.

I can't say I remember very much about 56th Field Ambulance. I know I was pretty sick with the wounds and malaria. I can say, what really jerked me around in there was the thin-faced York and Lancaster's Padre who came along and said 'Would you mind if I say a few prayers over your bed?' That was a real shocker, and I think from that moment I got better.

From the 56th Field Ambulance I went to hospitals at Cox's Bazaar, Comilla, Chittagong, Madras and Secunderabad. Thence to Bombay and from there invalided home to the UK. On arrival I was put in hospital in Winslow

Squadron Leader A.I. Mitchell MC (right) marches with 2942 Field Squadron at the Victory Parade at Rangoon, 15 June 1945. (Air Historical Branch RAF Crown Copyright)

before going to rehabilitation centres at Chessington and Loughborough. My final move was to Uxbridge where I was invalided out of the service.

After nearly nine months at Maungdaw 2942 Field Squadron was deservedly relieved from its monsoon duties and returned to the Depot for rest, retraining and reinforcement. For his actions the CO of the 6th Oxfordshire and Buckinghamshire Light Infantry recommended Mitchell[5] for the immediate award of the Military Cross. A highlight of the squadron's stay at Secunderabad was a parade on 19 December where Flying Officer Mitchell received his Military Cross, the only award for bravery received by an officer of the RAF Regiment in the Burma campaign.

During October 2946 Field Squadron had moved from Chittagong to Hathazari where better training facilities were available, but was to move by road via Agartala and Imphal to the Central Front during January. Airfield defence training was speeded up and additional Station Defence Instructors were posted to 224 Group to ensure large numbers of station personnel could be trained and readied for the coming offensive. Further effects of the 'third reorganisation' began to be felt in October with the formation of 1326 and 1327 Wing HQs. 1326 Wing was installed at Maungdaw and by November controlled seven squadrons at Dohazari, Cox's Bazaar, Jalia (13 miles south of Ramu) and Maungdaw (Map 2). With the campaigning season approaching Mountbatten toured his command, landing at Cox's Bazaar where he met and talked with Air Commodore The Earl of Bandon OC 224 Group and General Christison of XV Corps.[6] Bandon mounted a guard of the RAF Regiment for Mountbatten, who berated him in a kind way for such excessive enthusiasm.[7]

1327 Wing was to become the specialist Combined Operations Wing, and came under the command of Wing Commander G.S. Airey on 11 October at Chittagong. It moved a few miles south to the coastal village of Patenga during December to train and prepare for the amphibious landings on Akyab and Ramree Islands.

A further Wing HQ, 1308, arrived from the United Kingdom in early December, having previously been withdrawn from France on its disbandment in September 1944. It had reformed at Stoney Cross in the New Forest, under Wing Commander O.A. Guggenheim and had then proceeded overseas on 2 November. After arriving at the

A guard of the RAF Regiment marches past Lord Louis Mountbatten's aircraft 'Sister Ann' during an inspection tour of Bengal and the Arakan, September 1944. (Air Historical Branch RAF Crown Copyright)

RAF Regiment Depot Secunderabad in early December, it was sent to Forward Echelon Agartala for only five days' jungle training. There the Wing HQ was kitted up, given transport and ordered south on 2 January to take control of the five squadrons now defending the airstrips around Cox's Bazaar and as far south as Indin on the Mayu Peninsula.

2945 Field Squadron had been stationed at Feni airfield in Bengal following the return in April 1944 from their successful AMES protection role on St Martin's Island, which, however, had ended sadly with the death of one of their comrades. An AFV flight had been formed in early January 1944 but it was not taken to St Martin's Island. On 27 July 1944, while at Feni, three airmen of 2945 Field Squadron were to be involved in a horrific accident with one of the AFVs. The airmen were working on two AFVs, which had stood for some time in a pen under a thatched roof supported on poles. Access to the engine was by thick steel plate doors. While attempting to start the engine a faulty auto-vac pump sprayed fuel over the three airmen, which a spark from a battery then ignited. Corporal Keith Newey, the motor fitter attached to 2945 Field Squadron, aged 22 years, LAC Gordon E. Drain, 22 years, and LAC David Cook, 23 years, were all seriously burned. LAC George Bishop saw the accident and ran under the blazing roof, attached a tow rope and steered the vehicle out. The seriously burnt men were treated by the unit Medical Orderly, Albert Jones, before being transferred to Myanmati Hospital, near Comilla. Unfortunately, all three were to die within a few days from their injuries.

The AFV flight was later despatched to Chittagong to provide airfield defence. However, in mid-November, 2945 Field Squadron received orders to move forward from Feni to Maungdaw where, along with 2706 LAA Squadron, it was to relieve 2942. After a settling in period, regular patrols were instituted to the east and between 14 and 23 December each flight of the squadron moved on foot from Ngakyedauk Pass to Point 1619, one of the highest points on the Mayu Range.

The third Arakan campaigning season for XV Corps and 224 Group opened on 12 December. The first objective, under the code name Operation *Romulus*, was to clear the northern Arakan and Mayu Peninsula of the enemy and then advance south to Foul Point. It will be recalled that previous attempts in early 1943 to capture the strongpoints on the peninsula had ended in disaster for the attackers. The final Arakan offensive, however, proceeded with much greater speed than previously and by the end of December Donbaik[8] and Rathedaung had fallen and the operation was some fourteen days

LAC William Lewis and Corporal Joseph Bracchi cleaning and oiling a Bren gun outside the Armoury of the RAF Regiment camp at Maungdaw, December 1944. (Air Historical Branch RAF Crown Copyright)

ahead of schedule. The successes of the 25th Indian Division had been considerably aided this time by the advance of the 81st West African Division down the Kaladan Valley to the east.[9] The Japanese rapidly withdrew their forces to avoid envelopment and moved them to the southern Arakan to a firmer base.

The Allies now occupied the southern tip of the Mayu Peninsula and the next step was a combined operation to capture Akyab, now only 6 miles across the water. XV Corps now set about preparing for the first operation of this kind to be undertaken in SEAC. Knowing the value of Akyab airfield to the Allies, it was thought the enemy would hold it in strength, however, this was soon found not to be the case.

In preparation for the coming campaign, the LAA and field squadrons of the RAF Regiment were busy training and equipping for imminent moves to forward airfields. Colin Kirby describes the activities of 2966 Field Squadron as it prepared for its first action as a field squadron:

On 8 December we left for a new camp on the coast, near the port of Chittagong and just north of the Burma border. The Squadron was told that it was to train for Combined Operations before taking part in the assault on Burma from the sea. We had acquired some young new officers, and 'D' Flight now had Flying Officer Kocher in-charge . . . It was refreshing to be away from the jungle, paddy fields and the like, and on the first day we went for a swim in the sea.

On 11 December I was ordered to attend a course on mines and booby traps. How much more military knowledge was I expected to accumulate? A few of us attended daily along the coast at the Mines School where we were shown the different types of Japanese mines, how they worked, how to dismantle them etc, in the lecture room. Then began the business of how to deal with them. Also all the cunning booby traps that the Japs could leave behind. We scrabbled about on the sand prodding with bayonets until one unearthed a mine and disarmed it under the eyes of an expert. On my first attempt the instructor watched me for a moment and then said quietly, 'Corporal, you have just blown the two of us to smithereens.' I note that on 15 December I gave a lecture to the others on the Japanese mine Mark V. The following day we had a written test, which I passed, and returned to the Squadron with yet another string to my bow.

For the first time since its formation, SEAC finally had enough landing craft[10] and naval forces to contemplate an amphibious landing on the Arakan coast. The training methods were still relatively primitive and there was little scope for exercises with the real equipment before the landings were undertaken. Colin Kirby describes his squadron's initiation into the means and methods of combined operations:

On 18 December the whole Squadron practised embarking on mock landing craft, learning how to put a lot of equipment and vehicles into not very much space. It was quite hectic, and not without its humorous moments. The following night, just to remind us that all this was a serious business, the Japs delivered a heavy air raid on Chittagong, and the roads were choked with the populace scurrying out of the place. Between then and the year's end I note that I gave lectures on firing orders, Bren gun, passed on some mine knowledge, went over the assault course, attended lectures by an Army Captain and a Naval Officer about Combined Operations.

One night we practised on the mock landing craft rigged up on the sea shore, so that everybody got some idea of what the real thing would be like, with water up to the waist and vehicles churning though the sand and water. It was a dark night, which did not help, and the few torches were inadequate. 'We'll never get started to invade anywhere,' was the general rueful opinion.

New Year's Day 1945. We trained on insulating vehicle engines and equipment and drove the lorries through a long tank of water. It was a strange sensation driving with water almost up to the shoulders, looking out over an expanse of water. On 5 January there was torrential rain and our camp was swamped. On 6 January we were issued with mosquito repellent, sterilising pills, field dressings and, for those with a watch a condom to wrap it in. That night there was a hurricane, and the tents were blown over and belongings scattered.

The severe weather in early January that struck the domestic site of 2966 Field Squadron was to wreak considerable havoc on an important operation occurring at that same time many miles further south. With Akyab Island appearing to be only lightly held, it was decided to send a force to establish an AMES on Oyster Island, located off the southern tip of the Mayu Peninsula, 15 miles to the west of Akyab (Map 2). 2706 LAA Squadron had been ensconced at Maungdaw since arriving from the Depot in mid-November, when it received orders to send 'C' Flight north to Patenga. Arriving on 21 December 1944 and after receiving ten days' training in amphibious operations, gun drill and field craft, 'C' Flight learnt it was to provide AA and ground defence to a radar unit on the island and a radar barge to be anchored off shore. The Flight Commander, Flying Officer G. Leslie-Carter, was given little information about the island and could not be told whether or not it was occupied by the enemy. He, therefore, constituted an assault group should his small force find opposition on landing.

With the speed of the XV Corps advance down the Mayu Peninsula the operation was brought forward fourteen days. Thus, on 1 January, 'C' Flight proceeded by sea from Chittagong. Unfortunately, the mode of transport allocated was a rather precarious flat-topped wooden lighter, which would be towed to the island by the corvette HMIS *Bihar*. In calm waters this would not have been as great a problem, but in heavy weather it was likely to become unseaworthy, and possibly life-threatening. This wasn't helped by the lack of provision of life jackets for the airmen, adequate medical supplies or sufficient rations! In a bizarre twist the Flight Commander was given a map reference on the island as to where medical supplies could be obtained. In his report he notes with some humour:

> As, however, I had no maps issued to me, or means of communication indicated to me, it is presumed that all casualties had to swim three miles to mainland and then ask the nearest MP where the No 9's [field dressings] were!![11]

Following the *rendezvous* with HMIS *Bihar*, Leslie-Carter in consultation with its Captain, decided to transfer most of the guns and airmen onto the *Bihar* itself. Four Hispanos were placed where they could be brought into action if necessary, the remaining two with ammunition and equipment stayed on the lighter. The barge proved difficult to tow and it was soon brought alongside. At this point three naval cruisers passed at high speed and their wash caused the lighter to roll heavily against the side of the *Bihar*. Much of the equipment was thrown overboard, along with an airman who was a non-swimmer. Horrifyingly, he fell between the lighter and the corvette's side. But for the bravery of an LAC from the radar unit who dived in and pulled him clear, he would have been crushed between the two.

Returning to Chittagong, repairs and some recoveries were made and the force again readied to move off. This time all the guns had been loaded on the *Bihar* and they departed with an LCM towing the radar barge on 4 January. A second LCM was left anchored in the Naf River mouth. On arrival near the island, air photos of the island were suddenly produced by the officer in charge of the radar detachment, and Leslie-Carter was finally able to determine a suitable landing site. The island was approached under lighting generated by star shells fired from the *Bihar*. All was not well, however, as on the night of 5 January the weather deteriorated and when dawn broke it was found that in the heavy seas the radar barge been abandoned and was dragging its anchor. The *Bihar* attempted to take the barge in tow, which was by now listing heavily to port, and this was successfully achieved mainly through the gallant efforts of two Royal Indian Navy officers. At this time the seas were heavy and there were fierce squalls of wind and rain. At one point a number of water spouts formed and one came dangerously close to the *Bihar*. The Hispanos of the Regiment, along with the Oerlikons and Lewis guns on the *Bihar*, were brought to bear on it and it fortunately collapsed.

The usual January chota monsoon lasted only a few days. However, not before the LCM had sunk. The radar equipment on the barge was so badly damaged that it was unable to function and thus it was returned along with its crew to the Naf River. Credit must be given to the supreme seamanship on the part of Navy officers aboard the HMIS *Bihar* who enabled the radar barge to reach harbour.

The adventure was not yet over as the HMIS *Bihar*, with 'C' Flight on board and

A Hispano 20-mm gun manned and ready for action on an airstrip in the Arakan. (Air Historical Branch RAF Crown Copyright)

the radar barge in tow, was ordered south to Akyab Island. On 9 January at 1330 hours they entered Akyab harbour only to be greeted by an air raid by about six Japanese 'Oscars', which were attacking the shipping in the harbour. Unfortunately the range was too great for the Regiment's Hispanos to be of use, but the *Bihar's* 12-pounder gun was able to join in. A Sea Otter amphibious aircraft was seen attempting to take off during the attack but was shot down, crash-landing in flames on the beach.

Flying Officer G. Leslie-Carter was able to report his full complement of gunners and his guns were available for the AA protection of the airfield. To his disappointment, on contacting Akyab airstrip for orders he was initially told to return to Maungdaw, from whence 'C' Flight had come only a few weeks earlier. These orders were soon rescinded and on 11 January all guns and men were taken off the *Bihar* into landing craft and 'C' Flight was ordered into action on the airstrip. Further obstacles were surmounted when it was found that the near-ruined and unstable jetty was some eight feet above the landing craft. The guns were unloaded by hand with some difficulty and completed in darkness. Staying in ruined buildings for the night, the men proceeded to the airfield at dawn. Four guns were loaded on transport, while the other two were manhandled. By midday the Hispanos were in place and ready for action, despite the absence of equipment lost overboard from the lighter. By the next day a complete telephone system was in place and an early warning line was in operation by afternoon of the following day. The last and most optimistic word on this troubled operation is best left to Flying Officer Leslie-Carter, who wrote in the conclusion of his report:

> All personnel are fit and well . . . No disciplinary action had to be taken and all ranks behaved magnificently through a very unpleasant experience.
>
> I should like to take this opportunity of expressing my gratitude to Lieutenant Vandnell [Royal Indian Navy] and his crew, who at all times gave whatever assistance was possible. It was entirely due to his own conviction and courage of his two officers, Sub-Lieutenants Brown and Phillips, that the valuable radar barge was saved.
>
> Concluding, I would like to say that an operation of this nature must be carefully planned for its success and that all parties must have the opportunity for close liaison at the outset. Obviously there had been little, or no careful thought as to the best method of getting the barge to the island, and the weather conditions involved . . . Despite, however, all the disorganisation and what should in the circumstances been serious results, the adventure was not unpleasant and we all thoroughly enjoyed ourselves.[12]

Notes

1   2958 LAA Squadron did not remain for long with 224 Group and departed for Imphal in early August.

2   AIR 29/134 *Operations Record Books RAF Regiment Squadrons 2934, 2935, 2941–2943*.

3   The Tunnels area had been the scene of much bitter fighting in the previous two dry season's offensive. It was the site of one of only two motorable road crossings of the Mayu Range. The other vital crossing was Ngakyedauk Pass, referred to by many British troops as 'Okeydoke Pass'.

4   The Lance-Corporal was wounded by grenade fragments and threw himself down the hillside. The body of the Company Commander was brought back by Mitchell.

5   Flying Officer Angus Ian 'Mad Mitch' Mitchell was 23 years old when he received his MC. He had enlisted in the RAF in March 1941 and was posted to India in December 1942. He joined 2942 Field Squadron in September 1943 and remained with them until March 1946.

His saw post-war service with the RAF Iraq Levies, and with the Regiment in the United Kingdom, Germany and Cyprus. He joined the retired list in 1961. George Briggs who served in his flight described Mitchell as a tall, well-built man and a perfect example of officer material. I found him to be a fair and very able officer.

6   Since July 1944, 224 Group RAF had been under the command of the extrovert, unorthodox but delightful and charismatic Air Commodore (later Air Vice-Marshal), The Earl of Bandon (1904–1979). Paddy Bandon was affectionately known as 'The Abandoned Earl'.

7   Ziegler, P. ed. *Personal Diary of Admiral the Lord Louis Mountbatten. Supreme Commander, South-East Asia, 1943–1946.* London: Collins, 1988, p. 129.

8   Donbaik fell to 2942 Field Squadron's old friends the 6th Oxfordshire and Buckinghamshire Light Infantry.

9   Hamilton, J.A.L. *War Bush. 81 (West African) Division in Burma, 1943–1945.* Wilby, Norwich: Michael Russell, 2001, p.241.

10   Although adequate numbers of landing craft had been found for these operations, some had been rejected as being too old and worn out to be sent for use in the Mediterranean and North-Western European theatres of operations

11   AIR 29/73, *Operations Record Books RAF Regiment Squadrons 2706.*

12   ibid.

CHAPTER SEVEN

To the Irrawaddy Shore

'Infiltration tactics by the Japanese, in country and conditions which had never been experienced in any other major campaign made it vital that the RAF should be self-supporting in defence and the coordination of this defence was becoming a serious task which only senior officers of the Regiment were trained to perform.'
Operations Record Book, 1323 Wing, RAF Regiment

Lieutenant-General William Slim, the Commander-in-Chief of the Fourteenth Army, wrote of the importance of air supply and ground support in his classic account of the Burma Campaign:

> The fabric of our campaign was woven by the close intermeshing of land and air operations . . . As long as our squadrons, fighter or bomber, could operate from bases within reasonable range of their objectives this flexibility was obvious and marked.[1]

A massive air supply operation would be required if the Fourteenth Army was to re-conquer Burma and reach Rangoon before the monsoon. The further south the Army penetrated into Burma, the longer the supply lines would become and the greater its dependence on air supply. By January 1945 eleven squadrons of Commando and Dakota transport aircraft of the RAF, RCAF and the USAAF would be available to keep the Fourteenth Army supplied with rations, petrol, oil and lubricants, and ammunition. Moreover, the fighter-bomber squadrons were to be used as flying artillery and would be directed from Visual Control Posts moving with the forward troops. The mountain and jungle phase of the campaign on the Central Front was drawing to a close and the hot and dusty plains of the dry belt of Burma lay before the Fourteenth Army. With the jungle thinning, the aircraft could now see clearly the columns of Japanese and would wreak havoc on them. On the plains of north-central Burma, the armoured and motorised columns were free to range widely and disrupt the Japanese formations. Slim could use his forces in wide sweeping attacks against an enemy without the weapons or mobility to respond effectively.

Slim's original plan, code-named Operation *Capital*, had been to bring the Japanese to battle north of the Irrawaddy River on the Shwebo Plain and defeat them in detail (Map 6). However, as the Army moved forward in December, it had become apparent that the Japanese *15th Army* was rapidly withdrawing and planned to con-solidate south of the Irrawaddy. Slim quickly recast his plan, now renamed 'Extended Capital'. The most daring part was for IV Corps to move undetected down the Myittha valley and then strike across the Irrawaddy in a bold thrust and capture the vital supply and administration centre at Meiktila. To deceive the Japanese as to the real intentions of IV Corps, every effort would be made to convince the enemy that Mandalay, away to the east, was the main objective of the Fourteenth Army. The capture of Burma's second largest city held great political and propaganda value, but Meiktila was of greater military significance.

As part of Slim's new plan IV Corps was ordered to advance south from Kalemyo down the narrow Myittha valley road to Pakokku. The advance would be supported by supplies flown into landing grounds established at 50-mile intervals. To cover the movement the 28th East African Brigade would move ahead of the 7th Indian Division to mislead the enemy into thinking that they were merely an infantry column and that the objective was directly south at Seikpyu. RAF fighters would fly continuous sorties over the Myittha valley to keep the area clear of Japanese reconnaissance aircraft. Strict radio silence was to be kept during the advance and an elaborate deception plan called Operation *Cloak* was implemented, which included fake signals being transmitted to a false IV Corps HQ located well away to the east.

By mid-December 1944 all was in place and the Fourteenth Army and 221 Group, which had formed a joint land/air HQ, were poised on the banks of the Chindwin. The Fourteenth Army would push on to the east to secure the Monywa-Yeu-Shwebo triangle and to establish bridgeheads over the Irrawaddy for the attack on Mandalay from the north. It would advance on a broad front with three infantry divisions that would be heavily dependent on supply dropping by parachute until Japanese airfields could be captured. On New Year's Day 1945 Yeu airstrip was seized by the 2nd Recce Regiment of the 2nd British Division, followed seven days later by Shwebo and Onbauk. The 19th Indian Division established a divisional base at Onbauk in preparation for the crossing

An anti-aircraft gun crew of the RAF Regiment mans its 20-mm Hispano AA cannon during gun drill on a forward airstrip in Burma. The gun crew comprises (from left to right) Corporal W. Corcoran and LACs G.A. Shale, K. Madrall and G. Edgar. The gun pit wall is still in the early stages of construction. (Courtesy Imperial War Musem, London CF 343)

of the Irrawaddy north of Mandalay, which it did so on 11 January. It now prepared to fight off the inevitable determined counterattacks. At the same time the 20th Indian Division had moved south-east through trackless country along the east bank of the Chindwin, and was closing in on Monywa. The airfield at Yeu, which had originally been intended as a fighter airstrip, was turned over to the 2nd British Division on 10 January as it had overrun its fuel and supplies. It was soon found that the capacity of the RAF to support the advance by air drop had been optimistic, despite limited enemy resistance. A fortnight's halt was called to allow time to build up reserves and to concentrate forces before the advance to the Irrawaddy could recommence.

The captured airstrips were, in many instances, threatened by enemy parties, ranging from stragglers and marauding remnants, through to organised battle groups. The protection afforded by the RAF Regiment of the forward airstrips, located only a few miles behind the front line, or radar stations, at times forward of the front line, would be crucial. The LAA squadrons would provide primarily close AA defence of the airstrips in conjunction with the Army LAA batteries, but would also be used for ground defence patrols. In some instances the Hispanos would also provide supporting ground fire against incursions by Japanese troops.

For the Wing HQs and squadrons of the RAF Regiment, January was to be a month of constant movement. For the airmen, however, this served to emphasise that the Fourteenth Army was finally on the offensive and moving forward. The ORB of 1323 Wing HQ clearly articulates the special role that the RAF Regiment would now perform in the reconquest of Burma:

> The Wing was formed at the commencement of the campaign for [the reconquest of] Burma, at a time when the RAF Regiment was a new idea in so far as the Air Command, South-East Asia was concerned, and the operational necessity for local self-contained defence on forward airfields was a paramount concern. Infiltration tactics by the Japanese, in country and conditions which had never been experienced in any other major campaign made it vital that the RAF should be self-supporting in defence and the coordination of this defence was becoming a serious task which only senior officers of the Regiment were trained to perform.[2]

For the first two months of 1945 the advance of the RAF Regiment into Central Burma would be controlled by three Wing HQs (1307, 1323 and 1324), which would be responsible for a total of nine squadrons.[3] The first two field squadrons had arrived as reinforcements from the United Kingdom, but were still undergoing training at Forward Echelon and they would not be ready to take the field until the end of February 1945. Over the next three months the Wing HQs would take the following general paths: 1323 Wing would accompany IV Corps[4] as it made its clandestine way down the Myittha valley, while the remaining two wings would move with XXXIII Indian Corps.[5] 1307 would move in conjunction with 1324 Wing HQ on the west bank of the Irrawaddy north-west of Mandalay for a period, but it would eventually move west to the 20th Indian Division's area and provide protection to the airstrips and AMES around Monywa and Ywadon on the east bank of the Chindwin. From Onbauk, 1324 Wing HQ would follow up the advance of the 2nd British Division from the Shwebo Plain through Sadaung and Ondaw as it approached the key crossing points on the Irrawaddy.

The ORB of 221 Group describes the atmosphere as the RAF columns moved into Central Burma and why the RAF Regiment was an essential participant:

The Burmese night was eerie enough with its many jungle noises from bird and insect without adding further to the atmosphere in lonely areas of sudden shrieks of Japanese patrol parties who made 'jitter' raids on the forces holding the new airfields. Yet this was to be expected with the battle front so near and the enemy still roaming the west bank of the Irrawaddy. Roads leading to and from the airstrips were the happy hunting grounds of Japanese ambush parties and snipers at night. Protection of airstrips was provided [initially] by the Army and the feeling of uneasiness could be appreciated among aircrew and ground staffs at some of the strips around Shwebo and Onbauk, during January, when XXXIII Corps withdrew a company detailed for the protection of these without warning to 221 Group HQ.

In an area where the enemy was still operating, the newly occupied airfields, on this occasion had only small parties of the RAF Regiment to protect them.[6]

The first moves of the RAF Regiment were made in the first week of January by two of the newly formed SEAC squadrons, 2968 Field and 2961 LAA Squadrons. Both moved east through Kalewa to Mutaik and onto Yeu. With the Army advancing rapidly, the RAF had not been able to move the fighter wings forward quickly enough to provide protection to the supply aircraft and airstrips. Taking advantage of this vulnerability, the Japanese Air Force carried out limited and fleeting raids from 6 to 13 January on the forward airstrips. Fortunately most of the raids were ineffective. 2961 LAA Squadron was at Yeu North on 11 January when an armed recce aircraft attempted a hit-and-run raid:

The raid occurred with nil warning at five minutes before dawn stand-to. Following a general circuit of the area a bomb run was made and four anti-personnel bombs and phosphorus incendiary pellets were dropped east of airstrip. 2961 LAA Squadron manned eight HMGs of which six had snap sight of the enemy aircraft and accordingly opened fire. One gun site of two HMGs had a sharp engagement at close range and observed tracer in extremely close vicinity of the enemy aircraft. Subsequently the Squadron received very un-official reports of one enemy aircraft crashing in the Yeu-Shwebo district shortly after the raid, these rumours further declaring that strikes of 20 mm were distinguishable. Efforts to confirm, however, were to no avail.[7]

Despite their lack of success, their prompt action deflected the attacking aircraft from the target, a recently constructed bridge over the Mu River. A few days later a detachment from the same squadron escorted an R&SU party to recover a Japanese 'Oscar 2', which had been reported to have landed almost intact near Myiama.

On 13 January there was a further set back for the advance when a large number of enemy aircraft attacked Shwebo and Onbauk airfields, with four Dakotas being destroyed on the ground at the latter.[8] More effective air cover was urgently required. The short-range Spitfires and Hurricanes were still on the airstrips back in the Kabaw valley and the longer-range Thunderbolts were still flying patrols over central Burma from Imphal and Kumbhirgram. For the next few days only night landings were permitted at Onbauk until the fighter wings, with their RAF Regiment escorts, had been established at the forward airstrips and could provide air cover for the supply transport aircraft and extend their influence over the enemy airfields.

During the second week of January 2944 Field Squadron and two flights of 2958 LAA Squadron moved forward from Taukkyan under command of 1324 Wing. 1307

Wing HQ, with two flights of 2941 Field Squadron and the newly arrived 2963 LAA Squadron, took their place.[9] 1324 Wing HQ and its squadrons moved off during the first two weeks of January, travelling on a fair road north to Kalewa. After crossing the Bailey bridge over the Chindwin, they entered hill country where the roads worsened considerably and progress by motor vehicle was very difficult. Once onto the plain the pace quickened, and the rapid withdrawal of the Japanese was becoming more apparent as most bridges were found, fortunately, to be intact. The Wing HQ was established at Shwebo in a Burmese National School, with an offer of accommodation in the local jail and law courts being declined. Henry Kirk of 2944 Field Squadron recalls the abrupt and refreshing change in the character of the country:

> We left Taukkyan in early January 1945 and moved out onto the Shwebo Plain in central Burma. Lovely countryside, plenty of rice fields and it was good to be in open country again after all that rain and steaming heat of the jungle.

Staying only a few days at Yeu, on 13 January they were sent to Tabingaung, which was to be opened as a fighter airstrip for 906 Wing but was located only 10 miles from the Japanese lines. The airmen were soon joined by 2961 LAA Squadron, which was deployed to provide AA cover to the vulnerable positions on the airstrip, squadron dispersals and the AMES (Sketch Map 6).

While some of the newly captured airstrips could be put to immediate use, others required substantial repairs before they could be used. The ORB of 221 Group describes the attempts at sabotage by the Japanese before their departure:

> The enemy did not hand over his airfields as a present to the RAF but trenched, ditched or booby-trapped them before retirement. Taking over such air bases was no sinecure and called for laborious work by the engineers to put them right. At Tabingaung, trenches 5 feet deep and 6 feet wide were found spaced out on the airstrip. They stretched across the runway from one side to the other making landings impossible. But the taxi strip had been left untouched and this, the fighter squadrons used – dangerously narrow though it was – until the main landing ground had been made serviceable.[10]

More sinister, but fortunately ineffective, contraptions were found at Onbauk:

> . . . the enemy had hurriedly dug a series of large holes right down the centre of the runway and built into them some very amateurish and Heath Robinson-like booby-trap contraptions. They were designed, no doubt, for operation by volunteer parties who remained behind in cover, and consisted of a large bomb in each of the holes with a small pyramid shaped erection over the hole. A string, from which a large brick was suspended, dangled right above the warhead of the bomb, led to the place of secret cover taken up by the saboteur who, at the opportune moment put a light to the string causing the brick to fall on the warhead and detonate the bomb. They were a failure. The bricks, when released, glanced off the side of the bomb and fell into the hole. Then there was always the task of removing the bombs, not the safest of jobs, and then filling in the craters before the strip could be used.[11]

With the Tabingaung airfield secured by the RAF Regiment, 906 (Fighter) Wing, including the Spitfires of 17 Squadron from Taukkyan, flew in on 18/19 January. The

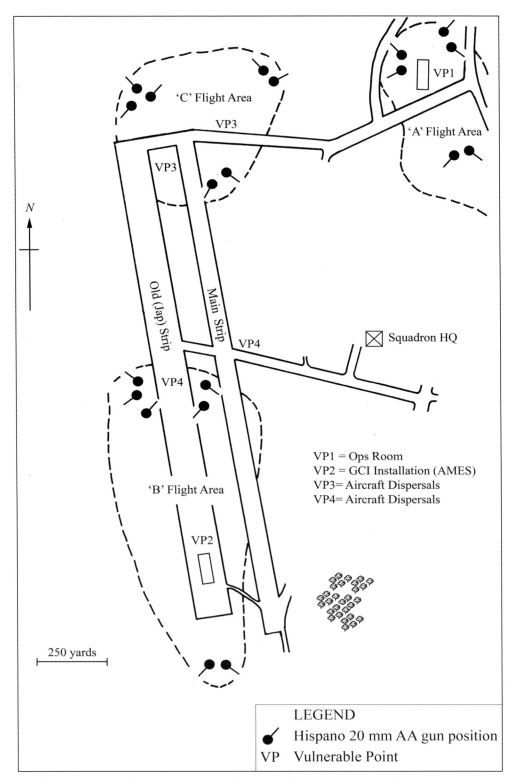

N

'C' Flight Area

VP3

VP3

'A' Flight Area

Old (Jap) Strip

Main Strip

Squadron HQ

VP4

VP4

'B' Flight Area

VP1

VP1 = Ops Room
VP2 = GCI Installation (AMES)
VP3= Aircraft Dispersals
VP4= Aircraft Dispersals

VP2

250 yards

LEGEND

Hispano 20 mm AA gun position

VP   Vulnerable Point

6 *The deployment of 2961 LAA Squadron at Tabingaung airstrip during January 1945.*

The improvised control tower at Tabingaung airstrip near Shwebo. On the airfield, Spitfire VIIIs of 221 Group RAF, flying in support of the Fourteenth Army's operations, await clearance to take off. (Air Historical Branch RAF Crown Copyright)

men were soon busy on air patrols, supporting the advancing troops and making ground attacks on Japanese supply convoys. Their arrival had not gone unnoticed when, during the early hours of 2 February, Tabingaung was raided by a single Japanese 'Lily' reconnaissance plane. At 0450 hours it swept from the east across the airstrip at a very low level and dropped its bombs on the dispersal area of 17 Squadron. The ground erupted in a line of explosions blowing dust, earth and rocks high into the air. The Hispanos of 2961 LAA Squadron had little opportunity to engage as the waning moon and no cloud meant the aircraft was only sighted after it had dropped its bombs. One Hispano of 'C' Flight opened fire and others soon joined in, but no strikes were seen and no hits were observed. Veering to the south-west, the remaining Hispanos on the centre and south of the airstrip fired at the fast-disappearing aircraft. By coming in low the intruder had evaded detection by radar, and the attack had been so sudden it had escaped unharmed. The damage toll had been one valuable Spitfire VIII destroyed and two more damaged.[12]

At the time of the attack a night patrol of 2944 Field Squadron, including LAC Stan Hutchinson,[13] had just returned to the airstrip and was in the 17 Squadron dispersal area amongst the Spitfires when the bombs dropped. One bomb fell in close proximity to the patrol but fortunately it had been dropped too low. The bomb was not activated and simply bounced off the wing of the squadron's CO 'Ginger' Lacey's Spitfire. This softened its fall, and it failed to explode, saving several aircraft from destruction. More importantly, Stan considered himself and the other airmen in the patrol to have been dead lucky not to have been seriously injured or killed.

Further dangers at Tabingaung came from an unexpected quarter in the form of the detachment of Beaufighters from 89 (Night Fighter) Squadron. Stan recalls moving with a night patrol across the runway in pitch darkness when they were forced to throw themselves flat, as a Beaufighter on a take-off run shot over them. Known as 'Whispering Death' by the Japanese because of their silent approach, this was also a problem to the RAF Regiment airmen sharing the airstrip with these aircraft.

The brazen advance of XXXIII Corps had trapped some 5,000 Japanese troops north and west of the Irrawaddy around Onbauk and Shwebo, and they constituted a grave threat to the security of the airstrips. The problem that was now developing was set out by the Supreme Commander:

> The Army was responsible in the first instance for the defence of these forward airfields: which was necessary even in areas some distance from the front, because night raids were frequently made by small parties of Japanese who had not been mopped up. As the battle increased in scope and intensity, however, Lieutenant-General Slim found it impossible to meet his commitment; and airfield defence became a joint responsibility of the Army and the RAF Regiment.[14]

Consequently, the airmen were to encounter parties of the enemy intent on hindering the build up on the airfields. Onbauk airstrip was at particular risk and this remained the case for the next two months. Onbauk had been busy with Dakotas landing and dropping supplies for the 19th Indian Division from 12 to 20 January. The airstrip was then turned over for use as a fighter-bomber airstrip. 2968 Field and 2960 LAA Squadrons were moved there quickly by road prior to the arrival of the fighters. On 14 January 2968 Field Squadron deployed two flights on airfield defence and occupied the well-sited Japanese bunkers. By midday on 16 January, 2960 LAA Squadron HQ and two flights were also deployed on the airstrip with full manning ordered.

The vulnerability of Onbauk was a major concern to the Regiment. Such was the danger of attack that within a week there would be the representatives of six Regiment squadrons, whole or in part, stationed at Onbauk. An incomplete 2941 Field Squadron was ordered forward and HQ and one flight arrived on 17 January. It had a difficult time concentrating for the move and the two dispersed flights would arrive separately. No 1 Flight was still guarding the AMES at Mawlaik, a long way back on the banks of the Chindwin, where the tracks had become impassable due to heavy rains. Following their relief by a flight of 2946 Field Squadron, they had to be evacuated by native boat and travel down the River Chindwin to *rendezvous* with the Squadron HQ at Kalewa before moving to Onbauk. No 2 Flight was at Sittaung even further to the north. They also had difficulty leaving and were ferried out by 15-cwt lorry to Tamu and then travelled independently by 3-tonner to Onbauk. No 1 Flight was dropped off at Yeu where an AMES required protection, while the remainder of the squadron moved through to Onbauk. With the airfield secured, the first Hurribombers of 42 Squadron RAF arrived, along with ground crews in Dakotas.

Some 10 miles to the east, the 19th Indian Division was involved in heavy fighting on the opposite bank of the Irrawaddy. On the morning of 20 January intelligence was received that 500 Japanese had crossed to the west bank of the Irrawaddy, and were only 8 miles from the Onbauk airstrip and further Regiment units were required. Fortuitously 2943 Field Squadron had been relieved of its AMES protection work at Kalemyo and, moving through Yeu, arrived at Onbauk that same day. Ted Daines of 2943 Field Squadron describes the journey and the situation at Onbauk:

At Yeu we did not have time to unpack, arriving in the late afternoon and were told to move the next morning, to Onbauk, an airfield that had fighting still going on around its perimeters, arriving here, to our place in the defence box, the ground trembled underfoot, the noise was incessant, with another I was placed in a recently captured bunker beside a signal unit. I had orders to stay until relieved. Was I happy when the relief came. During the night we lost a Corporal on patrol but gained a prisoner. Told to get my head down for a bit, was a joke, when you laid back you were lifted off the ground every few seconds by the guns. Two days later and very tired and bleary-eyed we noticed that the noise was getting a little further away. Going into Shwebo one day with the ration truck, on leaving the airfield area I noticed many dead Japs lying where they had fallen.

Heavy scrub grew right up to the edge of the airstrip and made it difficult to detect the approach of enemy parties. To allow for clear fields of view, the next few days were spent clearing the scrub for 50 yards around all aircraft dispersals. Full manning was maintained but no incidents were reported. The defence task was further expanded on 22 January when 113 Squadron arrived. The same day a flight of 2958 LAA Squadron arrived and was given a ground defence role. Wing Commander Lander and 1307 Wing HQ and No 2 Flight of 2941 Field Squadron arrived within the next few days, along with the Hurricanes of 34 Squadron.

On 26 January a new warning was received that a party of 150 Japanese had been seen 4 miles south of Onbauk. A captured Japanese operation order was found, giving

Armourers fit rocket-projectiles to Hurricane IVs in a dispersal area at an airfield in central Burma. The problems of defence of the airstrip are apparent with the thick scrub coming right up to the dispersal area. (Air Historical Branch RAF Crown Copyright)

them the task of attacking the airstrip. To assist the RAF Regiment with this threat, a company of the Assam Regiment and two troops of armoured cars from the 11th (Prince Albert Victor's Own) Cavalry arrived and deployed on the airstrip. Standing patrols of eight men each were placed on all tracks within a one-mile radius of the airstrip. At midnight the sounds of grenade explosions and small arms fire were heard to the south. A 'jitter' party of Japanese had attacked an Indian camp located at the entrance to Onbauk airstrip. While no attack occurred on the airstrip itself, explosives were left by the enemy, indicating that the airstrip was the ultimate objective.

The following night the airstrip was subjected to attack from the air at 0355 hours in bright moonlight by a single 'Sally' heavy bomber. In two runs over the fighter squadron dispersals the 'Sally' dropped high-explosive and anti-personnel bombs. A few airmen suffered slight shrapnel wounds and three tents were written off. Disappointingly, for the four nights prior to the air attack the Hispanos of 2960 LAA Squadron had been manned. No AA barrage was put up during the attack however, as that afternoon all guns, including the Army Bofors, had been withdrawn into the harbour due to the threat from Japanese ground patrols in the vicinity. During the second run Sergeant H. McKeown had leapt onto a Hispano and fired at the intruder from the gun harbour. After three rounds the gun jammed, but he immediately grabbed a Bren gun and continued to fire at the receding enemy aircraft. Despite his quick action against the aircraft the Airfield Defence Commander had ordered no firing and disciplinary action was taken against him. When asked for an explanation of his firing, Sergeant McKeown had stated that he couldn't resist firing on such a perfect target.[15]

Sensibly, Wing Commander Whitfield OC 1324 Wing instructed 2960 Squadron to resume moonlight manning of gun posts immediately. Gun posts would also, however, be responsible for protection of aircraft and other installations against sabotage. Some revenge was taken a few nights later on 31 January when another 'Sally' attacked the airstrip at 2105 hours while the flare path was alight. Diving from 2,000 feet and then flattening out at 1,000 feet, the bomber dropped eight bombs, all of which exploded harmlessly in the scrub north of the airstrip. On the second run across the airstrip twenty minutes later twenty-one Hispanos and the six Army Bofors guns were fully manned and ready. The 'Sally' was forced to take evasive action to avoid the AA barrage and hits were observed by the RAF Regiment airmen. This time the aircraft strafed the area occupied by 'C' Flight of 2968 Field Squadron, fortunately causing no casualties.

The threat at Onbauk remained throughout February, however, more Regiment squadrons were due to arrive and the opportunity was taken to redeploy to airstrips further south. These were in closer proximity to the points selected for the crossing of Irrawaddy by the Fourteenth Army. With air superiority and an efficient air transport organisation, it would become common practice for RAF Regiment squadrons to move by air to forward airstrips (Appendix 10). 2945 Field Squadron, which had been under command of 224 Group at Indin on the Mayu Peninsula, was flown in from 1 to 4 February. This allowed 2941 Field Squadron to concentrate at Monywa with 1307 Wing, and for 2968 Field Squadron to move further south:

> . . . the Squadron moved . . . from Indin. On 1 February, a single Dakota arrived at 1120 hours and took half of No 1 Flight with Flight Lieutenant W. le M. Brown in command. From the pilot it was learnt for the first time the squadron's destination. On 2 February an aircraft arrived at 0730 hours, took the remainder of No 1 Flight, and returned at 1130 hours. The pilot reported

that his aircraft was the only aircraft on the job, but even as he spoke another Dakota landed bearing news that yet a third was on its way. Fortunately enough aircraft loads were standing by in 3-tonners, and there was no delay. Aircraft No 1 returned at 1530 hours, so that by the end of the day all three rifle flights had been despatched. The Commanding Officer and Squadron HQ, including the newly formed Bren Support Group, together with one aircraft containing stores were transported, leaving one final load stores to travel the following day.[16]

One of the problems encountered with the moves by air was that squadrons were left without adequate transport and thus lost mobility and independence. Fortunately those arriving first at Onbauk were able to send a message on the return flight as to the paucity of transport and rations and that the nights were much colder than those they had experienced at Indin. Two motorcycles were loaded into the last aircraft, along with tents and a bedroll per man. Squadron Leader Garnett of 2945 Field Squadron assumed the role of Aerodrome Defence Commander at Onbauk and the squadron set about improving the defensive positions, organising patrols and dealing with domestic and transport problems arising from their arrival by air.

To give emphasis to the perils of life on a forward airstrip, on the first night after 2945 Field Squadron's arrival a grenade was thrown while a conference of officers was being held at Battle HQ. Fortunately it exploded on the rim of the dugout without causing any damage, but the assailant was not discovered. Squadron Leader Garnett, compiler of the 2945 Squadron ORB, describes the practical problems of establishing a squadron at an airfield and the steps taken to improve the defences:

The main difficulties of the first few days were a shortage of water so serious that each man was rationed to a water bottle a day for all purposes and a shortage of transport. The first was solved with the assistance of 906 Wing Satellite HQ and the second overcome by the cooperation of 2960 LAA and 2968 Field Squadrons, while a signal [was sent] to the MT party travelling from the Arakan via Imphal to despatch the water bowser in advance of the convoy. A crash guard was mounted (on the night of 11 February) on an aircraft which had overshot the strip.

The remainder of the week was spent organising defended localities around the aircraft dispersals. Weapon pits were dug and brushwood fences built. With the ground covered with dry leaves, silent approach would be difficult. . . Slit trenches were manned throughout the night by three men each, whose tour of duty was one hour on and one hour off. It was found that each flying squadron provided one Corporal and nine men nightly and their task had been a close patrol around the aircraft. This was changed so that each of the nine men was allotted a slit trench and the nine men of the RAF Regiment Squadron thus released took over the patrol, and provided a small mobile reserve under a Regiment Sergeant.[17]

Intelligence reports later in February indicated that Onbauk was still threatened by parties of Japanese intent on aircraft sabotage. The airfield defence now comprised: the newly arrived 2945 Field Squadron and 2968 Field Squadron HQ and 'B' Flight for ground defence, and 2960 LAA Squadron and six Army Bofors for AA defence (Sketch Map 7, Appendix 15). On 2 and 3 March, after four weeks on the road, the convoy of 2945 Field Squadron's motor transport arrived from Indin. The convoy had travelled some 1,430 miles in twenty-six days, with fourteen days of actual driving. Most of the vehicles had already completed 10,000 miles before they started and the performance reflected great credit on the drivers and MT maintenance personnel. The ORB continues:

The task of the Squadron continued to be the close defence of areas where the aircraft of 34 and 113 Squadrons were dispersed at night. These were at the north end of the airstrip in the midst of scrub, which stretched as far as the Irrawaddy nine miles to the east, indefinitely to the north, and for some miles to the south and west. A perimeter fence of brushwood had been built around the dispersal area, and a series of slit trenches were manned by three men each night as listening posts. A patrol of ten men under a Sergeant was maintained close round the aircraft both as an additional safeguard and to provide a mobile reserve inside the perimeter. By this time, the main scene of fighting undertaken by XXXIII Corps had moved 20 or more miles away, and the troops which had been allocated for outer perimeter defence, and for counter attack had been withdrawn. Under these circumstances it was tempting to relax the scale of manning; especially in view of Army assurances that danger was considerably less than it had been a month before, but

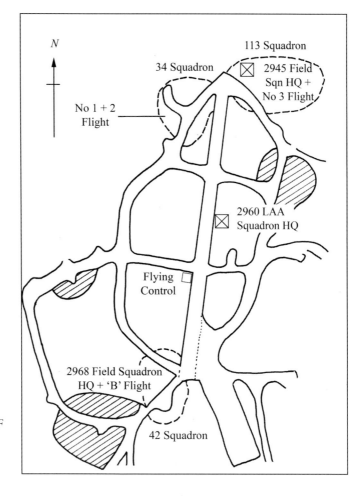

7 *The deployment of RAF Regiment squadrons and flying squadrons at Onbauk in February 1945. (Hatched areas are RAF domestic camps. Dashed lines indicate areas occupied by RAF Regiment squadrons and location of flying squadron dispersals.)*

personal instructions were received from the AOC 221 Group that 100% readiness was to be maintained.[18]

On 4 March a new report was received of a credible threat of ground attack from a Japanese raiding party that had been active 12 miles to the south of the airstrip:

> An enemy operation order had been captured that named Onbauk airstrip as an objective for such raids. Later in the day it was reported that Japanese in numbers which varied in different reports between a score and two hundred, had crossed the River Irrawaddy north of the strip. It was considered possible that an attack would be made on the strip under cover of another air raid. During the day the position was explained to the aircrew and ground staff of the strip, who dug further slit trenches sited with the advice of officers of this squadron.[19]

Events then proceeded at rapid pace:

> At 2000 hours that evening, the Naik on duty at the signal tent attached to the office reported that he had heard voices talking in a language, which he did not recognise. Flying Officer A.M. Terry [of 2945 Field Squadron] was ordered to take out the aircraft patrol of ten men and investigate. The patrol went northward for 400 yards as far as a bullock track, and reported that they heard a bullock cart and the driver shouting, but they had been unable to come up with it.[20]

As predicted the first action came not from the ground but from the air. At 0338 hours one of three 'Betty' twin-engine bombers dived from 2,000 to 700 feet, dropping high-explosive, anti-personnel and phosphorus bombs in and beyond the 42 Squadron dispersal areas, damaging one Hurricane. Despite more than thirteen bombs dropped on the airstrip, the only injury was to Corporal B.D. Johnson of 2960 LAA Squadron. He was struck by a piece of shrapnel from the bombs, which straddled the gun sites of 'B' Flight. One canister containing exploded anti-personnel bombs struck the wing of a 42 Squadron Hurricane and then some of the bombs exploded causing damage to the aircraft. Three 2945 Field Squadron men who were on duty by the edge of the airstrip, were caught with inadequate cover and had a narrow escape. The nearest bomb of a stick that fell within a dozen yards of them was one of the few that were not anti-personnel, and it buried itself too deep to do any harm. The AA barrage went up and tracer indicated the gunners were on target. They continued for one minute after the attack to indicate the direction to a patrolling Beaufighter of 89 Squadron. Grass fires had been started by the incendiaries and the Regiment airmen worked to bring them under control. They were quickly put out but three hours later another 'Betty' dived on the airstrip, dropping more than thirty bombs of various kinds. The first 'run in' destroyed three 906 Wing vehicles and an airmen suffered shrapnel injuries, while the second 'run in' badly cratered the runway rendering it temporarily out of use.

No more activity occurred that night, however, the Army allocated 'Robforce'[21] to provide long-range ground defence for the airstrip and it was now patrolling to the north and east of the airstrip. 34 (Hurricane) Squadron had moved one flight south to another airstrip and this allowed the defence task for 2945 Field Squadron to be contracted to one flight. No 1 Flight under Flying Officer R.A.W. Hollingdale was, therefore, stood down and the airmen were able to get their first full night's sleep for five weeks! This flight was still responsible for providing a mobile force should it be needed.

Matters quietened down until the night of 7/8 March, when at 0135 hours the same Naik in the Signals tent reported to Corporal S. Mallaghan of 2960 LAA Squadron that he had heard whispered voices in the undergrowth adjacent to his gun site. He had then seen a group of men mostly dressed like Burmese creeping into a clearing in the thick scrub. The Naik had challenged but had received no reply (Sketch Map 8):

> Regardless of any danger to his own person, Corporal Mallaghan crawled approximately 100 yards in darkness through the undergrowth to pass information to a Flight Commander of 2945 Field Squadron. Without wasting a moment he returned to his own post by the same route.
>
> On arrival at the gun site he immediately contacted the Squadron Commander, Squadron Leader S.J. Clark, at Battle HQ, by field telephone. The Squadron Commander, ordered Corporal Mallaghan to remain by his post, and warned him to keep a strict watch on the suspected area.[22]

Acting on the report from Corporal Mallaghan, Squadron Leader Garnett immediately ordered Flying Officer Hollingdale to take out his two sections and investigate:

> After a commendably short delay, the patrol moved off at 0150 hours. It proceeded along the track leading north, stopping at frequent intervals to listen. At 0215 hours the scouts discovered a bivouac area, from which a number of men dashed [noisily] off into the thick scrub to the west of the track. One man, however, dressed in Burmese clothes was seized by LAC R.W. Davis. It was now seen that a quantity of kit, including some rifles and two wireless sets, whose presence was given away by their luminous dials, was lying around. Flying Officer Hollingdale decided he must collect this, and return as quickly as possible with his information and prisoner. He therefore sent forward No 2 Section to collect the equipment, covered by No 1 Section.
>
> With this completed, he set off for Squadron Headquarters by a different route. At 0250 hours two grenades were thrown almost simultaneously over the heads of the leading scouts. The first grenade exploded to the east of the patrol and wounded LAC J.C. Bell and LAC G. Armitage, the second on the path at the feet of LAC Davis who was escorting the prisoner, killing him instantaneously. In the interval between the two bursts he was seen to strike the prisoner, who ran forward past the leading scouts. One of these, Corporal K. Drury, fired a burst from his Sten and the man fell. A few minutes later when he was seen to move, the other scout LAC C. Cruse fired a burst of Bren into him, and although the body was not recovered it is considered this man was killed, for in the morning a huge pool of blood was discovered where he had lain. Meanwhile the patrol, had taken up a position of all round protection at the track junction. It was found that the two wounded men were lying about 20 yards away.
>
> Corporal Drury and LAC G. Sutton at once volunteered to go out and collect the casualties. To do this they made two journeys and also verified that LAC Davis was dead. LAC G. Armitage had to be carried as he was badly wounded. Flying Officer Hollingdale had already sent back a runner, LAC W.G. Waters, to report what had happened. He came into the perimeter at an

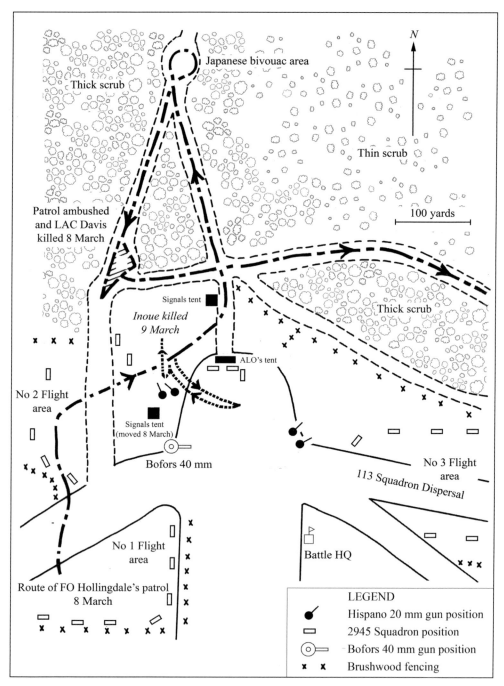

8 *The events at Onbauk airstrip 7–9 March 1945. (The heavy dashed line indicates the path taken by Flying Officer Hollingdale's patrol on the night of 7/8 March and the hatched area indicates the position taken up by the patrol when attacked. The short-dashed line shows the path taken by Inoue in the minutes prior to his death on the night of 8/9 March 1945.)*

unexpected place and failed to hear the challenge so that a grenade was thrown at him, fortunately without doing any harm.

Flying Officer Hollingdale was now in a difficult position. He was uncertain of the strength of the enemy, but estimated them as about twelve. The wireless sets and other equipment were obviously valuable and he had a seriously wounded man. He therefore decided to withdraw along a roundabout route by bounds, each section in turn covering the other. One wireless set had already been smashed against a tree stump, and the other he concealed in the scrub together with the rest of the equipment, which had been collected. He arrived back at 0430 hours without further incident.

It seems probable that when Flying Officer Hollingdale's patrol reached the bivouac area, a sabotage party, had already set out with designs on the aircraft, or for reconnaissance, and that it was this party that made the attack. It seems unlikely that the party which had panicked so badly as to leave all its arms and equipment behind would have laid an ambush between the bivouac and the airstrip in the short time available.

As soon as the action started the ground attack alarm had been given by Flying Officer A.M. Terry of No 2 Flight, and this was taken up by the master Bofors gun, so that the whole station stood-to. An attempt had already been made, as soon as the first report was received, to contact the Suffolks from Battle HQ but the telephone call was passed to a variety of Army formations, and it was not in fact till first light that a platoon arrived. Meanwhile at 0315 hours while the patrol was still out, with no information having yet been received from them, a further movement was reported from the original area. The OC 2945 Field Squadron still ignorant of the enemy's strength moved one flight of 2968 Field Squadron from the south end of the strip to act as reserve.

At first light a fighting patrol consisting of one platoon of the Suffolks and two sections of 2945 Field Squadron were sent out. They recovered all the equipment and while the Squadron brought this back, together with the body of LAC Davis. The Suffolks made a sweep of the area, but without finding anything. In the afternoon they made a wider sweep and found another rifle, two large sacks containing rice and bully beef, which they destroyed.[23]

The activity of this night certainly caused a stir in the higher echelons of the RAF and Army and the airstrip was overrun the following day by senior officers and their followers:

During the day visits were received from Air Vice Marshal Vincent, AOC 221 Group, Group Captain Goddard, Commanding 906 Wing, Wing Commander Mills, Group Defence Officer, Wing Commander Whitfield OC 1324 Wing and assorted others including an RAF Public Relations Officer and Intelligence Officers from Z Force, the Suffolks and Brigade.

All documents, money and maps, of which there were many, were sent at once to Corps HQ. During the day a Burman, who had appeared the day after the air raid was found on the strip again, was arrested, and taken to Shwebo. It was arranged that a platoon of the Suffolks should remain for the night as a mobile reserve at Battle HQ on the strip.[24]

The following night there was an unanticipated sequel to these events. At 0130 hours two men were seen running onto the north end of the airstrip and were fired on by a sentry on a Bofors post. One man appeared to have been hit. The two figures dropped down and then scrambled into the scrub from whence they had come. A few hours later a man appeared from the undergrowth near a gun post of 2960 LAA Squadron:

Whilst on Listening Post by the side of his Hispano gun, in the early hours of Saturday 9 March, LAC Room observed a suspicious movement in the under-growth some distance away.

Remaining quite still, Room kept his eyes trained on the spot and in the grey light observed the figure of a man approaching the gun site. The figure stopped behind a small tree and stood there. Meanwhile Room, as quietly as possible, trained his rifle on the suspect. After about five minutes of tense waiting the suspect moved slowly back towards the undergrowth again. Observing his quarry disappearing he fired a single shot from his rifle, and the figure im-mediately dropped to the ground. Whether or not he was wounded by that shot is not known, but almost immediately a pistol was fired from the spot towards Room.

Laying down his rifle, but making as little noise as possible, Room took up the Bren gun and fired three short bursts at the spot. He was rewarded by hearing groans coming from the area. Immediately afterwards he reported the incident by field telephone to the CO, Squadron Leader S.J. Clark at Battle HQ. The Squadron Commander warned Room to keep quite still, be on the alert, and keep the Bren gun trained on the spot, in case, as so often happens, any Japs returned to recover their dead or wounded. This order Room carried out, watching the spot keenly for approximately three and a half hours, until daylight made it safe to investigate.

These investigations revealed a Jap, dressed as a Burmese, lying dead in the undergrowth, and from papers and kit found on the body it would seem the man had been a Japanese officer.

He carried only an empty pistol and a bag containing personal effects, which included, as had the equipment captured the previous night, a surprising amount of medical stores. It seems possible that this was the Commander of the force, which had lost so much the night before, and that he had returned to the strip with the deliberate intention of being killed, in order to save face. After visits from the OC 'Robforce', Z Force and the Brigade Intelligence Officer, who took away the man's paybook and one or two other items, the body was buried.[25]

It was later confirmed that this was indeed the leader of the sabotage unit and the body identified as that of Captain Inoue Sukezo. The RAF Regiment had met him before but this time circumstances had not been in his favour. He had led the raid in early July 1944 on the Palel airstrip at Imphal, which had damaged seven aircraft.

With severe disruption caused to their operations, one would have thought the saboteurs would call a halt to their mission. Later that night, however, further incur-sions occurred:

During the day, the Suffolks were relieved by a company of Madrassis,[26] with whom contact was established, and arrangements made for them to put out a standing patrol of one section to the north-east of the strip. Z Force agents reported that during the afternoon, three Japanese had entered Myohit, a

1. A dawn attack by airmen of 1307 Wing RAF Regiment during the siege of Meiktila 6-28 March 1945. The painting was commissioned to mark the RAF Regiment's Fiftieth Anniversary in 1992. *(Painting by Michael Turner PGAvA) (Copyright RAF Regiment Fund)*

2. No.8 Staging Post, Meiktila, Burma, May 1945. *(Painting by Frank Wootton OBE)*

3. RAF Mingaladon, Rangoon, May 1945. A Dakota comes in to land through menacing monsoon clouds. In the foreground are a 20-mm Hispano AA gun crew of the RAF Regiment keeping watch. *(Painting by Frank Wootton OBE)*

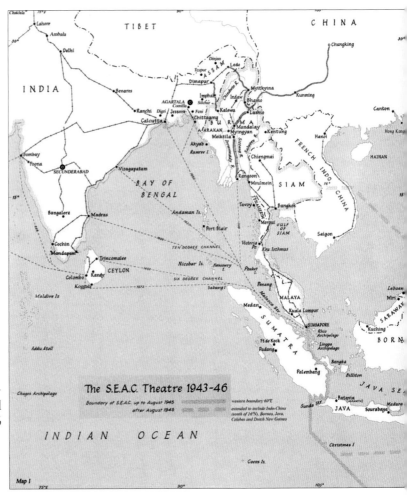

Map 1. The South-East Asia Command Theatre 1943-6

The S.E.A.C. Theatre 1943–46

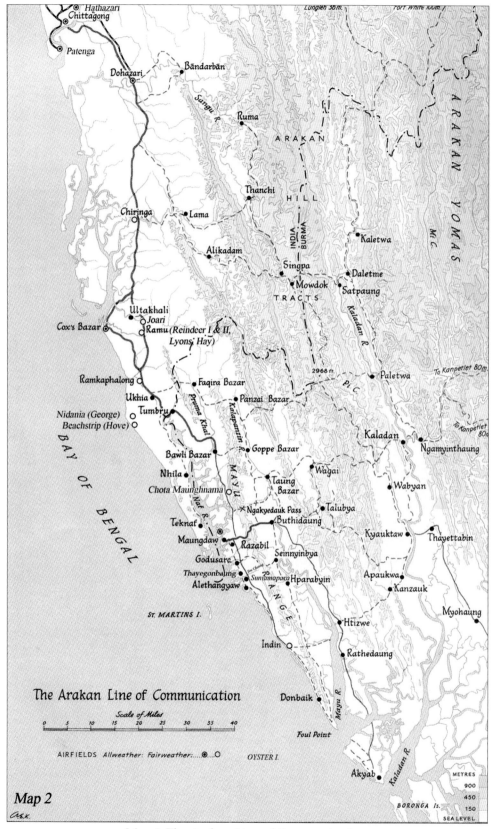

Map 2. The Arakan Line of Communication.

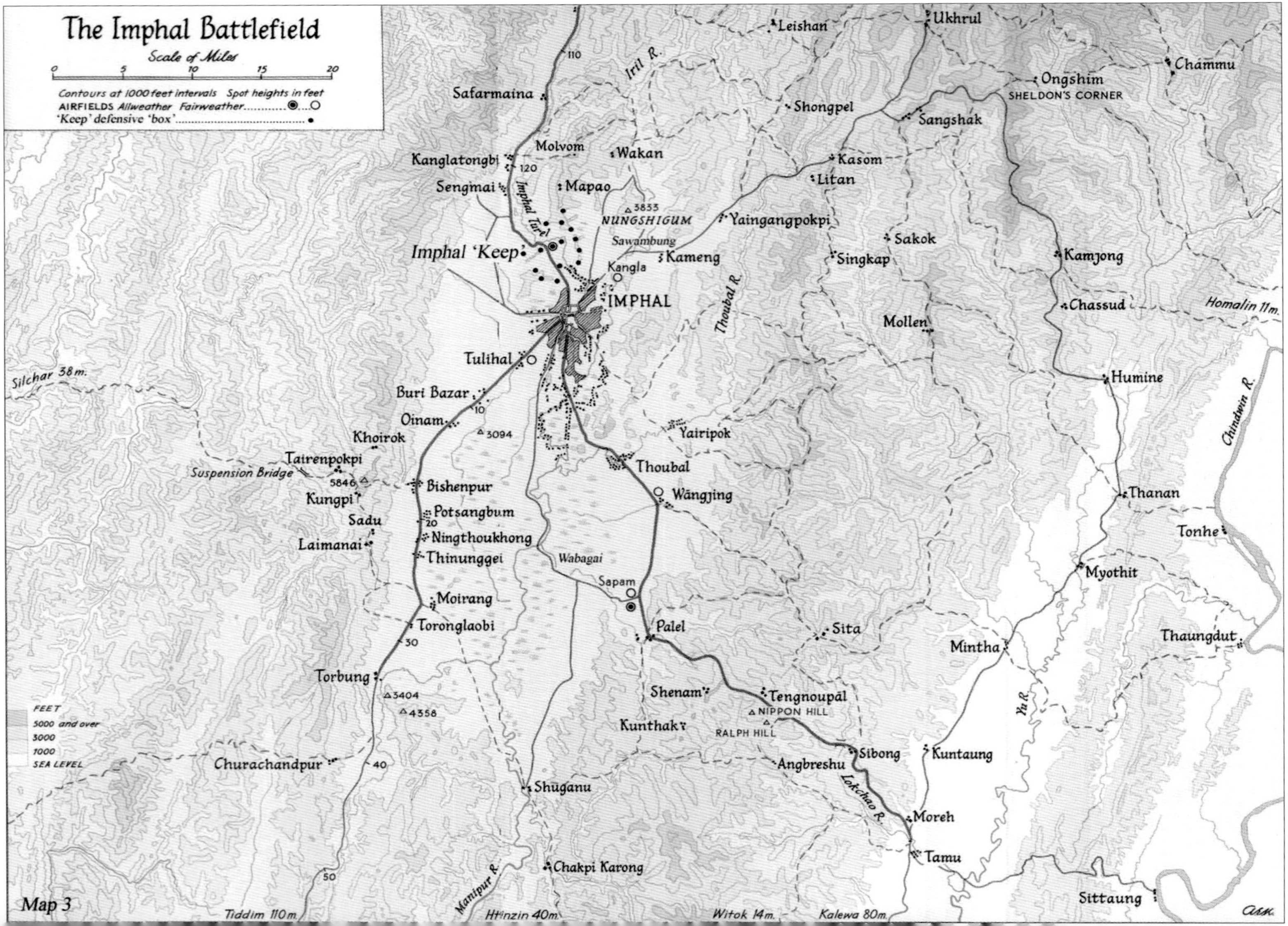

Map 3. The Imphal Battlefield.

The Imphal Battlefield

Scale of Miles

0   5   10   15   20

Contours at 1000 feet intervals   Spot heights in feet

AIRFIELDS All weather.   Fairweather............⊚...O

'Keep' defensive box..............●

Map 3

FEET
5000 and over
3000
1000
SEA LEVEL

Silchar 58 m.

Churachandpur

Suspension Bridge
Tairenpokpi
Kungpi
5846 △
Sadu
Laimanai
Torbung
△ 3404
△ 4356
40
50

Khoirok
Bishenpur
Potsangbum
20
Ningthoukhong
Thinunggei
Moirang
Toronglaobi
30

Buri Bazar
Oinam
△ 3094
10

Tiddim 110 m.

Hrinzin 40 m.

Manipur R.

Shuganu

Chakpi Karong

Kalewa 80 m.

Witok 14 m.

Tamu
Moreh
Sibong
Angbreshu
Lokchao R.
Kuntaung
Mintha

Sittaung

Thaungdut

Myothit
Thanan
Tonhe

Chindwin R.

Homalin 11 m.

Yu R.

Sita
Shenam
Kunthak
△ NIPPON HILL
Tengnoupal
RALPH HILL
Pallel
Sapam
Wahagai
Shugnu

Wangjing
Vairipok
Thoubal

Imphal 'Keep'
Tulihal
IMPHAL
Kangla
Sawombung
△ 3855
NUNGSHIGUM
Mapao
Molvom
120
Kameng
Yaingangpokpi

Imphal Turel
Serngmai
Kanglatongbi
110
Iril R.
Wakan

Safarmaina

Singkap
Sakok
Litan
Kasom
Shongpel
Leishan
Sangshak
Ulkhrul

Molku
Moller
Thoubal R.

Kamjong
Chassud
Humine
Sheldon's Corner
Ongshim
Chammu

Qak.

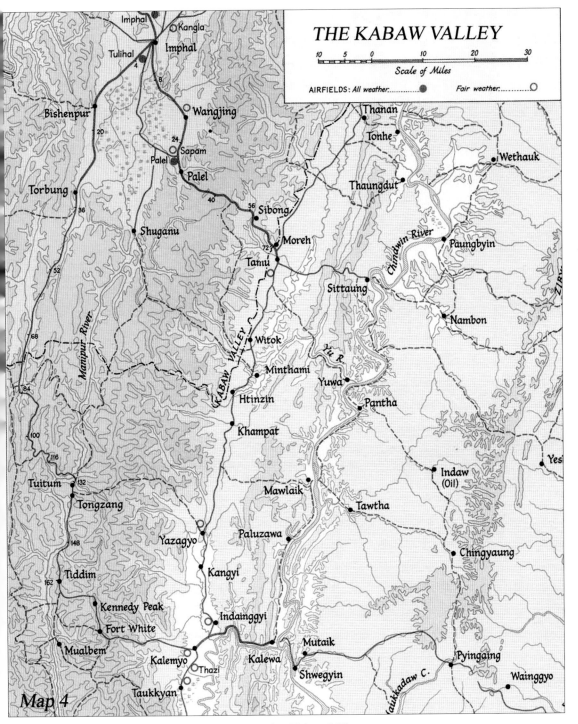

Map 4. The Kabaw Valley

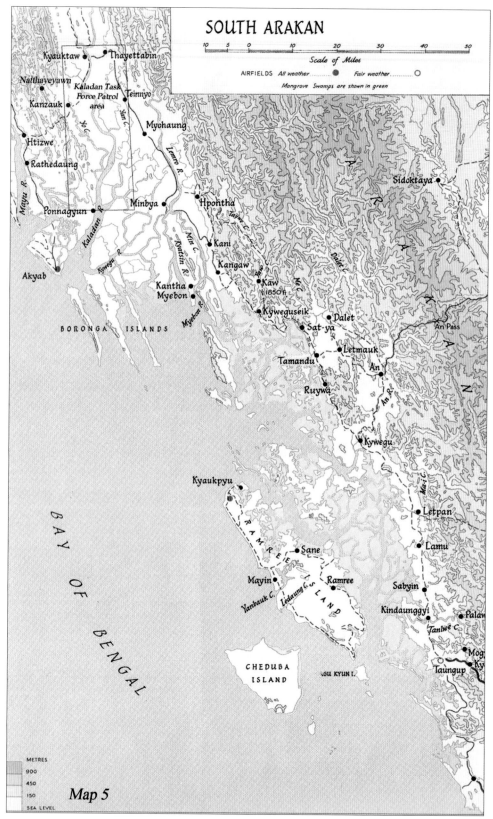

SOUTH ARAKAN

Scale of Miles

AIRFIELDS All weather ● Fair weather ○

Mangrove Swamps are shown in green

Map 5

Map 5. South Arakan

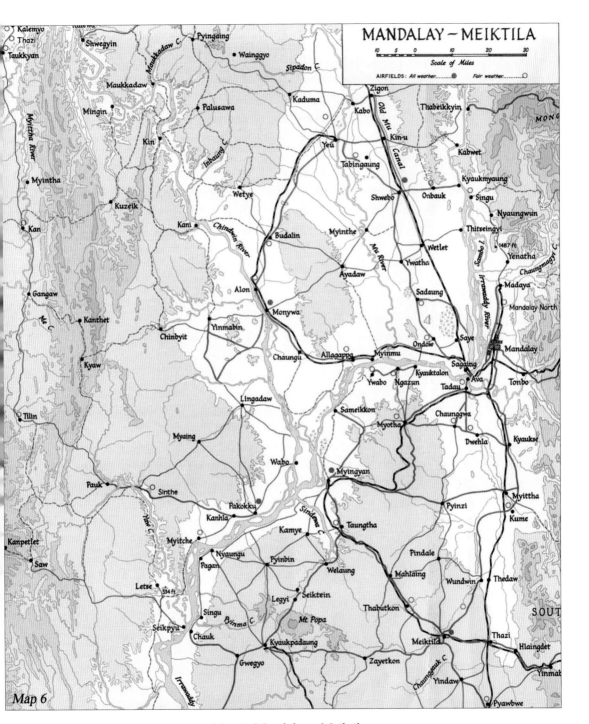

Map 6. Mandalay - Meiktila

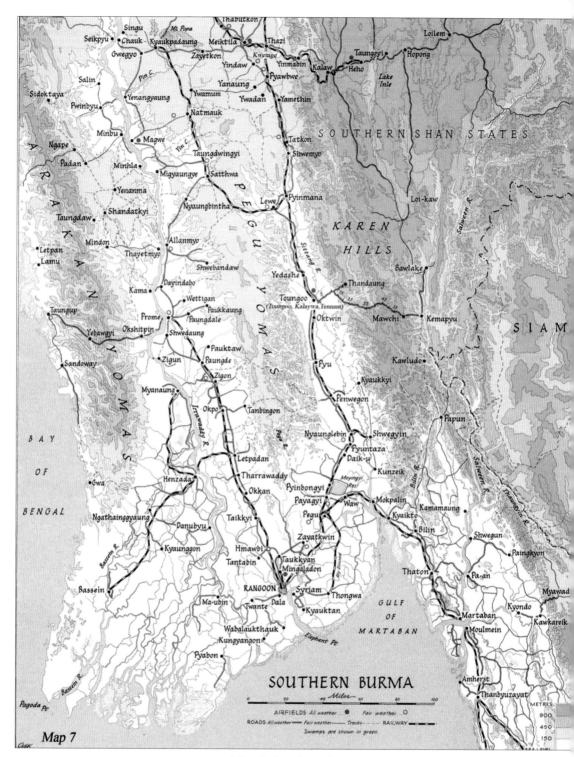

Map 7. Southern Burma

village 3 miles to the north of the strip, and had left going south. Relying on the Japanese tendency to repeat their tactics the defences were thickened up in the area where the earlier actions had taken place. At 2200 hours a Hispano post, on the west of the aerodrome, heard movement in the scrub a few yards away, towards which they threw a grenade and fired a burst of Bren. The fresh print of a boot similar to that worn by the dead Jap was subsequently found in the area.

At 2300 hours, the crew of a Bofors gun challenged five men at the south-east corner of the strip. One of these men fired at the challenger, and the fire was returned. Men in this post and in a neighbouring Hispano post claimed to have heard groans, but nothing was found. Shortly afterwards figures were seen close to the camp of another Hispano section, and almost immediately the tents were seen to be alight. Grenades were thrown, and at least two grenades were thrown back, but without doing any damage.[27]

In these situations the fire directed by your own side is just as deadly as that of the enemy and the remainder of the night was extremely uncomfortable for the airmen as some of the Army LAA units on the airstrip displayed poor fire discipline:

From then on until 0530 hours, five of the six Bofors posts on the strip kept up continuous but spasmodic fire from Brens and Stens. Much of this fire was tracer, and aimed either at movement, seen, heard, or suspected or in the general direction in which the master gun was firing. As most of this was northwards, and thus close over the positions manned by 2945 Squadron, the effect was most unsettling. One detachment was driven from its position, and more than one was compelled to keep their heads down, while Battle HQ was also in the direct line of fire. As the posts were not connected to the LAA Troop HQ by telephone, it was possible neither to control them, nor to learn what was going on. But as it did NOT appear that any large party was attacking, the alarm was not given, and the precaution was taken of informing 'Robforce' that they had better ignore the firework display until they received further information.

The communication system on the aerodrome by telephone and R/T, and the internal communication of the Squadron worked excellently, and the ability of Battle HQ to inform almost all others what was happening prevented much confusion. Great credit is due to LAC D. Etheridge, a gunner without any specialist training, who was mainly responsible for this efficiency. Meanwhile in spite of the confusion, it was clear that there was a party of enemy about. A machine-gun with a very slow rate of fire, quite unlike any British weapon, was heard to the south-west, and at about 0400 hours grenades and small arms fire were directed against the positions of No 2 Flight covering 34 Squadron dispersal area. This fire was returned and a Japanese 0.256 bullet was re-covered from one weapon pit. The coming of dawn was a relief, and the discovery that casualties were nil, and that the only damage to aircraft was a grenade splinter in the wing of one Hurricane.

During the day a Burman was picked up near the strip, but was vouched for by 'Z' Force agents, who themselves reported that four Japanese soldiers, one carrying a machine-gun, had entered a village two miles east of the strip at dawn that morning. It seems probable that this was the party, which had been active during the night. A standing patrol of 2968 Field Squadron at the

Station Commander's request was put out west of 42 Squadron Domestic Camp.[28]

The actions of the previous days and nights had caused considerable nervousness, as was evidenced the following night:

> The tension of the previous week had put everyone on edge and a sudden wind which sprang up . . . rattled all the tins [on the thorn fences] and stirred up the dry leaves [which] did nothing to improve nerves. A grenade was thrown from one post at suspected movements, but no results were discovered.[29]

The news received the next day must have provided a welcome relief as it was learnt that all the RAF Regiment units at Onbauk were to move south to Ondaw during the coming week. Furthermore, reinforcements arrived on 11 March in the form of 2743 Field Squadron, which flew in from Agartala in five C46 Commandos. They had come direct from Forward Echelon Agartala[30] and were under command of Squadron Leader Randle Manwaring.[31] By arrangement the men were mixed up with the airmen of 2945 and 2968 Field Squadrons for the first night to familiarise the newcomers to the layout and conditions and to gain experience.

The 2nd British Division had pushed south from Shwebo and had captured Sadaung and its airstrip in mid-January. The Group Defence Officer and Wing HQs continued to juggle the limited manpower available to maximise the defence of this airstrip and allocate squadrons for the protection of airstrips opening up further south. 1324 Wing had assumed full control of the squadrons in the Shwebo area during the

Group Captain J.H. Harris Command Defence Officer with Wing Commander Randle Manwaring and personnel of 2743 Field Squadron during a visit to a forward airstrip. (Photo courtesy Imperial War Museum London CF 566)

first week of February and now had seven squadrons under its command, with responsibility for ground and LAA defence at Yeu, Tabingaung and Onbauk and soon Sadaung and Ondaw airstrips (Appendix 14).

After moving across India by road to Imphal, 2942 Field Squadron was flown into Onbauk on 2 February and then moved to relieve 2944 Field Squadron at Tabingaung. This freed up 2944 to move south-west to join 1323 Wing. 2942 and 2943 Field and 2961 LAA Squadrons moved by road to Sadaung during early February to provide protection for three squadrons of 906 Wing.[32] The OC of 2961 LAA Squadron expressed his satisfaction with the situation at Sadaung compared with their previous location. With the short distance to the new airstrip and ample notice, a recce made it possible to place LAA flights so that they could perform a dual role of ground and AA defence. This contrasted satisfactorily with Tabingaung where the Operations Room had been distant from the airstrip and which rendered the AA guns of little value to protect the more distant dispersal areas (Sketch Map 9). Ted Daines of 2943 Field Squadron continues:

> Next it was to Sadaung, to defend an AMES unit overlooking the as yet empty airfield. At this point we were in front of the Army, guarding our rear was the 2nd Manchester Machine-Gun Battalion. The airfield was a long dirt strip suitable for fighters, and supply aircraft. To our front in the observable distance was a large Jap-held village. This was to be the next real engagement for the Army, but not just yet. The next days brought the supply planes in, then came the fighters all controlled by the unit we were guarding.
>
> One outstanding happening in my journey was about the very brave pilots of the L5 light ambulance aircraft. Unarmed and always at or very near the front line, often in places just about big enough to land if no errors were made in the process. Some of the aircraft were flown by American Quakers. These people refused to bear arms against anybody, and flew these tiny aircraft with a lot of skill and not a little courage. One such pilot flew low over us at Sadaung one day, waggled his wings and banked; flying back again he ejected a large parcel out over the camp. It had a makeshift parachute attached which slowed its fall slightly. Turning again he made a low pass over us, pulled up and flew away. When the parcel was opened it turned out to be a large carton of cigarettes. Scrawled on a piece of paper was 'From one of the good Yanks' . . . they flew these unarmed ambulance aircraft in the war zone with great courage. They were delighted to be awarded our medals.
>
> Sadaung was an open area, virtually no scrub in front but we were comforted by the fact that the Army covered us from the ridge just behind us. The heat was dry and it was much more pleasant without the humidity. Through binoculars we could keep an eye on the plain in front of us, as well as the Jap-held village. When the aircraft arrived on the airstrip for ground support operations we could tell how near the enemy was by the quickness of their return.
>
> At Sadaung we had only one pint of water per man per day. To shave one left a little tea in the bottom of your mug. Although we had purifying tablets on us, there was no river nearby. Not in fact until we came to the Irrawaddy, under two months away for us. We were here long enough to see the airfield develop. It became a large casualty clearing station for XXXIII Corps with the airfield good enough to take supply aircraft like Dakotas and Commandos and also house Spitfires and the much heavier Thunderbolt.

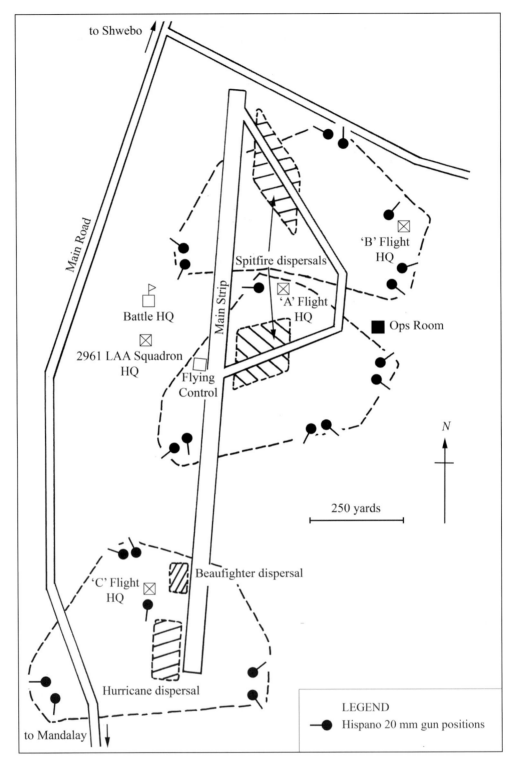

to Shwebo

Main Road

Main Strip

Spitfire dispersals

'B' Flight
HQ

Battle HQ

'A' Flight
HQ

Ops Room

2961 LAA Squadron
HQ

Flying
Control

N

250 yards

'C' Flight
HQ

Beaufighter dispersal

Hurricane dispersal

to Mandalay

LEGEND

Hispano 20 mm gun positions

9 The deployment of 2961 LAA Squadron at Sadaung airstrip during February 1945.
(The hatched areas are aircraft dispersals. The dotted lines are areas occupied by
2961 Squadron.)

The time was fast approaching to clear the Jap-held village. This happened one afternoon, preceded by a twelve Hurricane bomb and strafe raid that we could observe quite easily. We were then ordered to support the Army's right flank. This was soon over, and though the Army suffered one man killed, there were plenty of dead Japs lying about.

Some 10 miles south of Sadaung amongst some low hills on the north bank of the Irrawaddy is Ondaw. The airstrip at Ondaw was occupied on 24 January and became an important air supply point while the 2nd British Division cleared the Sagaing area and moved towards the crossing points on the Irrawaddy where it would threaten Mandalay. From 12 to 14 March 2743 and 2945 Field and 2960 LAA Squadrons proceeded south from Onbauk, leapfrogging the Regiment units at Sadaung, to take up residence at Ondaw. Squadron Leader Randle Manwaring was designated as Airfield Defence Commander. With the limited manpower available, the personnel from 906 Wing and 34, 42 and 113 Squadrons, who arrived on 14 March, were also required to provide ground defence for their domestic areas (Sketch Map 10).

Valuable lessons were still being learnt as the RAF Regiment advanced further into Burma. Arising from the experience gained at Onbauk, it was decided at Ondaw to group the control tower, briefing room, signals section and telephone exchange together, so that with a garrison of the RAF Regiment a single defensive 'box' could be formed around these vital installations. Furthermore, at Onbauk the RAF Regiment airmen had been required to camp within the dispersal areas as the scrub grew so close to the airstrip that there was a very real possibility of a surprise day attack. In addition, the combination of noise and dust from the aircraft and lack of shade made rest during the day almost impossible. Fortunately, Ondaw airstrip was more open and the RAF Regiment domestic camp was located in a pleasantly shaded and quiet tamarind copse sited ¼ of a mile from the dispersals. Positions were dug and thorn fences built, while daily bathing excursions to the banks of the Irrawaddy were instituted. As the dispersals were much wider than at Onbauk, 2945 Field Squadron formed a mobile force to fill the gaps and in each area one flight was detailed to man a ring of listening posts, while another was held in the centre as a reserve. This had the advantage that the flights in reserve were normally able to sleep, and to be fresh for duty the following day. Fighting patrols of one flight each were sent out to nearby villages and features but no encounters were reported.

Such an effective arrangement could not last however, as 2945 Field Squadron and most of the SEAC squadrons were now facing severe problems with regard to manpower and ordnance. By the end of March the situation was so serious as to require reorganisation of 2945 Field Squadron and changes to the tactical arrangements for airfield defence at Ondaw:

> With an effective strength of little over 80 men [the establishment laid down at this time was for seven officers and 166 men] it was proving very difficult to maintain three rifle flights as well as a Bren Support Group and Mortar Section in Squadron HQ. As an opportunity arose to borrow a 3-inch mortar for training purposes from 2743 Field Squadron, it was decided to disband No 2 Rifle Flight and bring HQ and the remaining two flights up to strength. This meant that each flight was on listening post duty two nights out of three, and instead of a mobile reserve in each dispersal area, it was held centrally between the two.[33]

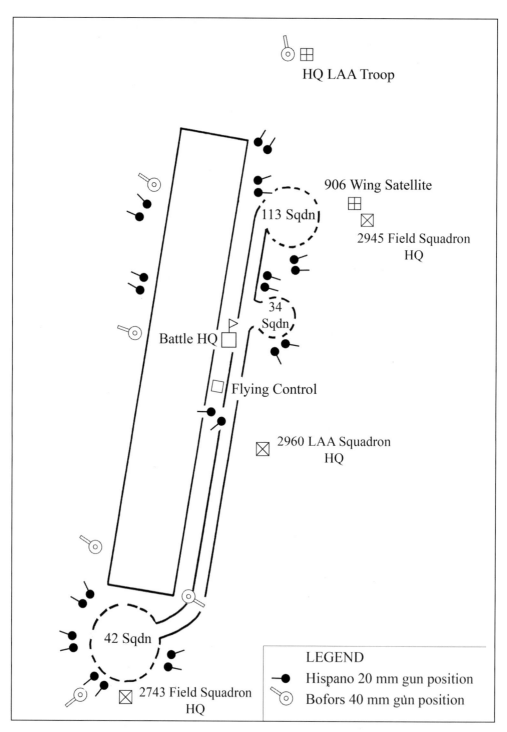

HQ LAA Troop

906 Wing Satellite

113 Sqdn

2945 Field Squadron
HQ

34
Sqdn

Battle HQ

Flying Control

2960 LAA Squadron
HQ

42 Sqdn

2743 Field Squadron
HQ

LEGEND

● Hispano 20 mm gun position

⊙ Bofors 40 mm gun position

10 *The deployment of 2960 LAA Squadron, 2743 and 2945 Field Squadrons and the*
allocated Army Bofors troop and flying squadrons at RAF Station Ondaw in
February 1945.

The ORB of 2743 Field Squadron provides a commentary on their sojourn so far, this from an author with an obvious literary bent and a wry sense of humour:

> First week of month spent in sport and cultural training in order to effect a therapeutic rehabilitation of the Squadron after the strenuous battle course at Agartala. At Onbauk the Squadron was plunged into an atmosphere electrified by Jap infiltration and found it galvanised along with everyone else on the strip into vigilance and resolve. At Ondaw conditions were greener, quieter, cleaner and altogether more pleasant, the strip having been constructed by the Allies for the Allies . . . [in contrast to Onbauk, a captured airstrip]. Morale excellent through all this despite diarrhoea for some, flies, sweat and dust for all, everyone remained efficient and in high spirits.[34]

Further to the west, 1307 Wing HQ had reached Monywa on 5 February (Appendix 14). The Wing HQ and the squadrons under command were to provide protection to 909 Wing following the capture of the Monywa airfields by the 20th Indian Division.[35] Wing Commander C.M. Lander of 1307 Wing reported on the obvious improvement in the outlook of the airmen now they were moving forward:

> The morale of the men in this wing is extremely high, they have been 'static' for so long that moves in recent weeks have made an incredible difference in everyone's outlook. A popular request is that they may be allowed to wear the flash of the 14th Army.[36]

In preparation for the crossings of the Irrawaddy the Fourteenth Army and 221 Group HQs had moved forward from Indainggyi to Monywa on 9 February. On 11 February the 19th Indian Division began the breakout from its bridgehead and headed south for Mandalay. The next to move was the 20th Indian Division, which crossed opposite Myinmu on 12 and 13 February and, as was planned, drew in heavy Japanese attacks. The final crossing in the north was by the 2nd British Division near Ngazun on 20 February, and once the bridgehead was secure the division moved east to capture Mandalay.

Preceding the move of the 1307 Wing HQ to Monywa were two flights of 2941 Field Squadron, which went to Alon and Okpo on AMES protection duties. By mid-February 2941 Field Squadron had moved in its entirety from Onbauk and was concentrated at Monywa and the satellite airstrip at Ywadon. The Spitfires of 17 Squadron had flown south from Tabingaung and were soon operating from Ywadon airstrip. 2963 LAA Squadron had been held at Indainggyi in the Kabaw Valley until it had been made up to strength with medically fit reinforcements from the Forward Echelon. It moved forward in late January and by the end of February also had flights at Alon and Monywa.

The AMES at Alon was No 569. This was the unit that had struggled through the mud and rain of the Kabaw Valley the previous December with the advancing Regiment squadrons. While at Alon the non-technical staff of the AMES were given a course of station defence training by the Regiment personnel. In mid-March the radar station and two flights of 2941 Field Squadron were ordered south to Myinmu on the banks of the Irrawaddy. This area had been the site of the crossing of the Irrawaddy by the 20th Indian Division and had only been cleared recently of the enemy and a strict stand-to between dawn and dusk was in place. The ORB of No 569 AMES describes the move to the new location and their dependence on the RAF Regiment:

. . . on the 17th Flight Lieutenant Aitken again visited the Myinmu area in company of Flying Officer Fox of 2941 Squadron RAF Regiment, who was Flight Commander and detailed for defence of the station. The area was devoid of all Army units . . .

. . . a full convoy of fourteen vehicles moved off . . . Nothing worse than a few minor mishaps occurred during the journey . . . The last six miles of the journey from Myinmu to the junction of the Mu and Irrawaddy were tricky for the tall Crossley vehicles and aerial vehicle . . .

Two flights from 2941 Squadron, one being the HQ Flight arrived at the same time under the command of Flight Lieutenant Brown. All necessary defence arrangements were made by him immediately on arrival. The site lent itself naturally to defence on a peninsular [sic] formed by the meeting of the two rivers . . . [37]

The AMES was set up and the next month was uneventful apart from a hurricane that swept the camp, blowing down the W/T masts and all but two of the sleeping tents, although the Regiment was to suffer a blow to its pride. The ORB continues:

A certain amount of defence training was given to unit personnel by the attached RAF Regiment Commander. A rifle shooting match was arranged between the two units and was won by the AMES. Instruction in the Bren and Sten guns and firing thereof took place.[38]

Meanwhile, a hundred or so miles to the west, 1323 Wing had been notified in early January to make preparations to accompany IV Corps down the Myittha Valley (Appendix 14). The advance had been held up at Gangaw since December. To avoid committing large numbers of troops, the RAF carried out an 'earthquake' attack on 10 January, using four squadrons of B25 Mitchell medium bombers, followed by three of

Loading a 20-mm Hispano of 2958 LAA Squadron into a Dakota for a squadron deployment by air. (Air Historical Branch RAF Crown Copyright)

Airmen of 2958 LAA Squadron board a Dakota for transport to a newly captured airfield. (Photograph courtesy of the Imperial War Museum, London, CF 440)

Thunderbolt and Hurricane fighter-bombers. A flight of 2946 Field Squadron had a 'ringside' seat for this full scale air and ground attack, having been located only 4,000 yards from the enemy on AMES protection duties for the previous week. The Lushai Brigade occupied the village without meeting further opposition and the 28th East African Brigade then moved through and the advance was resumed.

2946 Field Squadron and two flights of 2958 LAA Squadron then moved south from Taukkyan to the newly opened Kan airstrip in the Myittha Valley on 15 January. They arrived just prior to the fly-in of 907 (Fighter) Wing, which urgently required ground and AA protection. One flight of 2958 LAA Squadron was flown from Taukkyan while the other moved by road. It was eventually joined on 27 January by Squadron HQ and the remaining AA flight that had previously been sent east to Onbauk for a short time. This airstrip had been carved from a clearing by bulldozers and was located so near the Japanese positions that the ground-attack Hurricanes had to execute a steep climbing turn following take-off to gain sufficient height to attack.[39]

On 19 January, the 7th Indian Division and 255th Indian Tank Brigade, which had secretly concentrated between Kan and Gangaw, were ordered forward to the Irrawaddy. They set off in complete radio silence. The advance followed a narrow dusty cart track, which was widened and improved as they advanced. At first moving through teak forest the road turned sharply at Tilin to head east towards Pauk, where the dry belt begins, and then on to Pakokku, reaching the banks of the Irrawaddy by 1 February. Some 12 miles east of Pauk was Sinthe, an insignificant village on the edge of an expanse of flattish paddy field. This was selected as the airfield through which all the ammunition and vital engineers' stores for the river crossing had to pass. The Forward Airfield Engineers levelled the paddy bunds and filled in the ditches and enlarged the old Japanese airstrip. After a week's work with bulldozers and spades it was ready and on 10 February the airhead was opened.

The river crossings by the 7th Indian Division would be supported by 907 Wing, and maintained by air supply from Sinthe and the soon to be occupied airstrip at Myitche.[40] 2946 Field Squadron HQ, with two rifle flights from Kan and the flight at Gangaw, moved to Sinthe on 5 February. They were ordered to mount Brens on their vehicles for AA protection and ground-to-ground protection, while the airmen were to have personal arms ready as sniping had been reported on parts of the road. They were joined by 1323 Wing HQ on 9 February. Two flights were required for ground defence of the airstrip, while the remaining flight provided AA and ground defence to an AMES located nearby. Two flights of 2958 LAA Squadron also moved from Kan to provide AA cover for the airstrip.

The demands for protection of AMES were an even more vital task for the RAF Regiment as the radar units were being forced operationally into 'neutral ground' to maximise chances of interception of enemy aircraft intent on reconnaissance or air attack on the advancing columns. The advance of IV Corps could not afford to be revealed or slowed. Reinforcements were required to meet the AMES commitments and 2944 Field Squadron was, therefore, moved south-west by road from Tabingaung to reach Ywadon on 5 February. By now the airmen had become expert at packing up and moving and on 9 February the entire squadron was flown to Sinthe, coming under command of 1323 Wing. Henry Kirk recalls the departure from Ywadon airstrip and the problems arising from such hasty departures:

The airmen were loaded onto an aircraft with equipment . . . they loaded on as much ammunition as was possible as the Squadron were flying to a completely new location and, as far as they knew, might be unable to obtain ammunition and grenades for some time. The heavily-loaded Dakota headed off down the runway but soon came to a halt. The pilot entered the cargo and passenger compartment and announced that some airmen and equipment would have to leave the aircraft as he could not guarantee that the plane would get off the ground. We all eventually arrived safely at Sinthe.

In the early hours of 14 February, with the Japanese commanders' attentions fixed on the 20th Indian Division at

LAC Gore, the forward scout on an RAF Regiment patrol in central Burma, April 1945. (Air Historical Branch RAF Crown Copyright)

A patrol of the RAF Regiment crosses a river in central Burma on the alert for enemy parties cut off in the rapid advance by the Fourteenth Army, March 1945. (Photo courtesy Imperial War Museum, London CF 569)

Myinmu and the moves on Mandalay, the leading troops of the 7th Indian Division crossed the Irrawaddy near Nyaungu. This was to be the longest opposed river crossing attempted in any theatre of the Second World War. It was successfully completed and by 17 February the bridgehead was sufficiently secure for IV Corps to launch the 17th Indian Division and its armour eastwards to Meiktila.

2944 Field Squadron was given complete responsibility for AMES protection in the IV Corps area. On 26 February No 2 Flight had moved to Myitche on the west bank of the Irrawaddy to guard an AMES. LAC Stan Hutchinson of 2944 Field Squadron recalls the move and occupation:

> Myitche was a nice little town which had been abandoned. It was complete with houses, pagodas, Buddhist monastery and school and part of it walled around with a high brick wall. There was a large well complete with bucket. One of the lads lost his pay book and wallet from his breast pocket down this well. At the back of the monastery No 3 Flight were ordered to dig in and get below ground. It was overrun by cacti with very sharp spines that would easily go through the leather of your boots. When we got digging we realised why it was full of cactus, it was a graveyard. So we were sleeping in graves, with bones protruding from the side of our dugouts. On a night when all was quiet you could hear the little bells on the pagoda spire tinkling in the breeze; it would have been very romantic if Dorothy Lamour had appeared.

Sinthe was now being used by a flight of Thunderbolts of 146 Squadron, which flew in each day from the Arakan and maintained an air patrol over the fly-in corridor between Pagan and Meiktila. During March Sinthe was attacked from the air and although 2958 LAA Squadron went into action, no hits were credited. The air defence task was made more difficult by the habit of unfriendly locals regularly lighting fires beside the airstrip at night to guide in enemy bombers. On the ground the airstrip was subject to infiltration raids by parties of Japanese as the following incident demonstrates:

> On 8 March at 1800 hours two British officers were shot at and killed by a small party of Japanese about a mile from the airstrip. A rifle flight from 2946 Field Squadron immediately moved out and searched the area for a depth of two miles; no contact was made with the enemy party. At 0010 hours that night the body of one of the British officers was recovered and brought into the camp. [41]

The men of the Fourteenth Army and 221 Group knew that despite the bold moves of IV and XXXIII Corps the Japanese *15th* and *28th Armies* would not break off and withdraw; instead they would gather together every available unit and launch a determined counter-offensive. The next four weeks would be decisive in the campaign to retake Burma. The RAF Regiment, fighting alongside the Fourteenth Army, would be at the very core of the struggle and their actions would contribute in a small but vital manner to the eventual success of Operation *Extended Capital*.

Notes

1 Slim, W. *Defeat into Victory*. 2nd ed. London: Cassell, 1956, p. 543.
2 AIR 29/1120, *Operations Record Book, 1318–1338 RAF Regiment Wings, 1944–1947*.
3 These were 2941, 2943, 2944, 2946, 2968 Field and 2958, 2960, 2961 and 2963 LAA Squadrons.
4 IV Corps consisted of the 7th Indian Division, 255th Indian Tank Brigade, 28th East African Brigade, Lushai Brigade and the 17th Indian Division. The 5th Indian Division would arrive in March as reinforcement.
5 XXXIII Indian Corps eventually consisted of, moving from west to east, the 20th Indian, 2nd British and 19th Indian Divisions, supported by the 254th Indian Tank Brigade and 268th Indian Infantry Brigade.
6 AIR 25/910, *Operations Record Book 221 Group 1944–1945*.
7 AIR 29/137, *Operations Record Books RAF Regiment Squadrons 2960–2970*.
8 Thirty and twelve aircraft attacked Shwebo and Onbauk, respectively.
9 The manpower difficulties facing the RAF Regiment at this time in South-East Asia Command are exemplified by 2963 LAA Squadron. The squadron had been inspected by the Senior Medical Officer of 221 Group during December and had received orders not to proceed beyond Indainggyi until replacements could be found for the fifty medically unfit airmen. With the rapid advance of the preceding squadrons, it had been allowed to move on to Taukkyan and Kalemyo to replace those moving forward. At the end of January the reinforcements arrived from Forward Echelon Agartala and the unfit men were returned to the Depot.
10 op. cit., AIR 25/910.
11 ibid. AIR 25/910.
12 Bickers, R.T. *Ginger Lacey, Fighter Pilot*, Pan, London, 1969 (1962), p. 159. The perceptions of those in different places during a battle or other stressful incident can often differ widely. In R.T. Bickers' biography of 'Ginger' Lacey, he recounts Lacey emptying his thirty-eight revolver skyward during this raid and commenting with some theatricality, 'It was the only anti-aircraft fire delivered during the whole of the attack!' The gunners of 2961 LAA Squadron would beg to differ.
13 LAC Stan Hutchinson had been the batman to Squadron Leader George Arnold while at Imphal. He had arrived in India with the 99 (Wellington) Squadron Defence Flight in 1942 and had been transferred to 2944 Field Squadron at Secunderabad on its formation.

14 Mountbatten, Vice-Admiral The Earl. *Report to the Combined Chiefs of Staff by the Supreme Allied Commander South-East Asia, 1943–1945.* London: HMSO, 1951, p. 126.

15 AIR 29/137, *Operations Record Books RAF Regiment Squadrons 2960–2970.*

16 AIR 29/136, *Operations Record Books RAF Regiment Squadrons 2944–2959.*

17 ibid.

18 ibid.

19 ibid.

20 ibid.

21 ibid. The mobile outer defence was provided by 'Robforce', consisting of the 2nd Battalion, The Suffolk Regiment and a detachment of armoured cars of the 11th (Prince Albert Victor's Own) Cavalry.

22 AIR 29/138, *Operations Record Books RAF Regiment Squadrons 2941–2950, 2953–2955, 2957–2962, 2964, 2966–2970, Appendices Only.* Appendix No 5 March 1945.

23 op. cit., AIR 29/136.

24 ibid.

25 op. cit., AIR 29/138.

26 They had relieved the 2nd Suffolks on outer airfield protection.

27 op. cit., AIR 29/136.

28 ibid.

29 It is interesting to look at the ammunition expenditure for the night, which was as follows: 2960 LAA Squadron with 5 posts in action, 301 Bren rounds, 21 Sten 9-mm rounds and 17 grenades; 2945 Field Squadron with 9 posts in action, 328 Bren rounds, 100 Sten rounds and 15 grenades and the LAA Battery with 6 posts in action, 1,572 Bren rounds, 642 Sten rounds and one grenade. 2968 Field Squadron had only two posts in action and was relatively unmolested and fired only 2 rifle rounds and 1 grenade.

30 op.cit., AIR 29/138.

31 Randle Manwaring had been the OC 2896 Squadron at Bombay but was transferred to 2743 Field Squadron when the CO had fallen ill and been admitted to hospital at Secunderabad.

32 By 11 February, 28 (Hurricane IIC), 155 (Spitfire) and 607 (Spitfire) Squadrons and a Sector Operations Room were at Sadaung under 906 Wing HQ.

33 op. cit. AIR 29/136.

34 AIR 29/83, *Operations Record Books RAF Regiment Squadrons 2741–2743.*

35 20, 60 and 681 Squadrons were located at Monywa.

36 AIR 29/1118, *Operations Record Books 1300–1309, 1311–1317 RAF Regiment Wings 1944–47.*

37 AIR 29/182, *Operations Record Books and Appendices Air Ministry Experiment Stations 553,554, 566–570, 573, 574, 576–579, 581, 582, 589, 590.*

38 ibid. Whoops! The AMES unit had obviously been provided with good training in marksmanship by their RAF Regiment instructors.

39 Naydler, M. *Young Man, You'll Never Die.* Barnsley, Yorkshire: Pen & Sword, 2005, p. 133.

40 152 (Spitfire) Squadron, 11 (Hurricane) Squadron RAF and a Tactical Reconnaissance Flight of 1 IAF Squadron with Hurricanes.

41 *Review of RAF Regiment Squadrons under the control of HQ RAF Burma, 1st January 1945 to 3rd May 1945, Capture of Rangoon,* HQ RAF Burma, p. 5.

CHAPTER EIGHT

Meiktila – 'Bloody Renown'

'The RAF Regiment won bloody renown in the fierce fighting for repossession of the landing ground every humid morning.'
Squadron Leader 'Ginger' Lacey, OC 17 Squadron, RAF

The thrust for Meiktila was the master stroke of the Burma campaign and the operation that most clearly demonstrated the military brilliance of the Fourteenth Army commander Lieutenant-General Sir William Slim. The capture of Mandalay was of major importance for prestige purposes, however, Meiktila 82 miles further to the south, was the key to the retaking of Burma. Distracted by XXXIII Indian Corps, the Japanese divisions were drawn into fighting the 2nd British and 19th and 20th Indian Divisions in the north. The enemy were led to believe the crossing in the west was simply a diversion, but they would soon find themselves completely outflanked and they would be isolated from their main supply administrative base. The fall of Meiktila would deal the mortal blow to the Japanese *Burma Area Army*.

With the 7th Indian Division across the Irrawaddy at Pakokku, an armoured and motorised infantry column of the 255th Indian Tank Brigade and 48th Indian Infantry Brigade from 17th Indian Division set out for Meiktila. The first objective was Thabutkon airstrip, which was quickly captured on 26 February, and the fly-in of the 99th Indian Infantry Brigade was completed by 2 March. The 17th Indian Division did not have the troops to maintain its lines of communications to the west with the 7th Indian Division at Nyaungu and would, therefore, be entirely dependent on supply by air. By 2 March the 'Meiktila Striking Force' was on the outskirts of the town. Moving in three columns, two were sent to capture the town, while the third, the 255th Indian Tank Brigade column, swept around the north of Meiktila and secured the airstrip to the east of the town. Fierce house-to-house fighting occurred and even an *ad hoc* battalion of Japanese hospital patients fortified their compound and joined in. Some of the tanks were lost when the sluice gates were opened to the west and the ground flooded. By 4 March, after much bitter fighting, the Japanese garrison had been eliminated, the town was clear of stragglers and the final clean-up began the next day. Aware that the Japanese would not tolerate this stranglehold on their main line of communications, the entire force concentrated for the defence of Meiktila (Map 6).

Meiktila is 320 miles from Rangoon and 50 miles south of Mandalay and is situated on a branch of the Rangoon-Mandalay railway. This was the main Japanese base controlling everything an army needed: ammunition and stores dumps, reinforcement camps, hospitals and convalescent depots. It was the main administration area for the Japanese *15th Army*. Prior to the battle it was a small attractive town with red brick buildings and tree-lined streets dominated by a large gold-top pagoda. Built on a ridge, to the north and south were two large lakes fed by chaungs and a series of irrigation ditches controlled by sluice gates. The centre of the town was to be severely damaged

156

The devastation in Meiktila town following its capture in early March 1945.
(Air Historical Branch RAF Crown Copyright)

during the heavy fighting leading to its capture. The latter part of February and early March was the pre-monsoon period with the countryside very dry, everything parched, the red soil baked hard like concrete. The temperatures were in the region of 120°F, accompanied by high humidity and dust, which caused extreme discomfort. The surrounding country consisted of dried up paddy fields and scrub and was more like a desert. It was very different to the jungle that the Fourteenth Army and 221 Group had fought in and above for the last three years.

Meiktila was at the centre of a group of forward airfields that protected the main line of communications up to the Irrawaddy. The most important of these was located just outside of the town to the east and this airfield was developed as the main supply base for the 17th Indian Division. Essential to the success of this venture, the airstrip would allow the column to replenish its supplies, do essential maintenance and repairs on the armour and fly in a further air-transportable infantry brigade. It had two all-weather runways some 1,600 yards in length, these being separated by a belt of scrub, which ran in parallel from the north-west to the south-east. Meiktila East was the 17th Indian Division's lifeline and it had to be defended with absolute determination. The Japanese fully understood the need for its recapture and the division knew that it was surrounded and would soon be counter-attacked by numerically superior forces. With a limited number of troops, the ground could not be covered completely and, therefore, the defence was concentrated into six 'boxes' located at various points around the town. The 99th Indian Infantry Brigade was given responsibility for the defence of Meiktila, the airstrip and the FAMO depot, with orders to hold it as a secure base from which the division could operate. The other two infantry brigades and the tank brigade would then send out mobile columns to destroy and disrupt the Japanese supply lines from 6 March (Sketch Map 11).

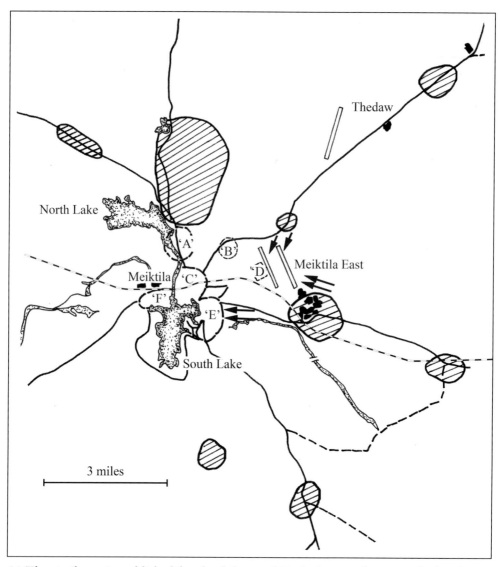

11 *The six 'boxes' established for the defence of Meiktila, March 1945. The hatching represents Japanese troop concentration areas and road blocks, and arrows the main enemy attacks.*

The defenders of the airstrip were to be concentrated in 'D' Box RAF Meiktila. Located on the airstrip itself, 'D' Box was to be jointly held by the RAF and the Army. It was positioned on the western side of the two runways. It was some 900 yards square, surrounded by apron-type barbed wire, which would be improved progressively as the battle developed. The box defence system had proven highly successful in 1944 during the siege of Imphal, however, the men were, by their concentrated nature, highly vulnerable to air attack and artillery and mortar fire. Looking out over the wire to the north-east on the extreme left was the Meiktila-Wundwin Road. There was a small pagoda with a few trees, a steamroller lying on its side and then dry scrub to runway ends (Sketch Map 12).

Wing Commander C.M. 'Bill' Lander, OC of 1307 Wing HQ, had been at

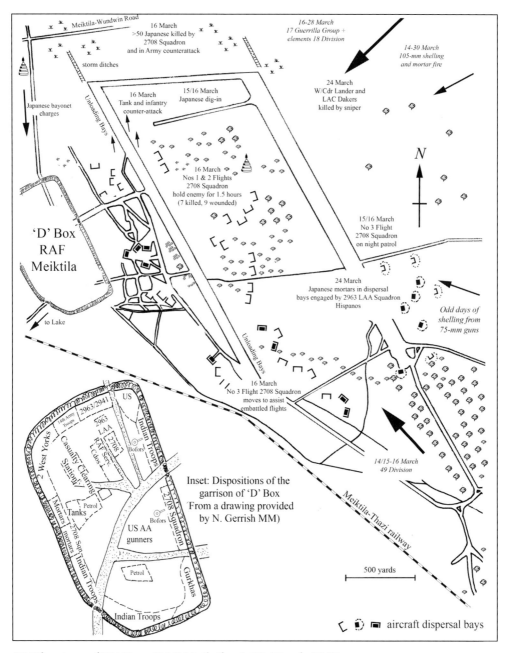

Map labels:

Meiktila-Wundwin Road

16 March
>50 Japanese killed by
2708 Squadron
and in Army counterattack

16-28 March
17 Guerrilla Group +
elements 18 Division

14-30 March
105-mm shelling
and mortar fire

storm ditches

16 March
Tank and infantry
counter-attack

15/16 March
Japanese dig-in

24 March
W/Cdr Lander and
LAC Dakers
killed by sniper

Japanese bayonet
charges

N

16 March
Nos 1 & 2 Flights
2708 Squadron
hold enemy for 1.5 hours
(7 killed, 9 wounded)

'D' Box
RAF
Meiktila

15/16 March
No 3 Flight
2708 Squadron
on night patrol

to Lake

24 March
Japanese mortars in dispersal
bays engaged by 2963 LAA Squadron
Hispanos

Odd days of
shelling from
75-mm guns

Unloading Bays

16 March
No 3 Flight 2708 Squadron
moves to assist
embattled flights

US

2963/2941

14th Army Troops

2 West Yorks

Casualty Clearing Station

5963

LAA

2708

RAF Serv.

L Cdos

Indian Troops

Bofors

Mortars

Tanks

Petrol

2708 Sep. Indian Troops

2708 mortars

US AA
gunners

Bofors

2708 Squadron

Gurkhas

Petrol

Indian Troops

Inset: Dispositions of the
garrison of 'D' Box
From a drawing provided
by N. Gerrish MM)

14/15-16 March
49 Division

Meiktila-Thazi railway

500 yards

aircraft dispersal bays

12 The siege of 'D' Box, RAF Meiktila, 6–28 March 1945.

Monywa for just under a month when orders were received in late February from 221 Group to prepare for the upcoming Meiktila operation. The wing was given responsibility for the defence of Meiktila airstrip and, as was usual, the general allocation was two AA flights and a field squadron for airfield defence, along with two flights for AMES protection. Unit tasks were allocated as follows and were to be ready to be flown in once the airstrip was open:

1. 2708 Field Squadron for ground defence of Meiktila East airfield,

2. Two flights 2963 LAA Squadron to provide AA protection to 17 (Spitfire) Squadron,

3. One flight 2941 Field Squadron to protect AMES 'Turkey' and

4. One flight 2968 Field Squadron to protect AMES 6178.

On 1 March, as the 17th Indian Division approached the outskirts of Meiktila, 1307 Wing was notified that all units were to be placed on 24 hours' readiness. On 1 March the required aircraft arrived, although belatedly, at 1300 hours. Loading of the two flights of 2963 LAA Squadron, with seven 20-mm Hispanos each, commenced immediately and they were airborne 1¾ hours later. For many, this was their first

An aerial photograph of Meiktila airfield, taken on 26 February 1945, a few days before its capture by the 17th Indian Division. (Australian War Memorial RC04394 - image modified)

Wing Commander C.M. 'Bill' Lander briefs airmen of the RAF Regiment at Meiktila a few days before the start of the enemy counter-attack. (Air Historical Branch RAF Crown Copyright)

experience of an airlift and an hour later the first aircraft, with Wing Commander Lander on board, touched down on Meiktila airstrip.

Lander immediately contacted Brigadier G.L. Tarver of the 99th Indian Infantry Brigade, learning that the Army had complete control of all defence including AA. The airstrip was surrounded by the enemy and parties of Japanese were roaming the area. As a result, all guns and equipment were being brought back into the 'D' Box each night. The arrival on the airstrip was a tense affair as the airmen were greeted by much small arms fire. They quickly moved into the box and started to dig slit trenches in the rock-hard earth and bring into use a monsoon storm ditch that ran into the box. Tarver expressed his gratitude at the arrival of the RAF Regiment and the much-anticipated arrival of 2708 Field Squadron as the brigade was short of fighting troops, given its widespread responsibilities. The two flights of 2963 LAA Squadron under the command of Flying Officer Wyatt and Keeling and accompanied by their CO, Squadron Leader R.H. Bond, made contact with an American AA detachment equipped with 0.50-cal and 40-mm AA guns already on the airstrip and they sited their Hispanos to fit into their defensive layout. The flights were to be kept busy manning AA posts by day and perimeter posts by night.

LAC Cyril Paskin of 2968 Field Squadron recalls the moment they were told to be ready to move and the ominous prelude:

My squadron were sent as reinforcements during the battle of Meiktila. We had to wait for aircraft to take us in. Whilst we were waiting, miles from anywhere, surrounded by the Japanese, the RAF sent a Padre in to give the

Squadron their 'last communion!' This was because the RAF did not expect us to survive this operation . . . However, I am Jewish and was the only Jew in the Squadron so I pointed that out and so soon after a rabbi arrived to speak to me. I don't know where they found a rabbi in the middle of nowhere but I have to say he must have blessed my life because I survived and I am still here. I cannot get over the fact that they found a rabbi just for me and think it is fantastic that the Regiment did this for just one man.

The flight of 2968 Field Squadron flew in at 1600 hours and was harboured with the AMES and its radar equipment in the box. The brigade then allocated each of the RAF Regiment units a commitment to holding a strong point at night on the perimeter defences of the 'D' Box. The cookhouse was located in a central position, along with a casualty clearing station and a command post, which was occupied by the Box Commanding Officer, Wing Commander Lander.

Lander kept a 'day-to-day' diary from 1 March, covering the operations at Meiktila. It was intended to be used as a guide for the official report, which would be written following the action. With a less formal style, it helps to convey the action from Lander's viewpoint and conveys something of his character:

Weapon slits dug feverishly and everyone settled for the night. No movement after 1900 hours. Firing not permitted unless in an emergency. Use only bayonets and grenades. The frequent ping of a Jap sniper's rifle was very close. At about 2000 hours an LMG opened up to the left of our strongpoint and this was followed by about a dozen grenades . . . The 3-inch mortars in our Box were firing on a defensive task. The enemy is strong to the north and a counter-attack is expected from that direction . . . four wounded Japs and two wounded 'Jifs' were found at first light by an Army patrol, obviously casualties of the previous night's scrap.

Lander visited Brigade HQ the following morning and volunteered to lead out a patrol of the flight from 2968 Field Squadron. As OC 1307 Wing this was not his personal responsibility, but Lander was determined to take a full part in the operation and establish the situation at first hand. As the flight's AMES commitment was currently located within 'D' Box, it was quite safe to leave it there during the day and go out on patrol. Lander expressed his satisfaction with the first sojourn onto the airstrip:

The area to be patrolled was to the north-west of the strip, snipers were suspected and the boys were thoroughly teed-up. My orders were to search every inch of the ground, every foxhole and bush. We set out at 1300 hours. The patrol turned out to be a piece of cake. We saw plenty of Japs – dead . . . Someone had a pot at us with a rifle, but he turned out to be a jittery Indian. We got back at 1600 hours and reported the area clear to Brigade. It was bloody hot, let none who hasn't taken the lads out on such a stunt say they are useless. I'd back them against any Army BORs. Their Flight Commander, Flying Officer Haymes, is first class. More 'jittering' at night and the odd spot of sniping but nothing of note really.

Despite being the largest component of the Regiment commitment, 2708 Field Squadron was not flown from Agartala to Monywa until 3 March.[1] Here the men remained until 8 March when the squadron received orders to move to Meiktila airstrip by air at first light. Lifted by five C46 Commandos from Monywa, the men landed 1¼ hours later at the contested airfield.

On 4 February 1945, 2708 Field Squadron had arrived at Agartala from Secunderabad. The Squadron in various forms had been providing AA defence on airfields in the United Kingdom since 1941 before conversion to a field squadron in October 1944. With the war in Europe heading towards its inevitable conclusion, the squadron concentrated with other SEAC-bound squadrons at RAF Davidstow Moor before departing from Liverpool Docks on 14 December 1944 for India.

Arriving at Bombay a month later the men travelled to the Depot at Secunderabad where they were kitted out to scale and reduced to Indian establishment. With the limited time available they quickly received lectures from the MO on medical matters, the equipment and the MT Officers on procedure, and did some range firing. Two weeks later 2708 Field Squadron moved by rail to Forward Echelon Agartala for a one-month 'Jungle Warfare' course under OC Wing Commander Donaldson and Chief Instructor Squadron Leader J.D. Warren. On 6 February the course began with range firing, weapons training and an assault course, of which the performance of 2708 Field Squadron was described by instructors as 'absolutely excellent, all men tried hard, and fitness of squadron is high-well done, marks 90%.' Training in 'Open and Jungle Section Attack', map reading and compass work, jungle cookery, river crossing and jungle lore were also covered. The training course culminated in a 36-hour exercise on 1 March.

The course had been organised in the form of a competition between 2708 and 2743 Field Squadrons, which had arrived in the same convoy. The prize for the winner was to be given a 'special job' and as it turned out this was not one to be treated with great relish. It is not clear from the ORB which unit won the competition, but as we have read 2743 Field Squadron was flown to Onbauk. Meanwhile, 2708 Field Squadron was rewarded with the 'special job', that of defending Meiktila East airfield.

Despite receiving the order to move, there was an initial delay as 2708 Field Squadron was four Bren guns short, and significantly deficient in cooking and medical equipment. 1307 Wing HQ agreed to supply these from its own resources to ensure the squadron's arrival. In the course of four months, 2708 Field Squadron had been transformed from an LAA squadron to a field squadron, arrived from the chilling wind and rain of autumn in Cornwall, spent a month on a troopship, trained for another month in the steamy jungle of Bengal and had then been deposited three days later in the heat, humidity and dust of the central plain of Burma. Many of the squadron's airmen would have been forgiven for thinking that the war in Europe was soon to be over and they would be returning to civilian life. Great credit is due to the officers and airmen of this, and indeed all, the United Kingdom RAF Regiment squadrons for their quick adjustment to new surroundings and pressures prevalent in Burma.

Following the arrival of 2708 Field Squadron, Lander attended a conference at Brigade HQ where he offered the brigade the use of the squadron's 3-inch Mortar Section. This offer was gratefully accepted and they were echeloned alongside 87 (Mortar) Battery of the 82nd Anti-Tank Regiment RA and were to be used frequently over the next few weeks on essential defensive fire tasks. Lander continued his diary, radiating his usual enthusiasm, and listed the tasks new arrivals would be allocated to keep the airstrip free from enemy incursions:

2708 arrived by air . . . They ought to thank their lucky stars that they are being given this opportunity to show their worth at such an early stage in this theatre. Morale of the men is excellent, I intend to maintain it. Action will help the lot of us keep it up . . . I put the Squadron on their location in the Box and gave the officers the low-down on the whole situation. They came slap bang into a sticky job – burying some dead Japs who had been written off probing the perimeter of our Box. There were about 14 of them and I thought the experience would serve in the nature of an inoculation.

I've given the Squadron the task of sweeping the east and north of the strip by day and by night they are inside the Box and are to be used in a counter-attack role. They are working with the Gurkhas and Rajputs on this job. They are to go out at 0545 hours and the whole Squadron will carry out their task of sweeping the area before any aircraft are allowed to land on the strip. After the area is swept one flight will remain on constant patrol and will not return until the strip is cleared at night, and everyone is in the Box.

The Squadron quickly settled down and were frantically digging in within a few minutes of their arrival. They will soon learn that it is a case of dig or die.

Meanwhile, 'A' Flight of 2963 LAA Squadron, which was still unemployed, was used to mark out and level the runway under supervision of the Flying Control Officer. By now the airmen had made the acquaintance of the other occupants of 'D' Box and their gruesome activities, such as the small number of the 1/3rd Gurkha Rifles proudly showing Japanese ears, which they had threaded onto wires hanging from their belts.

The third RAF Regiment unit to arrive was No 3 Flight of 2941 Field Squadron, under command of Flying Officer S.W. Cook. On 27 February the No 3 Flight had received notice to be ready to move on twelve hours' readiness to an unknown destination. Lander had expected them by 8 March:

Airmen of 2759 Field Squadron try out a Japanese foxhole. This squadron relieved 2708 Field Squadron in late March following the enemy withdrawal. (Air Historical Branch RAF Crown Copyright)

A snag cropped up today, the Flight of 2941 waiting at Monywa has not turned up. The airlift has slipped up somewhere. The AMES which they intended to cover, arrived and is setting up in the 17th Div Box at Meiktila. Fortunately 2968's Flight are kicking their heels as their commitments haven't arrived complete and they can't operate . . . I solved the problem by sending 2968's Flight on the job, they are tickled pink as the commitment is beside the lake in Meiktila.

Further problems were being encountered as a result of the Regiment's arrival by air Lander continues:

Transport is a terrific problem when you are lifted by air. We got motorcycles in OK and they are indispensable. The snag is, of course, rations and water carrying. The Army have been magnificent. FAMO has loaned us a Jeep complete with Sikh driver, a 15-cwt and 3-tonner. In addition they are pulling our guns at night.

No 3 Flight of 2941 Field Squadron finally arrived, along with 'A' and 'B' Flights of 3207 Servicing Commando RAF, some seventy men required to service aircraft, but who at the same time had been taught to a high standard in the use of firearms. The ORB of No 3 Flight describes the arrival and first patrol:

Allocated 70 yards of perimeter wire to man facing north. Four listening posts completed by nightfall. [On 9 March] defences strengthened by additional wiring . . . At very short notice the Flight went out at 2000 hours as a Recce patrol to investigate a large fire approximately 1 mile east of the strip. Box commander suspected Jap of starting fire to guide troop and aircraft movement.[2]

The first small Japanese parties probed the airfield on the night of 8/9 March and were surprised to find they were able to move freely on the airstrip as the British did not have enough troops or airmen to defend the entire area. Enemy activity was, however, detected by its guardians that night as Lander records:

The night was by no means quiet . . . At about 2200 hours, a small party of nine Japs brushed the Gurkha defences. They scurried north and probed our sector. In the dim light they could be seen by 2963 Squadron personnel who threw three grenades. A Rajput LMG opened up on our left flank, but both efforts were negative. A lot more 'jitter' firing took place on our flanks but there was no justification for it.

Lander was not the type to let them get away with this activity without exacting a toll and on the night of the 9/10 March he set up an ambush:

I was a bit peeved that we didn't have any success last night and a Gurkha and myself arranged a private war, whereby we were to put out an ambush in each of our sectors. I arranged our ambush on one of the most likely lines of approach and with six of the 2941 Squadron chaps we arranged that we would use grenades and automatics only. No-one would be engaged until they were within 15 yards of us. Sure enough at 2130 hours, seven of the brats were seen approaching by three of our men. They threw two 36 grenades at the Japs,

165

who dived for cover, with the result that we don't know if there were any casualties, it was damned annoying to miss such a bag . . . [the Japanese] mustn't have liked the experience because they didn't come back. Apart from this incident, the night passed quietly, with the exception of the roar set up by our artillery. They really went to town on a defensive fire task to the north-west. Apparently they were pranging a road block. If their firing was accurate, there couldn't be many Japs left in that road block.

By 11 March reports were being received that the Japanese had positioned an artillery piece to the south of the airstrip and the occupants of 'D' Box awaited the inevitable shelling from this and other artillery pieces. Lander wrote:

Everyone is wondering how the Jap is going to react to this party . . . Come what may, we are all thoroughly dug in. Our patrol out on the strip was sniped at about 0900 hours, one must expect that sort of thing as there were odd parties of Japs everywhere. The country lends itself to concealment. Sweeping an area is a hell of a task. The patrols have to put an occasional burst into the dense bush as the only means of clearing it. During the night, further 'jittering' took place, grenades were thrown all around the perimeter, but most of it was unnecessary.

On 12 March the usual daily sweep was carried out but the situation remained relatively calm and, therefore, Lander departed for Monywa in an L5 light plane to attend to 1307 Wing matters and to visit 221 Group. Here, he was able to explain the situation to the Command and Group Defence Officers and also to confirm that the HQ and the two remaining flights of 2968 Field Squadron would be arriving on 15 March. An airlift of mail and supplies for the airmen at Meiktila was also arranged, although this would become sporadic. In an ominous sign, the first three shells fell on Meiktila East airfield that morning and continued spasmodically throughout the day. With the Japanese 75-mm and 105-mm artillery pieces well hidden, the box would be subject to repeated and incessant shelling for the next sixteen days. Some guns were so well camouflaged that they were to remain undetected until near the end of the siege.

In the early days of the siege enemy troops had been seen moving across the north-east end of the airfield escaping to the south, but this was soon to change. Now the Japanese were gathering their forces and intensifying their attacks on Meiktila so as to strangle the air supply operation of the 17th Indian Division and reopen their route of withdrawal to the south. Orders had been given by the *Burma Area Army* Commander to recapture Meiktila airfield at all costs. To do so a crack sabotage unit, the *17 Guerrilla Company* of the *Mori Special Force*, with some 500 men under the command of Colonel Komatsubura Yukio, the *49th Division* and two battalions of the *18th Division*, victors of Malaya and Burma in 1942, were launched against the airfield. From this time the serious struggle for control of the airstrip would begin and it would continue for just over a fortnight.

Lander returned on 14 March and learned from intelligence reports that an attack was expected on 'D' Box that night. Following a brigade conference, he set in train his plans for the night of 14/15 March:

It was decided to send out a standing patrol on a likely line of approach about a mile to the north-east of the Box. No 2 Flight of 2708 Field Squadron under Pilot Officer Furlong was selected for the task. The Flight took up its position at 1850 hours and was instructed to remain in position until first light. At about 1900 hours, shelling recommenced from the north. The enemy have a number of 75s well concealed about 3 miles away. They constantly change position which makes it extremely difficult for our troops to find them. The tanks have had a good day, however, having knocked out four of them in a ground sweep.

The first major ground attack was launched on 'D' Box from the south-east by the column from the *49th Division* and this persisted during the night with heavy LMG fire and many grenades thrown. The result was only one dead Japanese soldier, but a search of the body revealed papers confirming that the defenders of Meiktila East could expect another attack in force. Although unsuccessful, the attacking force established itself close enough to the runway to seriously threaten landings the following morning.

The battle for Meiktila was now reaching a crucial stage and reinforcements were needed. The air-transportable 9th Indian Infantry Brigade of the 5th Indian Division was to be flown in on the morning of 15 March from Palel. The Japanese counter-offensive now made this exercise extremely hazardous. Fortunately, of fifty-four aircraft that flew in that day, only one was destroyed by shell fire. However, this allowed only half the brigade to fly in. Meanwhile the airstrip continued to be used by Hurricanes and Thunderbolts being used on ground-attack missions. These aircraft were rapidly refuelled and rearmed by a flight of 3207 RAF Servicing Commando.

At first light, a large party of Japanese soldiers was seen entering a village to the north-east of the airstrip. This was their lying up area during the day and a tank sweep was arranged to clear the village, which was successfully completed. The shelling in-tensified from about 0800 hours and became extremely accurate, falling in the box and on the unloading aprons on the airstrip. After an hour of this it was decided to close the airstrip and no aircraft were allowed to land. 1307 Wing HQ had a succession of shells land nearby, some coming within five yards of the trenches and two airmen of No 3 Flight 2941 Field Squadron were wounded when a shell hit a large tree and exploded down into their trench. Both were evacuated by plane the same day.

Lander decided to put another flight of 2708 Field Squadron out the next night under command of Flying Officer Kelly, this time to the east. One method for detecting the approach of 'jitter' parties and their like during the night was only tried for a short time. A one-man observation post was placed out forward of the box with a wire stretching back inside the box connected to some tin cans. The airman was a volunteer and the post was covered to prevent detection. When the enemy approached, he had to pull the wire and then kept down under cover. A Bren gun inside the box was positioned to fire on a fixed line over the post should the enemy party go near it. The strain of being put out on the observation post in complete darkness, on one's own, and straining eyes and ears for any sign of enemy movement was too great however, and the practice was stopped soon after it began.

During the small hours of 15/16 March the box came under attack from a party of unknown strength. Lasting about half an hour it was ineffective, but intensive shelling then began from the north and north-east. Around 0430 hours enemy movement was heard at the north end of the airstrip and they were presumed to be laying mines. As was normal practice, a patrol was sent out at dawn to clear the airstrip. Two flights of 2708 Field Squadron moved off through a gap in the barbed wire apron at 0600 hours. Considerable courage was required to move out onto the flat, featureless airstrip, which lacked cover, and walk slowly across it knowing that the Japanese were ready and waiting in prepared positions. There was a belt of scrub that grew up to the box wire for about 300 yards. One night, however, it was set on fire by the enemy, thus depriving the early morning clearance patrols of any cover. One of the flights was under the command of Sergeant Norman Gerrish. He humbly recounted the events of that day from his perspective many years later:

I was acting Flight Commander of No 1 Flight 2708 Squadron. Early in the morning long before daybreak I was told to report to the command post. On arriving there, Pilot Officer Furlong with No 2 Flight was also present, we were both informed that the Japs had been very active during the night on the airfield and could be heard using picks and shovels. We were told the Brigadier had decided that the Japs had been laying mines in the runways and we were both to take out patrols of two sections each from No 1 and 2 Flights, and I was to check the nearside runway and Flying Officer Furlong with No 2 Flight would check the far runway. I asked what equipment we would be using to do the check and I was told Mk 4 rifles with fixed bayonets and if we discovered any mines we would remove same.

I prepared two sections and then briefed them and I left the 'Box' just before first light and arrived at the junction with the runway just as it started to get light. From the junction to the north-east end of the runway was about 300 yards so I started to check this part first with one section on my left, myself in the middle and the other section on my right. We were in an extended line across the full width of the runway. We had checked a good portion of the runway and were starting to get towards the end. Mr Furlong had now come onto the runway and walked down the portion we had checked. Just before reaching us he moved right into the scrub so that he could move diagonally through the scrub and would then come out at the far end of the other runway . . . all hell was let loose and we came under LMG, HMG and rifle fire and very accurate mortar fire on the runway. The section on my left was pinned down, myself and the other section got off the runway and were scattered in the scrub, the mortars kept us all pinned down for a while, I decided I must get forward to a position where I could bring fire to bear on the machine-guns who were dug in at the end of the runway. I started to crawl forward through the scrub and I came alongside of Burns of No 2 Flight who had a Bren gun – I said I needed the Bren gun as I had to get a position where I could engage the machine-gun at the end of the runway. We exchanged his Bren for my rifle. I then ran forward firing the Bren from the hip until I reached a position where I could return fire on to the Jap machine-guns, the remainder of the section had moved forward through the scrub and were now formed into a line at the same time as Mr Furlong's patrol had merged with mine and we were now one. The section left on the runway were now immobilised and I could not see any movement from any of them and the only aid I could give them was to draw the Jap fire away from them. Burns had moved beside me and was busy filling the empty 'mags' so I had a constant supply of ammo to use. Mr Furlong was in the line about a couple of yards to my right so we were in constant touch with each other. Everybody in the line was engaging the Japs who were concealed in the scrub just beyond the perimeter where the Jap machine-guns were dug in pits at the end of the runway.

The two flights then held the enemy for the next one and a half hours, in the process not only taking all their fire but forcing the attackers back 200 yards to the north end of the strip.

It was eventually decided that we would have to make a withdrawal as we were now running short of ammo. We collected from every man in the line their remaining ammo and it was enough to fill two Bren magazines and five rounds for the third magazine. It was decided that the first section to withdraw would be one from No 2 Flight and I would give them covering fire. Away they went back down the runway and I brought fire to bear on the area of the Jap machine-guns. With the magazine empty, the second section from No 2 Flight was the next to go, including Mr Furlong. Away they went and I again fired at the Jap machine-guns until the magazine was empty.

About 40 yards from the junction there was on the side of the runway a disused Jap gun pit. On reaching this Mr Furlong jumped down into it to wait for me, his men carried on to the junction. The last to withdraw were the remains of my patrol. I told them I had only five rounds left and on the word go I would fire single shots at the Japs after which I would follow them with the magazine empty. I picked up the Bren gun and went after them. On reaching the Jap gun pit I saw Mr Furlong and jumped down into the pit with him. I had a breather for a few minutes then we both proceeded to the Junction where our men were waiting for us. The men filed back to the Box and I brought up the rear.

On arriving in the Box Mr Furlong who had fully participated in the all the action and had observed everything that had occurred since we came under fire reported to the CO and gave his report. I then reported to the CO and gave him my report of everything that had happened that morning. Flight Sergeant Billy Briggs was preparing a recovery party to bring back our casualties, most of them being fatal.

I would like to point out that there were others equally involved in the action. Every man in both patrols responded admirably containing an enemy who were in superior numbers, we made a withdrawal for one reason only because we had used all our ammunition.

Meanwhile, Flying Officer Kelly and No 3 Flight, which had been out on the night patrol had heard the gunfire and worked their way north. They then covered the withdrawal of the two flights and engaged the enemy until a counterattack could be launched. Wing Commander Lander mustered a flight from 2963 LAA Squadron to provide stretcher bearers along with the RAF Medical Officer, and took them out under fire onto the airstrip to bring in the wounded. Lander continues:

. . . Flying Officer Kelly was still engaging the enemy and the wounded evacuated to a First Aid Post which the MO set up on the side of the strip. Flight Lieutenant Wootten was in the thick of it here pulling the wounded off the Strip.

LMGs, mortars and snipers gave us hell and it took an hour before the casualties could be got clear. Bullets were flying in all directions which didn't make our task pleasant. Flying Officer Kelly withdrew his Flight when the casualties had been cleared. As a result of the action seven of our men were killed and eight wounded. The casualties inflicted on the enemy were thought to be 20 plus killed, actually I think this figure rather conservative. Flying Officers Furlong and Kelly each killed three or four snipers, I bagged one. Sergeant Gerrish i/c No 1 Flight, displayed courage and leadership of the highest order. He covered the withdrawal of his men with a Bren gun, firing from the hip. While doing this, he was seriously wounded in the leg, despite his wounds he

The main west runway at RAF Meiktila looking south on 5 March 1945. Three days later this area was heavily contested by the RAF Regiment and Japanese infiltration parties. (Australian War Memorial RCO 4395)

continued to fire until all his ammo was expended, he then moved across to another Bren, the gunners having been wounded, and resumed his action until all his men had withdrawn. Flying Officers Kelly and Furlong displayed powers of leadership and fighting qualities which stamped them as Officers far above the average. Not a man relaxed in his efforts, and the fact that a total of only 1500 rounds were expended during the whole of the action speaks highly for the fire control and discipline of the men.

The main west runway from the site of the RAF Meiktila defence 'box'. In the foreground are the entrances and air vents of Japanese bunkers constructed prior to the capture of the airfield, 5 March 1945. (Australian War Memorial RCO 4396)

For Norman Gerrish, his wounds were serious enough for him to require evacuation.

> During the morning action I had received a wound in my leg so off I went to the Casualty Station for attention. I remained there until late in the afternoon then with other wounded I was taken to the runway and put aboard a Dakota which was packed solid with wounded. I lay on the floor of the pilot's cabin then up and away. It was dark when we landed at Sinthe. I was taken to a Field Ambulance where I was examined by a couple of doctors, then to bed. Next morning I was flown back to India to 14th British General Hospital at Comilla where I remained a patient for a month, returning to the Squadron about the middle of April.

For the gallantry displayed that morning Sergeant Gerrish was strongly recommended for the Distinguished Conduct Medal, however, he received the lesser award of the Military Medal.[3]

Meanwhile, at Brigade HQ a counter-attack had been ordered but it took some 1½ hours to organise. Eventually a troop of Sherman tanks of an Indian cavalry regiment, Probyn's Horse, and two infantry companies arrived and the RAF Regiment withdrew. Beyond the runway ends, on either side of the flight path, was a monsoon ditch some 9 feet wide and 5 feet deep and these were what the enemy had occupied during the night. The tanks were sent out and they moved between the two ditches causing considerable slaughter in the ranks of the enemy. On the return of the tanks a Troop Sergeant called out to the Regiment airmen 'we made a mess of that b . . . .. lot, but you lads had killed a lot before we got in amongst them'. The Regiment was credited in the action with some fifty enemy killed, while they had lost seven killed and nine wounded.[4] The 99th Indian Infantry Brigade commander informed Lander that his men had put up a show that could not have been bettered by any infantry troops. On his return to the box Lander addressed the airmen, and complimented them on their actions during the day saying 'I am proud of you all. You certainly earned your laurels today'.

The Japanese now redoubled their efforts to take the airstrip. Despite the shelling intensifying and further enemy incursions the airstrip reopened on the afternoon of 16 March, and the remainder of the 9th Brigade was flown-in without great mishap by the evening of 17 March. Day after day the Dakota crews would bravely put their aircraft down on the contested airstrip, staying only long enough to unload their cargoes of men and supplies. At this stage of the battle it was often unclear to the pilots in the

Sergeant Norman Gerrish, 2708 Field Squadron, RAF Regiment, was awarded the MM for his part in the action at Meiktila on 16 March 1945. (RAF Regiment Museum)

Japanese dead lie on the ground after an unsuccessful counter-attack at Meiktila. (Photograph courtesy of the Imperial War Museum, London, IND 4592)

aircraft arriving soon after first light as to who held the airstrip or whether or not it had been cleared by the Regiment. Some pilots would circle the airstrip prior to landing in an attempt to identify the uniforms or facial features of those moving about the two runways, or wait for the green Very light indicating the RAF Regiment had done its job.[5] The aircraft would be emptied of supplies, which were quickly loaded into waiting 3-tonners, and were then filled as rapidly as possible with wounded. The planes would spend as a short a time on the ground as possible so that the Japanese artillery had no time to range on them. As soon as they lifted off they would then bank so as to avoid passing over the areas occupied by the Japanese. Despite the dangers the Dakotas continued bringing in the 250-pound bombs for the Hurribombers also flying from the airstrip, ammunition for the field and mountain guns and spares for the tanks. Despite the saying 'an army fights on its stomach', food was at the bottom of the priority list at Meiktila.

Once the fly-in was completed, the 9th Brigade took over responsibility for 'D' Box from the 99th Indian Infantry Brigade, which was released for mobile operations. With the new arrivals, 'D' Box had become even more crowded with British, Indian and Gurkha troops, American engineers and a field maintenance unit, and the RAF Regiment. The vehicles had to be dug down forward to protect their engines from shrapnel damage. Life in 'D' Box was grim and the airmen now lived like rabbits deep in dugouts. The small bivouac tents were now tightly packed together and the area was dotted with numerous slit trenches into which soldiers and airmen would dive, jump or roll at the sound of an incoming shell. The defenders were also exposed to the persistent cracks of sniper fire.

Heat and humidity were high as the pre-monsoon weather intensified and, with the supply line now incapacitated, rations were down to one-third and water rationed to one bottle a day. The only source of water was from the two lakes to the west in Meiktila town. Bill Raymond of 2941 Field Squadron was given the job of collecting water from the South Lake using a 44-gallon petrol drum and a jeep:

> The Japanese were using the same source and we would watch each other as we collected the water but we wouldn't fire. When they left you got the hell out of it quick, otherwise you got mortared. Two senior officers landed one day in an L5 and one asked why nobody had shaved. They never got a reply. The enemy started shelling and they left in a hurry and were not seen again at Meiktila.

Bill Raymond was eventually wounded by shellfire. He only survived more serious injury because he was wearing his .303 ammo bandolier around his waist rather than on one shoulder, as was usual, and this deflected the shrapnel.

There were only two aerial incursions by the Japanese Air Force during the siege of 'D' Box as the RAF fighters successfully kept the skies above Meiktila clear. During the night of 12 March two enemy bombers dropped five anti-personnel bombs on the airstrip but with no effect. The last raid was on 20/21 March when two enemy aircraft got through and bombed the 2963 LAA Squadron area. Flight Sergeant George Jones was seriously wounded in both legs, eventually losing one. The two flights of 2963 LAA Squadron were primarily occupied with a strongpoint on the eastern perimeter and they gave well-deserved praise to the work of the Cook, LAC T. Thornbury, assisted by Gunner Cooks LACs J. Darby and D. Thompson, as they prepared and served meals under very difficult conditions. Most importantly the tea was also constantly brewed and made available when firing was heaviest. The Hispanos were withdrawn into the box each night. Although willing to use their Hispanos at night, there was considerable reluctance by the brigade, as their ammunition was not self-destroying and posed a serious threat to units moving outside the perimeter during the night hours.

On the night of 17/18 March three Japanese reached the wire in front of No 3 Flight, 2941 Field Squadron, before one was killed. His body was removed by the remaining two while another group set fire to an abandoned Hurricane. The following night 'Bill' Lander was again in the thick of it when along with Flight Sergeant Briggs and Corporal Foster of 2708 Field Squadron he brought in an airman who had been wounded in a Japanese ambush while on patrol. On 19 March he returned again to Monywa to explain to 221 Group the seriousness of the situation and the requirement for reinforcements to sustain the necessary defence tasks.

The 17th Indian Division was now able to open a general offensive against the forces moving against Meiktila. On 20 March 'D' Box received its heaviest day of shelling since the siege had begun and this presaged an intensification of the enemy offensive. From 21 March and for the next five days there would be grim close-quarter fighting as the Japanese made an all-out attempt to retake the airfield.[5] Despite the arrival of the new brigade and the despatch by the 17th Indian Division of armoured columns to the surrounding areas to neutralise offensive action, the shelling continued. A section of 2941 Field Squadron went out on patrol and brought in a wounded Japanese soldier who had survived one of these offensive sweeps. Prisoners were hardly ever taken in Burma and this was indeed a rare find. He was able to provide Intelligence with much useful information. It was fortunate that the 9th Brigade had got in when they did as the following day the landing of aircraft was judged to be no longer safe and all supplies would have to be dropped by parachute. The Japanese were determined to wrest the airstrip from the 17th Indian Division's grasp and the events of the next few days would determine the success or otherwise of Slim's master stroke.

Following the losses suffered on 16 March, the airmen of 2708 Field Squadron had manned the perimeter wire from dusk till dawn from 17 March, but patrolling was halted for the next three days to allow for a reorganisation. Now suffering a shortage of officers and NCOs, No 1 Rifle Flight was absorbed into Nos 2 and 3 Flights. Lander returned to Meiktila on 21 March and resumed his role in leading Regiment patrols. For the next two days he went out with the two flights of 2708 Field Squadron on sweeps north and west of the airstrip, including one with a company of Gurkhas.

The Mortar Section of 2708 Squadron had some success when it wiped out an enemy post of twelve with six rounds. The enemy ambush party had pinned down a patrol of the 2nd West Yorkshire Regiment escorting supplies to an infantry outpost north of the airstrip. Later that day the Section also engaged some Japanese dug-in amongst the scrub to the north-east of 'D' Box with another effective concentration. A night attack on 22/23 March was driven off, leaving 103 enemy dead on the battlefield. On 23 March LAC Saint of 2941 Field Squadron provided support to the 2nd West Yorkshires with his Bren from the perimeter wire as they withdrew from the action and he directed his fire against enemy snipers who were proving dangerous.[6] Further 105-mm and 75-mm shells fell on the box, with the latter scoring a direct hit on the 9th Brigade HQ around 1100 hours, seriously wounding the Brigadier and Brigade Major.

The Hispanos of 2963 LAA Squadron had moved out each morning onto the airstrip. However, at midday on 23 March with mortar and sniper fire making their positions untenable, the guns were brought back into the box. Late in the afternoon of 23 March, two Dakotas landed and began unloading supplies. They were soon loading up with the badly wounded on stretchers. One of the aircraft took off successfully but the port engine on the second failed to start and it was soon a target for the Japanese artillery. It was heavily loaded with wounded and Sergeant Brown of 3207 RAF Servicing Commando immediately ran onto the airstrip to inspect the engine to see if it could be restarted. He refused to take cover despite shells falling in close proximity to the aircraft. In a short time, however, it was hit by shellfire from a Japanese anti-tank gun firing directly down the runway. The wounded were quickly carried from the stricken plane. However, one poor blighter had been left on a stretcher at the far end of the plane. It was the Brigade Major, W.S. Armour, who had just been wounded that morning in the shelling of the Brigade Command Post. He had been slightly wounded again at the dressing station and then again when the shell hit the Dakota, which was now blazing fiercely. Although conscious he was unable to talk or move and it was assumed he was dead. One man said 'He's had it!' He could hear his mortal state being discussed by those clearing the aircraft but he could not move to indicate he was alive.

The crew of a Douglas Dakota in a bomb crater beside their damaged aircraft after it was shelled by the Japanese before take-off at Meiktila. (Air Historical Branch RAF Crown Copyright)

Fortunately Sergeant Brown said, 'We're not leaving anybody in here dead or alive.' He then went back in and got Armour out and it was then discovered he was indeed alive. Meanwhile, an L5 in attempting to land received a direct hit and was burnt out. Sergeant Brown then saw another aircraft landing and he ran over and ordered it to take off immediately. For his quick action that day Sergeant Brown received the Military Medal.[8]

The RAF Regiment had now been at Meiktila for more than three weeks and, with the airstrip closed to further landings, the situation appeared to be worsening rather than improving. On 24 March the struggle was to reach its climax and the Regiment was to have more casualties and suffer a severe blow while carrying out its routine but vital tasks. The dawn patrol was again led by Wing Commander Lander and consisted of 2708 Field Squadron with 'D' Company of the 6/9th Jat Regiment. Moving to the north-east of the airstrip, enemy LMGs and small arms fire opened up from a strong and well-concealed enemy position and the airmen and jawans were immediately pinned down. The commander of the Jats and his 2 i/c were both wounded soon after the firing started. LAC Ron Finch was lying alongside Lander in the scrub when he heard a crack and saw the CO had been hit in the head. He was wearing a beret and a khaki short-sleeved shirt with rank slides, whereas the rest of the men had steel helmets and jungle green. Had the sniper identified him as an officer and picked him off? Finch remembers Lander's last words: 'Watch it the b . . . . are in the corner!' The CO's runner, LAC 'Jock' Dakers, was killed at the same time out on the right flank.

An Army Sergeant on a Bofors gun thought he saw the flash of a sniper's rifle from a nearby palm tree as one of his gun crew fell to the ground wounded. Siting his Bofors and firing, the top half of the tree was blown apart and a body was seen to fall from it as it disintegrated. The men of 2708 Mortar Section fired their mortars in support of the beleaguered patrol. In a demonstration of their skill in gun drill and accurate laying, they put down six rounds at range of 550 yards on an enemy position north-west of the box, which was sufficient wipe out by direct hits the entire party.[9]

Flight Lieutenant Wootton was now the only officer left in the patrol and he took command. Smoke was called for and the force retired to a better line, covered by the fire of Sergeant White's Mortar Section. They remained in this position for the next two hours until Brigade HQ ordered the force back to 'D' Box and they retired under cover of smoke. The Japanese position was then subjected to an air strike by Hurricane IICs, along with a heavy artillery concentration. During the afternoon a tank and infantry attack cleared the enemy positions. Unfortunately, it was impossible to bring in the bodies of Lander and Dakers owing to the strong enemy forces in the locality.

Morale, in spite of the appalling conditions had remained high. The example set by 'Bill' Lander had built into each man the belief that he was the best and that no Jap was going to walk over him. He had played a significant and active part in the defence of Meiktila airfield. He was a native of Liverpool, and studied at Liverpool University in the 1930s; jobs were difficult to get and he was recruited into the Somerset Police and was stationed at Bath. He joined the RAF when war broke out and became an instructor at the RAF Officers' College at Sidmouth in Devon as an officer in the RAF Police. From there he was posted to India in August 1944 in a draft of RAF Regiment officers.

The following appreciation was written of him by those who had served under him. 'The Commanding Officer Wing Commander Cuthbert Mons Lander, known as "Bill" Lander, was 30 years old when killed in action. He was, by any standard, an outstanding officer, superb in leadership, full of energy and enthusiasm, well liked and respected by all who served with him.' The late Wing Commander Tom McKirdy, one time the Commanding Officer of the RAF Regiment Depot at Secunderabad, said he was a friend of his and the men at Meiktila had a CO who was in a class of his own.

He has never able to understand why his bravery was never recognised. The standard he set others followed; one man remarked that he was a bright star that shone in the darkness at Meiktila.

As night fell on 24 March, along with the usual 'jitter' parties, another more disturbing noise echoed across 'D' Box. Japanese tanks were heard moving around the northern end of the airstrip. Brigade HQ ordered all fire to be withheld unless they committed a hostile act. Three tanks were recognised in the moonlight and they soon stopped directly in front of No 3 Flight of 2941 Field Squadron, only 20 yards from the wire. The Regiment possessed no weapons capable of responding to the threat so the airmen simply waited apprehensively, but remained firm and disciplined. The Box Commander bravely challenged them; there was confused shouting, and the tanks then simply turned about and rattled away, much to the relief and amazement of all. The tanks seemed to be more lost than acting with aggressive intent. Cyril Paskin of 2968 Field Squadron recalls one of the tanks moving past his own position:

> I remember being in the front trench at Meiktila one night when a Japanese tank came by. The Japanese officer got out and had a look round but luckily didn't see us and got back in and drove off. There were some Americans beside us and they had a bazooka anti-tank weapon. They didn't fire, which was a good thing, as things could have really kicked off.

The tanks could have caused serious havoc if used in a concerted fashion, although one

RAF Regiment airmen inspect a discarded Japanese 50-mm 'leg' mortar. The use of the mortar in this manner would result in a broken thigh. This weapon and the 81-mm mortar were skilfully handled by the enemy. (Air Historical Branch RAF Crown Copyright)

did later attack a post of the 3/2nd Punjab Regiment but was driven off by PIAT fire.

During the early hours of 25 March the enemy moved in and set up a mortar position in the earth-walled dispersal bays at the south-east end of the airfield. Other enemy parties used grenade-dischargers and machine-guns to try and draw fire from the defenders of 'D' Box. To add to this, an anti-tank gun was firing from the northern perimeter of the airstrip and another from near the pagoda. The mortars used by the Japanese were their most deadly and accurate weapons and the airstrip was now dominated by them. To remove this threat an infantry attack was launched on the dispersal bays while Hispanos of 2963 LAA Squadron and a Bofors gun blasted holes through the backs of these to prevent their further use. On one occasion the enemy mounted a mortar on a bullock cart and moved round the box at night from one firing position to another.

The heavy shellfire of 24 March had prevented the LAA flights of 2963 Squadron deploying and thus the men remained in their domestic areas. Their HQ tent was again pierced by shrapnel without harm, but unfortunately four members of a Hispano gun crew of 2963 LAA Squadron sheltering in a storm ditch were hit by shrapnel when a mortar hit the tree over their dugout. LACs Brown and Allen were killed immediately. Corporal Waite died the next day of the wounds he received, while LAC Morrish was evacuated but died of his wounds a few days later at a hospital near Comilla. By a stroke of luck a Regiment officer sheltering with them, but who was around the bend in the ditch, was unharmed. The three airmen were buried the following day at the Meiktila Military Cemetery where, due to the shelling, the funeral party was forced to take cover *en route*.

RAF Regiment airmen stand in their shrapnel-ridden tent, the result of the incessant Japanese shelling at Meiktila. (Air Historical Branch RAF Crown Copyright)

The shelling continued without let-up for the next three days as the enemy made repeated attempts to retake Meiktila. With the crowded conditions in the box it was inevitable that further casualties would ensue. On 25 March the Regiment's Casualty Clearing Station tent was hit and some airmen wounded a second time. The following day the 2708 Squadron Orderly Room took a direct hit, destroying the squadron's records and wounding the acting Squadron CO, Flight Lieutenant Wootten, the Adjutant, Flying Officer Henry, Corporal Saunders, LAC Dyer and the Padre, Squadron Leader M. O'Connor. The most severely wounded, Flight Lieutenant Wootton and Flying Officer Henry, were flown out to Mynamati Hospital near Comilla.

Norman Gerrish was at Comilla recovering from his wounds and remembers the arrival of the casualties from the shelling of the Orderly Room and the parlous state of 2708 Squadron with regard to officers and senior NCOs:

> While I was a patient at Comilla I learnt that my CO, Flight Lieutenant Wootten had been brought in wounded. I went and visited him; he was badly wounded in the hip. He told me that a Jap shell had pitched in the HQ tent and that as well as being wounded Flying Officer Henry, the Adjutant, had been killed . . . This now left the Squadron with only two officers and four senior NCOs. Mr Furlong (No 2 Flight) and Mr Kelly (No 3 Flight), Flight Sergeant Briggs, Sergeant Bill Syncup (No 2 Flight), Sergeant Johnny MacFarlane (No 3 Flight), Sergeant Eric 'Chalky' White commanding Mortar Section. So a heavy responsibility rested on the shoulders of these six men . . .

On 28 March reinforcements arrived in the form of a second flight of 2968 Field

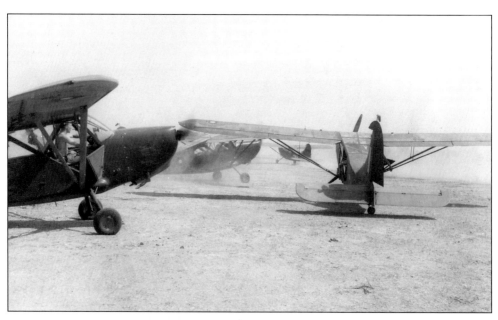

L5 Sentinels of 194 Squadron RAF queuing for take-off at a forward airstrip. These aircraft were capable of landing on very short or poor strips and played a crucial role in casualty evacuation and delivery of urgent supplies. They flew in the reinforcement flights of 2968 Field Squadron during the last days of the siege at Meiktila. (Air Historical Branch RAF Crown Copyright)

Squadron, but as the airstrip was still closed to the large air transports they were flown in by the pilots of 'C' Flight, 194 Squadron RAF, equipped with seven L5 Sentinel light planes. Cyril Paskin recalls their arrival:

> We could only use [L5] air ambulances which were small and, therefore, able to fly in undetected but this meant that we could only be flown in two at a time. The idea once the plane landed was to leap out and run as quickly as possible for the slit trenches [while] avoiding the shelling and sniper fire.

One L5 pilot recalled the incredible bravery of the men on the ground at Meiktila. A few days before the lifting of the siege, an RAF medical officer led a detachment of the Regiment in a morning bayonet charge to clear the airstrip so that a desperately needed consignment of blood plasma could be flown in. He was unable to recall his name and his bravery went unrecorded and unrecognised.[10]

There had been no shortage of volunteers to go out and recover the bodies of Lander and Dakers but it was considered too dangerous an operation. It was not until 28 March that Flying Officer Kelly with Corporal MacKenzie and LACs Finch, Hooson and Bartlett reached Wing Commander Lander's body. LAC Dakers' could not be recovered until two days later owing to sniper activity. Almost as a coincidence the shellfire was to cease on the day that Lander was temporarily buried on the battlefield.[11]

Wing Commander Gladding, previously of 1323 Wing, had arrived at Meiktila on 26 March to assume command of 1307 Wing. After assessing the situation he flew back to Monywa to 221 Group HQ and reported what he had found. He returned to Meiktila the same day and made contact with the 9th Indian Brigade Commander. The remaining flight of 2968 Field Squadron arrived by light plane the next day and this allowed for the relief of No 3 Flight of 2941 Field Squadron. This flight were now seriously depleted owing to the rigours of the previous weeks and the men were sent to the 1307 Wing 'Rest Camp' on the shores of one of the lakes in Meiktila, but still with responsibility for an AMES. Flying Officer A.A. Wyatt and his section from 2963 LAA Squadron were sent to support and reinforce No 3 Flight, but also to rest.

With the AA threat minimal, 2963 LAA Squadron relieved the RAF Servicing Commandos on the posts they had been hastily allocated during the desperate times of the previous days. While relatively untrained in infantry work, the airmen of 2963 Squadron did a considerable amount of day and night manning of strong points in the box defences and along with the other Regiment units were complimented by the Brigadier on their good fire control and discipline. 'Jitter' parties approached the wire each night and units in the box frequently expended thousands of rounds of ammunition. This was despite orders to hold fire until the enemy were on the wire, and then use grenades if possible. At all times the RAF Regiment units obeyed these instructions.

The Japanese attacks had been carried with their usual tenacity, however, surprisingly the siege ended abruptly on 28 March when the enemy finally conceded that they could not recapture Meiktila. To the west, two motorised brigades of the 5th Indian Division had crossed the Irrawaddy and were on their way to relieve the 17th Indian Division. Columns of the 17th Indian Division were fanning out from Meiktila and were soon in contact with the 20th Indian Division moving in from the north. On 1 April the airfield reopened for the landing of supplies and patrols were sent out but had nothing to report. The enemy had gone.

The Japanese had again been savagely mauled and they were ordered to withdraw south to form a new defensive line to block the road and railway to Rangoon. The *15th* and *33rd Armies* had suffered a major defeat and the *Burma Area Army* ceased to exist

Only four days after the siege had ended, three RAAF airmen, serving in 194 Squadron RAF, chat with two RAF Regiment officers on the airstrip at Meiktila while their Dakota transport aircraft is unloaded. The Dakota had flown in from Akyab. (Australian War Memorial SEA 0212)

as a fighting force. On 31 March the Japanese gave up hope of taking Meiktila. IV Corps was regrouping in the devastated town and was now preparing to move south. Slim's master stroke had succeeded and the Fourteenth Army and 221 Group brimmed with confidence. The urgency of their task remained, however. The objective was to reach Rangoon before the monsoon.

Over three weeks of strain and tension the Japanese came close at times to completely denying use of the airfield, but they were beaten back on each occasion by the dogged defence. The battle for, capture, and successful defence of Meiktila was one of the significant milestones in the reconquest of Burma. 'Meiktila' is one of the RAF Regiment's greatest and proudest battle honours. It had again played an important part in the ultimate success of the Burma campaign.

Whereas the operations in the Arakan and Imphal were primarily defensive, the siege of Meiktila was a significant offensive action for the Regiment. It was touch and go for a number of days as to whether Slim's thrust would succeed. The Fourteenth Army barely had enough troops to seize and hold the town and airfield, but ultimately succeeded through sound leadership and determination from trooper, sowar, gunner, private, rifleman, jawan, sapper and airman alike.

Less than two months after landing in India, 2708 Field Squadron had been flown to Meiktila, many miles ahead of the consolidated front line of the Army, and for three weeks stood up to repeated enemy attacks and shelling. Only a few months earlier 2708 Field Squadron had been back in the United Kingdom in a more benign environment. The squadron had gained the respect and admiration of all units in the area for its two actions against superior numbers of the enemy. Credit must also be given to airmen of the three other squadrons represented. Many had seen continuous service in India and Burma for three or more years. Most had had no leave or relief from their duties since mid-1943 and many were suffering from malaria, dysentery or various other tropical afflictions alone or in combination. The SEAC-formed squadrons were, therefore, already seriously depleted prior to reaching Meiktila. It must always be remembered when referring to the movements and actions of the Regiment that the field squadrons at full establishment were only equivalent in size to an infantry company and the flights to those of a platoon.

The fighting at Meiktila took a heavy toll on the Regiment. For the 270 airmen present during the siege, casualties were relatively heavy for such a small representation. The casualty rate for the operation was one airman in three and the officers in particular suffered in high proportion. Fourteen men were killed in action or died of wounds and twenty-five were wounded. Fifty airmen were evacuated from Meiktila due to sickness, slight wounds or suffering from nervous exhaustion caused by day after day of incessant shelling. The tension caused by exposure to unremitting, heavy and unpredictable shelling on a confined and crowded area for more than a fortnight, along with the ever-present threat posed by snipers and mortar fire, cannot be underestimated.[12]

Given the RAF Regiment put up such a determined fight at Meiktila, it was surprising that so few awards were made to those who took part. Lander's gallantry in particular seemed to have been noted but went unrewarded. Sergeant Norman Gerrish expressed his view of why the Regiment's work went unrecognised:

> Every day one thought that tomorrow would bring reinforcements and when they did arrive, it was all over, the gates were wide open to the south and Rangoon before the monsoon broke. I think that there were other members of the Squadron whose action during the siege *probably* warranted some form of recognition. The award made to me was the only one in the Squadron. Thinking back now it is probably because the Wing Commander was killed, the CO of the Squadron was in hospital badly wounded, the Adjutant killed, and the two remaining officers Flying Officer Kelly and Pilot Officer Furlong had plenty to contend with that possibly no other recommendations were made.

Mountbatten considered the RAF Regiment's contribution significant enough for its specific mention in his official report on the campaign in South-East Asia.[13] Words of admiration were also expressed for the work of the RAF Regiment at Meiktila by the CO of 17 (Spitfire) Squadron RAF, Squadron Leader 'Ginger' Lacey:

> [During the first week of March] 17 Squadron began carrying out patrols from the Meiktila airfield. But although the Fourteenth Army now held the town, they had to regain possession of the airstrip every day; they lacked the troops to occupy it during the night. At each sunset the force withdrew to the protection of its barbed-wire Box; the Japanese, knowing the airfield was left undefended, stubbornly returned to it. With first light, an attack was put in to clear them out. As soon as the airfield was reported to be back in British hands, 17 Squadron flew in. Invariably they had to help in removing enemy corpses from the runway. The RAF Regiment won bloody renown in the fierce fighting for repossession of the landing ground every humid morning. One day that the Squadron remembers, one of the aircraft dispersal bays was full of the bodies of RAF Regiment officers and men awaiting burial.[14]

The final words are left to Air Vice Marshal S.F. Vincent, the popular and highly regarded AOC 221 Group RAF, who wrote the following commendation for the actions of the RAF Regiment at Meiktila:

> The RAF Regiment proved themselves grand fighters . . . Those, mostly the RAF Regiment, of course held a Box on the edge of the strip, and the local Army troops withdrew . . . and left the strip open for recapture every night by the enemy, and our lads were, therefore, in the front position. During this time they had a considerable amount of fighting and inflicted very many casualties on the enemy, but of course, unfortunately, lost several killed and wounded themselves, including their CO, a first class Wing Commander by the name of Lander.[15]

Notes

1   Only four officers and 120 airmen were airlifted from Agartala. One officer and twenty-seven airmen remained as the rear party to collect transport, and convey heavy equipment by road, another twelve airmen were detached on a Mines and Booby Traps Course and another three airmen on a Signallers' Course.

2   AIR 29/138, *Operations Record Books RAF Regiment Squadrons 2941–2950, 2953–2955, 2957–2962, 2964, 2966–2970 Appendices Only.* Diary of events at Meiktila, 9–31 March, No 3 Flight, 2941 Squadron, RAF Regiment.

3   Norman Phillip Gerrish was born on 1 May 1921. He joined the RAF in May 1941 and was posted to 2810 Squadron. He served in the UK from 1942 to 1944 at Catterick, Handworthy, Hornchurch and Felixstowe. He joined 2708 Squadron in October 1944 and embarked with them when they were sent to India in December of that year. He recovered from his wounds and was able to remain with 2708 until he was discharged from the RAF in October 1946.

4   Airmen of 2708 Field Squadron killed in action on 16 March were Corporal A.C. Trebilcock and LACs A. Wilkinson, T. Turner, B. Rees, T.J. Roberts, D.C. Moore and G.H. Johnson.

5   Farquharson, R.H. *For Your Tomorrow. Canadians and the Burma Campaign, 1941–1945.* Victoria, BC [Canada]: Trafford Publishing, 2004, p. 237.

6   The first attacks were made by *II/196th Battalion*, which lost 160 men killed. Later when *18th Division* took over, the attacks were carried out by *55th* and *119th Regiments* and supported by *18th Mountain Artillery Regiment*.

7   The snipers had remained behind after the withdrawal and caused thirty-six casualties to the 2nd West Yorkshires.

8   The story of the RAF Servicing Commandos has been told in two books, Davies, J. and J.P. Kellett. *A History of the RAF Servicing Commandos.* Shrewsbury: Airlife, 1989, and Atkinson, T. ed. *Spectacles, Testicles, Fags and Matches. The untold story of RAF Servicing Commandos in World War Two*, Edinburgh: Luath Press, 2004.

9   AIR 20/4024, *The RAF Regiment in Action. 1943 July – 1945 December, Confidential Report*.

10   The pilot was John Dunbar of 194 Squadron RAF and his recollection was cited in Probert, H. *The Forgotten Air Force: A History of the Royal Air Force in the War against Japan.* London: Brassey's, 1995, p. 266.

11   Lander and Dakers were later re-interred at Taukkyan War Cemetery near Rangoon. LAC William Dakers was born in a small village called Brechin in Angus. In recent years it was discovered that his name had never been placed on the village war memorial. The RAF Regiment SEAC Association then arranged and paid for his name to be placed there.

12   Allen, L. *Burma. The Longest War 1941–1945.* London: Dent, 1984, p. 449, The Brigade Major of 255 Indian Tank Brigade, Colonel Alasdair Tuck, was of the opinion that too much had been asked of the RAF Regiment Commando [sic].

13   Mountbatten, Vice-Admiral The Earl. *Report to the Combined Chiefs of Staff by the Supreme Allied Commander South-East Asia, 1943–1945.* London: HMSO, 1951, p. 140,

'At Meiktila, when it was cut off, the fighting had been severe: the Japanese throwing in one attack upon another. A small force consisting mainly of the RAF Regiment was made responsible for Meiktila Main [sic] airfield . . . '

14 Bickers, R.T. *Ginger Lacey, Fighter Pilot*, London: Pan, 1969 (1962), p. 169.
15 Vincent, S. F. *Flying Fever*. London: Jarrolds, 1972, p. 176.

CHAPTER NINE

Arakan Advance – The Battle of the Arakan Beaches

> '... when he discovered that the RAF Regiment had a field squadron based on Akyab he had not hesitated in nominating us ... we would be coming into close contact with the native population ... he required troops who had the necessary military skills and toughness and also able to treat the Burmese with firmness where necessary, while being friendly and understanding toward them.'
>
> Corporal Colin Kirby, 2966 Field Squadron

The first land defeat of the Japanese by the Fourteenth Army had been inflicted in the Arakan in early 1944. By the middle of that year, however, this front had become of secondary importance to the advance in central Burma. The Allied command gave some consideration as to whether XV Corps should be reduced to a holding force while the major land advances were prosecuted elsewhere. Eventually it was decided that XV Corps would become independent from the Fourteenth Army and come under the direct command of Allied Land Forces, South-East Asia (ALFSEA).[1] With the firm principle that Army and Air Headquarters should be alongside each other at every level now well established, 224 Group RAF had moved in alongside XV Indian Corps HQ at Chittagong.

While the Fourteenth Army and 221 Group were pursuing the retreating Japanese forces down the Kabaw Valley and onto the central plain of Burma during November and December 1944, XV Corps[2] and 224 Group RAF had successfully cleared the north Arakan of the enemy fourteen days ahead of schedule. From now on the major advances on this front would not be made overland but by amphibious landing. The main objectives were the capture of the airfields on Akyab and Ramree Islands. Their value became more apparent as the Fourteenth Army pushed south. Rangoon had to be taken before the monsoon broke and the Fourteenth Army soon found it could no longer be maintained with the volumes of supplies delivered from the air bases in Bengal, Assam and Manipur. The economic range of the Dakota transports was some 250 miles and once the Fourteenth Army passed Mandalay they would be beyond that point. Flights from Chittagong would be of slightly greater economy but the only solution was to find new air bases that paralleled the advance. The most suitable would be the excellent airfields on Akyab and Ramree Islands (Map 5).

A large-scale amphibious landing, Operation *Talon*, had been planned for the capture of Akyab. It was first thought that the Japanese would, as they had since late 1942, defend it well forward and with their usual tenacity.[3] This was not the case, and the enemy forces were rapidly withdrawn to the south Arakan around Kangaw and Taungup. A small Japanese detachment was left on Akyab, and Ramree was to be held with light forces.

The Allies soon became suspicious that the Japanese had departed from Akyab, and, therefore, on 2 January a light plane was sent over the island. Flying at 50 feet the pilot was able to report that he could see no sign of the enemy and that the locals were indicating that the enemy had gone. The commanders of XV Corps and 224 Group, Christison and Bandon, flew in themselves and were enthusiastically greeted by the native populace. The enemy had indeed gone. The planned massive bombardment was called off and the landings proceeded peacefully.[4] Akyab town was occupied on 4 January. For very little struggle the Allies now possessed a valuable port, an airfield and seven satellite airstrips. The Japanese Air Force was determined to strike back and 67 (Spitfire) Squadron was quickly flown in to meet the anticipated response. It was a timely arrival as 67 (Spitfire) Squadron repelled the enemy air attack on the port of Akyab with heavy losses to the enemy. This was the attack seen by the men of 'C' Flight of 2706 LAA Squadron as they had sailed into the harbour with HMIS *Bihar*.

Since early December, 1327 Wing HQ had been at Patenga on combined operations training with the Regiment squadrons. This was completed by 1 January 1945 and 1327 Wing and two squadrons had readied themselves for the Akyab landings. Disappointingly, however, on 9 January Wing Commander G.S. Airey was told by Advanced HQ 224 Group, that the wing was not going to participate in that operation but would be given a new commitment in Operation *Matador*, the landings at Ramree (Appendix 14).

The protection of the airfields on Akyab Island would now be the responsibility of 1326 Wing and 2706 LAA Squadron, and so in mid-January they moved by the overland route from Maungdaw, down the coastal strip past Indin, and on to Akyab via the ferry at Foul Point. Despite the poor road conditions they were the first RAF convoy to reach Akyab complete. Here they were reunited with 'C' Flight of 2706 LAA Squadron, which was already in occupation, and were ready for action by late on 21 January. They were joined by 2966 Field Squadron, which had trained for combined operations under 1327 Wing HQ but had just been transferred to 1326 Wing. This squadron travelled by sea and was deployed on arrival to provide close protection to Akyab airfield. Colin Kirby describes the departure from Chittagong and the journey to Akyab:

We were told that we were to attack and effect a landing on Akyab Island, which lies just off the Arakan coast. On 9 January [however] we learned that Akyab was no longer defended. Such naval ships we had in the Indian Ocean had shelled the port and the Japs had left and moved inland. Instead of sailing down the coast in landing craft and attacking the island we could now go by steamer and go ashore unopposed. The Squadron practised a form of attack, whereby Sergeant Brown's mortars shelled an enemy position from the flank while the rest of the Squadron advanced. The trick was to get the timing spot on . . .

On 18 January we were up early and packed our kit, then hung around all day waiting for transport to take us to Chittagong . . . [But] spent the day 'playing' bridge. We left about midnight, and then spent another day and night sat on our kit on the quayside until we boarded the troopship at 0900 hours. We sailed at midday. It was a journey of about 24 hours down the coast to Akyab.

The port was flattened. What our ships hadn't shelled the Japs themselves had blown up. We marched a few miles inland, had a rest, and then marched some more. We were nearly across the island before stopping, and we slept on the spot. I recall it was very damp and there was not much sleep. The following day we were issued with K rations for the first time . . . Easy to handle and carry and nutritious. Later on in the jungle we relied on them a lot. They would have been a boon at Sapam and Kangla.

A further change was the arrival of the OC of 1326 Wing, and this was to have disturbing consequences for some of the airmen in 2966 Field Squadron. Colin Kirby continues:

> . . . at the beginning of February . . . Wing Commander Gow [OC 1326 Wing] arrived on the island, thus being the senior Regiment officer there . . . He quickly began to make himself unpopular with parades, drills, inspections of various kinds. All this was definitely not in the style of 2966!

Along with the ground defence tasks, 2966 Field Squadron now had to turn its hand to yet another task, as Colin Kirby describes:

> Life continued with . . . patrolling the airstrip, shooting on the range, drills and inspection. Our main job apart from all this, was fire fighting. Another task allocated to the Regiment which seemed to turn its hand to anything. Akyab is mainly flat, with large areas of scrubland. At this time the vegetation was tinder dry and there were numerous fires. It was suspected that many of them had been started deliberately by unfriendly natives. Every day one or two flights were on fire patrol, or standing by, ready to dash to the site of the latest outbreak. We had to beat out the flames with broom-like things fashioned out of bamboo and fronds. It was hot and tiring work, and as quickly as one area seemed to have been dealt with, it would blaze up again or the call would be received about another fire a few miles away. At the end of the day we had aching shoulders and parched throats.

However, there was a short respite from this toil when 2966 Field Squadron was called on to defend the honour of the Regiment:

> There was a unit of Royal Marine Commandos on the Island, and generally we were kept apart. When it was announced that a soccer match had been arranged between the two services it generated as much enthusiasm as a Wembley final. It was dour struggle, finishing 0-0. Clem Hales was a really good player, and he came off the field with his legs badly bruised, as did others. Honours were even!

Meanwhile, it was planned to make a direct assault on the Myebon Peninsula, located about 30 miles east of Akyab and close to the major enemy stronghold at Kangaw. Landings were made on 12 January by the 3rd Commando Brigade and the 74th Brigade of the 25th Indian Division. With heavy air support from Hurricanes, Thunderbolts and Mitchells, the bridgehead was secured. This was not the pushover that Akyab had been and there was a further week of severe and desperate fighting as the enemy counter-attacked. The Commandos and the 74th Indian Brigade, however, were able to gradually push north up the peninsula and form a solid defence line. Landings were then made to the east of the Myebon Peninsula at a place called Kangaw, where the Commando Brigade cut the escape route for the Japanese fighting to the north against the West Africans.

On 30 January, the day that Kangaw fell and the enemy escape route to the south was sealed, Flying Officer H.W. Kelly, an NCO, and twenty-two airmen of 2966 Field

Squadron embarked on an LCI at Akyab and sailed for Myebon. Their role was to protect a forward AMES on Myebon Peninsula, providing early warning to the landing areas of air attack. Although the initial landings had occurred more than two weeks earlier, the beaches to the north were still being shelled by the Royal Navy and the men were unable to land until just before midnight, and in three feet of water. Active day and night patrolling were begun and these were carried out to a depth of 3 miles from the radar site the next fortnight until the Army reported the peninsula clear of the enemy. Small arms fire and heavy MG were heard or seen during the first few nights as pockets of Japanese were cleared. A detachment was provided to guard a crashed aircraft located a mile from enemy positions across the Myebon River. Extensive patrolling was reinstituted when the AMES moved forward from the beachhead to an area with a flank unguarded by the Army. The operation was successfully completed without incident and on 24 February the flight returned to Akyab.

While heavy and bitter fighting was occurring at Myebon, Operation *Matador*, a further amphibious landing, was being made on Ramree Island. The objective was the port and airfield at Kyaukpyu. The Japanese commanders had concentrated their forces around Kangaw and Taungup and had handed over Akyab and the important airfields and bridgeheads without a great struggle. Ramree Island, located 50 miles south of Myebon, proved a slightly tougher proposition than Akyab. Therefore, on 21 January the 71st Indian Brigade of the 26th Indian Division landed unopposed at the northern end of the island at Kyaukpyu. A heavy naval bombardment, 360 tons of bombs dropped by eighty-six Liberators of the Strategic Air Force, along with air strikes by Thunderbolts and Mitchells, were preliminaries to the landings. The airfield was soon captured and the 4th Indian Brigade moved inland. The 71st Indian Brigade moved along the west coast and by 7 February was fighting with tank support on the outskirts of Ramree town. It was not until 17 February that Ramree was cleared of the enemy, although many continued to attempt escape to the mainland through crocodile-infested mangrove swamps.

While 1327 Wing had been disappointed at the cancellation of the Akyab landings, this had quickly disappeared when the men were told that Operation *Matador* would go ahead, and they continued with preparations and packing at Patenga. During the intervening period 1327 Wing also organised advanced Squadron Battle Training in Jungle Warfare, which proceeded with considerable success. The RAF Regiment Force allocated for Operation *Matador* was to consist of 1327 Wing HQ, 2967 Field Squadron, 2959 LAA Squadron and 'B' Flight of 2837 LAA Squadron. With limited shipping space, however, the arrival of the wing and squadrons at Ramree would be spread over eleven days.

On 19 January, the 1327 Wing Recce Party consisting of Wing Commander Airey and a runner, LAC J. Lamb,[5] reported to HMS *Flamingo* at Chittagong. The Recce Party was to accompany the Force Commanders and the 26th Indian Division HQ. After a pleasant and uneventful trip down the coast, Ramree was sighted at first light on 21 January. Surrounded by an imposing convoy, including the battleship HMS *Queen Elizabeth*, the bombardment commenced.

The assault landing craft then moved in and landed successfully, although those on HMS *Flamingo* witnessed a motor launch and an LCA going up on mines. Wing Commander Airey and his runner were soon transferred to a motor launch for the run in but taking heed of what they had just observed, removed their boots and socks and loosened their equipment. The launch landed them safely at 'Fox Red' Beach by 1400 hours where they made contact with the RAF Senior Commander. LAC Lamb was immediately ordered back to HMS *Flamingo* to retrieve important papers that this

An airman of the RAF Regiment wades ashore from a landing craft during the amphibious landings on Ramree Island. (Air Historical Branch RAF Crown Copyright)

officer had left behind. This was no easy task and Lamb had to make four changes of craft before returning with the papers.

The following day, Airey made an extensive recce of the airfield and selected sites suitable for the protection of the AMES that had also arrived. He made contact with the CRA 26th Indian Division, the local LAA Troop and HQ 4th Indian Brigade. That evening an enemy patrol came close to the radar site and an Army officer was killed in a skirmish. The next day the radar personnel questioned Airey as to when the RAF Regiment were going to arrive to give them some protection. The dual task of maintaining radar watch and doing guard duties as well was causing considerable strain. Similar opinions were expressed by 903 Satellite Wing HQ. These queries pointed to the need for the Regiment to arrive earlier in the landing timetable and in coordination with vital but vulnerable RAF installations.

Late in the evening of 26 January (D+5), Squadron Leader MacIntyre-Cathles (CO of 2967 Field Squadron), Pilot Officer Jones (the Recce Officer of 2959 LAA Squadron) and Flight Lieutenant Bairner with the 2837 AA Flight with its eight Hispanos were successfully landed. The guns were manhandled from the beaches to the previously selected sites. The following morning they were de-waterproofed, the gun arcs co-ordinated and were ready for action by 1100 hours.

Finally on 1 February (D+11), the main parties of 2967 Field and 2959 LAA Squadrons landed. Defence positions were dug in, tents erected and equipment sorted out. They soon settled into routine airfield defence tasks, with one flight of 2967 Field Squadron and one section of four guns of 2959 LAA Squadron moved well forward to the south-west of Kyaukpyu to protect an advanced AMES.

Spitfires of 273 Squadron were soon operating from Kyaukpyu, but it would be late April before the airfield would be ready for the Dakotas. The airfield needed considerable work to bring it up to a standard for supply aircraft and this would take nearly two months to complete. Thus, for the month of February, 2967 Field Squadron turned its hands to airfield construction, assisting with levelling and clearing the new airstrip. Meanwhile, the domestic arrangements of the squadron were well established and a new avian sub-unit was formed, although there were teething problems:

> . . . the Poultry Section is in good shape, except for the hen which will lay regularly in Flying Officer A.F. Carrington's bed, no matter how well he tucks in his mosquito net.[6]

A gun crew manhandles its Hispano 20-mm cannon through thick jungle. (Air Historical Branch RAF Crown Copyright)

An amusing incident occurred while an exercise was being held on the airfield. A sentry from 2967 Field Squadron saw a woman walking down a track he was watching. As she passed she grabbed his arm and whispered 'Jap!' She was being followed. Taking immediate action the sentry dodged behind a tree and awaited the arrival of the enemy. In a few moments he was relieved to see not a rampant Japanese patrol, but an Indian Anti-Malarial Squad complete with goggles and mouth masks. They did have the look of an enemy party intent on some form of hideous chemical warfare.

To take the place of the Regiment units that had moved forward following the capture of Akyab and Ramree, 1308 Wing was ordered to Maungdaw. The squadrons under the wing's control moved as follows: 2759 Field Squadron from Chiringa to Bawli North, 2739 Field Squadron from Ramu to Maungdaw. 2837 LAA Squadron remained at Cox's Bazaar, while 2945 Field Squadron, already at Maungdaw, now came under the command of 1308 Wing.

2945 Field Squadron continued patrolling around Maungdaw and the Mayu Range until 17 January when, along with 2854 LAA Squadron from Rumkhapalong, the men moved further south to Indin. This was the most southernmost point on the Mayu Peninsula that any RAF Regiment unit had previously reached during the campaign.[7] 2945 Field Squadron deployed with No 1 Flight covering the bridge over the Indin Chaung, No 2 Flight on a feature overlooking the domestic site and dispersal and No 3 Flight on a feature covering the airstrip. The AFV Flight was still in existence, and 'A' Troop deployed south of, and 'B' Troop north of, the airstrip. Following an inspection, the OC of 1308 Wing noted the 'excellent spirit' in 2945 Field Squadron.[8] Patrols of 2945 Field Squadron during late January moved up into the foothills to the east where they found deserted villages and relics of the 1943 campaign. They were soon, however, on the move to another front. Between 1 and 4 February, however, 2945 Field Squadron departed by air for Onbauk, north-west of Mandalay, where it was urgently required. We have read of the actions of the squadron at Onbauk in an earlier chapter.

Although the Arakan front had been seen as a secondary front, the tactical squadrons of 224 Group were playing a vital role, not only in the coastal advance, but also in sending squadrons to the east to assist 221 Group. The fighters and fighter-bombers were involved in close support of the amphibious landings, routine provision of fighter escorts to bombers and transport aircraft, maintenance of air superiority and interdiction of Japanese coastal craft.

With the preparations underway for the thrust for Meiktila, reinforcements in the form of 1st and 2nd US Air Commandos had arrived to provide close tactical support for IV Corps. They would, however, operate from the strips in the Arakan. As a consequence, on 19 February, one flight of 2837 LAA Squadron was temporarily deployed to 'Hay' airstrip at Ramu to provide AA protection to the airfield occupied by the 2nd US Air Commando Group. On 26 February, 2854 LAA Squadron moved by road and ferry from Indin to Akyab where the men came under command of 1326 Wing. They were followed the next day by the 224 Group Defence Officer Wing Commander Allen and his staff who moved with Advanced HQ 224 Group.

Despite the Allies' overwhelming air superiority, the Japanese Air Force was still able to fight back. Air raids were carried out during March as the enemy tried to disrupt the development and improvement of the ports and airstrips. At midnight on 3 March a large raid consisting of seven 'Lily' twin-engined bombers was launched against Akyab and its airstrips, while ten more attacked Ramree and Cox's Bazaar. Although ordered not to do so by the local Fighter Operations Room, the guns of 2706 LAA Squadron at Dabaing and Mawnubyn airstrips on Akyab opened fire but with no success. A fire-fighting squad of 2966 Field Squadron was immediately in action dealing with fires in the dry scrub started by the bombing. While fighting the blaze, the CO of the squadron, Flight Lieutenant Furneaux, was seriously wounded by an enemy strafing run. Meanwhile, an airman of 2706 LAA Squadron was killed and another wounded when bombs were dropped on their gun posts.

Late in the day of 26 March, Akyab town and harbour were again subjected to a heavy air raid consisting of seven 'Oscar' fighters and seven 'Sally' twin-engined bombers. Six guns of 2854 LAA Squadron went into action but no hits were claimed. However, Hispano fire during subsequent attacks served to divert the aircraft from their line of attack. Following the first attack, those airmen not manning the guns were called out to fight a fire burning near the 903 Wing HQ. The airmen moved off in the fire tender and some 3-tonners. They soon arrived at the site of the fire but at the moment the airmen were debussing, a further stick of incendiaries was dropped in close proximity. Sergeant Ernest Hills was killed while others received minor injuries. The gunners continued with their task and two hours later the fire was under control.

The loss of Sergeant Hills cast a gloom over everyone in 2854 LAA Squadron, which paraded the following morning as an expression of sympathy with the bereaved. The CO, Squadron Leader Leslie Chanter, said a short prayer. The funeral was held later that day at the local military cemetery. The coffin was draped with the Union Flag with fellow Sergeants acting as bearers. Full military honours were accorded and a firing party was present. A fund was also started by squadron personnel for the benefit of Sergeant Hills' widow.

Following the capture of Akyab, the attitude of the Burmese people had become of increasing importance to those wanting to re-establish the colonial government. Loyal Burmese had carried on guerrilla warfare against the Japanese with arms supplied by the British. It was inevitable, however, that a proportion of these arms should find their way into the hands of dacoits and pro-Japanese elements. As some of them had also obtained arms from the Japanese to use against the British and their own people, they had become a force to be reckoned with. In the Arakan hill tracts the situation became serious. After the 81st West African Division had cleared most of the Japanese from the Kaladan Valley, the strongly armed dacoits in this area began a reign of terror on the now peaceful villages. After raiding a village they would retire, often into the hills, with their spoils of poultry, grain, money and sometimes women. For some time they had no opposition. The XV Corps was too occupied in driving the Japanese out of the

Arakan, and the dacoits felt themselves safe in the assumption that the Allies could not spare the force necessary to round them up.

The airmen of 2966 Field Squadron were unaware of any of this until 4 March, when they received a visit from a Major Cliffe from the Burma Civil Affairs Service. Colin Kirby was present when Cliffe addressed the airmen:

> Cliffe was an Anglo-Burmese, a portly man of about 50. If we had any doubts about his ability to handle a tough military assignment, he soon put the notion out of our minds. He was in that respect like Squadron Leader Arnold.[9] We were to discover that he had an extensive knowledge of Burma and many native languages. He was in command of the party insofar as he decided where we went, our objectives at any particular time, etc . . . Cliffe, of course, wore the badge of a Major and carried a large revolver strapped to his waist.

2966 Field Squadron was to assist the Burma Civil Affairs Service to take the first steps in re-establishment of the colonial administration in the recaptured territory in the Kaladan area. The Task Force was also to search for dacoits, wanted 'known Japanese collaborators', political agitators, hidden arms and ammunition, and any stray Japanese soldiers. River craft were utilised by the Regiment at certain times owing to the nature of the country. The supply of rations and evacuation of prisoners captured would be carried out by river craft operating from Akyab base. Before setting out, Cliffe explained to the gathered airmen the reasons for the undertaking and made it clear why he had chosen the RAF Regiment in particular:

> . . . He told us of the great importance of the mission; so much so that he had been given the choice of any unit in Burma to accompany him, and that it had been suggested that as the Royal Marine Commandos were already in Akyab they would be an obvious choice. He then told us that when he discovered that the RAF Regiment had a field squadron based on Akyab he had not hesitated in nominating us. At this, we puffed out our chests and gave self-congratula-tory smiles. It could have been that Cliffe was indulging in a little 'bull' and flattery, but as we were to discover on closer acquaintance with the man, he had a blunt and direct personality and did not hesitate to voice his opinions for good or bad. He added that we would be coming into close contact with the native population on this and further operations, and that he required troops who had the necessary military skills and toughness and also able to treat the Burmese with firmness where necessary, while being friendly and under-standing toward them. He thought the Regiment admirably suited to his needs.

The first operation, lasting only three days and consisting of two and a half flights of 2966 Field Squadron, travelled up the Yo Chaung by motor launch and successfully apprehended a number of dacoits and captured arms. The second, however, was of much greater scope and size and saw the Regiment moving off into the jungles of the Kaladan for a month (Map 5).

On 18 March an RAF Regiment Task Force, under command of Wing Commander Graham Gow, OC 1326 Wing, and consisting of 2966 Field Squadron with elements of 2854 LAA Squadron, Flight Lieutenant Gardner, the Medical Officer, Flying Officer Leslie-Carter, the Signals Officer, Major Cliffe, various Civil Affairs officers and several Burma Police, set off to make a sweep up the Kaladan River as far as Kyauktaw. Corporal Colin Kirby describes their departure and journey up the Kaladan River:

. . . Alongside the jetty on the Akyab waterfront was the vessel which was to take the Squadron up the Kaladan, and act as base ship for the expedition. It resembled a Mississippi paddle steamer, although much smaller, with an upper and lower deck . . .

   After about an hour our Flight Commander, Flight Lieutenant Kocher, called us together and informed us that shortly we would be going ashore at the village of Pauktaw with Major Cliffe and some of the Burmese police. We were to work down from this point through the jungle to the Squadron base, and it was anticipated it would take about six days. It was about eleven when the boat came alongside Pauktaw and we went ashore alongside a ramshackle wooden jetty . . .

The Burma Police and Civil Affairs officers were constantly receiving intelligence and were sending out spies into nearby villages, and from this, numerous 'cordon and search' operations were planned by the Regiment over the next thirty days. Colin Kirby describes one of these operations:

   . . . we learned that three dacoits were in hiding at Wetmagwa some miles down river, and a dawn raid was decided upon.

   We were briefed by Flight Lieutenant Kocher on the part each man would play, and preparations were made for a departure at 0200 hours . . . The village slipped away behind us, and soon the only inkling of it was the glow from a fire. By this time the moon had gone, and everything was cloaked in rich blackness. An eerie silence was all the jungle had to offer, broken

Men from a patrol from Wing Commander Graham Gow's RAF Regiment Task Force are briefed as they travel up the Kaladan River prior to arriving at a village, March 1945. (Air Historical Branch RAF Crown Copyright)

occasionally by some wild cry from a jungle beast and the dipping of our paddles at regular intervals. Somewhere ahead, cloistered in the jungle, lay Wetmagwa. Somewhere in there were the three dacoits, and possibly renegade Japanese. There was the merest suggestion of grey light as we scrambled up the river bank sometime after 0500 hours. Within a short time we were ready to move off to the village about a mile away.

For the purpose of this raid some of us had left off our boots and were wearing plimsolls. We had not gone far before I regretted my decision. My plimsolls were an old pair and rather loose at the heel. Consequently I had to keep stopping to adjust them.

The Flight surrounded the village and the Major, with Tommy's section, moved quietly in until opposite the hut believed to house the wanted men. When in position Kocher would fire a green Very light and Tommy and his men with the Major would crash into the hut.

Henry and his section had one side of the place and the rest of us the other. As we had moved into position a patch of muddy ground had detached my plimsoll. I removed the other and continued barefoot. I had been bringing up the rear of my party, and the delay left me by myself. I carried on in what I believed to be the right direction.

It is very easy to become separated in jungle, and for about ten minutes I thought I was lost and feeling very uneasy, to put it mildly. Then I came to open ground beyond which appeared to be a corner of the village . . . As I was wondering which way to move a man came from the nearest hut. I shone my torch in his face. He was startled, as well he might be, and very frightened. I motioned to him to keep quiet and indicated my Sten gun. He looked innocent enough. It was at this moment the Very light lit the sky. Immediately there was pandemonium and yelling, and a few moments later some of my section came into sight. We searched our side of the village without any result before making our way into the centre. Here we learned that 'our bird' had flown.

From questioning it seemed that they had left a few days earlier, anticipating our arrival. It was disappointing, but we had the consolation of knowing that we were unsettling them and curtailing their activities. I retraced my steps with some of the others and fortunately found my plimsolls and was able to bind them with a spare boot lace somebody had . . .

From the Squadron HQ the flights radiated out to the surrounding villages or travelled up or down the river to inspect villages. Often they would stay for one or two nights in each village or establish a patrol base from which to work out through other more remote areas. In many villages they were welcomed with great hospitality, celebration and often singing. Most patrols up or down the river were by steamer or launch, but on some occasions more primitive forms of water transport were required. Colin Kirby describes one such patrol:

Today we took the steamer which had brought us from Akyab and travelled along the Kaladan to the village of Singyan. From here we trekked to Nyaunginle and completed our usual check and search . . . as it was . . . now late afternoon and we had a rendezvous with the steamer on the Kaladan . . . we paddled our small craft along the chaung and by the time we arrived at the Kaladan it was dark.

At this point the great river was very wide and running strongly and it took

An RAF Regiment patrol crosses a narrow bridge over a river while searching for dacoits and illegal arms and ammunition in the Kaladan region. (Air Historical Branch RAF Crown Copyright)

all our efforts to make for the centre. Land was lost to sight in the gloom, and the situation became very scary, like being out at sea, as the boats bobbed up and down. One sat on them rather than in, and we had to sit still to retain the balance, otherwise they would easily have capsized. For me it was particularly difficult as I had a Bren gun balanced across my knees. These boats were very shallow and we overlapped the edge when sitting so that looking down either side you could see the water, but no boats. There was no sign of the steamer and we fired several shots into the air as we bobbed precariously around, trying not to become separated.

After about twenty minutes of this nerve-jangling discomfort a white Very light shot into the sky and a few minutes later we heard the welcome sound of the ship's engines as she came up in the dark. Lights came on and ropes were thrown down to us. It was a tricky job climbing her sides. The river boats disappeared into the darkness with the natives who had come from the village, and the steamer set off . . .

A few days later the flight set out on another patrol but this time accompanied by a Corporal from the RAF Medical Branch. The patrols were now using a 'hearts and minds' approach to assist in restoring civil order to the villages. Colin Kirby continues:

. . . After an hour or so we stopped at a village and went through our usual routine as the captain questioned the villagers.

. . . [the] Corporal from the RAF Medical Branch (I never knew whether he had volunteered for the job or not) . . . had to be fit because he carried around a large, heavy bag of medical equipment. With regret I cannot remember his name, because it deserves to be recorded. He spent some time administering to the people, bathing and bandaging sores, applying ointments, and giving mepacrine tablets for malaria. Apart from the humanitarian aspect it was a good exercise in public relations! We travelled further along the river to another village and went through the same routine . . .

On Wednesday 4 April we were away by 0730 hours and had a busy morning along the river, taking in the villages of Pyinnyathe, Kwazon, Okkan, Tongmyin and Kansauk. During the afternoon we visited Sabotha and Aockchaung. At all these places the people seemed glad to see us, and it was a case of 'showing the flag' to indicate that even this remote part of Burma was back under British control. We stayed the night at Teigwabyin, and had another musical evening.

The following day they were away by 0700 hours, visiting four more villages, in the course of which the flight discovered a small arms dump of Japanese material: two boxes of rifle ammunition, five boxes of small grenades, two boxes of heavy grenades and three boxes of mortar bombs, which were carried back to base camp. The pursuit of the dacoits was renewed and on 7 April 'D' Flight, Major Cliffe and a ten-man coolie train set out:

. . . We trekked through thick hilly jungle most of the day on the track of a band of dacoits. The going was very tough, hour after hour, hacking away with our kukris, those in the lead having the worst of it, and being changed round from time to time. We arrived at Panpechaung in the evening. The terrorists had left just before our arrival. They had taken what they wanted from the village, gang-raped a young woman and beaten-up her mother who had tried to protect her daughter. The Corporal Medic set to work and ministered to both of them. Later that evening some of the Burmese police changed out of

their uniforms and set out as spies to see what could be discovered. It was a dangerous mission and certain death if they were rumbled.

The next day we set off back toward the river, but in a different direction to our route of the previous day. The police had brought intelligence of a good find to be made at a certain village. We approached after about three miles struggling through the usual thick jungle. We spread out around it and attacked. It was not easy to coordinate because of the

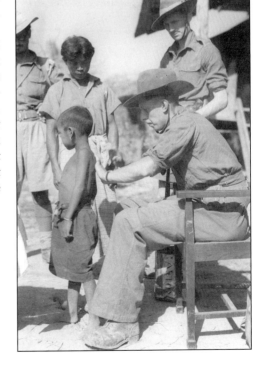

Flight Lieutenant A.M.M. Gardner undertakes a medical examination of a Burmese boy during the Kaladan operation to re-establish British administration in the region. (Air Historical Branch RAF Crown Copyright)

jungle, and we did not want to kill or injure innocent people. Firing into the air we charged in with a complete element of surprise, a tribute to our jungle craft. We found our quarry trying to hide in a hut. A Japanese Army Captain no less! Even Cliffe did not speak Japanese, but the villagers told him that he had been living with them for some time, apparently having decided to sit out the war. A rare bird for a Japanese officer. He was certainly surprised to see us in that remote area.

We left in the afternoon and headed away from the river and soon began climbing again . . . Kocher took his maps from the map-case he had dangling from his belt. 'Nothing to look at now,' he declared, 'We've run out of map. Up there is uncharted territory.' He indicated the jungle ahead of us. We headed for Kyauksadaung, the last village before the unknown. Our information was that the gang we had narrowly missed four days before was resting there . . .

The village was peaceful and the people glad to see us. Yes, the gangsters had been there, but had not stopped very long. They had split into separate groups and disappeared into the jungle. We had the satisfaction of knowing that our pursuit of them was making them 'jumpy.'

The pursuit continued the next day. Cliffe was relentless . . . We pressed on. In spite of the rigours, morale and discipline was first rate. At the last village, Kocher had taken a compass bearing on a place called Natthayeyawn, as indicated by the villagers. They believed it was a dacoit stronghold . . .

We came into an open space and a strange sight met our eyes. A large circular stockade, perhaps twelve feet high. It looked like the kind of fort erected by the earliest settlers from England on the American continent to give protection against marauding Indian tribes. There seemed to be no sign of life.

The RAF Regiment Kaladan Task force rounds up suspected criminals in a village. (Air Historical Branch RAF Crown Copyright)

We did a 'recce' around it and found an entrance on the other side, charging in with guns at the ready. We found three dacoits who willingly surrendered. They were tired of being chased through the jungle. The rest had flown. We brewed up some tea. The prisoners' hands were bound and they seemed grateful for the tea offered to them . . . .

'D' Flight then trekked on for two more days, heading up into the mountains following a lead with regard to the remaining dacoits. At one point they came face to face with hill tribesmen carrying poisoned blow pipes but who were fortunately of a friendly disposition. The Medic accompanying the flight raised his stocks significantly with them when he was called in to assist with a birth and then had the honour of having the child named after him. After a meal in the village the flight stayed the night and then moved on the next day:

> Our continual battle with the jungle recommenced . . . We pressed on until after several hours, with exhaustion setting in, we came, quite by chance on a track which seemed to lead somewhere. It did, to the village of Atetthinbondan. They were surprised to see us, particularly as we had approached them 'down mountain'.
> We carried out our usual search and uncovered several rifles and a few assorted pistols, for which there was no adequate reason for possession forth-coming. Cliffe decided against taking further prisoners. We still had three with us, who had been useful as porters. Instead he gave a stern lecture and burnt down two houses. We tramped out of the village feeling hungry and not very happy. The going was now a little easier, and we cut across the mountain to the village of Aukthinbondan.

Rations were getting low, however, the patrol was nearing its end:

> . . . We slogged toward Apaukwa, minds fixed on food and arrived by early afternoon. Yes, said the villagers, there had been a motor launch on the river that morning, but it had gone away. We found a shady spot on the river bank. Cliffe told us he thought he had made the right choice with the RAF Regiment. And particularly 'D' Flight which had accompanied him on most of the operation. Our chests swelled out and eased the emptiness in our stomachs.

The job given to the Regiment in the Kaladan had been completed. 'D' Flight was the last of the squadron to be withdrawn and the men embarked for the return journey late on 17 April. After a month in the jungle and constant patrol work, they looked forward to the relaxing trip down the Kaladan River and out to the squadron camp on Akyab. Kirby continues:

> It was late afternoon before the launch arrived, bearing jungle rations and ciga-rettes. They had not brought much in the way of rations with them, and we had scoffed the lot. Spirits lifted. It had been a trying day with no objective other than to wait. The crew of the launch would not navigate down the river in the dark, so it would be tomorrow before we could sail.
> The Flight was awake early, anxious to get under way . . . We chugged hour after hour along the great river, making us realise how far from Akyab our operation had taken. It was late afternoon and the river widened as we

approached our destination. The launch moved in toward the bank, searching for the landing jetty where we could go ashore a few miles from camp.

The launch lurched and bumped and stopped. Shouts from the crew, gesticulating, engine in reverse. Pushing with poles, jumping up and down. No good. We were grounded. 'We can't be far from terra firma,' said Kocher, 'we'll have to wade to it.' Curses and grumbles. We collected our kit together and lowered ourselves into the mangrove swamp. 'Watch out for crocodiles' somebody called . . . We splashed through the swamp for about thirty minutes and dragged ourselves on to firm ground, wet, dirty and hungry. The Flight formed up in section single file, with weapons at the trail, and squelched off down the road toward the Squadron camp a few miles away.

The month-long patrol by the Regiment Task Force had been a resounding success. They had covered an area of 2,600 square miles, visited or raided 250 villages, arrested 100 Japanese collaborators and dacoits and recovered twenty-six rifles. In addition, mortar shells and large quantities of small arms ammunition of British and Japanese make were recovered, together with Army clothing and equipment, parachutes and rations. The Regiment had again demonstrated its versatility and adaptability and had performed admirably. The training, skills and the physical stamina expected of the field squadron had allowed the men to be used in difficult and testing conditions, but also ones that required, on occasions, a 'light touch.'

In early April, 2739 Field Squadron departed from Cox's Bazaar on another Civil Affairs operation. The men moved south to Buthidaung, which had been the scene of desperate battles during the previous Arakan offensives. This time the Regiment's task was not so much concerned with restoration of civil order, but the clearing of ordnance from an area ravaged by three years of war. Although the war had moved on, there remained a number of mines, booby traps and bombs that needed to be removed or destroyed, as these were of grave concern and danger to the local population. Along with Civil Affairs officers and Burma Police, the squadron was to patrol and visit all the villages within an area of approximately twenty square miles north-west and east of Buthidaung.

Ordnance of various kinds was scattered across the region with, for example, an unexploded 500-pound bomb lying in the grounds of the local hospital, while six of the same were found in a nearby village. Many booby traps were found that had not been triggered and the approaches to a major bridge were found to be heavily mined. In just under a fortnight 2739 Field Squadron cleared and disposed of 7,000 2-inch and 3-inch mortar bombs, thirty-eight booby traps, fifty-two bombs of various sizes, twenty mines and two anti-tank traps, with the cost of only one airmen slightly wounded. Some of the bombs and booby traps were dealt with by 904 Wing Bomb Disposal Squad, who were called in to deal with the more complex and devious devices. One flight also successfully salvaged seven assault craft from the Kalapanzin River and these were used by squadron detachments to visit villages located up the river from Buthidaung. On completion of this worthwhile task they returned to Cox's Bazaar.

The firm establishment of air supply and ground support operations from Akyab and Ramree meant that by April 1945 the Mayu Peninsula airfields had become of minor importance. Consequently, 1308 Wing and 2739 Field Squadron were withdrawn from Maungdaw and moved north to Cox's Bazaar where they rejoined 2837 LAA Squadron. After two and half months on Ramree, 'B' Flight of 2837 LAA Squadron was freed to return to its parent unit, although shipping availability meant travelling via Calcutta!

The advance of XV Corps in the Arakan had, for a time, played an important role in holding down Japanese troops that could have otherwise moved east to repel the Allied advance in Central Burma. More importantly, it had captured Akyab and Ramree Islands, which were vital for their airfields and the support they would provide for the advance of the Fourteenth Army once across the Irrawaddy. Following their capture, the airfields and installations had to be built-up and stocked in time to supply the Fourteenth Army. Akyab opened for air supply operations on 20 March at the moment that IV Corps was preparing for the advance on Rangoon. Ramree was not ready until 15 April. However, this fortuitously coincided with the moment that IV Corps had moved out of the economic range of supply aircraft flying from Akyab.

Air supply to XV Corps had been deeply curtailed by early March, as priority was given to the Central Front. The more success XV Corps had, the sooner the central Burma operations would be resupplied, and resources would be diverted to that front. The 25th and 26th Indian Divisions were soon withdrawn from the Arakan as they could not be sustained. Consequently, the Regiment units in the Arakan were also re-deployed. Two more squadrons were flown to the Central Front during April. 2854 LAA Squadron flew in to Sinthe to bolster 1323 Wing, while 2759 Field Squadron went to Meiktila. Here they relieved the Regiment units, which had heavy suffered casualties during the defensive battle. 1326 Wing HQ was airlifted from Akyab to join 221 Group, and was replaced by the newly arrived 1331 Wing HQ, which came down from Agartala (Appendices 10 and 14).

The RAF Regiment was an integral part of the operations of 224 Group RAF. By February 1945 the officers and airmen of the Regiment had trained, learnt, developed and refined their skills in combined operations. The squadrons had performed their usual roles in AA and ground defence. They had also, however, demonstrated a capacity and adaptability for other roles such as pursuit and apprehension of dacoits, weapons disposal and maintenance of civil order. These activities would become of greater importance as the war in South-East Asia reached its conclusion.

The Fourteenth Army had soundly defeated the enemy around Meiktila and Mandalay, and the airfields that would support the land advance had been established on Akyab and Ramree by XV Corps. If Rangoon could be reached before the monsoon broke, the longest campaign of the Second World War would be over.

Notes

1   ALFSEA had replaced the 11th Army Group and was required to direct all land operations in Burma under the overall control of South-East Asia Command.
2   XV Corps was to consist of the 25th and 26th Indian Divisions, the 81st and 82nd West African Divisions, the 3rd Commando and 22nd East African Brigades and the 50th Indian Tank Brigade.
3   The 26th Indian Division and 3rd Commando Brigade were supported by medium tanks, medium artillery and LAA and HAA artillery. The Naval Bombardment Force consisted of three cruisers and the Arakan Coastal Forces. 224 Group had provided some 200 aircraft.
4   The remaining Japanese battalion had been withdrawn only 48 hours before the landing.
5   The runner had been taken on spec as no mention had been made of one in orders. Fortunately he was permitted on board.
6   AIR 29/137, *Operations Record Books RAF Regiment Squadrons 2960–2970*.
7   It will be recalled that the 'Tezpur' Flight had been sent to Indin to await the capture of Foul Point during the first Arakan offensive in early 1943.
8   AIR 29/1118, *Operations Record Books 1300–1309, 1311–1317 RAF Regiment Wings 1944–1947*.
9   Squadron Leader George Arnold of RAF Station Koggala and 2944 Field Squadron fame.

CHAPTER TEN

The Race for Rangoon

'I have it on record from one of my Group Commanders who moved with Fourteenth Army all the way through Burma, that he considered it probable that the Group could not have occupied airstrips as far forward as they did – with consequently better air support for the Army – had he not been confident that the RAF Regiment could have maintained the necessary security.'

Air Chief Marshal Sir Keith Park KCB KBE MC DFC,
Allied Air C-in-C, ACSEA

A top-level meeting was held in Calcutta during February 1945 between the Supreme Allied Commander, Admiral Lord Louis Mountbatten, and the C-in-Cs of the Navy, Army and Air Force of South-East Asia Command. At this meeting the newly appointed Allied Air C-in-C, Air Chief Marshal Sir Keith Park,[1] was asked whether the RAF could supply the 300,000 men of the Fourteenth Army by air during the advance on Rangoon. Despite having only just arrived in SEAC, he had unhesitatingly replied that the Air Forces would do so. At this time the emphasis had been placed on the capture of Rangoon overland from the north. The Japanese were unable to deal with the Allied use of motorised and armoured columns that were sweeping over the parched plain of central Burma. This still appeared to be the quickest and easiest means of reaching Rangoon.

Following the success of the Irrawaddy crossings, the resistance to these incursions and the relentless counter-attacks of the enemy had delayed the planned advance. By 22 March, with the fighting still raging around Meiktila, a meeting of senior commanders at Monywa was told that the plan for the land advance in Burma was now fourteen days behind schedule. To reach Rangoon before the monsoon, the Fourteenth Army would need to advance at 10 miles a day. This was very much a gamble and, if not achieved, the Army would probably have to withdraw to the north and see out yet another monsoon on tenuous lines of communication from Manipur. An all-out effort was required, with the supply aircraft and tactical squadrons of 221 Group flying at more than sustainable rates. If the land advance faltered, it would be necessary to revive plans for an amphibious landing by XV Corps near Rangoon.

By late March, however, the Japanese counter-offensives to recapture Meiktila and the Myitche-Nyaungu areas had failed. The Japanese *15th* and *33rd Armies* were ordered to retreat south, while the *28th Army* was to hold a line across the Irrawaddy south of Letse. Meanwhile, IV Corps and XXXIII Indian Corps[2] were regrouping for the final advance on two main axes. The latter would cross to the west and advance down the line of the Irrawaddy River, while the former, now concentrated at Meiktila, would move to the east and make a swift and more powerful thrust down the road and rail corridor from Mandalay to Rangoon. The rapid move of IV Corps would also serve another purpose. If the advance was rapid enough, it would trap a large part of the Japanese *28th Army* in the Pegu Yomas and prevent their escape eastwards into the jungle-covered hills of the Burma-Siam (now Thailand) border (Map 7).

As the Fourteenth Army moved south, it would yet again experience a change in climatic conditions. The end of the dry belt would soon be reached and the Army would enter the zone of Burma's maximum rainfall, and as the monsoon threatened, the conditions would worsen. Only a few months earlier the troops had been capable of marching long distances on foot and were able to go immediately into action, if required. With the deterioration in the weather, however, these capabilities would be severely tested. All the usual ailments, prickly heat, jungle sores and other skin complaints, would return, not to mention the reappearance of nefarious tropical diseases.

On 12 April, in preparation for the advance, the RAF began redeploying the flying squadrons. The squadrons of 221 Group were now highly mobile. The tactical wings supporting IV Corps, 906 and 909, were ordered to move as closely as possible behind the advance and would 'leap-frog' each other to maintain unbroken cover. To the west, 907 Wing, supporting the XXXIII Corps advance, would proceed at a slower pace. As these squadrons moved into central and south Burma, the long-range squadrons would then follow up from Assam and take over the airfields surrounding Shwebo and Meiktila. The advance of RAF units would, as much as possible, be by air so that lack of road transport did not impede their progress.

For the push to Rangoon the RAF Regiment would use 1307, 1323 and 1329 Wings with, eventually, a total of seventeen squadrons under command (Appendix 16). The UK-formed 1329 Wing had flown in from Agartala to Monywa on 13 March and had then moved by road to Shwebo. Here it took under command the four squadrons now concentrated at Sadaung and Ondaw and previously under command of 1324 Wing. This wing then departed Burma for Santa Cruz near Bombay, far away in western India, to begin a training programme for four of the recently arrived United Kingdom squadrons.[3]

2743 Field Squadron had been flown in from Agartala in mid-March, however, it took another three weeks for the unit's motor transport to reach Ondaw. LAC Alfred Vance was with the rear party and was shocked to hear on arrival what had happened at Meiktila to the squadron they had travelled from the United Kingdom with and with whom they had trained at Forward Echelon:

> . . . I had been retained to do a mines and booby trap course at the school and travelled by road with our MT . . . Our MTO was Pilot Officer Murdock. When we arrived at the Squadron HQ, Pilot Officer Murdock went to report our arrival and to brief us on what had taken place in our absence! The sad news was that 2708 Field Squadron had got a bashing at Meiktila and we were the next Squadron to move forward.

By early April 1329 Wing with its four squadrons had travelled south and crossed the Irrawaddy and were established at fair-weather airstrips at Kwetnge, 10 miles south-east of Meiktila, and Dwehla to the north. Ted Daines recalls the move:

> Our next trip was to the Irrawaddy to cross this mighty river by DUKW. Arriving at the river between the Ava Bridge on our right and Sagaing on our left we crossed in batches. I was in the first group and while waiting for the remainder we enjoyed a swim in the very fast flowing water. We finished a few miles south of Mandalay in a park-like area beside a small running stream

filled with shell holes. We were having a fortnight's rest. While the Army had a system of leave operating, the Regiment had no such system. Most went the three or four years without leave.

We did however, get to Mandalay on the ration wagon but I cannot say that I was enthralled from what I saw. When on arriving back we found that we had lost a man when fishing with grenades, he surfaced a week later. Needless to say a Corporal and I had to go through his possessions and to provide a list.

. . . we then moved to an airstrip near Meiktila [Kwetnge]. The airstrip that we now occupied was the southern-most of the Meiktila airfields. It was the most desolate looking of places yet encountered by us and the scene of most heavy fighting. It was plagued by huge millipedes and a vicious looking black scorpion. They were everywhere, under your blanket or in one's kit. If this was not bad enough the ground was littered with unexploded bombs both air and mortar.

At Meiktila, the squadrons that had fought during the siege slowly readjusted to the relative calm following the enemy withdrawal, although listening posts were put out over a large area around the airfield. The many Japanese dead had to be buried and booby traps found and dealt with by the sappers. The 221 Group Defence Officer, Wing Commander Gem, flew in and congratulated the airmen on their efforts of the last three weeks. A combined Regiment Church service for fallen comrades and the wounded was held on 1 April in 'D' Box. The following day the Regiment ceased to be under the command of the 9th Indian Brigade and moved out, while the airmen of 2708 Field Squadron received the sad news that their Adjutant, Flying Officer Henry, had died of his shrapnel wounds. The squadron was then sent for a week to the Wing Rest Camp by the lake. Having lost so many officers and men, this was a period of considerable reorganisation. The numbers were boosted with the arrival of the rear party under Flying Officer Anderson from Agartala after twenty-two days' travel.[4]

1307 Wing HQ was still at Monywa but would move forward by road to Meiktila on 5 April, along with 2963 LAA Squadron HQ and the remaining flight and 2941 Squadron HQ. 2965 LAA Squadron, which had been formed at the Depot from surplus personnel from the reorganisation of the United Kingdom squadrons, was flown in from Imphal a few days earlier and deployed its guns on the airfield. On 7 April, 2759 Field Squadron, another ex-United Kingdom squadron, arrived by air from Chiringa. They received an unfriendly welcome when at 2000 hours that evening a single 'Lily' bomber attacked the airstrip and three airmen of 2965 LAA Squadron were wounded.

The wing and its squadrons (less 2963 LAA Squadron) did not remain at Meiktila for long. From 8 to 12 April a move was made, by truck for some or on foot for most, to Thedaw, located 3 miles to the north-east of Meiktila. Here they were joined by 909 Wing, including 17 (Spitfire) Squadron. While 2708 Field Squadron was at Thedaw, Group Captain Harris, the Command Defence Officer, visited, along with other senior Regiment officers, to congratulate them on their fine efforts at Meiktila with Sergeant Gerrish receiving special and personal mention.

By early March, 2944 Field Squadron at Sinthe had deployed each of the rifle flights on close protection of an AMES. On the west bank of the river No 1 Flight had prepared and dug positions for close defence of an AMES which was located a half a mile outside the Army 'box' and was solely responsible for its protection. No 2 Flight was similarly occupied at Myitche, while No 3 Flight was across the Irrawaddy a few miles south of Nyaungu.

In mid-March the Japanese *28th Army* had launched a counter-offensive northward astride the Irrawaddy in response to the crossings and attack on Meiktila. A column was sent up the left bank of the river towards Letse and planned to strike towards Myitche. As a result, the latter half of the month saw a period of high tension and the Regiment increased its patrolling activities. By the last week of March, however, this offensive had also been halted.

During the first half of April the two Corps were ordered to push south on their respective axes. XXXIII Corps would fight what became known as the Battle of the Irrawaddy. The 7th Indian Division had been given the objectives of Seikpyu and Salin on the west bank of the river, while on the east bank they were to push for the oilfields around Chauk and Yenangyaung. Meanwhile, the 20th Indian Division would move south-west from Meiktila and move on Magwe, with its important all-weather airstrip, and then move further south to Prome.

After crossing the Irrawaddy at Pakokku, 2944 Field Squadron headed due south as the 7th Indian Division pushed forward. Having flown from Ywadon to Sinthe a month earlier, the squadron still had few vehicles and a few were borrowed from other squadrons to allow the movement forward of heavy equipment, ammunition and stores. The majority of the airmen, therefore, moved on foot. Henry Kirk recalls one of the perils encountered by 2944 Field Squadron as it moved towards Chauk:

Just after leaving Pakokku we were moving slowly in convoy and the lads marching each side of the road. There was black smoke from the burning oilfields at Chauk and Yenangyaung to the front. Out to the left was Mount Popa rising from an otherwise scrub-covered plain. There were clouds of dust ahead and shelling and small arms fire away to the east which we put down to our tanks. Our fighters circled overhead providing air cover to the advancing columns. Suddenly we came to a stop. With the column halted they would be sitting ducks should the Japanese open up with one of their 105-mm guns.

A bridge over a dried-up chaung had been destroyed. An officer in a jeep had come back enquiring if we had a munitions disposal man who could deal with mines. As Squadron Armourer I got the job, along with an Army Sergeant, to clear the mines down one long shallow bank of the chaung. The large anti-tank mines must have been laid in a hurry by the retreating Japs as it was easy to see their position due to the fresh soil disturbed on the red hard-baked surface. Using a very large bayonet it was easy to clear the top plate, check for booby trap wires, and lift it off. A few were booby trapped with a fuse wire leading to a grenade buried beneath the mine but they were easily detected. On the top of the mine was a thick coiled spring with a detonator in the centre. The spring when compressed by the top plate struck the detonator.

We made them safe and the lads heaped them up well clear of the road. By the time the job was finished the pile was about 12 feet high. We packed in some gun cotton and blew them up. This made quite a bang! No mines were found across the bottom of the chaung or the opposite bank. Their mines by our standards were crude but effective. Once cleared the few 3-tonners we had were emptied out and then towed across the chaung by the tanks. Another job completed by the Regiment in the race to Rangoon.[5]

2944 Field Squadron kept pace with the advance of the 7th Indian Division, having stopped at Kinka for a short period until Chauk had fallen. Despite meeting strong opposition, by 21 April the 7th Indian Division was soon approaching Yenangyaung. Further south, an armoured column of the 80th Indian Brigade had entered Magwe on

19 April, capturing a few Japanese troops but receiving the surrender of a large contingent of the Indian National Army. Most important was the capture of Maida Vale airfield, located 3 miles east of Magwe.

Maida Vale had sentimental as well as tactical significance. The RAF had suffered its greatest disaster of the 1942 retreat when most of the aircraft were knocked out by a Japanese air attack when caught on the ground. Now, just over three years later, the RAF was returning in force with near unchallenged air superiority. Following in the dusty wake of the tanks was 2944 Field Squadron, which took up residence. A few days later the Spitfires and Hurricanes of 907 Wing flew in from Sinthe. In the last week of April, 1323 Wing HQ, now with Wing Commander R.G. Manwaring as OC, moved south to Magwe to join 2944 Field Squadron, along with 2958 LAA Squadron. Randle Manwaring recalls one of the 'exciting' parts of his new job:

> I suppose my most exciting work was in a two-seater aircraft where I joined the Wing Commander flying to test out a new airfield of metal-mesh runways in an advanced position before he took his aircraft in, and I took my Regiment units. We were very close and, in one sense ahead of the Japanese lines. As we came back from a successful mission we congratulated each other.

Maida Vale was located in dry scrub-covered country with a few scraggly palms. The close proximity of the river meant that there were opportunities for swimming and fishing with explosives to supplement the usual rations. With Japanese parties still at large, this was all under the watchful eye of armed Regiment guards. With the pace of the advance on this axis now slowing, the Regiment airmen were able to clean up. Henry Kirk continues:

> We received new jungle green clothing and bush hats to replace what we had been wearing since late 1944 and which was now in tatters. We also had an unfortunate issue of 'white' 2-man bivouac tents. These stuck out like a sore thumb and were entirely unsuitable. Furthermore, when we first arrived at Magwe we were directed by one officer to set up our tents on a large concrete slab. Somebody else said 'Don't put 'em up here. Get into the bushes!' Realising the unsuitability of the location, we pitched our tents in nearby scrub. That night the airstrip was attacked by enemy aircraft which dropped anti-personnel bombs that blasted the hell out of the concrete area. If we had stayed there we would have been dead.

Meanwhile, the main thrust by IV Corps, in what became known as the Battle of the Rangoon Road, had been making rapid progress. In the second week of April the 17th Indian Division easily brushed aside the new Japanese defensive positions at Pyawbwe and the 5th Indian Division moved through to take up the southward march. Their opponents, the Japanese *33rd Army*, had reached breaking point. On the same day that Magwe had been occupied, Pyinmana and Lewe airstrip had been taken by the 5th Indian Division. Both ends of the all-weather road across the Pegu Yomas had been secured.

Lewe was to be used for the maintenance of the advance. Immediately following its capture, the Fourteenth Army's Forward Airfield Engineers set to work on repairing the airstrip, accompanied by bulldozers that were crash-landed in American gliders. The airhead was opened only four days later. 2943 Field Squadron was then ordered forward to Lewe from its positions near Meiktila. Ted Daines continues:

2944 Field Squadron after being kitted out with new clothes and bush hats at Magwe, May 1945. The airman (second from right) holds a captured Japanese officer's sword. Such trophies were frowned upon at this time. If an airman was captured with one in his possession it was likely to be quickly used on him by his captors. (RAF Regiment SEAC Association)

We were very relieved when we moved on ever nearer to the Burmese capital, fighting was still going on around us . . . Our next destination was to an operational airfield . . . called Lewe airstrip which was guarded, so to speak, by American Mustangs. The runway was lit by electric light bulbs. Sad to say as we were circling the runway on a patrol, lo and behold up came the Jap aircraft and well and truly plastered us with bouncing bombs. The ones that every time they bounced sent out largish ball bearing-like pellets that were lethal. The trouble was that as you dived for cover you had a good chance of being shot by your own side. Just imagine trying to tell an Indian or Gurkha soldier that you didn't know the password having only just got there. Can you imagine having to stand still with bombs exploding all around you while waiting for a British NCO to appear? They were not very helpful either, nor was their attitude. Needless to say we went after them the next day and one of two had to be forcefully restrained.

It was not long before we moved into a defence box, a rather heavily wooded area. Our position was from a narrow track on our left to a single railway line on our right. To our front we decided to booby trap. If you have never done it I can assure you it's a very dangerous occupation.

This was the last place I ever heard a bayonet charge go in, I even remember the time; it was twenty-five to three in the early hours of the morning, not a pleasant sound. We were frequently confronted by a Japanese officer coming up the track or along the railway, told by the Army to let him through and that they would look after him. Nobody ever approached our front . . . perhaps they knew of our booby traps?

IV Corps was now ordered by Slim to make haste to reach the important communication centre at Toungoo and capture the two all-weather airstrips, Toungoo Main and Tennant.[6] It was vital that these airfields be seized so as to provide air cover to the landings at Rangoon now being planned. They were taken on 22 April, three days ahead of the schedule, and with very little struggle. The Toungoo airfields were fit for use, although the runways were in a poor condition. The airfield construction engineers arrived soon after with extra earth-moving equipment, again flown in by glider. At Toungoo Main over 100 Dakota and Commando transports were landed on 24 April and the airstrip would soon become one of the busiest in Burma.

Before long it was ready to receive the fighter squadrons and six days later 906 and 909 Wings flew in with their Spitfires and Hurricanes, accompanied by the USAAF 166th Liaison Squadron with its L5 Sentinel light planes. They were soon followed by 910 Wing with their Thunderbolts, specifically charged with providing air support for the amphibious landings at Rangoon.

The flying squadron's RAF Regiment guardians had, however, preceded them. On 15 April a flight of 2941 Field Squadron had been sent south in anticipation of the capture of Toungoo. On 25 April 2759 Field Squadron flew into Tennant from Thedaw. It was followed by 1307 Wing and 2963 and 2965 LAA and 2968 Field Squadrons, which arrived by road on 27 April. A further United Kingdom-formed Wing HQ, 1330, arrived at Tennant, having travelled by road from Imphal via Monywa.

The 19th Indian Division was moved forward to consolidate the rapid gains that had been made and to counter threats from a large enemy force to the east of the Sittang River. The division was given the task of defence of the airfields in cooperation with the wings of the RAF Regiment. By this stage of the campaign the Army and Regiment units were maintaining close liaison so that each knew exactly what the other was doing. A company of the 1st Assam Regiment from the 19th Indian Division was assigned for ground defence at Toungoo, while the squadrons set up listening posts and carried out patrols of aircraft dispersals. The area was surrounded by large parties of Japanese and the Indian National Army that had been cut off by the rapid advance, as well as the formations moving in from the east. The airstrip was shelled on 1 May, and on the night of 4/5 May a strong Japanese force attempting to break into the aircraft dispersals was repelled by the sepoys of the Assam Regiment.[7]

To reinforce the area 2802, 2942 and 2943 Field and 2960 LAA Squadrons were sent south to Kalaywa airstrip, also near Toungoo. Ted Daines, with 2943 Field Squadron, continues:

> Toungoo was our next stop, a large railway junction, and the start of the metalled road to Rangoon, albeit a hundred miles away. We ran into trouble right away, having to camp on top of the ground at a small railway siding. Happily the night passed quiet enough, although noisy round about. Next day we moved into the defence 'box' and into our allocated area. Here booby traps abounded. Jap helmets wired together, new bayonets stuck into trees, trip wires most crudely erected. The first night in the defence 'box' was very noisy. Outside the box anything that was seen or suspected was heavily engaged. There were certainly plenty of bodies laying about the next morning.

Pyuntaza, 70 miles further south, had been opened as a divisional supply airhead by late April, and on 3 May two flights of 2968 Field and one flight of 2963 LAA Squadron were moved to defend and patrol the airstrip now being used for refuelling and rearmament. With weather conditions deteriorating, however, the flights were recalled to Toungoo five days later as the monsoon threatened.

2708 Field Squadron departed in convoy from Thedaw in the first week of May for Tennant. Travelling with the squadron was a flight of 2941 Field Squadron. But the delays in the journey meant that the remainder of 2941 Field Squadron with its CO, Squadron Leader Sullivan, soon caught up with them. The monsoon rains had washed bridges away and river crossings were difficult, however, despite a delay at one river while a new bridge was constructed and one of the squadron vehicles overturning, Tennant was reached only four days later.

Following its arrival 2708 Field Squadron immediately put out one flight for static defence of the airstrip and domestic site during the night, while the during the day patrols were sent out to the west of the Rangoon road. Another flight manned listening posts at night at the far end of the airstrip. Over the next few days flights were sent out to recce the surrounding area, reporting on serviceability of the tracks. Friendly villagers had reported Japanese moving in the area and that fifteen Japanese had arrived in a village with bullock carts and had stolen rice. A few days later No 1 Flight was able to confirm the presence of a group of Japanese with two elephants carrying artillery pieces and six bullock carts. Reports from other sources claimed up to 350 of the enemy in the area. Acting on this information No 1 Flight was sent out on a 48-hour fighting patrol with a company of the 1st Assam Regiment on 9 May, and although defensive positions were dug and ambushes were set no Japanese were seen. The patrol returned the following day, having covered 23 miles in 28 hours. Extensive patrolling was carried out by 2708 Field Squadron over the next few weeks and the area surrounding the airfield was kept clear of the enemy.

The 17th Indian Division took the lead from the 5th Indian Division and was ordered to push on towards Pegu. The entire enemy garrison of Rangoon was brought north in a desperate move to save Pegu and, though stoutly defended, the town was taken on 1 May. Few enemy troops of quality now remained between the leading elements of the 17th Indian Division and the Burmese capital only 50 miles away.

At nightfall on 2 May, however, heavy rain began to fall, the rivers rose, and even the 'all-weather' airfields at Toungoo flooded and were put out of action. The 17th Indian Division struggled to put a bridge across the Pegu River, but the rising waters and waterlogged approaches slowed progress. The division would not reach Rangoon. However, its rapid advance had not been futile as it had drawn out most of the capable fighting troops. With the last line of defence broken at Pegu, the Japanese evacuated the Burmese capital. But for the efforts of the 17th Indian Division, an opposed amphibious landing and bitter fight for the city by XV Corps might have ensued.

In early April Mountbatten had become concerned that the land advance by the Fourteenth Army could not be maintained for a long period and that the air supply system might 'crack-up'. As a consequence he had immediately ordered the plans for an amphibious operation aimed at Rangoon to be revived. D Day for Operation *Dracula* was set as 2 May. The forces would be drawn from those at Akyab and Ramree Islands and provision was made for significant RAF support.

On 10 April Wing Commander Airey, OC 1327 Wing, was informed that one field and one LAA squadron would be required for *Dracula* (Appendix 16). 2967 Field and 2959 LAA Squadrons were selected for the task and withdrawn from their operational role on Ramree. 2959 LAA Squadron was to land on D Day on the west bank of the Rangoon River, where a temporary airstrip would be constructed and enemy air attack was expected. 2967 Field Squadron would not arrive until D+6 on the eastern bank, where it would provide ground protection to RAF Signals, AMES and Fighter Operations units (Map 7).

On 25 April 2959 Squadron loaded its equipment onto motor transport and their vehicles were then sent for waterproofing. The twenty-four 20-mm Hispanos along with ammunition, three senior NCOs and forty-five gunners embarked on three LCTs at Kyaukpyu. As a further sign of the paucity of equipment in this theatre of operations, 2967 Field Squadron still had not received 3-inch mortars for its Mortar Section.[8] Unfortunately they were dropped some 14 miles from their intended targets and were only located after the despatch of frantic signals. They were loaded on the LCT still in the packing and unexamined.

The following day the airmen were visited by the Earl of Bandon, AOC 224 Group, and the Allied Air Task Force Commander, Group Captain Pleasance. Their speeches, rather than being rousing was rather indefinite, as it was still not certain whether the landings would be opposed. On 29 April at 0830 hours Wing HQ, 2959 LAA Squadron and OC 2967 Field Squadron and a Recce party embarked. The convoy sailed at 0600 hours the next day and sailed down the coast. Ominously several thunderstorms and heavy rain were experienced and this did not bode well for the landings and subsequent establishment of a fair-weather airstrip.

On D-1 a heavy air bombardment was carried out on likely enemy-defended positions at the river mouth and a battalion of Gurkhas was dropped successfully by parachute to capture Elephant Point. It was becoming apparent, however, that few of the enemy remained. Confirmation was provided the same day when an RAF plane

Operation Dracula. Men of the RAF Regiment and ground crews from 273 (Spitfire) Squadron RAF come ashore from an LCI at one of the landing beaches near Rangoon, May 1945. (Air Historical Branch RAF Crown Copyright)

The area selected by the invasion planners was waterlogged and entirely unsuitable as an airfield. RAF Regiment gunners haul their Hispanos through mud from landing craft. (Air Historical Branch RAF Crown Copyright)

flying over Rangoon had noticed a message painted in large white-washed letters on the roof of the Rangoon Jail, stating rather bluntly, 'JAPS GONE: BRITISH HERE' and in a near-completed state 'EXTRACT DIGIT'.[9] By 2 May Wing Commander Saunders of 110 Squadron flying a Mosquito had crashed-landed on the potholed runway at Mingaladon airfield in the north of the city. Further investigation by him revealed that the enemy had indeed evacuated the city and, after taking formal possession of the city on behalf of the Allies, he set off to notify the approaching landing force. Fortunately the Force commanders had taken the enemy's absence into account and the air and sea bombardment was significantly modified.

The 26th Indian Division was landed successfully on the west bank of the river as planned and moved north. By 3 May the men were into the docks and the city itself. They met only scattered opposition and suffered few casualties.

The RAF command contingent, including 1327 Wing HQ, landed on D Day on the west bank of the river from an LCI at 1730 hours on 'Fox White' Beach. After wading through chest-deep water and mud, the men found 2959 LAA Squadron already landed with its guns set out on the narrow muddy beach. Airey made contact with the OC of 273 Squadron, whose Spitfires and airstrip they were to protect, only to be told that the area selected by the invasion planners was waterlogged and entirely unsuitable as an airfield. As it was late the airmen remained there for the night. The flights of 2959 LAA Squadron formed a rough triangle and soon had fires going, were brewing tea and settled in for the night. Double sentries were posted and it soon began to rain and recurred during the night. Soaked through, the airmen did their best to remain comfortable. Wing Commander Airey describes the futile efforts of the Wing Medical Officer to ease his discomfort:

. . . Doc Dodds . . . completely stripped himself and seemed to squat on his haunches under a ground sheet all through the night, applying 'Scat' at odd intervals. Unfortunately ants seem to thrive on 'Scat' and the Doc's discomfort was complete.[10]

The weather the following day was clear and warm and a hot breakfast was prepared, however, no movement was made. On D+2 the airmen were soaked by heavy showers with many fine renditions of 'Singing in the Rain' to be heard, while, earlier in the day a grave-digging party was called on to bury five British servicemen killed earlier in the day when an LCT struck a mine. Digging in the mud and slush made the task all the more unpleasant.

At 1630 hours the Regiment personnel, guns and equipment finally embarked on an LCI. At all times the guns had to be manhandled as vehicles had yet to arrive. The LCI moved up the river and berthed alongside a severely damaged Rangoon jetty of debris, twisted girders and unexploded bombs. Spending the night on LCIs, the airmen moved up river the next day and landed at 1100 hours. A block of flats was located and the airmen were able to dry out clothes and equipment and a defence scheme was prepared.

Rangoon had fallen to the Japanese just over three years earlier and, as when the Japanese marched in, very few shots were fired. The populace turned out in some quarters to welcome the troops but were no doubt relieved that a pitch battle had not been fought over their already dilapidated and bombed city. Water supply, sanitation and hospitals had been neglected and the enemy had destroyed the electricity supply system. For such a bitterly fought campaign the fall of Rangoon had been achieved with relative ease. It must, however, be borne in mind that this was only because the decisive blow of the campaign had been struck back in March by Slim at Meiktila. The *Burma Area Army* never recovered adequately from this to establish strong-enough

During the Rangoon landings, a Dakota dropping supplies passes over the Hispanos of 2959 LAA Squadron. (Air Historical Branch RAF Crown Copyright)

RAF Regiment officers and airmen on the landing beaches await the end of a monsoon storm. (Air Historical Branch RAF Crown Copyright)

defensive positions that could slow the forward momentum of the Fourteenth Army.

Meanwhile, to the north at Pegu a bridge was finally put across the Pegu River on 4 May and traffic began to flow. An armoured column that had been pushing forward since 2 May had been held up by another river crossing, and the engineers lifted some 500 mines from the road. On 6 May troops from the 26th Indian Division coming from the south linked up with a Gurkha company of the 17th Indian Division. IV Corps had successfully pursued the enemy for twenty-six days and covered some 300 miles.[11] Operation *Capital*, which had been launched from Imphal the previous September, was over.

The RAF headed south along the road to Rangoon and took possession of airstrips closer to Rangoon. Ted Daines continues:

> The activity was very brief, it became very quiet and we were soon told a move was about to happen . . . getting out of Toungoo was very difficult owing to the heavy demolitions that had been done. The only way out was to be winched up on to the railway track, drive along the rails until one was diverted onto the road. This was a very slow job, but as we were going to an airfield we had some sort of priority. We found that the roads were indeed metalled but alas full of holes, some by wear, and some by Japs digging and sitting with an instrument to strike the fuse of the bomb held between their legs. It was pleasing to note that they had left the residue of soil around making it easy to notice. Less easy to notice was the piano wire stretched head high across the road, ready to decapitate the head stuck out of the oncoming vehicle. This was countered by welding a bayonet to the front of the lookout space.
>
> We were bound for Zayatkwin airfield . . . that was waiting for the bomb disposal boys . . . about the first thing I noticed, was this huge unexploded bomb sticking out of the ground about halfway down, also it was about central in the runway, whether it had been dropped or planted by the Japs I don't

know. There was also a 'Betty' [bomber] that looked in good condition; this was also looked at from a safe distance.

We started patrolling the outside of the airstrip, in the paddy field. We walked ankle deep in water, as usual myself or another Sergeant led the patrol and also the sweep that followed it, taking in the surrounding villages . . .

. . . There was not a lot happening at Zayatkwin, what we were doing got less and less, then came the news we were to move to the village of Mingaladon, we would be joining up with the rest of the Squadron.

For the RAF the main objective of Operation *Dracula* was Rangoon's principal airfield at Mingaladon. This had been the focus of RAF operations in 1942 before the retreat. On 7 May the Regiment units that had landed as part of *Dracula* were ordered to make for Mingaladon airfield. Following a recce by the Wing Commander and OCs of 2959 and 2967 Squadrons, an AA flight was ordered immediately to the airfield on the two 3-tonners available. They were to occupy the airfield and give local ground protection to the aircraft that had landed there. By 9 May the entire squadron was in place and AA positions had been prepared. Defensive plans were made for the aircraft dispersal and the only serviceable hangar, and the eight Spitfires of 273 Squadron, which had made risky but successful landings on the damaged runway.

Only three days later, Air Chief Marshal Sir Keith Park Allied Air C-in-C and Air Vice-Marshal The Earl of Bandon AOC 224 Group visited the airfield and inspected the Squadron HQs and a flight of 2959 LAA Squadron. Park had a cheery word for all and expressed pleasure and satisfaction with what he saw.

Finally, on 13 May, to the accompaniment of lusty cheers from those Regiment

2959 LAA Squadron RAF Regiment prepares to disembark from a landing craft at the Rangoon Docks, May 1945. (Air Historical Branch RAF Crown Copyright)

Airmen of 2959 LAA Squadron load equipment on trucks abandoned by the Japanese when they departed Rangoon. Note the trailer has wooden wheels. (Air Historical Branch RAF Crown Copyright)

personnel already present, 2967 Field Squadron arrived at Mingaladon after a five-day journey from Ramree. That afternoon they were all able to welcome 1329 Wing HQ, and 2960 LAA and 2942 Field Squadrons, the leading Regiment units of 221 Group, which drove from the north and were surprised to find 1327 Wing already in occupation. George Briggs of 2942 Field Squadron recalls the arrival in Rangoon:

> Upon my Squadron reaching Rangoon we were first quartered in a tented camp, and we did nightly patrols to seek out any Japs who may have been holed up and waiting their chance to do some damage. After a short time we were billeted in beautiful large houses, which had belonged to well-off civilians before the war broke out. What luxury after what we had been used to.

The need for AA defence had been declining steadily as the Allies cemented their superiority in the air and the Japanese Air Force withdrew east to airfields in Siam. The LAA squadrons, therefore, were called on more frequently to take on ground defence of airfields, convoys and AMES. For instance, over the next five months 2960 LAA Squadron's role was changed entirely to that of a field squadron, mainly acting in an anti-sabotage role, and its 20-mm guns were handed in to the Reinforcement Pool at Rangoon.

Prome had fallen to the 33rd Indian Brigade on 3 May, however, the advance of XXXIII Corps had become more difficult to supply by air and only a limited move forward could be supported with the aircraft and airstrips available. The primary role of XXXIII Corps, therefore, became that of destroying the remnants of the Japanese *54th Division* attempting to escape eastwards from the Arakan Yomas and to provide a diversion to the main efforts of IV Corps. The 7th and 20th Indian Divisions were

Wing Commander C.S. Airey (1327 Wing HQ) and Squadron Leader J.A. Boulton examine damage caused by repeated Allied bombing of Rangoon railway station. (Air Historical Branch RAF Crown Copyright)

placed across the most likely escape routes. The Japanese were fully aware of what they were facing and between 6 and 28 May they crossed the Irrawaddy in large numbers just to the north of Prome and the threat from enemy parties intensified.

1323 Wing received a replacement for 2958 LAA Squadron, now stationed at Magwe, when 2854 LAA Squadron flew into Sinthe from Akyab to join 2946 Field Squadron during the last week of April. 'C' Flight took up AA duties, while the other two flights were put on patrol duties by day, searching neighbouring villages for Japanese, and manning listening posts around the station at night.

On 13 May 'A' Flight of 2958 LAA Squadron departed from Magwe in convoy with an AMES and travelled south towards a village 23 miles from Prome. Making contact with a company of the 4/1st Gurkha Rifles, 'A' Flight took over their defensive positions, which were situated on the banks of the Irrawaddy. The Japanese *54th Division* was gathering in force on the west bank of the Irrawaddy to form a bridgehead only 8 miles north of Prome. The ORB describes the situation that now faced the flight:

> Many of the enemy were known to be in the village immediately across the river and constant nightly infiltration just north of our campsite by small bodies of the enemy was to be expected. Two further listening posts were, therefore, sited so as to give us all-round protection. Burmese were only allowed to sail up and down our side of the river if shewing a white flag. All other river craft were to be fired upon. During the night spasmodic fire was heard, both north and south of our position.[12]

Patrolling continued and on 15 May 'A' Flight took its first Japanese prisoner, a very rare occurrence. The Japanese were infamous for their reluctance to surrender and often would commit suicide and kill those attempting to apprehend or offer help to them. The ORB continues:

Three Burmese in a boat brought word that they had seen something in the water in the small bay, 100 yards north of our Camp. A party of men from 'A' Flight under Sergeant P. Upward was despatched to search the area. A recce for half an hour revealed nothing so the Flight Sergeant, taking a Bren gun with him and covered by the remainder of the party entered the Burmese boat and was paddled to the small bay. After some time and much diligent searching amongst the logs floating in the river, the Japanese was discovered. He surrendered and was brought back to the camp. Slightly wounded, but very hungry, the prisoner devoured a tin of salmon with a gusto which suggested he had not eaten for some considerable time. He had also intimated that, on being taken prisoner that he chose death by the Bren gun rather than the bayonets of the personnel who guarded him.[13]

The CO of the 4/1st Gurkha Rifles soon arrived with an escort and the prisoner and his belongings were handed over. The airmen were assured by the Gurkhas that he was a first-class capture.

The activities of the Regiment at this time were not all grim. On 8 May it was announced that the war was over in Europe. Soon after, 'A' Flight received its beer and spirit ration from the Squadron HQ. At times during this deployment the flight had been on quarter rations and so it was a pleasing change when the self-appointed Flight Welfare Committee arranged a small celebration and sing-song and the usual rations were augmented with a local purchase of chicken and fresh vegetables. The AMES, meanwhile, had found a suitable site and on 16 May 'A' Flight moved through Prome to the new location, 3 miles south of Shwedaung.

The situation was still fluid as more enemy parties moved east from the Arakan. An enemy party occupied a village to the south-east of 'A' Flight's positions. Small arms fire was heard throughout the day and heavy artillery fire during the night. A number of isolated Japanese parties were seen in the vicinity over the next few days, but enemy activity in this area was gradually settling down as those who were able had crossed into the Pegu Yomas. On 29 May 'B' Flight from 2854 LAA Squadron relieved 'A' Flight was and the men drove north to rejoin 2958 LAA Squadron at Magwe.

For all Regiment units this was a period of continual watch as enemy parties attempted to make their way eastwards and escape the trap. 2944 Field Squadron was protecting an AMES at Poktan on 17 May when a river crossing was attempted by a small group of Japanese:

A Regiment Listening Post gave warning of a country boat attempting to cross the river in the vicinity of the Radar Station. In accordance with Army orders, the country boat, not carrying a white flag was immediately engaged with Bren gun fire. The occupants promptly dropped over the side of the boat and disappeared; a search was made with no result.[14]

Incidents of this kind were to be repeated many times over the next three months until the Japanese surrender.

VE Day had also been celebrated many miles back at Sinthe, where 907 Wing arranged a supply of liquor and cake to the airmen of 2854 LAA Squadron. A large bonfire was lit and the squadron joined with the other units in a short thanksgiving service, followed by a sing-song around the fire. Only a few days later, the squadron moved 140 miles south to Magwe. Again, this was done with loaned vehicles as 2854 LAA Squadron, having been flown in, had no transport of its own.

The worsening weather in May inevitably caused a redeployment of the Allied Air Forces in southern and central Burma. The monsoon was reaching its full spate and many of the forward airstrips, some with all-weather surfaces, had become unusable. The tactical squadrons were ordered to withdraw to the 'drier' areas in the north. By late May, 907 Wing at Magwe and Sinthe had pulled back to Myingyan and Meiktila, and with them had gone 1323 Wing and the four squadrons. The road to Rangoon for 1323 Wing and its squadrons was not to be through Magwe.

Following the withdrawal of 1323 Wing to the north, 2968 Field Squadron was despatched to Prome airfield, nearly 320 miles north-west of Toungoo, to take over the AMES responsibilities. Toungoo Main was to remain in use for the air transports but with only one fighter squadron remaining for air defence. The air supply system still struggled as more and more airstrips were put out of action and movement of supplies off the major roads became impossible. IV Corps was placed on half rations and every effort was made to get the port of Rangoon open.

All Regiment squadrons were now consolidated within 221 Group; 1307 and 1330 Wing remained at Tennant, while 1326 Wing handed over to 1331 Wing at Akyab, and took control of the three squadrons at Kalaywa near Toungoo. 1327 Wing with five squadrons had sole responsibility for Mingaladon. In central Burma, 1329 Wing was located at Kwetnge, but with only 2943 Field Squadron under command far south at Zayatkwin. 1323 Wing remained at Myingyan and Meiktila. In the Arakan, where the RAF transport squadrons had been concentrated, there were only two Regiment Wings, 1308 concentrated at Cox's Bazaar and 1331 Wing at Akyab, with two squadrons each. However, by late June the Regiment had departed the Arakan for the last time.

On 15 June 1945 a Victory Day Parade was held in Rangoon. Representatives were

The end of the road. With the Shwedagon golden pagoda in the distance, an LAA squadron of the RAF Regiment moves through a Rangoon street on the way to Mingaladon airfield, May 1945. (Australian War Memorial P02491.071)

chosen from each of the Armed Services to provide fifty men for the guard of honour. In attendance was the Supreme Allied Commander of SEAC, Admiral Lord Louis Mountbatten. The Royal Navy were led by the Royal Marines, while the honour of leading the RAF contingent was given to RAF Regiment. While other squadrons were to march in the parade, it was 2942 Field Squadron that was chosen to provide the RAF guard of honour. This was seen as a reward for the squadron's long operational history in the Arakan and central Burma. Marching at the head of 2942 Field Squadron was the new CO, now Squadron Leader, Ian Mitchell, who had won the Military Cross in the Arakan the previous October.

The men of 2942 Field Squadron set to, and did considerable hard work to make themselves presentable, which including the wearing of white gaiters, belts and slings. It must be remembered that the Regiment had only been in existence for three and a half years, therefore, the turnout had to be of the highest standards and to ensure this drill work was taken on by Flight Lieutenant H.W. Eyrl. George Briggs continues:

> My Squadron had the honour to represent the RAF in the Victory Parade through the streets of Rangoon and we were inspected by Lord Louis Mountbatten before marching through the city. What a proud day that was.

During the address by Mountbatten and the March Past, which took over half an hour, the parade was subjected to two heavy monsoonal downpours. Rather than ruining the event, in some way it made it more impressive as this had been the blight of the Army and Air Forces since the struggle in Burma had begun in late 1941 and they had come through this and much worse from defeat into victory. This was more eloquently summed up in a comment made by a soldier to the journalist Frank Owen at the completion of the ceremony: 'We fought through the f . . . ing rain and it's bloody well right that the bull s..t should take place in this rain.'[15] The airmen of the RAF Regiment who had been in the Arakan, Imphal and Kabaw Valleys and into Burma proper would no doubt concur with his sentiments.

Following the parade Mountbatten commented to a Brigadier 'The Guards of Honour were excellent, particularly the RAF Regiment.' The new AOC 221 Group[16] said later in a personal message, 'I wish to add my own appreciation of the exceptional smartness of the guard of honour and the RAF Regiment Detachment as a whole who maintain the high standard I have always come to expect from the RAF Regiment.'

Despite the fall of Rangoon in May, the Burma campaign was not at an end. The rapid southward thrusts of IV Corps and XXXIII Corps had trapped more than 17,000 of the enemy between the Bay of Bengal and the Sittang River. To reach the relative safety of the Burma-Siam border they would have to cross the Mandalay-Rangoon road. Most of the *28th Army* was now concentrated in the hills and jungle-covered vastness of the Pegu Yomas. Although some of the enemy were in scattered groups, many were still part of a large coherent force and the breakout was already being planned by their commanders. The Japanese, by this time, were in a malnourished and diseased state and many were unable to fight effectively. Surrender, however, was considered a dishonourable act, and they would fight on and struggle to escape the trap that had been set for them. The *28th Army* made the move to escape from its trap in mid-July and, in what became known as the Battle of Sittang, there occurred some of the bitterest fighting of the campaign under appalling climatic conditions.

For the soldiers and airmen there were no longer the rapid armoured thrusts, but tedious day-after-day trudging through atrocious monsoonal weather, wading through paddy fields and plodding through mud, feet deep in soaking jungle.[17] Meanwhile, the

The RAF Regiment Band moves up to take its place in the Victory Parade at Rangoon, 15 June 1945. (Air Historical Branch RAF Crown Copyright)

pilots of 221 Group continued to fly through monsoonal deluges to strafe enemy troop concentrations, to provide close support to units of the Twelfth Army[18] and to carry out aerial reconnaissance flights to discover Japanese escape routes.

Efforts were made by Regiment personnel at Toungoo to improve the tented monsoon accommodation, with floor boards being made from railway sleepers. Welfare facilities were enhanced with the provision of two wirelesses and two gramophones. The Regiment activities concentrated on patrolling and watching for the anticipated breakout and intrusions around their airfields. The enemy parties surrounding Toungoo, in particular, posed a considerable threat. The magnitude of this threat was highlighted during June when 1307 Wing received a report that a column of 2,000 Japanese soldiers with 200 women had been seen passing through a village 12 miles to the north-west of Toungoo.

During July the Regiment Squadrons at Toungoo pursued coordinated action with the Army and RAF, carrying out patrols ranging to the west and as far as the Sittang in the east. Some eighty patrols were carried out, mainly by 2759 Field and 2965 LAA Squadrons. Their object was to close escape routes, guard the approaches to the airstrips, obtain information and intelligence and deal with any enemy encountered. While the patrols met little serious opposition, the activities did keep the airstrips free from enemy interference. They also collected arms and ammunition and killed some Japanese.

By early August the fighting had died down and only stragglers remained west of the Sittang. In the fighting between 7 May and 15 August 1945, the *28th Army* had lost 9,791 men killed with only 1,491 taken prisoner. This was in striking contrast to the losses to IV Corps of 435 killed, 1,452 wounded and fourteen missing.[19] The remaining depleted Japanese formations were now fatally weakened and disintegrating and were withdrawing south towards Tennasserim.

Since the fall of Rangoon most of the Regiment squadrons had been withdrawn to India to train for the amphibious landings to retake Malaya, code-named Operation *Zipper*. 2944 Field Squadron, along with many of the Burma squadrons, was earmarked for this operation. In late May 1945, 2944 Field Squadron, in company with 1323 Wing HQ and its other squadrons, had moved from Myingyan north of Meiktila down the Mandalay-Rangoon Road, staying for only a few days at Insein airfield north of Rangoon, then Mingaladon, and finally moved to the Rangoon docks, where they embarked on the HMT *Dilwara*. Sailing across the Bay of Bengal to Madras, they then moved inland to begin training at Warangal near the RAF Regiment Depot at Secunderabad for their new job.

By early August the only remaining Regiment representatives at Toungoo were 1307 Wing and 2759 Field Squadron, which was now solely responsible for the airfield. The wing and squadron were both under command of Squadron Leader Charles Killeen who was also Area Defence Commander. With this limited force he had a commitment of approximately 6–8 miles in length and 3–4 miles in depth. The monsoon conditions were still horrendous but 2759 Field Squadron continued to patrol the area vigorously and man listening posts at nights. Charles Killeen continues:

> The defence of the airstrips and its flying squadrons was my main concern . . .
> Guerrilla and native information were fully investigated assisted by a Burmese
> who attached to us who could speak English reasonably well. This man's wife

'*The Supremo' Lord Louis Mountbatten speaks to an airman of 2942 Field Squadron. Squadron Leader Ian Mitchell MC stands to the right. (Air Historical Branch RAF Crown Copyright)*

and daughter had been murdered by the Japanese some time previously.

A few days before the first atom bomb was dropped on Hiroshima, I was asked by 19th Indian Division if my Squadron could deal with a party of Japs some 20 miles west of the airstrip. Volunteers were asked for and the number required soon obtained. The unit was desperately short of officers due to illness while others had been detached for other duties. Corporal Miller [therefore] . . . led the patrol. His orders were simple i.e. to locate and destroy any Japs in the area of Tabetgwe. The patrol lasted from 8 August to 14 August 1945.

The patrol . . . were the only members of the RAF to go into action on elephants against the Japs.[20]

Corporal Alexander Miller recalls the circumstances of his involvement in the patrol:

Our CO called for volunteers for a patrol, with the definite meeting of Japs thrown in, so being kinda fed up with typing all day, I stuck my name down, and with permission being granted for me to proceed . . . [I then spent] seven days . . . with this patrol.

They moved off on foot early on 7 August, with local scouts who were to guide them to where they knew a large number of the enemy were living, and reached a nearby village late in the afternoon where they spent the night. Corporal Miller, another Corporal and eighteen men were organised in two sections, which were to be transported by elephant through the foothills of the Pegu Yomas to clear a village of Japanese troops. Though the Regiment had trained repeatedly for many tasks, none of the airmen had ridden an elephant before, except for Corporal Miller. He had done so as a child at Regent's Park. He continues:

[The next day] . . . we were up at usual time, had a wash at the local well . . . Then after breakfast, we collected our gear and awaited the arrival of the elephants – yeah, you heard . . . elephants. They eventually strolled (or lumbered) up, were made to kneel down and we loaded on all our gear, ammunition, stores, etc, then these creatures set off to ford the chaung, whilst we in two parties crossed the river in a canoe. By the time we were all over, the elephants were likewise and on to their backs we clambered. We were on our way and the time was 0915 hours.

The country over which we bumped and slipped was completely covered with water, and at the commencement was thickly wooded, so great care had to be taken that branches did not knock the odd eye. Leaving the woods behind we set off over miles of flooded paddy fields and so we splashed on. Suddenly there was a fusillade of shots, and we in the rear thought 'Here it comes already', but with another burst, all was silent once more. We arrived at our first stop, a village named Kyattaiknyaungbin, where we unloaded into a big warehouse place, and where we had a meal.

The time of arrival here was just after 1200 hours, and we now awaited the return of the elephants for a further trek to our night quarters, where we hoped to establish Patrol Headquarters. After all having had a refreshing snooze, we again set off on our huge steeds, leaving at 1530 hours. We all took the same mounts as previously and once more we paddled through the paddy fields with even deeper water. Then to crown it, the rains came – raining like hell with a strong and rather cold wind. Very quickly we were completely soaked, as there is no protection from the elements in the open baskets which serve as sitting accommodation on these elephants . . . One of the elephants slipped and sent one of the lads into some quite deep water, but as he was wet already, it did not make much difference. This bloke, Heath, was a cheerful chap, so amid bursts of merriment he just grinned and clambered back on to his chariot.

There was another fusillade of shots and one of the men who fired was the Scout on my elephant, and it has now transpired that it is a warning to the villagers that friends were approaching. Then we arrived at our HQ village, named Shwekaung Ywathit, just after 1730 hours, very cold and very wet . . . We had some well-deserved grub, but some silly so-and-so had left the tea behind, so for a hot beverage we had boiled milk – well boiled too, as cholera is an ever present danger.

On 9 August the patrol received credible intelligence that there was there was a group of Japanese in Tabetgwe village. Leaving two airmen behind to make the midday meal, the patrol set off at 0745 hours armed with rifles, Stens and two Bren guns. Corporal Miller describes events as they approached the village:

Leading us was a Burmese scout and bringing up the rear was another. Also attached to the patrol were six armed villagers. The going was hellish tough for the first part, as it was through thick and evil-smelling mud, and then it was through deep water, well over the knees of the tallest of us. After the flats, we hit wooded land (or jungle) and then we climbed a hill by means of a rough path and at the top was a large basha. We were ordered to get down, and a message was passed back that six Japs were in the village below; 'Tabetgwe' by name.

No. 1 Section went left flanking to the south and No. 2 (mine) went right to the north. Fire control was excellent and we were within ten yards of the occupied bashas before the first burst of fire came, immediately after the throwing of a grenade by Corporal Doverty. The returning fire was light, but I saw one bullet cut the grass alongside Lorraine's head, and another planted itself at my posterior, peppering my pants with mud. I shot like hell into the shrubbery – not my rifle, but both of us. Corporal Doverty threw another grenade and we dashed into the courtyard between the two bashas.

Corporal Doverty and four [airmen] went to the right of the first basha and Lorraine and I went to the left. I had only taken a few steps when I saw a Jap head being raised between two legs of the basha, the distance from me being just over 15 yards. I fired from the shoulder and hit him right behind the left ear. He lay still [and] I fired again just to make sure, and one of the right flanking lads gave another Jap a burst from his Sten, and that seemed to account for the occupants of that particular basha and firing had ceased from the other parts of the attack. I reckon the bloke I hit behind the ear was the one who had been unlucky (for him) in not hitting Lorraine and I.

Among the loot taken were five grenades, three rifles and one revolver, a small quantity of ammunition, and a lot of other articles including three flags. Full kill for the attack was four dead Japs, and two who had escaped but had been wounded in so doing.

No casualties on the patrol's side, and we returned to Patrol HQ at 1045 hours, rather muddy, very wet but with spirits high. Scouts returned from [the] village and they had followed blood stains of one of the wounded escapes, and had found that he had blown himself up with a grenade. Other now occupying another basha across the river, but he was definitely wounded.

On Friday 10 August the patrol received a further unconfirmed report that two more Japanese had arrived in Tabetgwe and set out again to investigate. Corporal Miller describes the day's events:

> Left for Tabetgwe again, Friday at 0830 hours, and raining was beating down, causing deeply flooded fields to be even deeper. Arrived at hill-top overlooking village, without seeing any signs of the enemy, our patrol today had extra recruits from villages around, attachment now being about 20 strong.
>
> Anyway, we decided to enter the village from the west, and had to hack our way through thick undergrowth. The villagers all took up positions around, 'just in case there was any break-out'. We anticipated fording a small chaung running through the village, but as banks were high and the water running rather too fast, we decided to cross by the narrow bridge. Crossing of the bridge was made singly, the bashas covering the bridge having received three bursts from the Bren in the hands of Morgan. We all got over safely, and one party went west and the other east and then both north. No actual opposition was encountered, but each basha was potentially in danger, especially the two-storey affairs.

This part of the village seemed to be a 'graveyard', with the body of a Japanese soldier laid out in or under each basha. A few were in an advanced state of decomposition, but most looked newly dead. In all, fourteen bodies were counted. No live enemy were encountered until the edge of the village was reached where two more, both of whom had been wounded in the previous day's encounter, were killed. Another ran from a basha and committed suicide by placing a hand grenade on his stomach. It was also confirmed that the soldier who had committed suicide had been wounded the day before. The patrol returned to its HQ just after noon.

The following day was spent resting until late in the day when a patrol moved off to Kyattaiknyaungbin. Corporal Miller and the patrol received some good news *en route* to the village:

> . . . left Patrol HQ at 1600 hours on foot again. Destination was village with long name where we had broken first elephant trip on Wednesday. We probed the jungle for signs of the enemy but none seen. Halfway to village, Bennet returned on his elephant with a message. The message stated that the Japs were asking for unconditional surrender, and also that our destination had been changed, and that we were to proceed to Thabyegon. Great was the rejoicing among the lads at the news of the end of the war, and various remarks were passed about the early release and back to our homes.

No enemy were seen and the patrol was diverted to Thabyegon where it stayed the night. Two more villages were checked on 12 August and footprints of Japanese rubber shoes found in the mud. The tracks led to two Japanese bodies, which had been dead for a week. The patrol checked two more villages but the area was clear of the enemy. Corporal Miller continues:

> For about a half mile we hiked up the middle of a small river and then hit the hills, where the going was dry and solid for a change, but still hard going.

Passed through the jungle and eventually reached Taungbohla, but this village was completely clear of the enemy. Arrived back at Patrol Headquarters at 1330 hours, as hungry as we could be . . . this was the biggest patrol of all, as there were at least 30 armed scouts, guides and villagers with us. Conditions overhead were much better, and we nearly got dry above the waist when our destination was reached . . . Area now presumed clear of Jappy, and good show patrol.

With confirmation from scouts the following day that the area was clear, arrangements were made to obtain the patrol's mounts for the return journey. Corporal Miller continues:

Trying to contact elephants, and if not successful we intend walking – over 15 miles. . . . 14 elephants will be here first light. Doing trip in one hop this time, taking just over three hours.

Set off on our slow steeds shortly after 0900 hours, after saying cheerio to all our Burmese friends. Shortly after starting, the basket on my elephant collapsed and kit tumbled into the water. Simpson changed to another elephant and I was left balancing the basket with one leg to prevent the whole caboodle slipping off the back. Also, the elephant on which Dixon and Currie were travelling refused to carry on, so we left them far behind. My elephant was not so sure footed as she might have been, and we were all glad when the village of Kinseik was reached, and this time we forded the river on the backs of the elephants, and not by canoe as previously. Squadron transport turned up almost immediately after our arrival, and with our return to camp at 1500 hours, so our patrol came to an end.

We heard later that the elephant carrying Dixon and Currie had died as a result of being bitten by a snake in the tip of the trunk. These two lads eventually reached camp at 2230 hours having come all the way in the dark, and having crossed the river as well. This crossing shook them rotten. So endeth my brush with the enemy, and I would not have missed the outing for anything.

The dropping of two atomic bombs on Hiroshima and Nagasaki forced the Japanese Government to seek surrender terms. On 15 August, the same day that Corporal Miller and the men from 2759 Field Squadron were returning on their elephants from their patrol, Emperor Hirohito announced on the radio that Japan had officially surrendered. By 20 August Lieutenant-General Montagu Stopford of the Twelfth Army ordered General Kimura, the Commander of the *Burma Area Army*, to cease hostilities immediately and to make arrangements for the surrender of all his forces. This did not necessarily mean that all the Japanese soldiers remaining in the jungles of Burma would immediately lay down their arms or knew that the war was over. The Twelfth Army was to halt operations but remain prepared to take adequate precautions should local Japanese commanders appear reluctant to cease hostilities.

At Hmawbi airstrip, 12 miles north of Mingaladon, victory celebrations were well underway on 15 August when about eighty Japanese soldiers made a quick dash across the airfield making for the officers' lines. The enemy party threw hand grenades and Molotov cocktails and eight RAF officers were injured and taken to hospital suffering from blast injuries, while a Mosquito of 47 Squadron was severely damaged and three tents burnt down. The incident was quickly dealt with by 2802 Field Squadron who then had to organise the removal of unexploded bombs and high explosive remaining on the airstrip. Despite the end of the war, this incident kept the RAF Regiment and the flying squadron personnel at Hmawbi on full alert for the next few days.

The Air Forces in Burma were now under the control of HQ RAF Burma based in Rangoon. In late May, 221 Group had taken sole command of the air support for the Twelfth Army in Burma, the fighter defence of Rangoon and air defence of Burma as far north as Mandalay. From May to August 221 Group was deployed with 906 Wing at Mingaladon, 908 and 910 Wings at Meiktila and 909 Wing at Toungoo. 224 Group RAF had been withdrawn in late May and moved to southern India, where it began preparations for the invasion of Malaya.

The speed of the advance and successful capture of Rangoon now meant that Forward Echelon Agartala was now far behind the front, whereas at the time of its establishment it had been only a short distance. The reason for its formation had been, first, to overcome the difficulties of transporting RAF Regiment reinforcements quickly from Secunderabad to the front in Manipur and the Arakan, and, second, to prepare and train a readily available reserve of replacements for units in forward areas. Between early January and June 1945, seven field squadrons had completed their advanced battle and jungle training at Agartala before being sent to join 221 Group, while smaller groups of airmen had completed signals, mines and booby traps, mortar, and other specialist courses. The last unit to pass through Forward Echelon was 2964 Field Squadron, which had been formed in late 1944 as an LAA Squadron but had, as a result of changing requirements, been retrained as a field squadron. The reasons for the establishment of Forward Echelon Agartala were no longer relevant. It was now a 'back area' and most of the squadrons had now been withdrawn to India to prepare for Operation *Zipper*. In June 1945 a centre was established in Rangoon to provide a reinforcement and replacement pool for the Regiment units remaining in southern Burma, and subsequently Forward Echelon Agartala closed.

On 1 January 1945 there were ten field squadrons, seven LAA squadrons and seven Wing HQs working with 221 and 224 Groups in Burma. By the fall of Rangoon on 3 May, this had been increased to fourteen field squadrons, nine LAA squadrons and eight Wing HQs. The increase had only been made possible by the arrival of eight squadrons from the United Kingdom in December 1944. The last word on the critical role of the RAF Regiment in the successful conclusion of the Burma campaign should go to Air Chief Marshal Sir Keith Park, who said:

> . . . as the army units advanced, it frequently proved impossible, despite the presence of enemy troops lurking in the neighbourhood, to leave garrisons behind to protect the airfields they had overrun. The defence of the latter thus fell to the squadrons of the RAF Regiment. On their shoulders there thus rested the defence of the army lifeline and also of the air bases indispensable for air support and defence, and they were accordingly moved forward step by step with the progress of the campaign . . . [21]

Notes

1   Air Chief Marshal Sir Keith Park GCB KBE MC DFC MA (1892–1975). A New Zealander by birth, Park had come to prominence early in the war as OC No 11 Fighter Group RAF during the Battle of Britain and again in 1942 for his astute and vigorous command of the air defence of the besieged island fortress of Malta.

2   Following the regrouping IV Corps would consist of the 5th, 17th and 19th Indian Divisions

and the 255th Indian Tank Brigade and XXXIII Indian Corps, the 2nd British and the 7th and 20th Indian Divisions, the 254th Indian Tank Brigade and the 268th Indian Brigade.

3   Consisting of 2748 and 2810 Field and 2846 and 2852 LAA Squadrons.

4   This was not a successful period on the sports field for 2708. They were beaten 2–3 by 2968 Squadron and 0–1 by 2941 Squadron at football, then went on to lose 81–94 in a cricket match against the latter.

5   Henry Kirk met the same Army Sergeant again a few weeks later in Rangoon. By this time the Sergeant was wearing the medal ribbon for an award for distinguished conduct for his mine-lifting work on that day.

6   So-named after a brand of beer popular in the Far East at the time.

7   Steyn, P. ed. *The History of the Assam Regiment.* Vol. I, 1941–1947. Calcutta: Orient Longmans, 1959, p. 200.

8   The RAF Regiment Depot Secunderabad had received twenty 3-inch mortars on 11 April and these were quickly despatched to Agartala for distribution. Such a poor situation with regard to armaments would not have existed for RAF Regiment units in North-West Europe and Mediterranean theatres for two or more years.

9   This was where a large number of British and Commonwealth POWs were being held, however, their captors had fled.

10 AIR 29/1121, *Appendices 1319–1323, 1327–1329, 1331 & 1333, 1335 & 1336 RAF Regiment Wings 1944–1947.* Flight Lieutenant Dodds, the Wing Medical Officer, had only arrived on posting on 27 April, two days before embarkation for the landings.

11 On average, just over 11 miles a day.

12 AIR 29/138, *Operations Record Books RAF Regiment Squadrons 2941–2950, 2953–2955, 2957–2962, 2964, 2966–2970, Appendices Only.*

13 ibid.

14 *Review of RAF Regiment Squadrons under the control of HQ RAF Burma, 1st January 1945 to 3rd May 1945, Capture of Rangoon,* HQ RAF Burma, p. 7.

15 Ziegler, P. ed. *Personal Diary of Admiral the Lord Louis Mountbatten. Supreme Commander, South-East Asia, 1943–1946.* London: Collins, 1988, p. 213.

16 Air Vice-Marshal S.F. Vincent had completed his successful tour of duty on 13 June and sailed from Rangoon that day. As a result his place on the Victory Parade dais had been taken by Air Vice-Marshal C.A. Bouchier (1895–1979) who had taken command of 221 Group RAF.

17 The monsoon was taking a steady toll on many of the RAF Regiment units. The ORB of 1307 Wing refers to the poor state of one of the squadrons under its control. It was desperately in need of rest and re-equipping and in particular there were some airmen who had had only seven days' leave in the last three years.

18 The Fourteenth Army in Burma was renamed the Twelfth Army on 1 June 1945.

19 Kirby, S.W. et al. *The War against Japan. The Surrender of Japan.* Vol. V. London: HMSO, 1969, p. 443.

20 Most probably the only RAF personnel to go into battle riding elephants against any foe.

21 Air Chief Marshal Sir Keith Park KCB KBE MC DFC, *Third Supplement to the London Gazette,* Tuesday 6 April 1951, Air Operations in South-East Asia from 1 June 1944 to 2 May 1945, p. 1990.

CHAPTER ELEVEN

Keeping the Peace – Singapore, Malaya, Hong Kong, Siam, Vietnam and Indonesia

' . . . Squadron personnel were quickly selecting positions for defence, siting guns and gave a fine example of how the Regiment, given a real job of work, will work untiringly and with efficiency to achieve the almost impossible. On the first five days . . . though the men . . . had had no sleep and were wet through by the continued monsoon conditions, their vigilance never wavered.'

Wing Commander W.R. Allen, OC 1307 Wing, RAF Regiment

Operation *Zipper*, the landings on the Malay Peninsula, would be the largest single undertaking the Regiment had participated in as part of SEAC. Five RAF Regiment wings of nine field and five LAA squadrons, composed of nearly 2,500 officers and airmen, were allocated for the landings to protect captured airfields and AMES. To prepare for this, the Regiment had withdrawn four Wing HQs and thirteen of the longest-serving squadrons from Burma to rest, refit and train at Secunderabad. Thus, the month of June at the Depot was occupied with preparations for the return of the squadrons from Forward Areas, formation of new Training Wings and the establishment of a new camp at nearby Warangal to accommodate the largest influx of airmen the Depot had dealt with in its three-year existence[1] (Map 1) (Appendix 17).

Following the Kaladan patrols, 2966 Field Squadron had remained on ground defence at Akyab until ordered back to Secunderabad. For many of the airmen this was their first return to the Depot in a long time. Colin Kirby describes the return to the Depot that he had departed from with 4440 AA Flight two years and seven months earlier:

On the 3rd May we heard that Rangoon had been taken by the Fourteenth Army, and that seemed about it so far as Burma was concerned. On the 11th June we were told that we were returning to the Depot in India. During this period the monsoon was in full flow, and life under canvas was especially damp and wearing. On the 14th we embarked on a naval landing craft and sailed to Madras. Being a vessel designed to get close in-shore during combined operations the ship had a very shallow draught, and heaved and rolled in the choppy sea. Within two hours I was suffering in extremis from *mal-de-mere*. I found a corner to stretch out in on deck and did not move for 48 hours, when

Madras came into sight. I managed to drag myself to the bow and thankfully watched Madras coming closer.

We disembarked and set off marching to a transit camp which was some distance away. We had all our kit, kit-bags, webbing, arms, etc. It was very hot in the middle of the day and I felt very weak, but managed to stagger on to the camp. We stayed there until 8th July, and fortunately had a fairly easy time with some duties and fatigues, but also swimming and cinema.

We left Madras by train and arrived at Warangal the following day. This place was a satellite camp to Secunderabad, a secondary depot a few hours from it by road. We arrived at Warangal to hear that some of the Squadron were posted back to the United Kingdom [while the remainder were sent on leave] . . .

The depleted Squadron boarded a train at 0200 hours on the 26th and it moved off to arrive in Bombay in the early morning of the 28th July. We were transported to the Ship Hotel, an unprepossessing establishment that had been taken over by the military to accommodate troops on leave. There were no furnishings to speak of, just bare rooms with bunk beds. The important thing for us was that we were left alone. We could get meals there, and could come and go as we pleased at any time. They gave us lots of back pay and told us to enjoy ourselves. We did not have to report to anyone and could 'lose' ourselves until 2359 hours on the 11th August.

[On 12 August] . . . we were on the train to Warangal, a few pounds heavier, if lighter in our pockets. There was talk that Japan had surrendered – the Allies had dropped some super bombs on Japan. On the 14th August we were at the Warangal Depot, where my mate and I were met with the news that we had, along with a few others, been posted to another Squadron, presently at Secunderabad. We were devastated. Leaving 2966? 'But we are under strength as it is.' 'The numbers are being made up from Blighty' we were told. 'It's the same with other squadrons. Experienced men are being moved around to get a fair mix.' . . .

Secunderabad seemed to have improved in some respects since I had last seen it. For one thing there was a Corporals' mess run on the same lines as a Sergeants' mess. That night we listened on the radio to speeches by General Slim and Lord Mountbatten. On the 18th Air Vice-Marshal the Earl of Bandon paid us a visit . . . We also had anti-cholera injections. Immediately the Squadron went into intense training; on the range, over the assault course, various battle drills. 'Hasn't anybody told them that the war's over?' was the plaintiff cry.

By July the Secunderabad and Warangal Depots would be home to 1,200 and 1,800 airmen, respectively. Those squadrons earmarked for *Zipper* received concentrated training, particularly in Combined Operations. By early August 1945, all these units had been brought up to strength in personnel and equipment and awaited further instructions. Despite this, few reinforcements had been received from the United Kingdom since early 1945 and the units were still composed predominantly of men who had served in India and Burma. The Regiment was now facing the ongoing and increasing difficulty in keeping the squadrons up to strength with the requirement for release and repatriation of time-expired airmen, which operated under a scheme known as Operation *Python*. At the end of 1944 the qualifying time for repatriation had been shortened from five to three years and eight months. As a result, many of the Royal

2941 Field Squadron at the RAF Regiment Depot, Secunderabad in mid-1945. Re-equipping and receiving reinforcements following the end of the Burma campaign, the men display Japanese battle flags captured at Meiktila. (RAF Regiment SEAC Association)

Navy, Army and RAF units in SEAC were finding it difficult to sustain operations, and in particular, were losing large numbers of specialists. Some of the infantry divisions that had been allocated for Operation *Zipper* were badly affected and therefore units that had only just completed monsoon operations around the Sittang and Pegu Yomas in southern Burma were detailed to go to Malaya in their place.

All that remained of the Regiment in Burma by early September 1945 were three Wing HQs with six squadrons, and these were concentrated in southern Burma on the Insein, Zayatkwin, Hmawbi and Mingaladon airfields in close proximity to Rangoon (Map 7). The latter three airfields were to be essential staging posts for squadrons flying into Malaya and Singapore and later Siam and French Indo-China. Three Wing HQs and ten squadrons were to remain at Warangal and Secunderabad but they would also be required in the next few months, while three Wing HQs and fourteen squadrons would soon be heading for Malaya, Singapore and Hong Kong and other destinations in South-East Asia (Appendix 18).

With the announcement of the Japanese surrender on 15 August 1945, SEAC assumed responsibility for an area of approximately one and a half million square miles with a population of 128 million (Map 1). Along with the British colonies of Malaya, Singapore and Hong Kong, it would have the job of disarming Japanese troops and restoring civil order in the Dutch and French colonies of Netherlands East Indies (now Indonesia) and French Indo-China (now Vietnam), until their colonial governments could send troops and re-establish their own administration. In most of these countries there was no reliable civil police or government and the economy was in a parlous state as a result of three years of Japanese occupation. The troops would find themselves dealing with delicate political as well as military problems in many of these countries. In South-East Asia there remained three-quarters of a million Japanese, including 630,000 armed troops. Despite the capitulation, it was unclear whether they would all obey the surrender terms. There was also the urgent need to locate, feed, clothe and treat some 123,000 prisoners-of-war and internees spread across these territories. To accomplish these tasks, Mountbatten had limited forces at his disposal: the Twelfth Army in Burma and the Fourteenth Army located in India, and shipping adequate only for operations in Malaya and Burma. For the next fifteen months the Regiment would be performing an important part in the reoccupation of South-East Asia. This role was summed up as follows, though it does fail to mention the new challenges arising from the emergence of strong nationalist and communist movements in the former colonies of Britain, the Netherlands and France:

> The role that the Regiment played was as a part of the liberating force. In most cases the Regiment had to accept the surrender of Japanese forces numerically far superior and whose morale and fanaticism were an unknown quantity. Fortunately Japanese discipline over-rode fanaticism and the surrender went off fairly quietly.[2]

The initial focus for SEAC was the recapture of Malaya and Singapore. They had always been the main strategic objectives of the British campaign in India and Burma, however, lack of naval, air and military resources meant that such an expedition was unable to be contemplated until the second half of 1945. Comprehensive plans for Operation *Zipper* had been drawn up in early 1945 for amphibious landings on the western coast of Malaya. At the insistence of the Americans, however, any reoccupation of Japanese-held territory was not to be implemented until the formal surrender document had been signed by General MacArthur on the USS *Missouri* anchored in Tokyo Bay. This was delayed by inclement weather and was not signed until 2 September.

As a precautionary move Mountbatten made contact with the senior Japanese

On 26 August 1945 the Japanese emissaries, Lieutenant-General Takazo Numata and Rear Admiral Kaigye Chudo, arrived at Mingaladon airfield, Rangoon, to discuss arrangements for the surrender of the Japanese Southern Army. Wing Commander Randle Manwaring RAF Regiment (right) was a member of the escort party.
(Air Historical Branch RAF Crown Copyright)

commander in South-East Asia, Field Marshal Count Terauchi, of the Japanese *Southern Army* at Saigon. A delegation was ordered to Rangoon to sign a preliminary surrender agreement on his behalf. A party, led by his Chief of Staff, Lieutenant-General Numata, flew into Mingaladon on 26 August in an aircraft painted with a large white cross to indicate it had no hostile intent. An RAF Regiment officer, Wing Commander Randle Manwaring, was responsible for the reception of the delegation and the ceremony was conducted by Air Vice-Marshal Bouchier of 221 Group. Some suspicion remained as to how the enemy would respond and Regiment units were placed on alert to ensure nothing untoward should occur during the surrender ceremony. LAC Cyril Paskin with 2968 Field Squadron was now stationed at Insein north of Rangoon. He recalls:

> . . . we worked our way down the length of Burma with the Fourteenth Army down to Rangoon. I remember I was on a hill overlooking Rangoon where the Japanese surrender took place. We had our guns aimed ready in case there was any treachery but the Japanese just came, took off their swords and signed the peace treaty.

The assault force for Operation *Zipper* had been gathering for some time and although the Japanese had surrendered, there was still a reasonable concern that Allied troops should be despatched as soon as possible to receive their surrender, occupy strategic points and aid in the re-establishment of civil administration (Appendix 19). It would be launched during late August and required the complex coordination of a number of slow and fast convoys, which were to depart from six widely spaced Indian ports of Bombay, Cochin, Madras, Vizagapatam, Calcutta and Chittagong in India and Rangoon in Burma.

Men of the RAF Regiment board an LCI in preparation for going ashore at Georgetown near Penang. (IWM CF 739)

The formal ceremony held at Victoria Green, Georgetown, on 12 September 1945 where 1329 Wing RAF Regiment took over garrison responsibilities from the Royal Marines. (Air Historical Branch RAF Crown Copyright)

Penang, with its airstrips, was the first location in Malaya to be reoccupied by the Allies when a detachment of Royal Marines landed without opposition on 3 September. The same day 152 and 155 (Spitfire) Squadrons and 84 and 110 (Mosquito) Squadrons flew in from Rangoon to await the capitulation of Singapore. Two LSIs immediately set sail from Penang for Rangoon where they collected an RAF Regiment Wing HQ and four squadrons. On 10 September, 1329 Wing HQ, under command of Wing Commander A. Yates, with 2759, 2802, 2854 and 2964 Squadrons disembarked at Georgetown, Penang. Two days later, at a formal ceremony held at Victoria Green, the Regiment formally took over garrison responsibilities from the Royal Marines. The following day the squadrons moved out to occupy Port Butterworth, the Prai area and Province Wellesley. The main threats now came from looters and, therefore, guard details were placed on essential facilities, including supply dumps, the dockyard, power station and a large stores depot located at the racecourse. On 13 September an editorial in a Penang newspaper had the following generous words to say of the Regiment:

Fortunately, in reconciling ourselves to an all too short stay by the Royal Marines, we are able, at the same time, to greet the arrival of their no less welcome successors. The RAF Regiment which makes its official debut in Penang today brings with it the same high traditions of justice and fair play that are the pride of the British Fighting Forces. The RAF, no less than the other Services, has played its full part in the Allied victory in South-East Asia; to the Regiment which 'took over' the 'going concern' which the Royal

Marines have set up in Penang, we are pleased to extend a cordial welcome, confident as we are in the knowledge that the Marines could not have entrusted their work, so well begun, in better, more sympathetic hands.[3]

Further reinforcements arrived by air from Hmawbi near Rangoon on 23 September, in the form of 1326 Wing HQ and 2965 LAA and 2960 LAA Squadrons. Following the arrival of the Army and its assumption of responsibility for internal security, the Regiment was given responsibility for the protection of RAF equipment and installations at Butterworth and on Penang Island itself.

In the closing days of August 1945 it was decided to launch an emergency operation code-named *Tiderace*, the objective of which was the quick occupation of Singapore. This operation was mounted using resources other than those allocated for *Zipper*. On 5 September, following formal negotiations between General Christison and the Japanese commanders aboard the invasion convoy flagship, XV Corps and the 5th Indian Division landed without opposition on Singapore Island.

The first unit of the Regiment to arrive was 2896 Field Squadron under command of Squadron Leader Lennox, which had travelled by sea from India with the main occupation force on the HMT *Derbyshire*. Following embarkation the airmen had taken responsibility for manning the ship's Oerlikons and assisted with the Bofors and 6- and 12-pounder guns. Most of Singapore was quiet on their arrival, although there was still fighting going on in the north of the island between Japanese and Chinese forces. Landing at 1430 hours, they proceeded in requisitioned Japanese lorries to the civil airport at Kallang in the south-east of the island. Twenty-four hours later this single squadron had taken responsibility for all four major airfields on the island: Kallang, Changi, Seletar and Tengah. Only one of these airfields had required 300 police to guard it in peacetime. The following day the two Spitfire and Mosquito squadrons flew in from Penang to Tengah and Seletar. The Regiment in Singapore would soon be reinforced by 2810 and 2944 Field Squadrons which were travelling in a later convoy.

Three members of the RAF Regiment on foot patrol in Georgetown, the capital of Penang, Malaya. (Air Historical Branch RAF Crown Copyright)

A former Japanese Navy fast patrol boat now in the hands of the RAF Regiment prepares to leave Glugor Pier for a patrol in the Penang area, Malaya. (Air Historical Branch RAF Crown Copyright)

Four days after Singapore had surrendered, and 150 miles to the north-west, the first landings of Operation *Zipper* were made. The 25th Indian Division and a brigade of the 23rd Indian Division landed on the Morib beaches, and further south near Sebang in the Port Swettenham-Port Dickson area, respectively. It was fortunate that they met no opposition as some of the beaches selected by the Allied planners turned out to be entirely unsuitable for landing craft. They were far too shallow and most vehicles and troops had to move up to 600 yards in three feet of deep water and sticky mud.

Flying Officer Gogarthy of 2941 Field Squadron supervises the collection of abandoned Japanese weapons at Prai Power Station, Port Butterworth, Malaya. The collection of arms and equipment was vital to stop them falling into the hands of nationalist fighters or criminal gangs. (Air Historical Branch RAF Crown Copyright)

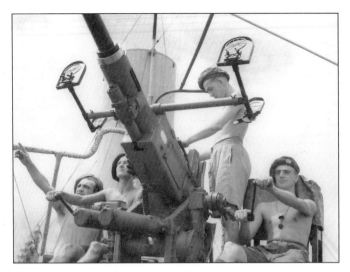

The RAF Regiment mans a Bofors 40-mm AA gun on board HMT Derbyshire *as part of Operation Tiderace, September 1945. (Air Historical Branch RAF Crown Copyright)*

Although the first wave of troops was landed successfully and able to move inland, the ebbing tide meant the discharge of vehicles was chaotic as many landing craft grounded too far from the beach. Vehicles were soon bogged in the mud or had their engines flooded and only a few were able to reach the shore.

The first airfield, Kelanang, was handed over peacefully by the 100 Japanese soldiers assigned to guard it and was found to be in good condition. Spitfires from 11 and 17 Squadrons were flown off from aircraft carriers and were later joined by the Austers of 656 Air OP Squadron. Advanced HQ 224 Group was established on the airfield by that evening.

The Regiment was represented in the landings at Morib by 1324 Wing HQ, under command of Wing Commander Laurie, along with four squadrons. On 11 September 2748 Field and 2846 LAA Squadrons were transferred offshore from a ship to an LCI and then an LCM for the run inshore. Unfortunately, the landing craft grounded in four feet of water and the airmen had to wade 50 yards with water up to their chests. After sorting themselves out on dry land, a recce party of wing and squadron officers moved off to the airfield at Kelanang. Here they made contact with Wing Commander Rae, the GDO of 224 Group who had landed on D Day. The airfield was secured by noon that day with guards and patrols being sent out immediately to sweep the area for Japanese troops. Three days later 2941 Field Squadron landed on the Morib beaches. The ORB continues:

A landing was effected without opposition at Morib Beach, Malaya, on 14 September. The Squadron moved the next day to Kuala Lumpur, and engaged on anti-looting work, and protection of threatened civilians, and liaison with the RAF Provost, as well as mounting security guards . . .

Kuala Lumpur was to be the home of the Squadron until 'finis' was written by a Command Disbandment Order . . . During the stay in Kuala Lumpur many Guards of Honour were provided for VIPs including Lord Louis Mountbatten, Governor General of Malaya, the Governor of the Malaya Union, and the Air Officer Commanding in Chief, and the Squadron represented the RAF at the Victory Parade on 8 June [1946].[4]

Men of the RAF Regiment disembarking from the first troopship to dock at Singapore following the Japanese surrender, 5 September 1945. (Air Historical Branch RAF Crown Copyright)

They were joined at Kuala Lumpur a few days later by 1324 Wing HQ and 2852 LAA Squadron. Meanwhile, the other half of the wing, 2748 Field and 2846 LAA Squadrons, had been sent south to Singapore by road. One party of two officers and fifty airmen was diverted to Seramban, representing the RAF at the local Victory Parade on 15 September. During the advance through Burma there had not been the same excitement from the population that was experienced as the squadrons moved through the liberated Malayan villages. A report written at the time describes the journey south:

> At every town triumphal arches had been placed across the road and gifts of fruit and garlands of flowers were showered on the advancing forces. When the 2846 Squadron entered Malacca, people mobbed the trucks and knelt down to kiss the feet of the liberators . . . [5]

Some 80 miles further on at Muar the convoy came across a large force of Chinese guerrillas. Their numbers had been built up during the Japanese occupation as the Allies developed a clandestine guerrilla force to harass the Japanese occupiers. The road at this point reached a river that could only be crossed by ferry. However, as most of the decent boats had been taken by the Japanese, a Corporal from the MT section of 2846 Squadron set to work and got two 1913 vintage motorboats going. Using two old wooden rafts, the Regiment vehicles were transported across one at a time over a six-hour period. Meanwhile, on the far bank the CO of 2846 Squadron, Squadron Leader

Cameron, was invited to inspect a large guard of honour of the guerrillas, as well as have a meal with the village headman and the senior guerrilla commander.

A soldier belonging to the 2nd Argyll and Sutherland Highlanders was discovered in the local hospital. His battalion had surrendered along with the remainder of the garrison when Singapore fell in 1942. He had, however, escaped and spent the last three and a half years in the jungle. As he had become familiar with the work of the Chinese guerrillas, they had decided that he should be shot. A 2846 Squadron officer was told of his presence and his plight and he was collected quietly in an RAF truck, hidden under a tarpaulin, and driven to safety through the guerrilla lines. At Johore Bahru he was delivered safely to the military hospital and from there he was able to provide a considerable amount of useful intelligence.

At 0930 hours on 17 September 2846 Squadron arrived at RAF Seletar, while 2748 Squadron moved to nearby RAF Tengah. They were the first British troops to have passed down the Singapore road from the north and across the causeway, since the Argylls had withdrawn across the causeway to the sound of their pipers playing 'Heilan Laddie', just prior to the fall of the fortress almost four years earlier.

On 12 September 2896 Field Squadron provided the RAF component of a joint service guard of honour at the signing of the Instrument of Surrender by the Japanese at the Municipal Building at Singapore. Flags of all the Allied nations were hung in the hall of the Council Chambers while an armed guard represented each of the Allies. Two long tables were placed six feet apart, with one for the Allied delegates and the other for the Japanese. Prior to the ceremony the guards of honour, including the 2896 Field Squadron, were inspected by Lord Louis Mountbatten. Following the inspection he moved into the Municipal Building for the surrender ceremony. Before proceedings began, however, he had noticed that there was no representative of the RAF Regiment in the chamber. A request was sent out by Mountbatten to the CO of 2896 Field Squadron for an airman to come in to witness the signing. Corporal W. Vance, the smartest airman on parade, was sent in. The official photograph taken at the time is well-known, but few realise the context of why an RAF Regiment airman stands prominently to attention in the near background.

Officers and airmen of 2896 Squadron RAF Regiment provide the RAF guard of honour at the Japanese surrender at Singapore, 12 September 1945. (Air Historical Branch RAF Crown Copyright)

The signing of the formal instrument of Japanese surrender at the Singapore Municipal Building, 12 September 1945. Corporal W. Vance of 2896 Squadron RAF Regiment stands to attention against a pillar in white belt, gaiters and blue beret. (Air Historical Branch RAF Crown Copyright)

Following the signing, all those involved moved to the terrace and steps leading up to the Municipal Buildings. Mountbatten read out the Order of the Day and a Union Flag, which had been concealed in Changi Jail by British prisoners-of-war for more than three years, was hoisted to the strains of the National Anthem. After the disasters of 1942 and the ignominy of the fall of Singapore, many would have been forgiven for thinking this day would never come.

Following a fortnight's rest after arriving at Warangal, 2944 Field Squadron had begun training for the landings in Malaya. The squadron then travelled to Calcutta and embarked on HMT *Egra*. Accompanying the squadron was the 5th Parachute Brigade, which had arrived only recently from Europe. This unit expressed considerable unhappiness at the shipboard conditions they were required to endure during the voyage and were obviously not aware of the standard of transportation available in SEAC. Colin Kirby remembers the train journey to Calcutta and the unpleasant conditions on the ships of these convoys:

> . . . the Squadron was on a train to Calcutta. I was tired of these long sweaty train journeys . . . We left the camp in Calcutta and transferred in heavy rain to the docks and embarked on a troopship. It was overcrowded with RAF and army personnel. We were herded below deck into the cargo hold with its primitive facilities, which would have been bad enough even with fewer men there

. . . The ship eventually got under way, and when it was dark some of us collected our kit together and found a spot under the lifeboats. It was still raining, although the boats kept us dry, and cold. We stayed there for the rest of the voyage. It was not long before I felt sea-sick as the sea was choppy, but fortunately it was not as bad as on the voyage to Madras, and passed within a day [Six days later] we were following the Malayan coastline, and docked in Singapore at 2100 hours.

2944 Field Squadron was originally assigned to take responsibility for Butterworth airfield following its capture by the 5th Parachute Brigade. The Japanese surrender, however, had led to the cancellation of their role in the landings and although the Parachute Brigade travelling with their convoy had been landed at Morib they were re-embarked on 18 September. The convoy then steamed south for Singapore. Stan Hutchinson recalls the arrival in Singapore:

. . . we stayed in the RAF Service Police HQ at the corner of Orchard Road, quite near the YMCA building, which had been used by the *Kempei Tai* [the notorious Japanese Military Police]. Then up to Tanglin Barracks, where we were put into married quarters, which were luxurious to us. [Sadly] After we had got them tidied up they moved us out into the barrack blocks.

During the planning for the landings on the Malay Peninsula in mid-1944, the RAF was concerned that there should be an airfield in closer proximity than India or Burma that could be used as a staging post and airbase from which to launch attacks and air re-connaissance missions over Java and Malaya, and as a stepping stone in the move on Singapore. Phuket Island in Siam had been considered but this option was abandoned when the monsoon weather intensified. The alternative was to develop and all-weather airfield on the Cocos Islands located to the south in the Indian Ocean. About six hundred miles south-west of Java and 1,040 miles south-south-west of Singapore, they were the same distance as Rangoon from the planned landing beaches at Port Swettenham. The airfield could, however, be developed beyond the influence of the monsoon. A large RAF contingent landed on the Islands on 20 March and an airbase was established. By July, bomber and photo reconnaissance missions were being flown from the Islands.

The Regiment was represented by 2962 LAA Squadron, which had been formed at Secunderabad in December 1944 from a large draft of personnel from the United Kingdom. On 3 April 2962 LAA Squadron disembarked with its Hispano 20-mm cannon on the Cocos Islands where it assisted Army units in the defence of the landing area, the airstrip and the various islands during and after the airfield's construction. 2962 LAA Squadron was to remain there until mid-July1945 when it returned the Warangal Depot.

Despite an agreement that SEAC would only handle the surrender of the Japanese south of 16 degrees latitude while the Chinese would take the surrender to the north, the British Government was determined that it should restore British administration in Hong Kong. After much discussion and negotiation an agreement was reached with the Chinese and on 29 August 1945 a British naval task force arrived off Hong Kong. After discussion of surrender details, the fleet sailed into the harbour the following day. Five days later the task force was joined by a large three thousand two hundred-strong RAF contingent predominantly composed of No 5358 Airfield Construction Wing. This unit

A Hispano 20-mm AA gun crew of 2962 LAA Squadron on the Cocos Islands, April 1945. (Photo courtesy Imperial War Museum, London C11501)

had been making its way through the Panama Canal and across the Pacific and was to have established several airfields on Okinawa. From these airfields the RAF would join the US Air Forces in the bombing of Japan and support the planned invasion of the Japanese mainland. With the sudden announcement of the surrender of Japan, however, they were diverted to Hong Kong.

The naval task force commander, Admiral Harcourt, had plenty of ships but no troops to take the surrender of the 7,000-strong Japanese garrison of a total of 21,605 Japanese in the Colony and welcomed the presence of the RAF personnel. While the Royal Marines would look after Hong Kong Island, the RAF would be responsible for Kowloon. Among the fitters, joiners, electricians, bakers and cooks on board the *Empress of Australia* was also a contingent of the RAF Regiment, led by Squadron Leader James and consisting of three Flight Sergeants and four Sergeants. Their job had been to drill and train the airmen of the Construction Wing in airfield defence. With the new responsibilities the Regiment personnel were soon hard at it, giving tradesmen some intensive shipboard training in marksmanship.

After receiving his orders from Admiral Harcourt, the OC of the Construction Wing, Group Captain Barker, took steps to assume control of Kowloon. He continues:

> When we entered the British naval base we did not know if the Japanese would offer any resistance. I disembarked with a small advance party of the RAF Regiment. We decided to head for Kai Tak airfield. We found around fifty Japanese there. We disarmed them and left them in charge of one OR. We made for the centre of the city and contacted the local police who acted as our guides and we proceeded to the POW camps.

Our next job was to look after our own internees. We arranged for their accommodation and feeding. We also distributed rice to the Chinese which we took from the Japanese. All the officers and men did a splendid job . . . [6]

The RAF responsibilities at Kowloon involved the disarming of thousands of Japanese troops, along with the prevention of serious looting, repair and operation of essential public services, the commandeering of all civilian transport and the maintenance of law and order. The senior RAF Regiment officer, Squadron Leader James, was appointed Assistant Provost Marshal and a Flying Squad was formed with Flight Sergeants F.J. Jones, Norris and Light of the Regiment to take charge of policing in Kowloon. They were to supervise three patrols of six men, two Royal Navy, two Commandos and two RAF. Their main role was to prevent looting and pick up any wayward soldier, sailor or airman who might get out of hand or who had crossed into areas marked as 'out of bounds'. Flight Sergeant Jones also participated in the capture and delivery for interrogation and trial of two of the most wanted Japanese war criminals in Hong Kong.

On 11 September the convoy carrying the 3rd Commando Brigade arrived in Hong Kong harbour. With them came the major component of the RAF Regiment force designated for Hong Kong. The force consisted of 1331 Wing HQ, along with 2708 and 2743 Field Squadrons and 2706 LAA Squadron. The wing moved immediately to Kai Tak airfield, while Spitfires of 132 Squadron were flown in from the aircraft carrier, HMS *Smiter*. The 3rd Commando Brigade did not have enough men to occupy the Island and territories and so the presence of the RAF Regiment was of great assistance.

The official surrender of Hong Kong took place five days later. The Commandos and Regiment Wing performed their tasks until late December, when they were reinforced by an Indian Brigade. The soldiers of Chiang Kai-Shek's Army had arrived in Hong Kong prior to the British naval force and caused some trouble. The Regiment,

Airmen of the RAF Regiment stand guard over Japanese prisoners they have rounded up in the hills around Hong Kong, 22 September 1945. (Air Historical Branch RAF Crown Copyright)

while carrying out security duties and assisting civil police, therefore, also had to deal with the problems arising from their presence and hostile attitude to the return of the British. After a short time however, the Chinese forces fortunately withdrew from the colony. Repatriation was arranged for the Japanese prisoners-of-war and civilians when around 2,000 were escorted down to the docks by 2708 Field Squadron in December 1945. For 2706 LAA Squadron, the last major task before disbandment was to provide the guard of honour for the proclamation of the new civil governor of Hong Kong and the end of military rule on 1 May 1946.

Two smaller commitments were given to the Regiment in early 1946. 2854 LAA Squadron was sent by sea from Malaya to Labuan Island in British North Borneo to provide defence for the airstrip and 110 (Mosquito) Squadron. The Island had been captured by a brigade group of the 9th Australian Division in June 1945 and their commitment was taken over by the 32nd Indian Brigade in January the following year when SEAC took formal control. The British Commonwealth Occupation Force was also despatched to Japan at this time and a flight from 2964 Squadron then stationed in Singapore was detached to form part of the RAF element.

The successful outcome of the recovery of Allied prisoners-of-war and internees (abbreviated to RAPWI) and Japanese disarmament operations in Siam (now Thailand) and French Indo-China by SEAC were to be strongly dependent on air supply, and the availability and security of airfields, until sea communications could be established with Bangkok and Saigon. Before a force could be flown into Saigon in French Indo-China it was necessary, due to the long distances involved, to secure an airfield at Bangkok as an air staging post. Operations would be controlled from Hmawbi and Mingaladon in the Rangoon area with five Dakota squadrons flying in 100 sorties a day to the two countries.

Although the Siamese Government had declared war on Britain in 1942, it had become clear early on that the King of Siam did not support this move. As soon as Japan surrendered, the Siamese Government had been overthrown and the declaration of war withdrawn. On 1 September 1945 an agreement was signed with SEAC and leading elements of the 7th Indian Division were quickly flown from Hmawbi to Don Muang airfield, just outside Bangkok. They were warmly welcomed by the high-ranking Siamese officials and a guard of honour.

2945 Field Squadron under Squadron Leader Garnett had returned to the RAF Regiment Depot in June from central Burma. It travelled by sea in September to Siam where it assumed sole responsibility for the defence of RAF assets at Don Muang airfield. Although there was no nationalist movement in Siam, the threat to the airfield came not from terrorist attack but from locals attempting to steal equipment and fuel. There were, however, still significant dangers facing the airmen. In February 1946 a group of infiltrators was discovered by a patrol from 2945 Field Squadron. In the confused struggle that followed one airman was separated from the remainder of the patrol. Unfortunately, he was set upon by the intruders and killed. His rifle and ammunition were taken and his body was thrown into a nearby lake. 2945 Field Squadron would disband at Don Muang in June 1946, while the task in Siam would continue until its completion in September when the last Allied troops left the country.

Nationalist and communist resistance movements had expanded significantly in French Indo-China over the period of the Vichy Government and later Japanese occupation from 1942 to 1945. When Japan surrendered in August 1945, the states of Tongking (under the Vietminh) and Annam (collectively known as the Annamites) had declared a republic under the name of Vietnam. By agreement, SEAC forces were to take the surrender of the Japanese in French Indo-China south of the 16th parallel.

North of the parallel the responsibility lay with the Chinese, which actually meant that the Vietminh under Ho Chi Minh in the north would remain in power and take the Japanese surrender. The Vietminh were also organising a resistance movement in the south to resist the arrival of the British forces being sent to take the Japanese surrender. Meanwhile, the French were gathering together an expeditionary force to recover their old territories in South-East Asia.

Major-General Douglas Gracey and his 20th Indian Division were given the multiple tasks of taking the Japanese surrender, rescuing Allied prisoners and internees, and keeping order in French Indo-China until the arrival of the French. However, Gracey was ordered not to use his division to reconquer the country for the French, but only to occupy as much as allowed him to complete his tasks. It was inevitable that, with the country having declared its independence, there would be fighting between the British and Indian troops and the Vietminh and Annamites.

The first British and Indian troops arrived by air at Saigon on 8 September, but being few in number they concentrated on getting as many prisoners-of-war out of the country and disarming the 45,000 Japanese still present. The nationalist government was considered a puppet of the Japanese by the Allies and was soon removed, and this aggravated the situation further. The deposed government did not believe the French intended to grant independence and began attacking French civilians and British and French soldiers. Attacks were made by the Annamites on docks, power stations, radio stations and other vital points. These attacks intensified later in the month and many of the Japanese troops, who still had a role in upholding law and order, seemed reluctant to act.

The only link with the rest of the world at this time for the British, Indian and Gurkha soldiers and airmen was through the Tan Son Nhut airfield located 4 miles north-west of Saigon. It covered an area of 3 square miles, had two runways, very wide dispersals, and was well endowed with buildings, having eight serviceable hangars, large stores and armoury and three communal sites. The Annamite forces in the surrounding area were well armed and supported and by late September 1945 the situation had become extremely tense. RAF personnel were becoming anxious as an invasion of the airstrip by hordes of Annamites was expected at any moment. The local Annamite force was estimated to be in the thousands and most were armed with automatic weapons.

An urgent request was made for the RAF Regiment and on 1 October, with only 24 hours' notice, 1307 Wing HQ and 2963 Squadron were flown in from Hmawbi after a six-hour flight, interrupted only by a refuelling stop at Bangkok. The men of

Wing Commander W.R. Allen, OC 1307 Wing, leads 2963 LAA Squadron during the Victory Parade held in Saigon, French Indo-China, in late 1945. (RAF Regiment SEAC Association)

2963 Squadron were warned that they might have to fight immediately they disembarked from the Dakotas. Their 'battle drill' as they left the aircraft and took up all-round defensive positions much impressed the Dakota crews. It also cheered up the ninety RAF personnel on the airfield, who had been standing-to in anticipation of an attack by the Annamites surrounding the airfield. A report written at the time by the OC Wing Commander W.R. Allen describes the prevailing mood at Tan Son Nhut and the first night of occupation:

> One could sense the tense atmosphere pervading immediately on landing since the previous hours of darkness had been nightmarish, pitched battles having been fought within 300 yards of the airfield. Never has the Regiment been more warmly received and as a result of an immediate conference between Wing Commander Allen and the OC 908 Wing, Group Captain Sturgiss OBE, the former took over command of all forces defending the airfield. These were meagre indeed, there being only the Advance Parties of 908 Wing, 273 Squadron, 98 MFCU and 917 ALG – a total of 150 officers and airmen of the RAF. They were supplemented by two companies of Dogras and a Japanese battalion commanded by Major Matsuzato . . . of 1000 Japanese, 300 only of whom were armed.[7] It was a situation of some irony when Wing Commander Allen met the Japanese Major and discussed the disposition of the Japanese forces.
>
> 2963 Squadron personnel were quickly selecting positions for defence, siting guns and gave a fine example of how the Regiment, given a real job of work, will work untiringly and with efficiency to achieve the almost impossible. On the first five days at Saigon, though the men of 2963 Squadron had had no sleep and were wet through by the continued monsoon conditions, their vigilance never wavered.
>
> Tension grew as night fell on October 1st, since the Annamites had announced their intention of taking the airfield at 0300 hours the following morning . . . The night was an anti-climax and the airfield did not come under direct fire, although there was spasmodic shooting from dusk until dawn.[8]

At 1300 hours the next day, however, the serious intent of the rebels was brought home to the defenders of the airfield when it was learnt that the CO of 2963 Squadron, Squadron Leader H.D. Ward, had been shot and wounded while carrying out a recce. He had been travelling in a jeep with his second-in-command Flight Lieutenant A.A. Wyatt, the 'C' Flight Commander, Flying Officer T.H. Keeling and the Squadron Warrant Officer Flight Sergeant F. Seaby. They were returning to the airstrip when a burst of automatic fire from a Sten hit Ward, who was at the wheel. Flight Lieutenant Wyatt had the presence of mind to reach over and grab the steering wheel and put his foot on the accelerator to keep the vehicle under control. Keeling and Seaby put down covering fire but the nearside tyre was hit and burst and the jeep careered into a tree. All the occupants were thrown out, but Seaby quickly reverse the jeep while the two officers saw to the CO's wounds. Staunching the flow of blood, he was lifted onto the jeep and with no firing they were able to make their escape, albeit on two flat tyres. They made it safely back to the airfield, where Ward was evacuated to hospital in Saigon and Flight Lieutenant Wyatt took command of 2963 Squadron.

The situation worsened over the next few weeks, with firing heard on some part of the airstrip every night and stand-to was ordered on many occasions. Truces were attempted but as the rebel leaders seemed to have little control over their forces they quickly broke down. Eventually all three brigades of the 20th Indian Division arrived and the RAF Regiment was able to coordinate the airfield defence with the 32nd Indian Infantry Brigade, which had responsibility for this sector of Saigon.

1307 Wing was appropriately reinforced on 11 October with the arrival of 2967 Squadron under command of Squadron Leader Redston. The duties were now shared between the two squadrons but the 'off duty' squadron had to provide a domestic guard and a mobile reserve flight should any emergencies arise. Although this eased the Regiment workload, the commitments were also growing. More RAF aircraft, equipment and installations were arriving, including 684 (Mosquito) Squadron and some 360,000 gallons of 100 octane fuel. This was a tempting target, if any, for the Annamites and one they did attempt to ignite. Regiment sections constantly patrolled vulnerable points around the airstrip and particularly just before dawn when most trouble seemed to occur.

On Saturday 13 October the Regiment experienced its heaviest action so far at Tan Son Nhut. A report written at the time describes the events of that day:

> Just before dawn . . . armed Annamites approached from the south-west of the airfield and fired at a house occupied by 16th Indian Cavalry . . . There was a sharp exchange of shots and bullets entered the house occupied by 273 Squadron officers and were heard whistling over the HQ of 1307 Wing. The 6th Air Formation Signals Officers Mess was under direct fire and for 20 minutes the situation looked serious. However, the attackers were driven off by fire from the 16th Cavalry and Japanese guards and there were no casualties . . .[9]

The Regiment was located to the east and south-east and had not come directly under fire. Wing Commander Allen ordered a sweep to be made of the area by two squadrons and a company of the Japanese Air Force battalion, including the village of Tan Son Nhi. Following a briefing of his squadron and flight commanders, they departed at 1100 hours with the aim of giving the Annamites an unmistakeable show of force and to thoroughly search the area for arms. 2963 Squadron took the left flank, 2967 Squadron the centre and the Japanese the right. Wing Commander Allen established his Attack HQ at a crossroads and directed the operation.

Almost immediately No 2 Flight of 2967 Squadron came under fire from a building, however, well-placed Bren and rifle fire dispersed the rebels and they fled. No 1 Flight, under Flying Officer Casserley, was also soon in action and an attack was launched on a graveyard and the rebels again retired although two of their number were captured. Thickening jungle meant that the two flights and the Bren group became separated as the latter chased two armed Annamites, discovering in the process evidence of rebel occupation of a temple. Meanwhile, another flight found ammunition stored in a temple. 2967 Squadron completed its sweep and returned at 1430 hours. 2963 Squadron returned at 1300 hours, having found no evidence of rebels as they had completely vacated the area. The Japanese on the right were kept busy until 1600 hours without loss, but found only small amounts of ammunition and thirty bamboo spears and arrows.[10]

The sweep had been of value as no further trouble was experienced from that quarter for some days. It was the first carried out by the Regiment in Saigon and was found to be a successful reply to the incursions of that morning. Offensive patrols over the next month by Gurkha, Dogras and Punjabi battalions began to take a toll on Annamites during numerous encounters and French troops began to play a larger role.

Incidents continued around the airfield, and on 23 October at 0130 hours firing was heard to the east. Stand-to was ordered for the next two hours, although no attack occurred. Annamites were reported to be planning a follow up action the next day, this time on the old Japanese Naval Arsenal. Flying Officer Keeling and his flight took up positions on the anticipated line of advance of the enemy party and at 0300 hours they heard movement and dimly saw the Annamites advancing. The Bren and rifles opened up, the attack was thwarted and it was later confirmed that six rebels had been killed. The Regiment had prevented a potentially serious incident as the dump contained a number of depth charges, which would have caused a huge explosion should the attackers have got hold of them or blown up the arsenal.

While at Saigon the Regiment also developed a specialised role as bodyguards to RAF officers moving about the area and beyond. On 18 October Corporal Heath and LAC Taylor accompanied Flying Officer Hayes of 273 Squadron in a Japanese aircraft to Dalat in north French Indo-China. Should it become necessary, the airstrip was being considered as a base for 273 Squadron to use on ground support missions against the Annamites. There was some concern as the airstrip was precariously held by only thirty-five Japanese soldiers. The Annamites, although lacking modern weapons, were known to be proficient in the use of poisoned darts. The party was 'regally received' by the Japanese and, after finding the facilities were poor and dispersals overgrown with elephant grass, returned safely to Saigon. On a second trip two days later LACs Trundle and Cook escorted two officers whose mission was to obtain the keys to the vaults of the Bank of Indo-China from a Frenchman in Dalat. The Japanese considered a trip into the town to be unsafe for the party and agreed to go in their place. Unfortunately the Frenchman refused to hand over the keys and the party returned to Saigon empty-handed.

Grenade attacks as well as sniping became a regular occurrence during October.

The ceremony marking the handover of the airfield at Saigon from Japanese to British control. The guard of honour was provided by the RAF Regiment. Their arrival was the cause of great relief for the occupants of the previously undefended airfield. (Photograph courtesy of the Imperial War Museum, London CF 932)

An officer of 2963 LAA Squadron receives the sword of a Japanese officer at the surrender ceremony held at Tan Son Nhut airfield. (RAF Regiment SEAC Association)

Wing Commander Allen was on the receiving end one evening while driving his jeep from the Officers' Mess to his quarters. A grenade was thrown at him but he managed to avoid it and accelerated away without injury. Over the next week the Regiment patrolled the villages that had sprung up around the airfield and discovered caches of ammunition and stolen RAF equipment. It became necessary to warn locals that severe action would be taken if stolen goods were found in the future. An incident of a more serious nature for the Allied troops occurred when the Annamites fired the Saigon market, a cigarette factory and wrecked the brewery!

Enemy activity eased somewhat as the brigades of the 20th Indian Division had pushed the insurgent elements further from the airfield. Guards of honour were provided during October when 2963 Squadron turned out for the AOC Air HQ Burma, while 2963 and 2967 Squadrons and the RAF 3209 Servicing Commandos turned out for the visit of Air Chief Marshal Sir Keith Park and Lady Park. He later sent a congratulatory message:

> Please thank the pilots of 273 Squadron for their excellent escort and congratulate all ranks of the RAF Regiment on their smartness and efficiency. One felt proud of both.[11]

At a surrender ceremony on 17 November 1945, the Japanese battalion commander Major Matsuzato formally surrendered his sword to the senior RAF Regiment officer, with the Regiment being represented by 2967 Field Squadron. 1307 Wing, which had played such an illustrious part in the history of the Regiment at Meiktila in March 1945, was disbanded soon after. Four of its airmen had served in the wing for the entire two-year period of its existence, from its formation in the United Kingdom, through Normandy, Burma and onto Vietnam.

The British and Indian forces remained in French Indo-China for six months, dealing on a daily basis with the highly complex and insoluble political problems that were now being played out between the French, Vietnamese and Chinese. The Regiment continued to ensure the safety of RAF personnel and assets and the unhampered operation of the Tan Son Nhut airfield until handed over to the French *Armée de l'Air* in February 1946.

In mid-1945 a decision was made by ACSEA to form a specialised RAF Regiment Parachute Field Squadron. The unit chosen for conversion was one of the United Kingdom squadrons, 2810. It would, however, be composed entirely of volunteers who were selected following interviews by OCs at Wing HQs, and would be drawn from Regiment squadrons all over SEAC. The CO was to be Squadron Leader Tony Sullivan, previously of 2941 Field Squadron.[12] 2810 Squadron had been on airfield defence duties since 1941 at various RAF Stations in the United Kingdom. Prior to its despatch to India in December 1944 it was converted to a field squadron. Arriving in India on 14 January, it spent a short time at the Secunderabad Depot before moving to RAF Hathazari in Bengal to continue field squadron training. From the latter half of March, groups of five to ten airmen had volunteered to work as 'ejectors' on supply missions being flown by 31 Squadron RAF out of the Hathazari airstrip.[13] April was spent at Forward Echelon Agartala, where LAC McKillop set the 'Battle School' Grand National record of fourteen minutes.

At Agartala on 1 July 1945 it was officially notified of its conversion to 2810 (Parachute) Field Squadron. Over the next month the squadron moved off to RAF Begampet near Secunderabad.[14] Parties of volunteers arrived by various means. The difficulties of drawing such a unit together at the height of the monsoon could not be underestimated. A party from Agartala attempted to fly out on three occasions; the first attempt they were forced back by bad weather and wireless failure, the next day the allocated Dakota was sent on another more urgent task and on the third attempt the landing gear collapsed as the aircraft taxied for take-off. The aircraft was evacuated 'extremely rapidly' with no casualties. A detachment from Rangoon was eventually sent by sea and rail after flying conditions became impossible.

On 23 July Squadron Leader Sullivan took over the command of 2810 from

2810 (Parachute) Field Squadron. Clockwise: LAC Hartley Blairs on Parachute Training at No 3 Training School Chaklala; driving one of the squadron 3-tonners; disarming the Japanese following the surrender. (Hartley Blairs)

Squadron Leader Barrett who went to command 2944 Field Squadron at nearby Warangal. The following day the first party of airmen departed for No 3 Parachute Training School at Chaklala near Rawalpindi and parties then moved off at regular intervals over the next few weeks. Hartley Blairs recalls the journey and training:

I joined 2810 at Agartala from 2748 Squadron to go on a week's parachute course at Chaklala. We travelled by train for a week. We did six day jumps and one night jump. I was a transport driver and picked up lorries to travel down India to Madras. We were assembled there ready for the invasion of Malaya.

Those not on jump training busied themselves with mortar training, field training and developing a high standard in foot and arms drill and high efficiency in the handling of squadron weapons. Sullivan described his squadron as follows:

The volunteers for this new type of Squadron are fine material. Young, keen and fit, they should mould into a fine unit. The urge to get on operations is obvious among the officers and men and the worst punishment I could give a man would be 'Return to Unit.'[15]

On 8 August Flying Officer Josh and seven airmen departed for the Visual Control Post (VCP) School at Ranchi. Following completion of the course, they would return to train the remainder of the Squadron. VCPs had been found to be an essential component in providing close air support for the columns advancing towards Rangoon.

2810 Squadron, led by Squadron Leader H.T. Sullivan, parades at the Cenotaph in Singapore on Remembrance Day 1945. The squadron wore its distinctive parachute wings above the right breast pocket. (Photo courtesy Imperial War Museum, London CI1734)

Made up of an RAF officer with flying experience and two signallers with either a jeep or light pack set, they were of immense value directing fighter bombers onto enemy positions. A VCP party had been parachuted into Elephant Point prior to the parachute drop and had called in air support on the few occupied Japanese positions. In preparation for Operation *Zipper*, some of the VCPs were formed into an Airborne Control Unit, which would parachute in prior to the landings. Such a unit required armed protection and it was decided that personnel of 2810 (Parachute) Field Squadron would be trained for this specialist role.

It came as a blow to 2810 (Parachute) Field Squadron when, on 15 August, the Japanese surrender was announced. Sullivan was concerned at the effect on morale and was keen to maintain the level of enthusiasm. He noted the change in attitude once the airmen had completed the very tough jump training at Chaklala:

> Those already parachute trained are interesting. They have a standard of morale higher than when they went on the course . . . I realise why. The course is well run and the instructors are magnificent. The superiority one feels on completion of a jump successfully is unbelievable.[16]

A specially selected group of four airmen under command of Corporal Lane proceeded to Bombay to act as protective personnel for No 25 VCP, which was to accompany 3rd Commando Brigade on the planned landings for Operation *Zipper*. Further large parties moved off to Ceylon and Jessore to participate in operations now being planned for the reoccupation of former colonies. Unfortunately, however, with the Japanese surrender, the Airborne Control Unit was not used in *Zipper* and, by late September, the squadron reverted to a standard field squadron organisation.

The squadron's training, however, was not to be wasted when on 25 August Wing Commander Tull of the RAF Airborne Control Unit informed 2810 (Parachute) Field Squadron it would have a central role in Operation *Mastiff*. This was the second phase of the operation (RAPWI) to find, feed and recover internees and prisoners-of-war in the recaptured territories. Food and medical supplies were to be dropped and medical teams with wireless operators were to be parachuted into known camps as soon as possible. The operation proceeded relatively smoothly in Burma, Siam, French Indo-China and Malaya, but greater difficulties were encountered in the Netherlands East Indies.

The boundaries of SEAC had been extended to include the Netherlands East Indies only days before the Japanese capitulation. Little intelligence was available at SEAC HQ in Kandy on the political and military conditions operating there and, in particular, the state of the pre-war independence movement. The British and Indian soldiers and airmen soon found themselves embroiled in a complex and hazardous situation that would take a year and many casualties before they could extricate themselves.

The responsibilities of the Allies in the Netherlands East Indies were to find and evacuate prisoners-of-war and internees, disarm and concentrate surrendered Japanese in preparation for their repatriation, and arrest those wanted for war crimes and maintain law and order in key areas. There were some 80,000 internees in Java, mostly Dutch, over 6,000 prisoners–of-war, with just under 2,000 British, Indians, Australians and Americans. The initial response by the local populace to the arrival of British soldiers and airmen was relatively benign. The atmosphere soon turned violent when it was realised that the former Dutch colonial rulers, for whom many Indonesians had a burning hatred, were to return.

A significant Indonesian independence movement had developed during the years of Japanese occupation, which had been further encouraged by some Japanese officers. Following the surrender an Indonesian Republic was declared, while the Japanese handed over their weapons to the Indonesians and went into self-imposed internment to await the arrival of the Allies. Therefore, by the time the Allies arrived a month later in September 1945 there was a large Indonesian military force, trained and armed by the Japanese, an established Indonesian Government and the situation had reached a point where a peaceful reoccupation was impossible. Although the war against Japan had ended, the ferocity of the struggle can be seen in the casualty figures for the British-Indian Forces, which lost some 2,340 killed, wounded and missing in the first two months spent on Java.[17]

In early September one of the first 'Mastiff' parties, consisting of a Medical Officer, a POW Contact Officer and Corporal Lionel Groome, a nursing orderly, from 2810 (Parachute) Field Squadron, and four Dutch soldiers, was parachuted into Surabaya on the eastern end of Java after moving via the airfield on the Cocos Islands.[18] Groome had been part of 2810 Squadron before its conversion for parachute work and had remained with it as a specialist. Initially the party was well received by the Indonesians, however, there was a suspicion that the British were also preparing to hand the Netherlands East Indies back to the Dutch. Matters turned sour on 19 September when a Dutch military detachment hoisted the Dutch flag. This led to a riot among the local population, which was only quelled after the flag was lowered. Matters gradually worsened and eventually developed into an extremely bitter and vicious conflict.

The situation in Surabaya exploded in late October when thousands of Indonesians set upon and slaughtered a large part of a column of 400 Dutch women and children being escorted by sixty Indian troops.[19] On 28 October the 'Mastiff' party, including Corporal Groome, came under small arms fire and was forced to withdraw to a hotel organised as a defensive position. In company of a platoon of the 5/6th Rajputana Rifles, the party came under heavy sniper fire. Four hours later the Indonesians made a fierce frontal attack and they were forced back from the front of the building. Many of the riflemen were wounded and Corporal Groome rendered first aid to them under fire. Although a nursing orderly, Groome then took a Bren gun from a wounded Rajput and handled it so effectively that he assisted significantly in preventing wave after wave of Indonesians from reaching the upper levels of the hotel. He then continued to give first aid to the wounded and while doing so he was taken prisoner. Fortunately, he was released unharmed on 3 November. For his actions that day Groome was awarded the Military Medal.[20]

The initial uprising in Surabaya incited trouble further to the west in Batavia (now Jakarta). A 'Mastiff' party was dropped there on 8 September and was followed by a British naval force on 15 September. The men arrived to find large numbers of internees and much looting and a lack of basic infrastructure and transport. Whereas the Allies had been welcomed as liberators by a large part of the Malayan population, there were no flags waving or triumphal arches for those arriving on Java, other than the red and white flags of the Indonesian nationalists. The political situation was tense.

Two brigades of the 23rd Indian Division arrived in late September and the first week of October. Air support for the Army was provided by 904 Wing, flying Thunderbolts, under the control of Air HQ Netherlands East Indies (formed from the old 221 Group HQ in Rangoon). 904 Wing departed Madras in a small convoy of one LSI and two MT and stores ships with airmen of the two flying squadrons and support units. Accompanying them was 1308 Wing HQ, under command of Wing Commander Sullivan,[21] with 2943 Field and 2962 LAA Squadrons.

Arriving off Batavia, the commanding officer of 904 Wing was uncertain of the

Marmon-Herrington armoured cars of 2962 LAA Squadron patrol Kemajoran airfield, Batavia, in December 1945. The armoured cars had originally been captured by the Japanese when the Netherlands East Indies fell in 1942. (Courtesy Imperial War Museum, London CF853)

state of play onshore, having been under radio silence while moving to Java. Fortunately he had the two Regiment squadrons, which he readied either for a peaceful ceremonial entry into Batavia, or an assault landing! Fortunately a naval force had preceded them and they sailed without incident to the Batavia docks. The Regiment provided the OC 904 Wing with a heavily armed escort the following morning when he drove to inspect the state of the airfield at Kemajoran. 2962 LAA Squadron deployed immediately to Kemajoran airfield, while 2943 Field Squadron occupied defensive positions in the rear approaches to the airfield in the Kramat area of the town. The airfield was a mess but the first Thunderbolts flew in on 21 October and, with the gravity of the situation now appreciated, three Mosquito squadrons and one Dakota squadron were also sent.

Incidents with the Indonesian nationalists gradually intensified and the airfield was attacked on most nights. The two Regiment squadrons were tasked with enforcing a curfew and carrying out raids on nearby villages for stolen equipment. At times they were caught up in clashes between Indonesian extremists and 'hot-headed' Dutch Ambonese troops.[22] The Regiment was also called on to provide escorts and firing parties for the funerals of RAF airmen who had died as a result of the ravages of life as a prisoner–of–war or who had been killed by the nationalist insurgents. One such firing party was fortunately present at a funeral being conducted on 20 November in the city cemetery when it came under heavy fire from a large force of Indonesians. The NCO in charge of the firing party, Sergeant Alec C. Haines of 2962 LAA Squadron, quickly took stock of the situation and covered the withdrawal of the party to a safe area without loss. Deploying the firing party in defensive positions, he withdrew them only once all the RAF personnel were clear. The funeral party was then successfully guided back to the airfield by Haines along a road where an ambush had been laid but which failed to halt the convoy. He then returned to the cemetery with other Regiment airmen, once he had satisfied himself personally that the situation was safe, and re-covered the coffin. In the words of his citation for the award of the Military Medal:

> . . . This non-commissioned officer displayed courage, initiative and leadership in a very difficult situation. He was instrumental in saving many lives.[23]

The hideous nature of the Indonesian conflict was brought home to the Regiment on 23 November. A Dakota of 31 Squadron RAF, with four crew, twenty Indian jawans and a medical orderly, made a forced landing a few miles from the airstrip at Kemajoran. An escorting Thunderbolt fighter reported seeing five Europeans and several Indians standing by the smouldering aircraft. The CO of 31 Squadron, Wing

Commander MacNamara, set out with a small party from the squadron and a detachment of 2962 LAA Squadron. The crash site was soon found but there was no sign of the survivors. The search party came under attack from hostile Indonesians but the retaliatory fire killed twenty-five of their assailants. No immediate concern was shown for the aircrew and passengers as all had been armed and it was thought they were making their way back to the airfield. Further attempts to find the missing party proved futile. It was later discovered that the crew and troops had been captured by Indonesian soldiers near Bekassi village and jailed overnight. The following day they were taken one by one to a nearby river to be hacked to death in a bestial manner and were then decapitated. This became known as the 'Crime of Bekassi' and as a consequence British and Indian Army units went out to exact retribution, burning down several villages and killing known hostile natives.

Eventually the 5th British Parachute Brigade was brought in from Singapore during December as the situation worsened and 2943 Squadron was withdrawn with the Army to the barracks at Tanah Tinggi at Batavia.[24] This did not lessen the airmen's task or reduce its unpleasant nature, as they were kept at full stretch doing up to 72-hour stints on guard duty. The heavy rain also meant that they were, at times, nearly washed out of their tents by foot-deep torrents. Eventually many airmen were accommodated in entire streets of abandoned houses on the outskirts of Batavia.

During December 2943 Squadron fought a night battle when its section of the barracks was attacked by a large party of Indonesians. For more than three hours the airmen beat off continuous attacks and inflicted heavy losses, with the only illumination coming from the flames of blazing buildings. One airman was fortunate to

A roadblock of 2943 Field Squadron established near Kemajoran, Batavia, Java, 1945. (Air Historical Branch RAF Crown Copyright)

escape death when a bullet hit the end of his Bren gun, grazed the length of the barrel, tore away the magazine opening and stopped inside the magazine. His only injuries were from hot lead splashed up from the bullet.[25]

By January, 2748 Squadron had joined the wing and was deployed to Surabaya. The squadron remained there until 30 March 1946 when it was broken up to provide airmen for the other now badly-depleted squadrons of the wing. At the same time Wing Commander S.C.E. Norris was posted to command 1308 Wing, following the disbandment of 1323 Wing and the repatriation of Wing Commander Sullivan. Evacuation of internees continued apace, interrupted by the flare up of rebel activity and disturbances caused by the handover to Dutch control of parts of the island by the British-Indian forces. On 30 November 1946 the last elements of XV Corps departed from Java.

Small Allied intelligence detachments had been parachuted into Sumatra in early September and along with RAPWI search parties set about finding prisoners-of-war and internment camps. By the end of the month 2,200 prisoners-of-war and 1,000 internees had been evacuated to Singapore. With Japanese help, the 26th Indian Division concentrated 13,550 Dutch and Asiatic prisoners and internees at Medan, Palembang and Padang. Political unrest was also evident on Sumatra, with clashes between Indonesians, and Ambonese and Chinese, along with kidnapping and murders of many Dutch civilians. The situation at first seemed to calm down but the withdrawal of the remaining Japanese troops in January disturbed the balance of the armed forces available to police the island and extremist activity intensified.

Further Regiment reinforcements were required and, as a consequence, 1323 Wing and three squadrons were sent from Singapore, arriving at RAF Medan in late October 1945.[26] The 1323 Wing ORB describes their time at Medan and their important role in organising and coordinating the defence of the airfield:

> February and March [were] interesting months in dispersal at Medan, [with] lots of work keeping the aerodrome clear for operations, and the aerodrome equipment out of the hands of pilferers, a difficult job, which required tact and diplomacy of a high order on the part of all concerned. A peaceful operation against a resentful people, and one whose success depends entirely on the actions of the personnel involved.
> . . . the promulgation and practice of a combined defence scheme by Wing Commander S.C.E. Norris, on behalf of Wing Commander D.I.C. Eyres, Commanding RAF Medan, bringing every airman on the Station into the defence plan, and thus creating a sense of Defence confidence down to the lowest other rank, have combined to add to the passing of the Squadron and Wing a feeling that the Station has not suffered, but rather has been unlucky.[27]

2944 Field Squadron despatched two flights to RAF Medan on rotation from Singapore. The airmen were accommodated in tents, however, many were reluctant to sleep in them and sought more solid indoor accommodation. The reason for this may not be initially apparent and was not necessarily related to a craving for comfort. The Indonesian locals had the disturbing habit of creeping onto the airstrip at night and cutting the canvas from tents for their own use. The insurgents might do the same but would then attempt to slit the throat of any occupant.

While the British commitment in Sumatra would take until November 1946, the Regiment would remain only until August. Maintaining a viable airfield defence force became more difficult as officers and airmen were repatriated to the United Kingdom at increasing rates. 2739 Squadron had to be sent from India to reinforce 1323 Wing in January 1946. Further reinforcements of one officer and seventy-five airmen from 2941 Field Squadron flew in a few weeks later to assist 2739 Squadron as it was also becoming seriously depleted by the departure of time-expired personnel.

Tensions on Sumatra were soon inflamed when rumours began to circulate that the Dutch Army was readying itself to return in large numbers. A section of 2739 Field Squadron guarding a radio installation was attacked just after midnight on 10 June 1946 by a force of forty Indonesians. With no warning, a grenade was thrown and the tented camp came under attack from two sides by parties armed with swords and knives. The section commander, LAC Holbrook, with complete disregard for his own safety, led his men in a counter-attack. Four of the assailants were killed but he and another LAC were hacked to death, two more seriously wounded and the remaining three treated for shock. The OC of 2739 Squadron, Squadron Leader Williams, launched an attack at the head of the reserve flight and was able to drive the enemy back. Later in the month a flight of 2810 Squadron was flown in from Singapore to assist Indian troops to rescue a group of internees being held at an Indonesian rebel camp near Padang airstrip on the southern coast of Sumatra. The operation was a success, with fifty-two internees released and ten insurgents taken prisoner. On its return journey the column was ambushed but was able to kill seventeen attackers and captured another three. Two Indian soldiers were killed and one wounded. Further attacks were made by 2810 Squadron on insurgent camps, killing nineteen and capturing five. In all these actions the Regiment suffered no losses.

The experience of the RAF Regiment in the Netherlands East Indies is best summed up by Flight Lieutenant E.G. Robinson, who wrote the following in his final report on the disbandment of 1308 Wing in late April 1946:

> The period in the Netherlands East Indies was generally one of great activity, the political situation of the islands was in the melting pot and the economic situation left by the Japanese aggravated the matter. Looting and shooting incidents and alarms were the lot of the Squadrons of the Wing, but yet in the period of great nervous strain and operational tension at no time did the Gunners of the Regiment allow their standards of conduct and duty to fall below the high level attained in the Burma campaign. This is more worthy of praise when one considers that the War was over, everyone quite naturally waiting for their turn for release, and also that the higher policy of the whole operation was beyond the realisation of the uninformed.[28]

Notes

1   By June 1945 the Commandant of the RAF Regiment Depot was Wing Commander A. Donaldson.
2   AIR 20/4024, *The RAF Regiment in Action, Report No. 37*.
3   *The Straits Echo*, 13 September 1945, cited in AIR 20/4024.
4   AIR 29/134, *Operations Record Books RAF Regiment Squadrons 2934, 2935, 2941–2943*.
5   op. cit. AIR 20/4024.
6   *The South China Morning Mail*, late 1945.
7   The remainder were armed with pick helves and shovel handles.
8   AIR 29/1118, *Operations Record Books 1300–1309, 1311–1317 RAF Regiment Wings 1944–1947*.
9   ibid.
10 It must have caused some astonishment for those airmen who only two months earlier had been fighting the Japanese but now had the same enemy under command. They were soon reporting on their reliability in their airfield defence duties. Ironically, those Japanese who

had surrendered and were now assisting the Regiment on the airfield were likely to be killed by their own weapons, which were in the hands of Japanese soldiers fighting with the rebels, or which had been given to the Annamites when the Japanese-occupiers had installed them as the government.

11 ibid., AIR 29/1118. Similar high compliments were paid to the Regiment by Major-General D.D. Gracey CB CBE MC the GOC 20th Indian Division on the occasion of Park's visit.

12 Later Group Captain H. Sullivan CBE, Commandant RAF Regiment Depot 1961–3.

13 When dropping supplies by parachute, 'ejectors' or 'kickers' were responsible for pushing supplies out of the plane over the drop zone when given the signal by the pilot.

14 This had been the location of the No 1 RAF Regiment Training School, which had first opened in October 1942.

15 AIR 29/103, *Operations Record Books RAF Regiment Squadrons 2810–2813*.

16 ibid.

17 This was about half the number of casualties that Burcorps had suffered in the retreat from Burma in 1942 and more than the 23rd Indian Division had lost in an entire year's fighting in Burma.

18 Three Liberator squadrons flew from the Cocos Islands as part of Operation *Mastiff*.

19 The bravery and sacrifice of the Indian troops during this incident and other during the troubles in Indonesia is well described in Doulton, A.J.F. *The Fighting Cock: The Story of the 23rd Indian Division 1942–1947*. Aldershot: Gale & Polden, 1951.

20 Tucker, N.G. *In Adversity. Exploits of gallantry and awards made to the RAF Regiment and its associated forces 1921–1995*. Oldham, Lancashire: Jade Publishing, 1997, pp. 108–109.

21 Ex-2810 (Parachute) Field Squadron.

22 Lee, D. *Eastward. A History of the RAF in the Far East 1945–1972*. London: HMSO, 1984, p. 51.

23 ibid., pp. 110–111.

24 At one time the Squadron CO had been arrested and imprisoned by the Indonesians along with four other British officers, though they were eventually released after an uncomfortable period of imprisonment.

25 *The Evening News*, Saturday 2 March 1946.

26 The wing was initially composed of 2968 Squadron and two flights of 2944 Field Squadron and 2961 LAA Squadron.

27 AIR 29/1120, *Operations Record Books 1318–1338 RAF Regiment Wings 1944–1947*.

28 op. cit. AIR 29/1118.

CHAPTER TWELVE

Disbandment and Home

'If the RAF Regiment in South-East Asia has done nothing more than provide vital protection for our airfields, the record of its achievements would still read with commendable credit. That it was able to perform further additional services and maintain a smartness and discipline which called forth praise from Army and Navy alike, demonstrates the value of our Regiment as an adjunct of the Royal Air Force.'
Air Chief Marshal Sir Keith Park, Allied Air C-in-C, ACSEA

With the post-surrender tasks in South-East Asia nearing completion and Operation *Python* having a debilitating effect on the manpower resources of the RAF Regiment, it became necessary, from January 1946, to progressively disband the RAF Regiment Wing HQs and squadrons. One Wing HQ and three squadrons had remained at the Depot and had not participated in the operations in Malaya, Singapore, Siam, Vietnam and Indonesia and these were the first units marked for disbandment. The activities of the Training Wings had come to a standstill, and in December 1945, the RAF Regiment Depot had been notified that it was to close and it was to move to a new location in southern Malaya. Planning and packing were undertaken but it was not until early the months of 1946 that staff finally received their movement orders.

Ted Daines of 2943 Squadron had reached Mingaladon north of Rangoon in May 1945 but it would not be long, however, before he was heading home:

> . . . it was to be my last posting. I had been unwell for quite a long period, you may imagine how difficult it was to report sick, we only carried a medical orderly. I had three Sten guns blow up on me, then there was the wound I got at Yazagyo when the Mosquito crashed, so I had plenty of scars although most were on the small side. Thank goodness, most of these had not turned septic. The largest scar on my back had a boil starting to appear [in the] middle of it. Although at the time I did not realise it I had something far more serious wrong with me. I had contracted amoebic dysentery, this was in the same league as sprue and cholera, and not to be confused with the normal dysentery.
>
> Four days later I embarked on a hospital ship bound for Calcutta and was sent to 9th British General Hospital to undergo five weeks of uncomfortable and at the start, painful treatment, but I must admit in very pleasant surroundings. There was also four weeks sick leave at the end. I had a visit from Corporal Rose from the Squadron who informed me that my kit was lost overboard when loading at Rangoon Docks. I was to indent for more. At least half the Squadron gear was lost when the loading net split. How can you indent for snaps and a log book and other bits and pieces? Treatment over, with three others it was up to Nainital for a very restful and delightful sick leave, no out of bounds for other ranks here.

Then it was back to hospital for the really painful examination to see if the insides had healed, then with the words of the Group Captain ringing in my ears, 'No more Burma for you,' and back to the Depot to await the call for repatriation, about a month I think . . . But for me and the ten others that I had on my list it was up to Bombay (Worli) then to Poona and on to Mauripur, Karachi. Changed from a Dakota into a Stirling, then it was takeoff to Shaiba, on to Lod, Castel Benito and lastly RAF Stradishall.

There was no great welcome on his return to England. He continues:

I thought the greeting we received at Stradishall was appalling, you would have thought we were straight out of a leper colony, there was no meal laid on for us, until breakfast the next day. I could not because of my rank use the NAAFI. That is until I borrowed one of the lads' tunics. Even when on returning from disembarkation leave we had to attend lectures on basic weaponry given by lower ranking bare-breasted instructors. They could see trouble was brewing up, and I for one with two or three others was posted to recruit take-in centres. I remained there until I got my demob.

I am glad that I served abroad, there seemed to be much more comradeship overseas. People who were never in Burma cannot even start to understand what is was like, low rations, little water, holes in the ground to live in, mail in short supply. My rank entitled me to a bottle of spirits once a month. In the twelve I was in Burma I received one bottle, Christmas 1944. Who got the others, base wallahs I suspect. It never really bothered me, I used to give it away, but I'm sure the lads would have liked a drop. Even the cigarettes became non-existent. In central Burma we used to get seven every three days.

The other thing that appeared to be in short supply was provision made for leave. The Army had it. They used to send their troops back to Shillong which was a garrison town as well as a hill station. The Regiment idea of leave was to give units a rest in a place that was still on the trail so to speak. This was the cause of much under-current of anxiety among the men. Some of the leave pages were blank for all of their overseas tour of duty, others only had sick leave to show for it. Those that had sick leave were not in a fit state to enjoy it. Another thing that often puzzled me was that we were always or appeared to be under strength.

I think they more than did their job in a war zone that was recognised as the world's worst against a very barbaric foe, all this was with the bottom of the league weapons, rationed food and water. The Forgotten Army, Navy and Air Force they may have been so called, but you must admit, they were terrific.

Les Jewitt who we met in the first chapter had remained at the RAF Regiment Depot as the first Drum Major, however, polio cut short his career with the Regiment and he was invalided home. Others such as Ian Welch, who had joined the RAF in March 1941 when he was 17½ years old, having put up his age, had served in 2945 Field Squadron from its formation in 1943, in Bengal and on St Martin's Island then through Burma including Onbauk. He returned to India in August 1945, where 2945 Field Squadron was re-formed, and then sailed from Madras to Siam and was stationed at Don Muang airfield. He left the squadron in November 1945 and arrived back in England on 20 December, after being abroad for the required three years and eight months.

Henry Kirk had served a similar time overseas. Arriving in India in early 1942, he had served initially with 99 Squadron Defence Flight. He had suffered from a number of diseases contracted in the humid climate of Bengal, a snake bite, a strafing attack and was hit and knocked unconscious by a jeep being driven by a drunken American serviceman while walking down a street in Calcutta. He had served in the Arakan, at Imphal, had travelled the length of the Kabaw Valley, and had then reached Rangoon, before being sent to Singapore and Medan in Sumatra. Following his near fatal attack of pneumonia and pleurisy in 1942, he probably should have been sent back to the United Kingdom. As it was, he remained in the East for another three years. He thought he was finally heading home by early November 1945:

> . . . I left Singapore and flew to Air Trooping Station Arkonam at Madras on my way to pick up my gear at Secunderabad. However, on arrival at Arkonam I found that the enteric dysentery I had contracted just prior to leaving Singapore had worsened and I was sent to the MO. He was shocked at the poor physical state I was in and declared me unfit to travel. More delay was to follow as my service history file had gone astray and there was a strike by RAF servicing personnel in India which badly affected the schedules of the repatriation flights back to the UK. I eventually left Madras early March 1946 and flew direct to Karachi by Dakota and then on a priority Liberator flight to the UK, landing at Abingdon in Berkshire. We had engine trouble and the flight took five days and included an emergency landing at night on two engines at Lod in Palestine.
>
> I walked off the aircraft at Abingdon and went into the large dining hall. My skin was yellow from years of taken mepacrine, I was thin and emaciated. I was still in jungle green, had a 20 lb pack, carried a bag of jaffa oranges and an RAF greatcoat, this four years after sailing away. When I entered the entire station was in having lunch. Everyone to a man stopped eating and stared at me. It was as if I had come from another planet. Apparently I looked completely strange to them.
>
> My looted tin trunk arrived by sea in June 1946. I was discharged in May 1946, a rare bird – an LAC with two good conduct stripes . . . Like all others who served in the Far East I arrived home shattered, unable to sleep in a bed and suffered nightmares for years.

Colin Kirby, who had served in Ceylon, at Imphal and then at Akyab and in the Kaladan, had remained in Singapore well into 1946, carrying out routine guard duties and awaiting his orders for repatriation. He and five of his mates decided they would be happy to serve on in the Regiment. Suddenly, a request appeared in daily routine orders for volunteers to go on special hazardous duty in Japan. Unfortunately they left their run too late and, with their names already on the repatriation list, their offer was refused. Colin continues:

> Five of the lads and myself had no wish to return. We would have been quite content to continue serving in the Far East, and we clung together like a forlorn group waiting extradition.
>
> I left Tanglin in the early morning of the 17th November . . . We drove through almost deserted streets to the docks, where we went aboard the *City of Canterbury*. . . . the conditions . . . on troopships, had been dreadful. Now

they were much improved. We learned that for some time she had been transporting prisoners of war. Probably due to the Geneva Convention, POWs had been afforded better conditions than our own servicemen.

We sailed for Calcutta, with six men leaning over the stern sadly watching Singapore fade into the distance, and arrived in Calcutta on the 22nd. From there we travelled on to the Depot at Secunderabad to get our clearance from SEAC, on to Bombay and home via South Africa on the *Ile de France*. . . .

We docked at Southampton when 1946 was only a few days old. Lady Astor, a prominent figure in British politics at the time had, a short time before, made a speech in Parliament declaring that all servicemen returning from the Far East were infected with VD, and should be placed in quarantine. That just about set the tone for our reception in the UK generally. I served on until August before being 'demobbed'. 2966 Squadron was disbanded the same month. Quite apt really.

Cyril Paskin of 2968 Field Squadron had spent more than four years overseas with the Regiment. He was also sent back to the United Kingdom by plane rather than by boat. His service in the pestilential Kabaw Valley, the central plain of Burma and the race to Rangoon counted for little on his return home and he received a bewildering posting. He continues:

This still took a few days as we had to land in Aden and in Lod in Palestine. When I finally arrived back in Lincoln, believe it or not, they wanted to send me on a 'jungle course'. I think you will agree, that it was a bit late for that! A couple of months after returning to England, I was finally demobbed.

With the losses of men through repatriation, and with the Regiment now spread out over five countries and many thousands of miles apart, the units were to be disbanded or amalgamated as their tasks were completed or as they became unviable. The disbandment of 2943 Field Squadron serves as an example of the Regiment Wing HQs and squadrons that served in SEAC. In February 1946 the remaining seventy officers and airmen paraded for the last time. The other half of 2943 Field Squadron had already returned home and those remaining were to be divided between 2962 Squadron, stationed at Kemajoran airfield, and 2748 Squadron at Surabaya. A newspaper article written at the time describes the final parade after two and half years of active service:

There was an impressive 'farewell' parade on the Koningsplein, Batavia when the CO Squadron Leader R.R.J. Digges inspected his men for the last time, and took the salute at the march past by the forty-four NCOs and airmen before they left to join 2962 Squadron. The remainder of the squadron, under Flying Officer K.J. Wallen, formed a guard of honour for their comrades as they marched off. Also present at the parade was Wing Commander H. Sullivan, officer commanding No 1308 Wing RAF Regiment.

Squadron Leader Digges addressed the parade and told them, 'Since we landed in Java, this has been one of the hardest worked units in the RAF.' But sterling service in Java had been the culmination of the Squadron's long fighting career.[1]

2943 Field Squadron was formed at Secunderabad in May 1943, and had been the first Regiment squadron to move to the Imphal Valley, where it took up station at Palel airfield in November. One flight had been sent over the Shenam Pass to Tamu at the head of the Kabaw Valley. It had participated in patrols with the 2nd Border Regiment before the airfield was evacuated in the face of the Japanese advance in February 1944. It then withdrew into a defensive 'box' at Palel and formed defensive positions around the airstrip for the length of the siege of Imphal from February until June 1944. Meanwhile, the AFV flight carried out patrols with the 20th Indian Division on the Shenam Pass. In August 1944, the Japanese were retreating and a flight from the squadron accompanied the 13th Frontier Force Rifles on a thirty-one-day patrol, which penetrated into Burma and came within 4 miles of the River Chindwin. After resting and refitting in the valley, they followed the advance from Tamu to the Chindwin at Kalewa. On many occasions during the advance to Rangoon, the squadron moved by forced marches and, on one occasion, a flight did thirty-five miles wearing full kit in twenty-four hours. After landing in Java, the squadron was involved in many actions against the Indonesian nationalist forces.

The other 'original' SEAC-formed squadrons, 2941 to 2946, had just as long and an illustrious a story to tell.[2] 2941 Squadron was the last of the SEAC-formed squadrons to disband, which it did on 31 July 1946, at Kuala Lumpur. 2962 and 2739 Squadrons continued with their tasks in Java and Sumatra and were disbanded in August. The Wing HQs were all disbanded by April 1946. The final Regiment unit to go was 2810 Field Squadron. In April 1947 it paraded for the last time at Changi and in its place the first steps were taken to form the RAF Regiment (Malaya).[3]

For many of the men who served in the RAF Regiment in South-East Asia Command and, certainly for many of those who fought in Burma, it had been a long war. From late 1941 to mid-1942 when the British colonies in South-East Asia appeared likely to fall, the British Government had been forced to divert Army, Navy and Air Force units from the Middle East to India and Burma. The war in Egypt and Libya hung in the balance at that time, but the situation in the Far East had become desperate and limited resources were scraped together. Flying squadrons diverted from the Middle East were flown in to India and others were shipped directly from the United Kingdom.

It was at this time that many of the airmen who would one day make up the SEAC-formed AA flights, field and LAA squadrons and Wing HQs of the RAF Regiment arrived. Their job was made all the more difficult by the Air Ministry requirement to cut the size of the Regiment in India and re-muster the airmen to trades. The next major influx of airmen for the Regiment did not come until late 1944, when the United Kingdom squadrons arrived and were soon in the thick of the fighting for central Burma. They had come from the relative comfort of a home station but they had to adapt quickly to a completely different war against an implacable enemy. Most of these new squadrons performed sterling work in the advance through Burma with the most striking example being the actions of 2708 Field Squadron at Meiktila.

The ever-present factor overlying the war in Burma was the scourge of numerous tropical diseases and the generally unhealthy conditions on the plains and jungle-clad mountains of Manipur, the Kabaw Valley and the Arakan. Mountbatten and Slim had, however, made every effort to introduce drugs and preventative procedures to minimise the effects of these diseases and considerable progress had been made by the end of the campaign. However, when reading of the deployments and responsibilities of the Regiment, it must always be borne in mind that not only were there inadequate numbers for the tasks often asked of them, but that many of the airmen who were considered 'fit' for active service were suffering to varying degrees from more than one tropical malady.

The RAF in SEAC, which was at the end of the Allied supply chain both in distance and in priority, had to make do with aircraft well into 1945 that were out of date in North-West Europe and the Mediterranean. Similarly, for the RAF Regiment, the equipment provided whether as AA weapons or armoured fighting vehicles, was obsolete by standards used in other theatres. One of the major problems that the Regiment faced was that it could only provide airfield defence in diminution of the Army commitment i.e. if it had allocated more airmen to ground defence, it would have proportionately more airfields or ground to defend. The ceiling on manpower imposed by the Air Ministry made a proposal of this kind hypothetical in any case.

With regards to AA weapons, consideration was given towards the end of the campaign to issuing the LAA squadrons with Bofors 40-mm guns, with which the squadrons in North-West Europe and the Mediterranean had been equipped from 1943 onwards. This proposal was eventually rejected as it was assumed that the Army would simply withdraw its own LAA batteries from airfield defence in proportion and there would be little gain for the Regiment. There were relatively few opportunities for the Regiment to actively engage enemy aircraft, both through opportunity and given the limitations of the weapons they were given. With the RAF gaining a large degree of air superiority over Burma by late 1944, at the very time the LAA squadrons were being deployed, there were limited occasions for the Hispanos to fire on enemy aircraft. At that same time, there were often much bigger guns belonging to the LAA and HAA regiments of the Army, though in limited numbers, firing at the same time. The further problem that limited the use of the Hispanos was that they did not fire self-destroying ammunition. The deterrent effect of the Regiment's Brownings and Hispanos in diverting enemy fighters and bombers from their targets, however, should not be underestimated. Furthermore, the Brownings, and later Hispanos, positioned around an airfield could also provide considerable ground-to-ground fire support. This would also have been a deterrent to an enemy force planning an assault on an airfield. The AA flights and LAA squadrons did not confine themselves purely to an AA role and were more often than not used in a similar manner to the field squadrons. This was particularly the case following the Japanese capitulation, when the Regiment assumed a major role in accepting the surrender, reception and processing of Japanese troops and in dealing with the various insurgent and nationalist movements that had arisen in the former colonies.

Very early on in the development of the RAF Regiment, armoured fighting vehicles were established as an important element of airfield defence. As such, they were an integral part of the establishment of the field squadrons operating in the United Kingdom from 1942. At times they were also a crucial factor in the efficiency of the work of the RAF Regiment and the RAF Armoured Car Companies in North Africa and the Middle East. Indian-pattern AFVs were allocated to the SEAC squadrons in early 1944. However, they were found to be unsuitable for the terrain and in particular unable to climb paddy bunds. Such vehicles could not be moved by airlift, which meant that the AFVs and up to one quarter of the fighting strength of the squadron might have to be left behind to catch up by road, if that was at all possible. There were instances of the AFVs performing a useful role, for example, the work of the AFV flight of 2943 Field Squadron in patrolling the road over the Shenam Pass during the siege of Imphal. If the AFVs could have been moved into central Burma they may have been of some use for transport, but as the squadrons were down to only three and in some cases two rifle flights by this time, there would not have been enough airmen to man them and perform the ever present and crucial foot patrols. As most of the threat came from small parties of Japanese attempting to infiltrate onto airstrips, the prowler patrols and listening posts were of far greater value.

The extensive use of air supply and, consequently, the need for Allied air superiority were distinctive features of the Burma campaign and this had a profound influence on the eventual successful outcome. The RAF Regiment was well placed to take advantage of the flexibility for deployment to areas of greatest need that air transport provided and this was used to a limited extent in 1944 but gained in intensity as the Fourteenth Army rapidly moved through central and southern Burma. The only limitation to this was that the squadrons when moving forward to the next airstrip had to beg for or borrow transport to at least carry their heavy equipment, stores and ammunition. An apt description of their plight was provided by LAC Sid Wood of 2944 Field Squadron who said:

> We must have walked nearly a thousand miles from Imphal to Rangoon. Even when the squadron had some gharries we were usually marching either side of them in the dust storm they threw up.

A crucial factor in the success of the RAF Regiment in SEAC was related to the organisational changes that were made from early 1943 onwards. These changes resulted in

'In many tours and inspections throughout this Theatre I have noticed the almost "jealous-like" pride which the Regiment Squadrons have in their own service.' The Allied Air C-in-C, ACSEA Air Chief Marshal Sir Keith Park inspects airmen of the RAF Regiment. (Air Historical Branch RAF Crown Copyright)

the creation of an airfield defence force that had been trained to a consistent and high standard at the Depot and Forward Echelon, and with training pursued with great vigour when deployed. The second aspect was the reorganisation of the original station, squadron and other RAF asset defence flights into recognisable units, which could be deployed to the task required according to priority. This meant they were not simply 'hanging around' an airfield or installation in a rear area where the parent unit was stationed. It was the airfield that had to be defended and in a tactically coordinated manner. Following the first reorganisation, the AA flights and squadrons were able to be sent to where they were most required, on the forward airfields and with the AMES, often well in front of the Army positions. This flexibility and tactical control was further enhanced by the introduction of the Wing HQs.

By early 1945 it was accepted practice that the RAF should, in all instances, be self-supporting in ground defence and that Regiment officers be consulted as to its organisation and coordination at all RAF forward airfields.[4] In his despatches on the campaign in South-East Asia, Air Chief Marshal Sir Keith Park wrote:

> . . . the RAF Regiment proved itself a force capable of carrying out more than the tasks its originators claimed the Regiment could accomplish. It was not a force of men dressed up as guards and picqueted around some airfield or supply dump with guns propped in their hands. These men were so trained in the art and strategy of ground defence and jungle warfare that they were able to undertake with success countermeasures against Japanese infiltration parties who might set themselves up near the perimeter of some airfield and constitute a menace until hunted down and destroyed.[5]

Arguably, however, the most profound effect of the reorganisation of the RAF Regiment in SEAC was the development of a strong *esprit de corps*, high morale, comradeship and sense of purpose amongst the officers and airmen. This was again eloquently put by Park who wrote:

> If the RAF Regiment in South-East Asia has done nothing more than provide vital protection for our airfields, the record of its achievements would still read with commendable credit. That it was able to perform further additional services and maintain a smartness and discipline which called forth praise from Army and Navy alike, demonstrates the value of our Regiment as an adjunct of the Royal Air Force. In many tours and inspections throughout this Theatre I have noticed the almost 'jealous-like' pride which the Regiment Squadrons have in their own service.[6]

That the Regiment was able to carry out its tasks so effectively and efficiently despite inadequate numbers, outdated equipment and often with a significant proportion of the unit debilitated with tropical ailments, is a tribute to the diligence, tenacity, persistence and professionalism of its officers and airmen. The RAF and, in particular, Air Command, South-East Asia, could not have asked more of the men of its youngest Corps.

Notes
1   *The Evening News*, Saturday 2 May 1946.
2   The process of disbandment of the RAF Regiment in all theatres at the end of the Second World War was unfortunately carried out without consideration of the continuation of the

battle honours gained by the squadrons. As a result none of those earned by the Regiment in South-East Asia are carried today by any RAF Regiment squadron. The Regiment and its derivatives would continue on after the war as it had clearly demonstrated its utility. It has been on active service since then in the Malayan Emergency, the Indonesian Confrontation, Cyprus, Aden, Oman, Germany, the Falklands, Kosovo, Northern Ireland, the Gulf War, Iraq and Afghanistan. It provides the hard core of Force Protection for the RAF.

3   The RAF Regiment (Malaya) was formed in 1947 to provide locally raised RAF Regiment squadrons for airfield defence in the Far East. It was to play a major and continuous role in the successful outcome of the Malayan Emergency, which lasted from 1948 until 1961.

4   The Regiment had gained such a reputation that the USAAF had requested the loan of an RAF Regiment officer to organise the defence of its forward airfields in the Assam Valley.

5   Air Chief Marshal Sir Keith Park KCB KBE MC DFC, *Third Supplement to the London Gazette*, Tuesday 13 April 1951, Air Operations in South-East Asia from 3 May 1945 to 12 September 1945, p. 2166.

6   ibid, pp. 2166–7.

Appendices

Appendix 1.
The establishments of RAF Regiment units formed by Air HQ India and Air Command South-East Asia 1943–5.

			Officers				Airmen					Total	Total
Unit	Date	Organisation	WC	SL	FL	FO	WO	FS	Sgt	Cpl	AC	Officers	Airmen
AA Flight	Apr 1943	Headquarters				1			1	1	1	1	3
		Section x 3								1	10		33
												1	36
Field Squadron	Apr 1943	Headquarters	1	1	1			1		1	7	3	9
		Rifle Flight x 3				1			1	3	34	3	114
		Support Flight							1	5	21		27
												6	150
LAA Squadron[1]	May 1944	Headquarters	1			1	1		1	6	16	2	24
		Flight HQ x 3			1	1		1		1	4	6	18
		Flight x 3							2	8	28		114
												8	156
Field Squadron[2]	Jul 1944	Headquarters	1	1	2		1	1		9	22		
		Mortar Section							1	4	8	4	46
		Rifle Flight x 3				1			1	3	32	3	108
		Armoured Flight				1			2	4	26	1	32
												8	186
Wing HQ	Jul 1944	Headquarters		1		1				2	3	2	5
												2	5
Field Squadron[3]	Jan 1945	Headquarters	1	1	2		1	1		9	21		
		Mortar Section							1	4	8		
		Bren Section							1	2	10	4	58
		Rifle Flight x 3				1			1	3	32	3	108
												7	166
Armoured Squadron	Jan 1945	Headquarters	1			1	1	1		6	16	2	24
		Armd Flt x 2				1			2	5	26		
		x 1			1				2	5	26	3	99
												5	123

Notes

1 Transport: Four jeeps, twelve motorcycles, sixteen 3-ton tenders (one 3-ton tender per gun plus four extra 3-ton tenders per flight) and one water tender. Squadron armament: 24 Hispanos 20-mm guns with each flight manning 8 x 20-mm Hispanos (Mobile), of two four-gun sections.

2 Transport: One jeep, six motorcycles, six 3-ton tenders, six 15-cwts, one water trailer, eight AFVs distributed as one Squadron HQ AFV, an Armoured Flight HQ AFV and two troops each of three AFVs. Squadron armament: Two 3-inch mortars in HQ Flight and each AFV armed with two Bren LMGs.

3 Transport: same as for Field Squadron (July 1944) but without AFV Flight. Squadron armament: Bren Section (Support Group) armed with four Bren LMGs.

Appendix 2.

The RAF Regiment units formed in India or arriving from the UK. All were formed or received initial training at the RAF Regiment Depot Secunderabad unless noted.

Year	Month	SEAC		UK Squadrons	Wing HQs
		AA Flights	Squadrons		
1943	Apr	4401–4404	2941 Field		
	May	4405–4408	2942 Field		
	Jun	4409–4412	2943, 2944 Field		
	Jul	4413–4416	2945, 2946 Field		
	Aug	4417–4427			
	Sep	4428–4438			
	Oct	4439–4450			
	Nov				
	Dec				
1944	Jan	1–12 (India)			
	Feb				
	Mar				
	Apr				
	May		2958 LAA		
	Jun				
	Jul		2959, 2960, 2961 LAA		
			2966[1], 2967[2] Field		1323, 1324
	Aug				
	Sep		2968 Field		
			2963 LAA		
	Oct			2706, 2837, 2854 LAA[3]	1325, 1326, 1327
	Nov			2739, 2759 Field[3]	
	Dec		2962 LAA		1307, 1308, 1329[4]
1945	Jan			2708[5], 2743[5], 2748[6] Field	1330, 1331[4]
	Feb		2965 LAA[7]	2802[8], 2810[9] Field	
				2846, 2852 LAA	
	Mar		2964 Field [10]	2896 Field[5]	
	Apr				
	May		2970 Armd[11]		

Notes

1   Formed at Comilla and moved to Patenga for combined operations training.
2   Formed at Agartala and moved to Patenga for combined operations training.
3   All deployed after two weeks at Depot to 224 Group.
4   All Wing HQs from the UK.
5   Departed for Agartala after two weeks at Depot.

6 Departed for Comilla and then to Agartala after two weeks at Depot.
7 Formed from spare airmen from UK squadrons and departed directly for Battle Station.
8 Departed for Feni and then Agartala after two weeks at Depot.
9 Departed for Hathazari and then Agartala after two weeks at Depot.
10 Departed for Agartala. Formed in August 1944 at Dimapur then moved to Alipore. Originally an LAA squadron, it returned to Secunderabad and was used to provide airmen for the Bren Support Groups and Mortar Flights of field squadrons. Then reformed as a field squadron using spare airmen remaining at the Depot.
11 Formed at Agartala.

Appendix 3.
The disposition of ground defence units of 224 Group RAF on 21 November 1942.
Locations ordered from north to south.

Location	Unit	Ground Defence
Bengal and Assam	Thirteen AMES	13 Sections
Tezpur	–	1 Flight
Agartala	169 Wing (forming)	½ Flight
	5 Squadron	1 Flight
Feni	–	1 Flight
	877 AMES	1 Section
Calcutta	75 ASP	1 Flight
	101 R&SU	1 Flight
Red Road	17 Squadron	1 Flight
Belvedere	224 Group HQ	½ Flight
Dum Dum	165 Wing HQ	½ Flight
	135 Squadron	1 Flight
	136 Squadron	1 Flight
Kanchrapara	HQ	1 Flight
	79 Squadron	1 Flight
	60 R&SU	1 Flight
	304 MU	1 Flight
Jessore	166 Wing HQ	½ Flight
	607 Squadron	1 Flight
	615 Squadron	1 Flight
	853 AMES	1 Section
Alipore	293 Wing HQ	½ Flight
	67 Squadron	1 Flight
	146 Squadron	1 Flight
	155 Squadron (to 169 Wing)	1 Flight
Amarda Road	–	1 Flight
	848 AMES	1 Section
Chittagong	–	1 Flight
	864 AMES	1 Section
Cox's Bazaar	–	1 Flight

Appendix 4.

The disposition of ground defence flights on forward airstrips with 165 Wing of 224 Group RAF on 16 April 1943. Locations ordered from north to south.

Location		Ground Defence
Ramu	Reindeer	165 Wing HQ Flight
	Lyons	136 Squadron Flight 'Bombay' Flight
	Hay	79 Squadron Flight
Nidania – George		607 Squadron Flight
Beachstrip – Hove		135 Squadron Flight
Teknaf		R&SU Flight
Maungdaw		'Chittagong' Flight 'Tezpur' Flight (Indin until 26 March)

Appendix 5.

The disposition of the RAF Regiment on monsoon airstrips of 224 Group RAF on 25 May 1943. The Secunderabad-trained RAF Regiment units appear in the Order of Battle. Locations ordered from north to south.

Location	Unit	RAF Regiment
Agartala	169 Wing HQ	½ Flight
	–	2 Flights
	–	2941 Field Squadron
Comilla (165 Wing)	–	1 Flight
		2942 Field Squadron
Feni	167 Wing HQ	–
	–	1 Flight
	–	4404 AA Flight
Chittagong	224 Group HQ	–
	21 Ops Room	½ Flight
	166 Wing HQ	1 Flight
	–	1 Flight
	–	4405 AA Flight
	AMES	4407 AA Flight
Dohazari (167 Wing)	–	1 Flight
	–	4402 AA Flight
Cox's Bazaar (165 Wing)	–	2 Flights
	–	4403 AA Flight
Ramu – Reindeer	165 Wing HQ	½ Flight
	Ops Room/AMES	4401 AA Flight

Appendix 6.

The disposition of the RAF Regiment in 224 Group RAF from June 1943 to June 1944.
Locations ordered from north to south.

Location	1943		1944	
	June	December	March	June
Singarbil		4426	4426	
				4411
Agartala	2941	2941	2941[1]	
		4401	4401	4401
		4425	4425	4425
				4402
Comilla	2942			
		4421		
		4439	4439	4439
			4412	4412
			3	
			5	
				4414
Bhatpara		4415		
			4414	
Lalmai		4414		
Chandpur	4409	4409		
Feni		2945	2945[2]	2945
	4404			
			4407[3]	
		4424	4424[3]	
		4433		
			4437	
		4441		
Parashuram		4407		
Fazilpur			4433[3]	
Hathazari				4422
Chittagong		2944		
		2946	2946	2946[4]
				2958 LAA
	4405	4405	4405	
	4407			
	4411	4411		
		4438	4438	
			7	
Dohazari			2944[5]	
	4402			
		4404	4404	
		4442	4442	
			4	

Location	June	December	March	June
		1943		1944
Chiringa		4402		
				4421
				4410
Joari			4402	
Cox's Bazaar	4403	4403		
	4410	4410	4410	
		4431		
			4411	
				4404
				4443
Ramu		2942		
	4401			
		4422	4422	
		4432	4432	4432
		4443		
			4406	
			4421	
			4447	
Rumkhapalong			4415	
Nazir (Ramu)			4431	
Bawli Bazaar			4443	
			8	
Maungdaw			2942	2942

Notes

1   Less three flights airlifted to Imphal.
2   At St Martin's Island on AMES protection duties February to March 1944.
3   Airlifted to Imphal May 1944.
4   Less one flight airlifted to Imphal.
5   To Maungdaw twice on AMES duties and then airlifted to Imphal.

Appendix 7.

The disposition of the RAF Regiment in 222, 225, 227 and 231 Groups RAF from June 1943 to June 1944.

Group	Location	1943 Jun	1943 Dec	1944 Mar	1944 Jun
231 Group	Jessore	2943			
	Barkakana	2944			
	Amarda Road	4406	4406		
				6	
				10	
				11	
	Kharagpur	4412	4412		
			4446		
	Cuttack		4420	4420	4420
	Baigachi		4435		
			4447		
				4436	4436
	Char Chapli		4436		
	Diamond Harbour		4437		
	Alipore				4405
227 Group (RAF Regiment Depot)	Secunderabad	2945			
		4413			
		4414			
		4415			
		4416			
		4420			
225 Group	St Thomas' Mt		4428		
	Vizagapatam		4449		
	Madras			4428	
222 Group	Koggala		4413	4413	4413
	Ratmalana		4419	4419	
	Vavuniya		4429	4429	
	Sigirya		4450		
	Minneriya			12	

Appendix 8.
The disposition of the RAF Regiment in 221 Group RAF from June 1943 to June 1944.

Location	1943		1944				
	Jun	Dec	Mar	Apr	1 May	30 May	30 Jun
Imphal Plain							
Imphal			2946 (½ Flt) 2941 (2 Flts)	2946 (½ Flt)	2946 (½ Flt)	2946 (½ Flt)	2946 (½ Flt)
					2944	2944	2944
	4408	4408	4408 4423 1	4408 4423 1	4408 1 4440	4408 1 4440	4408 1 4440
Ukhrul Road		4418					
Sawambung						4424	4424
Kangla					2941 (2 Flts)	2941 (2 Flts)	2941 (2 Flts)
			4418 9	4418 9	4418 9 4423 4434	4418 9 4423	9
Tulihal						2941 (1 Flt)	2941 (1 Flt)
			4427 2	4427 2	4427 2	4427 2 4407 4435	4427 2 4407 4435
Yairipok						4433	4433
Wangjing			4434 4440	4434 4440		4434	4434
Sapam		4440					
Palel			2943 4430 4444	2943 4430 4444	2943 4430 4444	2943 4430 4444	2943 4430 4444 4418 4423
Assam Valley							
Dergaon				2941 det. 4448	2941 det. 4448	2941 det. 4448	2941 det. 4448
Dimapur		4448	4448				
						4445	4445
Surma Valley							
Silchar		4445	4445	4445	4445		
Kumbhirgram		4416 4417	4416 4417	4416 4417	4416 4417	4416 4417	4416 4417
Rayjeswapur		4434					

Appendix 9.

Time allocation for the three-month training programme for 2944 Field Squadron while stationed at RAF Station Barkakana (near Ranchi) in Bengal from July to September 1943.

Training	Activity	Time allocated (hours)
Weapons	Rifle, Bren, Sten, grenade, ammunition, sighting	121
Field	Uses of ground, cover, fire positions	12
	Judging distances including indication of targets	12
	Fire orders	8
	Attack and defence	18
	Anti-Tank mines – laying practice	2
	Road blocks	2
	Scouts and patrols	16
	Field engineering	3
	Tank hunting	1
	Aircraft recognition	3
	Anti-gas	3
	Map reading	6
	Drill – foot, arms, squadron	24
	Bayonet fighting, PT, unarmed combat	53
	Assault course, route marches, night operations	72
	Organised games	48
	Lost time	28
Total		432

Appendix 10.
Airlifts of RAF Regiment units from March 1944 to October 1945.

Year	Date	Wing	AA Flight/Squadron	From	To
1944	30 Mar		2941 Field (1 Flt)	Agartala	Imphal
	1 Apr		2941 Field (1 Flt)	Agartala	Sapam
	22 Apr		2944 Field	Dohazari	Kangla
	11 May		4407, 4424, 4433	Feni	Kangla
	25 May		2941 Field (1 NCO, 20 ORs)	Agartala	Tulihal
1945	15 Jan		2958 LAA (1 Flt)	Taukkyan	Kan
	1–4 Feb		2945 Field	Indin	Onbauk
	3 Feb		2942 Field	Imphal	Onbauk
	9 Feb		2944 Field	Ywadon	Sinthe
	16 Feb	1330		FE Agartala	Imphal
	3 Mar		2708 Field	FE Agartala	Monywa
	6 Mar		2963 LAA (2 Flts)	Monywa	Meiktila
			2968 Field (1 Flt)	Tabingaung	Meiktila
	8 Mar		2708 Field	Monywa	Meiktila
	9 Mar		2941 Field (1 Flt)	Monywa	Meiktila
	11 Mar		2743 Field	FE Agartala	Onbauk
	12 Mar	1329		FE Agartala	Monywa
	28–9 Mar		2968 Field (2 Flts)	–	Meiktila
	Apr		Reinforcements (168 ORs)	FE Agartala	Forward Airstrips 221 Group
	3 Apr	1324		Monywa	Comilla
			2965 LAA	Imphal	Meiktila
	7 Apr		2759 Field	Chiringa	Meiktila
	15 Apr		2802 Field	FE Agartala	Dwehla
	19 Apr		2743 Field (1 officer, 17 ORs)	Ondaw	Kwetnge
	21 Apr		2802 Field	Dwehla	Kwetnge
	23 Apr		2854 LAA	Akyab	Sinthe
	25 Apr		2759 Field	Thedaw	Tennant
	28 Apr		2802 Field	Kwetnge	Kalaywa
	3 May	1331		Ramree Island	Akyab
	17 May	1326		Akyab	Kwetnge
	15 Sept		2941 Field (1 officer, 20 ORs)	Kelanang	Kuala Lumpur
	20 Sept		2743 Field (3 officers, 27 ORs)	Kelanang	Tengah
	21 Sept	1326	2965 Field	Hmawbi	Penang
	23 Sept		2960 LAA	Hmawbi	Penang
	1 Oct	1307	2963 LAA	Hmawbi	Saigon

Appendix 11.
Anti-aircraft engagements by the RAF Regiment from November 1943 to March 1945.

Year	Date	Location	AA Flight/ Squadron	Calibre	Claim — Destroyed	Claim — Damaged
1943	1 Nov	Agartala	4401	.303		
	9 Nov	Palel	4430	.303		
1944	9 Feb	Ramu	4432 4443	.303		
	3 Mar	Cox's Bazaar	4411	.303	1	
	17 Mar	Palel	4444	.303	1	
	13 Apr	Imphal	2941 Field	.303		1
	15 Apr	Imphal	4408	.303		2
	26 Apr	Palel	4430 4444	.303	1	
	1 May	Ramu	4422	.303		
	6 May	Ramu	4432	.303		
	5 Nov	Palel	2944 Field	.303		
			2961 LAA	20-mm		3
		Tamu	2941 Field	.303		
			2958 LAA	20-mm		
	23 Dec	Kyawzin	2961 LAA	20-mm		
1945	11 Jan	Yeu	2961 LAA	20-mm	1	
	31 Jan	Onbauk	2960 LAA	20-mm		1
	1 Feb	Tabingaung	2961 LAA	20-mm		
	2 Mar	Sinthe	2958 LAA	20-mm		1
	3 Mar	Ramree	2837 LAA 2959 LAA	20-mm 20-mm		
	4 Mar	Onbauk	2960 LAA	20-mm		1
	26 Mar	Akyab	2854 LAA	20-mm		

Appendix 12.
The disposition of the RAF Regiment in 221 and 224 Groups RAF in late November 1944.

Group	Wing HQ	Location	Squadron Field	LAA
221	1323	Imphal		2963
		Kangla		2960
		Wangjing		2960/2961 (1 Flt ea.)
		Tulihal	2946	2960 (1 Flt)
		Sapam		2961
		Palel	2943	2961 (1 Flt)
		Tamu	2941 (HQ+AFV Flt) 2944	
		Mawlaik	2941 (1 Flt)	
	1324	Yazagyo	2968	2958
		Kalewa	2944 (1 Flt)[1]	
		Kalemyo	2941 (1 Flt)[1]	
		Agartala	2967	
224	1327	Chittagong		
		Dohazari	2966	
		Cox's Bazaar		2959
	1326	Jalia		2706
				2837
				2854
		Maungdaw	2945	
In transit	To 1326 Wing		2739	
			2759	
	To Depot		2942	2964

Notes

1   Attached to the 11th East African Division in the Kabaw Valley.

Appendix 13.

The operational role of 2944 Field Squadron at Taukkyan Air Landing Ground issued on 2 January 1945.

OPERATION INSTRUCTION No 4

Operational Role of 2944 Field Squadron RAF Regiment at Taukkyan ALG

INFORMATION. General.

Taukkyan ALG is primarily used for:-

(a)   A Base for No 17 Spitfire Squadron.

(b)   For landings supplies by DC3 aircraft.

(c)   A Base for No 1 Detachment Communication Squadron (221 Group).

(d)   A Base for No 60 Hurricane Squadron.

Own Troops.

Defence Commander – Squadron Leader E.S. Gosnell, No 2944 Field Squadron RAF Regiment

No 2944 Field Squadron RAF Regiment

No 909 Wing (Satellite) RAF

No 17 Squadron RAF

No 60 Squadron RAF

No 1 Detachment Communication Squadron (221 Group)

Defence Coy VII Rajput

INTENTION. The above troops will protect Taukkyan ALG from ground attack.

METHOD. (1)   The area surrounding Taukkyan ALG will be divided into three sectors to a depth of 3000 yards.

Map Kalemyo – Kalewa Sheet No. 3

(a)   Ref Pt 5157 to a depth of 3000 yards between bearing 320° to 195°.

(b)   Ref Pt 5157 to a depth of 3000 yards between bearing 320° to 90°.

(c)   Ref Pt 5157 to a depth of 3000 yards between bearing 90° to 195°.

(2)   Each area will be patrolled by one Flight daily as detailed from 0730 hours to 1800 hours.

(3)   One Flight will be detailed as mobile reserve to be at Squadron HQ at half hour readiness.

(4)   One Flight will patrol the close proximity of the ALG from 1800 hours to 0730 hours.

(5)   Three Flights will be detailed as mobile reserve to be at Squadron HQ at half hour readiness from 1800 hours to 0730 hours.

(6)   Squadron HQ personnel will be responsible for the protection of the camp area.

(7)   In the event of ground attack alarm 2nd i/c will assume command of the Squadron.

ADMINISTRATION.

All Flight weapons and full scale operational ammunition will be carried.
Reserve ammunition will be held at Squadron HQ.

Dress – Battle Order.

Rations will be drawn in advance by Flights on full day patrol.

Water and rations for 72 hours will be held as reserve at Squadron HQ.

COMMUNICATIONS.
Location of HQ.

Defence Commander – No 2944 Squadron Office	E of ALG.
No 2944 Field Squadron, RAF Regiment	Orderly Room.
No 909 Wing (Satellite)	SE end of ALG.
No 17 Squadron	SE end of ALG.
No 60 Squadron	NE end of ALG.
No 1 Det. Communication Squadron (221 Group)	W end of ALG.
Defence Company VII Rajput	4 Corps HQ.

Warning Systems.
Ack-Ack.

Alarm – Three rounds fired by Master Bofors.

All clear – One round fired by Master Bofors.

Ground Attack.

Alarm – Series of short blasts on whistles.

All clear – Series of long blasts on whistles.

On receipt of Ack-Ack or ground attack alarm all troops will immediately 'Stand to' and all lights will be extinguished.

RT.

All Flights on patrol will be in RT communication with Squadron Headquarters at times detailed in Squadron intercommunication Orders.

2958 Squadron and Defence Company VII Rajputs will be in RT communication in event of alarm.

2944 Squadron telephone land line to PORTLAND via 17 Squadron exchange.

2944 Squadron telephone land line to HESTON via 17 Squadron exchange.

2944 Squadron telephone land line to BROADWAY via 17 Squadron exchange.

NOTE:-

4 Corps Telephone Exchange	– PORTLAND
909 Wing HQ Telephone Ex	– HESTON
909 Wing Ops Telephone Ex	– BROADWAY

All other communications will only be by telephone, 'Jeep', DR and Runner.

PASSWORDS will be issued daily.

ACKNOWLEDGE.

(Sgd) (E.S. Gosnell)
Squadron Leader, Commanding,
No 2944 Field Squadron RAF Regiment

Appendix 14.

The disposition of the RAF Regiment in 221 and 224 Groups RAF from January to March 1945.
Locations ordered from north to south.

Group	Wing	January	February	March
221				
	1323	Mawlaik		
		Indainggyi		
		Kalemyo		
		Taukkyan		
		Tabingaung		
		Gangaw		
		Kan		
			Sinthe	Sinthe
			Myitche	Myitche
			Nyaungu	
				Kinka
		2944 Field	2944 Field	2944 Field
		2946 Field	2946 Field	2946 Field
		2963 LAA		
			2958 LAA	2958 LAA
	1324	Indainggyi		
		Mutaik		
			Tabingaung	
		Yeu	Yeu	
		Shwebo	Shwebo	
		Onbauk	Onbauk	Onbauk
		Sadaung	Sadaung	Sadaung
				Ondaw
		2943 Field	2943 Field	2943 Field
		2960 LAA	2960 LAA	2960 LAA
		2961 LAA	2961 LAA	2961 LAA
		2968 Field	2968 Field	2968 Field
			2942 Field	2942 Field
			2945 Field	2945 Field
				2743 Field
	1307	Sittaung		
		Mawlaik		
		Indainggyi		
		Taukkyan		
		Kalemyo		
		Onbauk		
		Okpo		
		Alon		
			Ywadon	Ywadon
			Monywa	Monywa
				Meiktila
				Myinmu
		2941 Field	2941 Field	2941 Field
		2958 LAA		
		2963 LAA	2963 LAA	2963 LAA
				2708 Field

Group	Wing	January	February	March
224	1327	Chiringa		
		Bawli North		
		Patenga		
		Ramree	Ramree	Ramree
			Kyaukpyu	Kyaukpyu
		2837 LAA	2837 LAA	
		(1 Flt)	(1 Flt)	
		2959 LAA	2959 LAA	2959 LAA
		2967 Field	2967 Field	2967 Field
		Oyster Island		
	1326	Akyab	Akyab	Akyab
			Mawnubyn	Mawnubyn
			Dabaing	Dabaing
				Kaladan
		2706 LAA	2706 LAA	2706 LAA
		2966 Field	2966 Field	2966 Field
				2854 LAA
	1308	Cox's Bazaar		Cox's Bazaar
		Chiringa	Chiringa	Chiringa
		Ramu	Ramu	
		Rumkhapalong		
				Buthidaung
		Maungdaw	Maungdaw	
		Indin	Indin	
		2739 Field	2739 Field	2739 Field
		2759 Field	2759 Field	2759 Field
		2837 LAA	2837 LAA	2837 LAA
		2854 LAA	2854 LAA	
		2945 Field		
Not operational				
1329		Depot	Agartala	Monywa-Shwebo
1330		"	"	Monywa
1331		"	Depot	Agartala
	2962 LAA	"	"	Depot
	2896 Field	"	"	"
	2743 Field	"	Agartala	(1324)
	2708 Field	"	"	(1307)
	2802 Field	"	Feni	Agartala
	2846 LAA	"	Depot	Depot
	2852 LAA	"	"	"
	2748 Field	"	Comilla	Agartala
	2810 Field	"	Hathazari	Hathazari

Appendix 15.

Operational order for the defence of Onbauk airstrip against ground attack, February 1945.

DEFENCE OF ONBAUK AIRSTRIP AGAINST GROUND ATTACK

INFORMATION.

ENEMY. Any large scale threat is thought to have disappeared, but it is extremely possible that small parties up to 20 in number will attempt to infiltrate particularly at night in order to sabotage aircraft.

OWN TROOPS.

OUTER PERIMETER PROTECTION – 3 Coy 4/3 Madras Regiment.

CLOSE DEFENCES
    (a) 2945 Field Squadron RAFR
        2968 Field Squadron RAFR (less 2 Flights)
    (b) 2960 LAA Squadron RAFR
        42 Squadron RAF   Ground defence
        113 Squadron RAF   is only the
        34 Squadron RAF   secondary task
        R&SU Detachment   of these troops.
        No 1 Troop 9 Battery LAA

COUNTER ATTACK FORCE – 1/15 Punjab Regiment

INTENTION.   This force will prevent the enemy destroying aircraft and equipment.

METHOD A.   OUTER PERIMETER.
    4/3 Madras will maintain standing patrols at 3 points outside the aerodrome area, and man 3 localities on the outer perimeter.

    CLOSE DEFENCE.
    2945 Squadron HQ & No. 3 Flight will be responsible for 113 Squadron dispersal area. – Squadron Leader Garnett i/c.
    2945 Squadron No. 1 & 2 Flight will be responsible for 34 Squadron dispersal – Flying Officer Terry i/c.
    2968 Squadron HQ & B Flight will be responsible for 42 Squadron dispersal – Flight Lieutenant Dutton i/c.
    Each of the flying squadrons will provide 10 men at stand-to each evening for duty inside their dispersal area.
    All other troops will be responsible for their own protection and for giving the alarm if any incident occurs in their area.

METHOD B.   In each locality pits will be sited to cover all possible approaches to the aircraft. At stand-to each evening a picket of 1 Sergeant, 1 Corporal and 9 men will be posted among the aircraft. Of this picket 3 men will patrol continuously round the aircraft, each man keeping at least 10 yards from the others. This force will be available under the Sergeant for immediate counter attack <u>inside</u> the locality perimeter.

ACTION TO BE TAKEN.

(a) BY NIGHT – From stand-to at night to stand-down in the morning, each pit will be manned by one man with two others at immediate readiness. During stand-to all 3 men will man the pits.

(b) BY DAY – Each locality will post 1 sentry to watch for alarm signals and any untoward incident.

Bayonets will be left fixed from dusk stand-to until dawn stand-down. The enemy will be met with bayonet, kukri and grenade, and there will be no firing except at point-blank range. After dusk stand-to any movement will be assumed to be hostile.

ADMINISTRATION. – ARMS AND AMMUNITION. – All ranks will carry their personal arms and ammunition at all times. All reserves will be distributed among localities. Magazines will be charged from dusk to dawn. At dusk 2 grenades will be issued to each man. They will be checked and handed in at stand-down in the morning.

MEDICAL. Casualties to be taken to RAF Regiment or Squadron MI Room.

WATER. All water bottles will be kept filled and inspected at dusk.

RATIONS. 4 days rations will be kept in each locality.

COMMUNICATION.

Alarm signals

(a) BY DAY (i) AIR ATTACK – 3 rounds Bofors – to be taken up by sentries on whistles.

(ii) GROUND ATTACK – Continuous short blasts on whistles.

(b) BY NIGHT (i) AIR ATTACK – 1 Red Very Light.

(ii) GROUND ATTACK – 3 Green Very Lights.

Signal Code -		
Battle HQ	– Lulworth.	
4/3 Madras Regiment	– Croydon.	
42 Dispersal	– Shark.	
34 Dispersal	– Pike.	
2960 Squadron	– Doodlebug.	

All units will be connected by telephone. Close defence troops will have R/T in reserve (frequency 86.65 megacycles – control name 'WHISPER'). Runners will be used in an emergency.

GENERAL.

(i) Dusk stand-to – 1815–1845 hours.
Dawn stand-to – 0545–0615 hours.

(ii) After 1815 hours no fires are to be shown; blackout is to be as complete as possible and all noise reduced to a minimum.

(iii) If it is necessary for RAF personnel to move into dispersal areas on duty between dusk and dawn, the locality commander must be informed by telephone.

(Sgd)
(T.R. Garnett) Squadron Leader
Aerodrome Defence Commander,
RAF Onbauk

DISTRIBUTION:-

RAF Admin Unit, Onbauk
HQ 1324 Wing, RAFR
4/3 Madras Company
No. 1 Troop LAA
113 Squadron
42 Squadron
34 Squadron

2960 LAA Squadron
2968 Field Squadron
2945 Field Squadron
Air Formation Signals

Appendix 16.
The disposition of the RAF Regiment in India and South-East Asia Command from April to June 1945.

Wing HQ	April	May	June
			Myingyan
			Meiktila
	Sinthe	Sinthe	
1323	Magwe	Magwe	
	2944 Field	2944 Field	2944 Field
	2946 Field	2946 Field	2946 Field
	2958 LAA	2958 LAA	2958 LAA
	2854 LAA	2854 LAA	2854 LAA
1329	Dwehla		
	Kwetnge	Kwetnge	Kwetnge
	Lewe	Lewe	
	Kalaywa	Kalaywa	
			Zayatkwin
	2960 LAA	2960 LAA	
	2961 LAA	2961 LAA	
	2802 Field	2802 Field	
	2942 Field	2942 Field	
	2943 Field	2943 Field	
	2743 Field	2743 Field	2743 Field
	2945 Field	2945 Field	
1330	Tennant	Tennant	Tennant
	Meiktila		
1307	Thedaw	Thedaw	Thedaw
	Toungoo	Toungoo	Toungoo
	Tennant	Tennant	Tennant
		Prome	Prome
			Shwedaung
		Pyinmana	Pyinmana
	2708 Field	2708 Field	2708 Field
	2941 Field	2941 Field	2941 Field
	2963 LAA	2963 LAA	2963 LAA
	2965 Field	2965 Field	2965 Field
	2968 Field	2968 Field	2968 Field
	2759 Field	2759 Field	2759 Field
1326	Akyab		
		In transit	
			Kalaywa
			2802 Field
			2942 Field
			2943 Field
1308	Cox's Bazaar	Cox's Bazaar	Cox's Bazaar
	Ramu		
	Maungdaw	Maungdaw	
	2739 Field	2739 Field	2739 Field
	2837 LAA	2837 LAA	2837 LAA
1331	Akyab	Akyab	Akyab
	2706 LAA	2706 LAA	2706 LAA
	2966 Field	2966 Field	2966 Field

Wing HQ	April	May	June
1327	Ramree		
		Rangoon	
		Mingaladon	Mingaladon
	2959 LAA	2959 LAA	2959 LAA
	2967 Field	2967 Field	2967 Field
			2960 LAA
			2961 LAA
			2945 Field
1324	Santa Cruz	Santa Cruz	Santa Cruz
		2810 Field	
		2852 LAA	2852 LAA
		2748 Field	2748 Field
		2846 LAA	2846 LAA
RAF Regiment Depot	2852 LAA		
Secunderabad		2964 Field	
FE Agartala	2896 Field	2896 Field	2896 Field
			2964 Field
			2810 Field
Cocos Islands	2962 LAA	2962 LAA	2962 LAA
In transit	2846 LAA		
	2748 Field		
	2810 Field		

Appendix 17.
The disposition of the RAF Regiment in South-East Asia Command on 24 August 1945.

Group	Wing	Location	Squadron
221	1307	Toungoo	2759 Field
		Zayatkwin	2963 LAA
		"	2965 Field
	1329	Mingaladon	2896 Field
		"	2960 LAA
		Hmawbi	2802 Field
		HQ RAF Burma	2961 LAA
	1326	Insein	2968 Field
		"	2854 LAA
	1330	Pegu	2964 Field
		HQ 221 Group RAF	2942 Field
224		Agartala	2970 Armoured
225	RAF Regiment Depot	Secunderabad	2943 Field
		"	2945 Field
	1327	Warangal	2967 Field
		"	2959 LAA
	1331	"	2966 Field
		"	2944 Field
		"	2706 LAA
	1323	"	2946 Field
		"	2958 LAA
	1308	"	2739 Field
		"	2837 LAA
		"	2708 Field
		"	2743 Field
		"	2962 LAA
	1324	Santa Cruz	2748 Field
		" "	2846 LAA
	–	Begumpet	2810 (Para) Field
	–	Madras	2941 Field
	–	"	2852 LAA

Appendix 18.
The disposition of the RAF Regiment in South-East Asia Command on 12 September 1945.

Group	Location	Wing	Squadron
221	Zayatkwin	1307	2963 LAA
			2965 Field
	Hmawbi	1326	2960 LAA
	Insein		2968 Field
	Rangoon	1330	2942 Field
	Mingaladon		2961 LAA
	Agartala		2970 Armd Car
225	Secunderabad and	1308	2943 Field
	Warangal		2962 LAA
		1323	2958 LAA
			2959 LAA
			2966 Field
		1327	2739 Field
			2837 LAA
			2944 Field
			2946 Field
	Begampet		2810 Field
en route	Singapore	1324	2748 Field
			2846 LAA
			2852 LAA
			2941 Field
	Penang	1329	2759 Field
			2802 Field
			2854 LAA
			2964 Field
	Hong Kong	1331	2706 LAA
			2708 Field
			2743 Field
	Bangkok		2945 Field
	Saigon		2967 Field
Operation *Tiderace*	Singapore		2896 Field

Appendix 19.

The arrival dates of RAF Regiment units in the Malay Peninsula and French Indo-China operations of September to October 1945.

Date	Location	Wing	Squadron
5 September	Singapore	1324 later	2896 Field
10 September	Penang	1329	2759 Field
			2802 LAA
			2854 Field
			2964 Field
11 September	Morib Beaches	1324	2748 Field
			2846 LAA
14 September			2941 Field
17 September			2852 LAA
19 September	Singapore		2944 Field
21 September	Penang	1326	2965 Field
			2960 LAA
1 October	Saigon	1307	2963 LAA
11 October			2967 Field

Bibliography

COMMANDERS' DESPATCHES AND REPORTS

Air Marshal W.A. Coryton CB MVO DFC, *Despatches covering operations of 3rd Tactical Air Force from 1st June–4th December 1944.*

Air Chief Marshal Sir Keith Park KCB KBE MC DFC, *Third Supplement to the London Gazette*, Tuesday 6 April 1951, Air Operations in South-East Asia from 1 June 1944 to 2 May 1945.

Air Chief Marshal Sir Keith Park KCB KBE MC DFC, *Third Supplement to the London Gazette*, Tuesday 13 April 1951, Air Operations in South-East Asia from 3 May 1945 to 12 September 1945.

Air Marshal Sir R.E.C. Peirse KCB DSO AFC, *Third Supplement to the London Gazette*, Tuesday 13 March 1951, Air Operations in South-East Asia from 16 November 1943 to 31 May 1944.

Air Commodore S.F. Vincent DFC AFC, *Despatches covering operations of 221 Group during the Manipur Campaign, 1st March–31st July 1944.*

Mountbatten, Vice-Admiral The Earl, *Report to the Combined Chiefs of Staff by the Supreme Allied Commander South-East Asia, 1943–1945.* London: HMSO, 1951.

AIR AND WAR OFFICE FILES (held in the National Archives, Kew, UK)

AIR 20/4024, *The RAF Regiment in Action.*

AIR 23/2050, *1942–44 Aerodrome Defence: RAF Regiment Instructions, HQ 224 Group to OC AA Flights.*

AIR 23/2051, *Policy concerning the reduction and reorganisation of the RAF Regiment.*

AIR 24/1374, *Operations Record Books Appendices, SEAC, Indian Observer Corps, Gas Defence, Ground Defence, Engineer 1943–1944.*

AIR 24/1375, *Operational Record Books Appendices, SEAC, Indian Observer Corps, Ground Defence, January–August 1945.*

AIR 25/910, *Operations Record Book 221 Group, 1944–1945.*

AIR 25/915, *Operations Record Book and Appendices, 221 Group, May 1944.*

AIR 25/917, *221 Group Appendices Only, July 1944.*

AIR 29/73, *Operations Record Books RAF Regiment Squadrons, 2706.*

AIR 29/83, *Operations Record Books RAF Regiment Squadrons, 2741–2743.*

AIR 29/103, *Operations Record Books RAF Regiment Squadrons 2810–2813.*

AIR 29/134, *Operations Record Books RAF Regiment Squadrons 2934, 2935, 2941–2943.*

AIR 29/136, *Operations Record Books RAF Regiment Squadrons 2944–2959.*

AIR 29/137, *Operations Record Books RAF Regiment Squadrons 2960–2970.*

AIR 29/138, *Operations Record Books RAF Regiment Squadrons 2941–2950, 2953–2955, 2957–2962, 2964, 2966–2970 Appendices Only.*

AIR 29/182, *Operations Record Books and Appendices Air Ministry Experiment*

Stations 553,554, 566–570, 573, 574, 576–579, 581, 582, 589, 590.

AIR 29/716, *No 1 RAF Regiment Training School, later RAF Regiment (ACSEA) Secunderabad (with Appendices).*

AIR 29/884, *Operations Record Books RAF Regiment 4401–4408 AA Flights.*

AIR 29/886, *Operations Record Books and Appendices RAF Regiment 4436–4450, 5756, 6201, 6203, 6204, 6206 AA Flights.*

AIR 29/1118, *Operations Record Books 1300–1309, 1311–1317 RAF Regiment Wings 1944–47.*

AIR 29/1120, *Operations Record Books 1318–1338 RAF Regiment Wings, 1944–1947.*

AIR 29/1121, *Appendices 1319–1323, 1327–1329, 1331 & 1333, 1335 & 1336 RAF Regiment Wings 1944–1947.*

WO 172/4193, *4 Corps R.A., Jan–Dec 1944.*

MISCELLANEOUS REPORTS

Review of RAF Regiment Squadrons under the control of HQ RAF Burma, 1ˢᵗ January 1945 to 3rd May 1945, Capture of Rangoon. HQ RAF Burma.

Official Press Note Com/236, 5 November 1944.

Ground Defence and the RAF Regiment in India and South-East Asia 1942–1945, Document held at RAF Regiment Museum, RAF Honington, Suffolk.

PUBLISHED PAPERS

M.S. Witherow, ' "Flying Soldiers in Blue Khaki"–The Royal Air Force Regiment Part 1', *Army Quarterly & Defence Journal,* Vol. 118, 1988.

NEWSPAPERS

The South China Morning Mail, late 1945.

The Statesman, Delhi, 19 September 1944.

The Straits Echo, Penang, 13 September 1945.

The Evening News, Saturday 2 March 1946.

The Evening News, Saturday 2 May 1946.

OFFICIAL HISTORIES

Khera, P. N. and S. N. Prasad, eds. *Reconquest of Burma 1942–45: June 1944–August 1945.* Vol. II, *Official History of the Indian Armed Forces in the Second World War, 1939–45.* New Delhi: Combined Inter-Services Historical Section, India & Pakistan. Orient: Longmans, 1959.

Prasad, S. N., K.D. Bhargava, and P.N. Khera, eds. *Reconquest of Burma 1942–45: June 1942–June 1944.* Vol. I, *Official History of the Indian Armed Forces in the Second World War, 1939–45.* New Delhi: Combined Inter-Services Historical Section, India & Pakistan. Orient: Longmans, 1958.

Kirby, S.W. et al. *The War against Japan. India's Most Dangerous Hour.* Vol. II. London: HMSO, 1958.

——. *The War against Japan. The Decisive Battles.* Vol. III. London: HMSO, 1961.

——. *The War against Japan. The Reconquest of Burma.* Vol. IV. London: HMSO, 1965.

——. *The War against Japan. The Surrender of Japan.* Vol. V. London: HMSO, 1969.

PUBLISHED BOOKS

Allen, L. *Burma. The Longest War 1941–1945*. London: Dent, 1984.

Anon. *The Eleventh (Kenya) Battalion King's African Rifles 1941 to 1945*. Ranchi, Bihar: Privately published, 1946.

_____. *Wings of the Phoenix. The Official Story of the Air War in Burma*. London: HMSO, 1949.

Atkinson, T. ed. *Spectacles, Testicles, Fags and Matches. The untold story of RAF Servicing Commandos in World War Two,* Edinburgh: Luath Press, 2004.

Bickers, R.T. *Ginger Lacey, Fighter Pilot*. Pan, London, 1969 (1962).

Brett-James, A. *Ball of Fire: 5th Indian Division in the Second World War*. Aldershot: Gale & Polden, 1951.

Chaplin, J.B. *Action in Burma 1942–1945*. London: Publisher's details not shown, 1984.

Davies, J. and J.P. Kellett. *A History of the RAF Servicing Commandos*. Shrewsbury: Airlife, 1989.

Davis, P. *A Child at Arms*. London: Hutchinson & Co., 1970.

Doulton, A.J.F. *The Fighting Cock: The Story of the 23rd Indian Division 1942–1947*. Aldershot: Gale & Polden, 1951.

Edgerly, A.G. ed. *Each Tenacious. A History of No. 99 (Madras Presidency) Squadron (1917–1976)*. Worcester: Square One Publications, 1993.

Evans, G. and Brett-James, A. *Imphal: A Flower on Lofty Heights*. London: Macmillan, 1962.

Fairbairn, T. *Action Stations Overseas*. Sparkford, nr Yeovil, Somerset: Patrick Stephens Ltd, 1991.

Farndale, M. ed. *The Far East Theatre 1941–1946, History of the Royal Regiment of Artillery*. London: Brassey's, 2002.

Farquharson, R.H. *For Your Tomorrow. Canadians and the Burma Campaign, 1941–1945*. Victoria, BC [Canada]: Trafford Publishing, 2004.

Forty, G. *XIVth Army at War*. Shepperton, Surrey: Ian Allan, 1982.

Franks, N. *First in the Indian Skies*. Lincoln: Life Publications/RAF Collection, 1981.

——. *The Air Battle of Imphal*. London: William Kimber, 1985.

——. *Spitfires over the Arakan*. London: William Kimber, 1988.

——. *Hurricanes over the Arakan*. Wellingborough: Patrick Stephens, 1989.

Hamilton, A. *Canadians on Radar in South-East Asia 1941–1945*. Fredericton, N.B. [Canada]: ACH Publishing, 1998.

Hamilton, J.A.L. *War Bush. 81 (West African) Division in Burma, 1943–1945*. Wilby, Norwich: Michael Russell, 2001.

Hingston, W. *Never Give Up. History of the King's Own Yorkshire Light Infantry 1919–1942*. Vol. V. York: Published by the Regiment, 1950.

Jacobs, V.K. *The Woodpecker Story: As Told by No. 136 (Fighter) Squadron, Royal Air Force 'The Woodpeckers'*. Durham: Pentland Press, 1994.

Jefford, C.G. *The Flying Camels. The History of No. 45 Squadron RAF*. High Wycombe, Bucks: CG Jefford, 1995.

Johnson, C.D. *The Forgotten Army's Box of Lions*. Norfolk: Published privately by the author [Printed by Catton Print, Norwich], 2001.

Lee, D. *Eastward, A History of the RAF in the Far East 1945–1972*. London: HMSO, 1984.

Moyse-Bartlett, H. *The King's African Rifles. A Study in the Military History of East and Central Africa, 1890–1945*. Aldershot: Gale & Polden, 1956.

Naydler, M. *Young Man, You'll Never Die*. Barnsley, Yorkshire: Pen & Sword, 2005.

Neville, J.E.H., ed. *The Oxfordshire & Buckinghamshire Light Infantry Chronicle: The Record of the 43rd, 52nd, 4th, 5th, [6th, 7th, 70th] and 1st & 2nd Buckinghamshire Battalion in the Second German War.* Vol. 4. June, 1944–December, 1945. Aldershot: Gale & Polden, 1954.

Oliver, K.M. *A Short History of the RAF Regiment.* RAF Regiment Fund, 1974.

——. *Through Adversity: The History of the Royal Air Force Regiment 1942–1992.* Rushden, Northamptonshire: Forces & Corporate Publishing Ltd, 1997.

——. *The RAF Regiment at War 1942–1946.* Barnsley, Yorkshire: Leo Cooper, 2002.

Orange, V. *Sir Keith Park.* London: Methuen, 1984.

Probert, H. *The Forgotten Air Force: A History of the Royal Air Force in the War against Japan.* London: Brassey's, 1995.

Richey, P. and N. Franks. *Fighter Pilot's Summer.* London: Grub Street, 1999 (1993).

Roberson, N.J. *The History of No. 20 Squadron Royal Flying Corps Royal Air Force.* Weeze: Privately Published [Printed by Palka-Verlag], 1987.

Roberts, M.R. *Golden Arrow. The Story of the 7th Indian Division in the Second World War 1939–1945.* Aldershot: Gale & Polden, 1952.

Ross, J. and W.L. Hailes. *War Services of the 9th Jat Regiment.* Vol. II. 1937–1948. Redhill, Surrey: Becher, 1965.

Routledge, N.W. *Anti-Aircraft Artillery 1914–55, History of the Royal Regiment of Artillery.* London: Brassey's, 1994.

Sandes, E.W.C. *From Pyramid to Pagoda: The Story of the West Yorkshire Regiment (the Prince of Wales's Own) in the War, 1939–45, and Afterwards.* York: West Yorkshire Regiment, 1952.

Sansome, R.S. *The Bamboo Workshop: The History of the RAF Repair & Salvage Units India/Burma 1941–1946.* Braunton, Devon: Merlin Books, 1995.

Shores, C. *Air War for Burma: The Allied Air Forces Fight Back in South-East Asia, 1942–1945.* London: Grub Street, 2005.

Slim, W. *Defeat into Victory.* 2nd ed. London: Cassell, 1956.

Stevens, G.R. *History of the 2nd King Edward VII's Own Goorkha Rifles (The Sirmoor Rifles).* Vol. III, 1921–1948. Aldershot: Gale & Polden, 1952.

Steyn, P. ed. *The History of the Assam Regiment.* Vol. I, 1941–1947. Calcutta: Orient Longmans, 1959.

Tucker, N.G. *In Adversity. Exploits of gallantry and awards made to the RAF Regiment and its associated forces 1921–1995.* Oldham, Lancashire: Jade Publishing, 1997.

Turnbull, P. *Battle of the Box.* Shepperton, Surrey: Ian Allan, 1979.

Vincent, S.F. *Flying Fever.* London: Jarrolds, 1972.

Willis, G.R.T. *No Hero, Just a Survivor. A Personal Story with Beaufighters and Mosquitos of 47 Squadron RAF over the Mediterranean and Burma, 1943–1945*: Emley, Huddersfield: Robert Willis Associates, 1999.

Ziegler, P. ed. *Personal Diary of Admiral the Lord Louis Mountbatten. Supreme Commander, South-East Asia, 1943–1946.* London: Collins, 1988.

Index

n indicates an entry within the notes